A Museum

.

A Museum

The History of the Cabinet of Curiosities
of the
American Philosophical Society

MURPHY D. SMITH

———••◦••———

American Philosophical Society
Independence Square • Philadelphia
1996

ISBN:0-87169-960-5
Library of Congress Catalog Card No. 94-78522

For Margaret, Evelyn, and Avis

Contents

Introduction

The eighteenth century, the "Age of Enlightenment," honored philosophers (the word philosophy referred to "hard" sciences, such as physics or astronomy) for their ability to discover the laws of nature and apply them for the betterment of mankind. This century looked for solutions to practical problems and in the Newtonian system they saw the key to the wisdom of the ages.

The experience of the ages shews, that by such institutions, arts and sciences in general are advanced; useful discoveries made and communicated; many ingenious artists, who might otherwise remain in obscurity, drawn forth ... and ... every domestic improvement that may help either to save or acquire wealth, may, by such means [as the American Philosophical Society] be more effectively carried on. [1]

For there appears from the whole order & disposition of the Universe, a manifest contrivance & design in the Creator, nor can it be reasonably suppos'd, that the least Attom, was form'd by chance, or without some View to a particular end, to be a Link in the grand Chain of Nature; and if each Attom was form'd with design, we must conclude, they were afterwards combin'd in such proportions, as best Answer'd the purposes of the Creator. [2]

During the eighteenth century the value of the various scientific academies of Europe were recognized. The Royal Society of London, formed in 1662 "for Promoting Natural Knowledge," became the model for the English-speaking world, and the American Philosophical Society was based on it. The Royal Society's *Philosophical Transactions,* the source of America's knowledge of current science, published some papers written by Americans.

By the 1740s several colonial scholars were recognized as philosophers by the European savants. Most of the Americans, however, were unacquainted with each other. Philadelphia, the largest American colonial city, was the home of John Bartram and Benjamin Franklin. Fellows of the Royal Society of London, they based their concept of a learned Society on it: "That One Society be formed of Virtuosi or ingenious Men residing in the several Colonies, to be called *The American Philosophical Society* who are to maintain a constant Correspondence." The subjects which would be of the most interest were:

All new discovered Plants, Herbs, Trees, Roots, &c., Methods of Propagating them, and making such as are useful, but particular to some Plantations, more general, Improvements of vegetable Juices, as Cyders, Wines, &c.; New methods of curing or preventing diseases; All new discovered Fossils in different Countries, as Mines, Minerals, Quarries, &c.

Mathematics, trades and manufactures, chemistry, arts, mechanics, agriculture, husbandry, and geography also were mentioned. The Society, formed in 1743, was to embrace all natural philosophy and natural history: "all philosophical experiments that let light into the nature of things, tend to increase the power of man over matter, and multiply the conveniences or pleasures of life." [3] There was to be no dependence on governmental support because Franklin and his friends believed there were enough wealthy men interested in science who could do valuable work if the Society provided a focus for them.

A later fusion of the American Society and the American Philosophical Society became the present American Philosophical Society for Promoting Useful Knowledge. Interest in the Transit of Venus of 1769 spurred the rebirth of the Society because the Royal Society of London wanted reports of observations from as many different areas of the world as possible.

The pursuit of science in eighteenth-century America has been well explored by Brooke Hindle in his Ph. D. thesis, "The Rise of the American Philosophical Society" [4] and his *Pursuit of Science in Revolutionary America.* [5] The emergence of the scientific aspects of the Society has been carefully explained by Carl Van Doren in "The Beginnings of the American Philosophical Society. [6] John Greene's The Death of Adam is one of the best sources for background material from this period. [7]

Much has been published on the history of the American Philosophical Society. John Vaughan and Peter Stephen Du Ponceau wrote the earliest histories.[8] The Society's bicentennial celebration of its history in 1942 included a symposium entitled: "The early History of Science and Learning in America with Especial Reference to the Work of the American Philosophical Society During the Eighteenth and Nineteenth Centuries" which was published in the Proceedings. The director of the Leander McCormick Observatory at the University of Virginia, Samuel Alfred Mitchell, read a paper on "Astronomy During the Early Years of the American Philosophical Society." This science was the major focus in the first volume of the Transactions. Other papers in the Symposium were by Horace C. Richards, Professor Emeritus of Physics at the University of Pennsylvania, who spoke on "Some Early American Physicists," featuring both early David Rittenhouse and, more especially, Franklin, as the outstanding physicists. Massachusetts Institute of Technology Professor Emeritus of Electrical Engineering and Dugald C. Jackson presented "Engineering in Our Early History," with Franklin again the main focus. "The Survey of Scientific Agriculture" by M. L. Wilson, director of Extension Work, United States Department of Agriculture, stressed the importance of the early papers on agriculture in the Transactions. Merritt L. Ferrald, Harvard University Fisher Professor of Natural History and the director of the Gray Herbarium, described "Some Early Botanists of the American Philosophical Society." while Francis Packard, editor of Annals of Medical History, explained "Medicine and the American Philosophical Society." Detlev Bronk, then Director of the Eldridge Reeves Johnson Research Foundation at the University of Pennsylvania, read "[Member] Joseph Priestley and the Early History of the American Philosophical Society." A paper on "Benjamin Smith Barton as Naturalist" was read by Francis W. Pennell, curator of plants of the Academy of Natural Sciences of Philadelphia. George Gaylord Simpson's "The Beginnings of Vertebrate Paleontology in North America" recorded the early attempts of the Society to gather fossil bones, praising especially the president of the Society, Thomas Jefferson, for his insight and honoring Caspar Wistar as the first of American vertebrate paleontologists. The Cabinet of the Society looms large in this paper. Curator of anthropology of the American Museum of Natural History Clark Wissler, commented on "The American Indian and the American Philosophical Society." He concluded that both the study of linguistics and archaeology owed much to the Society. The "Introductory Remarks" by the vice-president, Edwin G. Conklin, stated:

This year marks the close of the second century of this Society which was organized by Benjamin Franklin in 1743 "for the promotion of useful knowledge among the British plantations in America." Therefore, it has seemed fitting to mark this bicentenary by a review of some of the notable work of the Society in various fields of learning, and accordingly different persons were asked to prepare papers on the contributions of the Society in the fields of their special interests.

Further consideration led to the conclusion that it would be more useful to make this occasion a general review of the Early History of Science and Learning in America, with especial reference to the work of this Society during the eighteenth and nineteenth centuries. Such a review would have a broader interest than the work of one institution, and it would have the practical result of assessing the wealth of our library and archives in this field of learning its principal needs, if it is to be an important research library, as was recommended by the special committee on the library at the General Meeting last April.

Accordingly this program was planned to begin with the mathematical and physical sciences and then to proceed to the geological and biological and finally to the social sciences and the humanities.[9]

Many of these papers made reference to various aspects of the Cabinet of Curiosities, but other than a brief history of the early Cabinet by Whitfield J. Bell, Jr. (it

Introduction

can be found in *A Cabinet of Curiosities Five Episodes in the Evolution of American Museums*) no major study has been attempted on the Cabinet.

From these studies three basic factors emerge:

(1) The Society published a successful volume of *Transactions* in 1771 and thereafter, at home and abroad, it was known as *the* American scientific society. Consequently, the Society never had to compete with the local specialized societies which proliferated after the Revolution.

(2) The Society owned a permanent home, so it continued to exist even during periods when interest in it lapsed.

(3) Donations to the Cabinet were integral parts of the basic history of the Society.

In considering the history of the Cabinet of Curiosities one must know the homes of the Society over the years for it has occupied many places for its meetings. In 1768 it met at "Mr. Byrne's, the Indian Queen and the State House (Independence Hall)"; in 1769, at the "College (University of Pennsylvania)"; in 1770, at the "Schoolhouse in 2nd street" and in 1771 the "Society's Hall" (a rented room with no other location given); in 1773 it met in the State House and the "Society's Hall." In 1775 it met "in the College" and in 1779 in "Society Hall." It met at Benjamin Franklin's home from 1784 to 1790 for he was too ill to move about easily and, as president, he presided over the meetings. Finally, on 21 February 1789 the first meeting of the Society was held in it own building, Philosophical Hall, on Independence Square.

In 1993, major meetings of the Society were moved to the newly renovated Benjamin Franklin Hall at 427 Chestnut Street.

It should be noted that until the completion of Philosophical Hall, the Library and Cabinet were kept in various places: homes of certain members, meeting rooms, and elsewhere. The Minutes refer several times to the attempts to gather together all these objects.

The sources for this study seem complete until one does research. The curators kept records, at times, and, being busy with their own professions, evidently found it difficult to take time to describe the gifts. All such references are in the Minutes, and some of the lists which the curators compiled are included in this study. The Minutes are of paramount importance, but the correspondence, publications, and the Society's records augment them. And yet many items, while discussed, studied, and admired by the Members, are merely listed as gifts, with no written comments.

In most organizations, a few men maintain a keen interest, and the Society is no exception. Preeminent among its most steadfast supporters were Benjamin Franklin, Thomas Jefferson, and John Vaughan. Franklin, founder of the Society, kept members informed of inventions and discoveries when he was in England and France. He introduced other scientists, acted as a clearing house for correspondence, and gifts, and lent the Society $500 to put a new roof on Philosophical Hall. Jefferson, with his immense prestige, was more active than Franklin (each was president of the Society), in presenting the Society with artifacts for its Cabinet, as well as introducing other learned men, forwarding books and manuscripts. John Vaughan, a bachelor who lived in Philosophical Hall from about 1803 until his death in 1841, was a merchant with an intense interest in the exploding world of scientific knowledge of his day, He was treasurer, secretary, librarian, and curator, and was on hand to lend books, show guests and visitors through the "apartments," pay bills, and manage everything.

These three men kept alive the interest of science, and, through their encouragement, the Library and the Cabinet of Curiosities of the Society flourished. Vaughan shipped gifts to and from the Society and kept the records of gifts and accessions. At the time of his death, interest in the Society began to wane, because many scientific organizations with specific interests, such as the Academy of Natural Sciences of Philadelphia, geographical societies, and geological societies, and then the Smithsonian were founded—with the last becoming the American scientific society. As the focal point of scientists turned to narrower interests, the American Philosophical Society became a less active organization, but it still held meetings and published its *Transactions* and *Proceedings*. The library of the Society continued to grow but the cabinet's growth was slower.

The Cabinet of Curiosities

At first, when the Society moved into Philosophical Hall, it occupied the two south rooms on the second floor, and as the cabinet and the library grew, space was needed. A third floor was constructed for the library in Philosophical Hall in 1890 and the Society, realizing that it could not continue to support and house its cabinet, began depositing parts of it with various local institutions. As more time passed, the Society took over many rooms which had been rented in Philosophical Hall, especially during the 1890s when the City of Philadelphia moved the courts into the new City Hall. The courts had occupied the old Supreme Court building on Independence Square and rented the northern rooms of Philosophical Hall; an extension which connected the Court House to Philosophical Hall had been built.

Although the Society continued to rent parts of the Hall to others, much of it was used by the constantly expanding library, and in 1931, the Society received a splendid bequest from the estate of Richard Alexander Fullerton Penrose made the possibility of a separate library building feasible. The library was removed from the third floor of Philosophical Hall and installed in rooms on the second and third floors (the Stock Exchange) of the Drexel Building, directly across Fifth Street from the Hall. Additional space in the Drexel Building was rented as needed. When the Independence National Historic Park was established, the Drexel Building was the first major building destroyed. The Library, in 1955, moved into the United States Fidelity and Guarantee Building, on the site of the old Philadelphia Infirmary (or Dispensary), just south of Library Street on Fifth Street.

As soon as the Drexel Building was destroyed, the Society began construction of Library Hall on the site and the Library moved into it in 1958. In 1981 the Society purchased the Merchants Exchange Bank Building on Chestnut Street, between Fourth and Fifth Streets. It was partially rebuilt to hold the ever-expanding Library. This building is now undergoing continued reconstruction and will be used by the Society as a meeting place in the large auditorium therein, and continued expansion for the Library. It will also hold parts of the Cabinet still in the possession of the Society: the instruments and models, the antiques, and some of the objets d'art.

The story of the available space for the Society's use is important, for space was always needed. Although the attic and basement of the Hall were used by the Society, the huge bones of the mastodons and elephants, fossils and mineralogical specimens, other segments of the Cabinet and the growing Library forced the members to agree to the deposit of many items with other local learned institutions. Because many of the members were also active in these sister institutions, especially the Academy of Natural Sciences of Philadelphia, some of these members suggested these institutions as places of deposit.

The curators are elected officers of the Society and are chosen by the general membership. Their duties varied over the years. Some records exist, but often the Minutes merely state what the Curators wished to report, or that they had made a report, and many of the reports and minutes of the curators meetings simply no longer exist. Nor, unfortunately, do many of the lists of the Cabinet which the Society asked them to prepare.

It cannot be overstated that the Cabinet's history consists chiefly of a listing of gifts, donors, and dates of accession. Very few entries of the minutes make a detailed listing of the gifts, and some of the entries are remarkably skimpy: "a box of coins," "some bones." Sometimes the secretary merely noted the name of a donor of an item for the cabinet, with no description of the gift. A more complete listing was made by John Vaughan, the secretary, librarian, and treasurer, of the Society until his death in 1841 in the Donation Books, begun in 1809. At first, the Transactions contained a listing of items presented, both for the cabinet and the library. These are valuable lists, but are not complete. In fact, no record seems to be complete, for when the Proceedings began to appear in 1838, an abstract of the minutes, as well as the presentation of gifts, are intermingled with papers presented to the Society. After Vaughan's death, the Donation Books show fewer and fewer gifts for the cabinet and by around 1850 lists only the publications presented. In this study, the item, name of the donor(s), and date of acquisition have been united wherever possible.

In order to stress the fact that this cabinet was a cabinet for the members, and was created and preserved by the members, each time a member is mentioned for the first time, in each chapter of this work, the identification word, "member" precedes his name. In preparing this work, the items of the cabinet of curiosities fell into twelve distinct categories: Native American artifacts: Antiques; Botany: Coins and medals: Fossils; Instruments and inventions; Manufactured goods; Maps; Mineralogical specimens; Objets d'art; Oddities, or Miscellany; and, Zoological specimens.

Four of these categories have been studied and published by the American Philosophical Society as separate volumes. The antiques are listed and depicted in *Due Reverence: Antiques in the American Philosophical Society*, by Murphy D. Smith. The instruments are listed and described in *A Catalogue of Instruments and Models in the Possession of the American Philosophical Society* by Robert P. Multhauf. The maps are catalogued in *Realms of Gold A Catalogue of Maps in the Library of the American Philosophical Society*, by Murphy D. Smith. The objets d'art are depicted and listed in *Catalogue of Portraits and Other Works of Art in the Possession of the American Philosophical Society*. Therefore, this study of the cabinet of curiosities does not include any of these four volumes. The members, in depositing much of the Cabinet of Curiosities in sister Philadelphia institutions, acted wisely. The Cabinet was made by the members for the members, but over the years it was felt that the cabinet should be made available for scholars everywhere. Therefore, three major Philadelphia institutions, the University Museum of the University of Pennsylvania, the Academy of Natural Sciences of Philadelphia and the Wagner Free Institute of Science now have the items which the Society no longer could house and display, thereby these items are open for research at these sister institutions.

MANUSCRIPTS

American Philosophical Society Archives

The most important archival item in any history of any organization is its Minutes. The Minutes contain the skeleton of the society and its happenings.

There is no reference to the ASP Minutes in these footnotes, for the date is included in any description of the item. A person, therefore, can locate the reference, without the use of footnotes.

The Minutes of the Society include the Minutes of the American Society. The two Societies united in 1769 and formed the present American Philosophical Society for the Promotion of Useful Knowledge. In 1884 an abstract of the *Minutes of the Society* from 1769 was published. However, the *Minutes of the American Society* to 1769 remain unpublished.

Because this study is about one specific organization, references in the footnotes which pertain to the Archives of the Society do not include a reference to the APS. Rather, the footnotes refer to the specific group of papers in the Archives.

When one researches the history of an old organization, one finds that over the years, various people use different names for records that were placed in the Archives later. Even the term, *Archives,* was used at one time to segregate a group which was called Archives. When the Society first began to consider care and cataloging of its Archives, a huge mass of individual letters, papers, etc., were divided into two collections and named: Miscellaneous Manuscripts Collections, and, the "Archives." (*Archives.*)

Description of further breakdowns of the Archives, and their abbreviated use in the Footnotes, follows:

Card Catalogue for Coins and Medals.
Committee Records = Com. Recs.
Curators Cards in the Library = Curators Cards.
Curators Records = Cur. Recs.
Curators Donation Book = Cur. Donation Book.
Donation Book. [This series of volumes is, in fact, an accession record. The gifts for the Cabinet of Curiosities were listed, as well as books for the Library. Over the years, the gifts to the Cabinet were discontinued.]
Donations to Cabinet.
Historical and Literary Committee Letterbooks.
Manuscripts Communicated to the APS = MS. Com.

Secretary's letters. [These continue, but the last fifty years have not been reorganized, or individually studied. Therefore, the references to Luther Pfaler Eisenhart and Edwin Grant Conklin must refer to this breakdown.]

Manuscripts used other than the Archives of the Society:

Miscellaneous Manuscripts Collection = Misc. MS. Col.

Academy of Natural Sciences of Philadelphia. Archives and Collections. Charlottesville: University Press of Virginia: 1967. See article by Whitfield J. Bell, Jr.

INTRODUCTION—References

1. APS. Trans., vol. 1, p. xxiv.
2. American Society. Minutes, 28 Nov. 1766.
3. Franklin, B. A Proposal for Promoting Useful Knowledge among the British Plantations in America. Philadelphia, 14 May 1743.
4. Hindle, B. The Rise of the American Philosophical Society, 1766-1787. Dissertation. Ph. D. in History at the University of Pennsylvania. 1949.
5. Ibid. The Pursuit of Science in Revolutionary America, 1735-1789. Chapel Hill, University of North Carolina Press, 1956.
6. Van Doren, C. "The Beginnings of the American Philosophical Society...," APS. Proc., vol. 87, no. 3, pp. 277–289.
7. Greene, JC. The Death of Adam: Evolution and its Fact on Western Thought. Ames, Iowa State University Press, 1959.
8. Du Ponceau, PS. An Historical Account of the Origin and Foundation of the American Philosophical Society held at Philadelphia for Promoting Useful Knowledge. 19 June 1840. Manuscript. John Vaughan. An Account of the American Philosophical Society, 1841. Copy. Manuscript.
9. "The Early History of Science and Learning in America, with Especial Reference to The Work of the American Philosophical Society During the Eighteenth and Nineteenth Centuries," APS. Proc., vol. 86. Philadelphia, APS: 1943.
10. A Cabinet of Curiosities; Five Episodes in the Evolution of American Museums. Charlottesville, University Press of Virginia, 1967. See article by Whitfield J. Bell, Jr.

Chapter 1.

The Role of the Curators

The curators were, generally, very careful of their role and acted to preserve items given to the Society. Basically, the objects were kept for the amusement and instruction of the members. However, the Society has always been generous in lending or making copies of its holdings available to sister institutions. Plaster casts of fossil bones were made for exchange or sale to other organizations. Artists were permitted to visit and study or copy portraits. Herbaria were consulted frequently by both members and non-members. Consequently, the history of the Cabinet consists of the amassing of the objects and their final disposition. Whenever particular use of an item demanded attention, the curators made the ultimate decision, and, insofar as possible, whenever such decisions were to be made, and records exist of the actions of the curators, these actions are recorded herein in the chapter on the type of item(s).

Curators were protective of the objects and saw to it that the portraits and other works of art were kept in good order and hung as prominently as possible. Philosophical Hall was small, and the quarters of the Society were the two rooms on the second floor on the south side of the building. Consequently, crowded with books and tables, there was little room for exhibiting items. Photographs of the rooms in 1884 show how cramped they were. Books were, quite properly, placed in the hands of the librarian and, as time passed, maps and charts, engravings and etchings, and prints, became part of the library's holdings, as did the residue of the Cabinet when items were deposited elsewhere. In large part during the first century of the Society's existence, the accumulations were of gifts or publications acquired through exchange with other learned societies or from members. Indeed, the gifts of members constitute by far the larger part of the collection. Many discussions of various artifacts must have occurred as time passed and the artifacts were studied, but with no written record, one can only guess.

The Cabinet was fairly well known, at first, but in time was replaced in interest as larger buildings were constructed by sister institutions in Philadelphia, and in the United States at large, especially the Smithsonian Institution. And, in due time, the growth of objects of natural history reached such a point that the Society could not preserve and display them.

Today, the Cabinet is much reduced. Botanical and zoological specimens and the minerals and fossils are now in the Academy of Natural Sciences of Philadelphia. Native American artifacts were deposited in the University Museum of the University of Pennsylvania, as were many of the Oddities (e.g., Polynesian objects, a Greek kylix). Some mineralogical specimens are in the Wagner Free Institute of Science, Philadelphia. In Philosophical Hall the instruments and inventions, many antiques, and the mass of the portraits and busts are preserved and in the care of the curator today. A few segments of other collections have somehow escaped being deposited and are in the library. At the end of each chapter in this book there is a listing of what is left of the Cabinet in various buildings of the Society..

The formation of a Cabinet of Curiosities was implicit in the proposal for the founding of the American Philosophical Society

That the Subjects of the Correspondence be, All new-discovered Plants, Herbs, Trees, Roots, &c.; their Virtues, Uses, 7c.; Methods of Propagating them, and making such as are useful, but particular to some Plantations, more general. Improvements of vegetable Juices, as Cyders, Wines, &c.; New Methods of Curing or preventing Diseases. All new-discovered Fossils in different Countries, as Mines, Minerals, Quarries; &c. New and useful Improvements in any Branch of Mathematicks; New Discoveries in Chemistry, such as Improvements in Distillation, Brewing, Assaying of ores; &c. New Mechanical Inventions for saving Labour; as Mills, Carriages, &c. and for Raising and Conveying of Water, Draining of Meadows, &c.; All new Arts, Trades, Manufactures, &c. that may be

proposed or thought of; Surveys, Maps and Charts of particular Parts of the Sea-
coasts, or Inland Countries; Course and Junction of Rivers and great Roads,
Situation of Lakes and Mountains, Nature of the Soil and Productions; &c. New
Methods of Improving the Breed of useful Animals; Introducing other Sorts from
foreign Countries. New Improvements in Planting, Gardening, Clearing Land,
&c.; And all philosophical Experiments that let Light into the nature of Things, tend
to increase the Power of Man over Matter, and multiply the Conveniences or
Pleasures of Life.[11]

      The American Society held in Philadelphia for Promoting and Propagating
Useful Knowledge, united with the American Philosophical Society in 1769, forming the
American Philosophical Society held in Philadelphia for Promoting Useful Knowledge.[2]
As early as 18 March 1768, the American Society had received some gifts related to
American natural history, and expressed its gratitude in a newspaper:

> The Society return thanks to the Several Gentlemen who have sent them Specimens
> of the Silk Cotton, Labradore Tea & American Bole an account of which is duly
> entered upon their Minutes & proper measures will be taken to inquire into &
> inform the public of what Use these particulars may prove to the Community. A
> very acceptable present of a Curious Collection of Fishes from a Gentleman of taste
> & public Spirit in this City is received for which the Society make him their grateful
> acknowledgements. They doubt not but these instances of public spirit will
> encourage other persons who have it in their power, to make similar presents, or to
> Communicate whatever is Curious or useful, to the Society.[3]

      On 25 March 1768 the members ordered that all of the "Curiosities" were to
be given to Owen Biddle "untill a proper Place is provided to deposit them in." By 23
September 1768 the American Society had three curators of natural history "viz one for
each Kingdom" [animal, mineral, and vegetable], and asked Isaac Paschall, James
Pearson, and George Roberts to have a cabinet made "suitable for keeping the Curiosities
&c. belonging to the Society." The cabinet cost 13 pounds, 12 shillings 4 pence and the
preliminary agreement with the American Philosophical Society stated on 2 December
1768:

> 5. That the books of the former Societies be delivered to the Curators and deposited
> in the Cabinet.

> 6. That the models of machines, the specimens of ores, minerals, &c. and other
> Curiosities belonging to either of the former Societies be delivered to the new
> curators and deposited in the Cabinet.

This was revised 9 December 1768: "That the Books and all the Curiosities of the former
Societies be deposited in a Cabinet, or elsewhere as the united Societies shall direct." [4]
      The laws and regulations of the united Society specifically stated that a
Cabinet was to be collected and that three curators would care for it:

> The business of the Curators shall be to take charge of, and preserve, all *Specimens
> of natural Productions,* whether of the Animal, Vegetable or Fossil Kingdoms; all
> Models of Machines belonging to the Society, which shall be committed to them; to
> class and arrange them in their proper order, and keep an exact list of them, with the
> names of the respective donors, in a book provided for that purpose; which book
> shall be laid before the Society, as often as called for.

> The Curators, on entering upon their office, shall give such a receipt for everything
> that is committed to their charge, as the Society shall think proper; and, at the end of
> their term, shall deliver up the same to their successors. For the faithful
> performance of their duty, and of the trust reposed in them, they shall give bond to
> the Presidents, and Vice-Presidents, in such a sum as they, or any three of them,
> shall require.[4]

The curators took their role seriously and reported "A scheme for encreasing the Cabinet of Natural Curiosities," which was discussed and "returned for some alterations against next meeting" [16 March 1770]. These proposals were rewritten and presented to the Society on 20 April:

The Curators of the said Society having considered What steps would be most proper in Order to procure an Increase of the Subjects of Natural History, as well as everything else which would enrich the Cabinet beg Leave to submit the following Proposals to the Consideration of the Society.—

1. That a Request be made in the News Papers in each Colony on the Continent in the name of the Society to all merchants—Officers in the Army—Captains of Vessels & Others to collect & preserve all such new & unusual Plants—animals & Fossils as they may meet with on this Continent & in foreign Countries, & to transmit them to the Curators of the Society.

2. That the Names of all Persons who present anything to the Society be inserted in their Books, & a public acknowledgement made of their Donation when it may be thought to deserve it in the news Papers.

3. That the Curators may have an Order from the Society to write in their Names to all the foreign Members, & to such Other Persons as they are acquainted with in foreign Parts to solicit their Assistance in completing the Museum provided they first submit their Letters to the Inspection of the Society.

4. That Orders be given to the Members to deliver all the Effects of the Society which belong to the Cabinet to the Curators, as many Things have been entrusted to the Care of the Members which have never yet been delivered up to the Society.

Should the Society be pleased to comply with these Proposals of the Curators, they flatter themselves a Plan will be established which will in a few years procure a Collection worthy of the Care of the Society.[5]

As late as 18 February 1774 the curators were "desired to collect the Books and other valuables belonging to the Society and place them in the Cabinet."

The curators also cared for the manuscripts submitted and listed those available for publication when requested to do so by the Society, from these manuscripts that the contents of the Transactions was selected.[6] Models were often presented in these papers, for the eighteenth century used the term "model" for any description, sketch, or three-dimensional projection of whatever was under discussion. Curators were entrusted with three-dimensional models, also, and the collection of these items has been published: *Catalogue of Instruments and Models,* by Robert P. Multhauf [Philadelphia: 1961].

"Promoting useful knowledge" was a major interest of the Society and in the early years, it advertised for ideas and offered premiums; these advertisements are listed in the early volumes of the *Transactions,* with the amount of money or medal to be awarded. One such advertisement in a London paper of 29 September 1796, prompted William Cauldery to write Thomas Jefferson on the better lighting of streets.

During these early years astronomy was the major hard science of interest to the Society and David Rittenhouse was chief proponent. The Society purchased from Edward Duffield an astronomical time piece, and gifts of telescopes, quadrants, and other material were received.

From the first, the curators preserved and cared for items in the Cabinet. During the early history of the Society, the curators were seldom referred to per se. Generally, a committee was formed for the study of gifts and once the report was made, the committee was discharged and the gift turned over to the curators.

Although great men were members of the Society, few active members attended meetings. Local members raised funds for the Society, oversaw the publications, preserved the cabinet, and enriched and protected the growing library.

The librarian, as the only salaried member of the Society, became the manager of the Cabinet of Curiosities, keeping the rooms open for certain hours, greeting and helping the researchers and visitors. Because he had to exhibit materials upon request, he had to know where and what the various objects were, so he could make them available for use. Donations for the Cabinet and books were quite uneven until the publication of volume I of the *Transactions*. Then gifts increased. By 18 May 1770 the curators were told to "enter the List [of donations] in their own Books," but those books have disappeared. The Revolution intervened and the Society scarcely met for several years, but the possessions of the Society concerned the members. David Rittenhouse, curator, along with Edward Duffield and Pierre Eugene Du Simiti`ere, gathered as much as they could, but some objects escaped them and the vice-presidents, William Smith and Thomas Bond, directed the curators on 7 September 1777:

> Agreeable to a former Vote of the Society, you are requestd immediately to collect the different Copperplates belonging to the first Volume of the Society's Transactions, which were left in the Hands of Mr. Kennedy and Mr. Nevil, who roll'd off the Impressions, of which may be in any other Hands, and deposit the same in the Cabinet.
>
> The Canal Plate particularly, as it is the Theatre of War at present, & has been made Use of by Mr. Brooks without the Knowle[d]ge of the Society, & in a way that may give Offence, you are desired immediately to take up, & the Impressions made from it; allowing Mr. Brooks what may be reasonable for his labor & Paper.[6]

These attempts to regain possessions continued and on 6 March 1783 the curators were requested to report on the Cabinet. On 2 April Samuel Duffield and Ebenezer Hazard did so:

> Pursuant to the Order of the Society at their last Meeting, we report the State of the natural Curiosities in the Museum as follows, Viz.
>
> We find some of them to be absolutely perished: from others the Spirit has totally evaporated; but we think they may still be the preserved:—others stand in need of an Addition of Spirit;—and the Remainder are in good Preservation.[7]

The members therefore instructed the curators on 4 April to take all necessary steps to "preserve the natural curiosities from further decay."

David Rittenhouse, now the librarian (the first ever to hold this position) on 21 November 1783, announced on 5 December 1783 that part of the library and the Cabinet had been removed to his home. The following month, on 2 January 1784, he received the papers and seal of the Society which were in the possession of Timothy Matlack.

The Society was not totally dependent upon gifts of natural curiosities, although practically everything in the Cabinet was presented to it. When Pierre Eugene Du Simitière, owner of the first public museum in Philadelphia, died, a committee was appointed 5 November 1784 to examine and price this collection. A special meeting was called with a notice that money was to be expended, thereby stating the seriousness of the meeting and provoking a larger attendance. This warning was in vain, for the committee reported, 12 November at this special meeting, that DuSimitière's collection was unsorted as to lots and selection and, consequently, it was impossible to estimate its monetary value. Nothing else was ever entered in the minutes of the Society about this unique estate.

Items continued to be presented and by 15 January 1790 a By-law to "enable such of the members...as reside in the Western countries, to prosecute the objects of this institution with greater effort." This by-law was to be published in the newspapers.

The desire to augment the growing collection continued and on 26 March 1797 a committee reported its "Plan for collecting information respecting the remains of ancient natural and artificial productions in North America." This was read by paragraphs, commented upon, and returned to the committee for a "Code of Rules for the Government of the permanent Committee contemplated in the aforesaid report." On 16 June the draft of rules was reported and tabled: members of this permanent committee were to be chosen at the next meeting, 21 July. Decisions were difficult, it seems, for this report was ordered to be reconsidered at a special meeting to be held on 4 August.

The Committee appointed to draw-up Rules & Regulations for the Standing Committee recommend in their last report on "A plan for collecting information respecting the Antiquities of North America," beg leave to Report the following

Institution of a Standing Committee for collecting information as to the Antiquities of North America

Organization of the Committee

1st. The Committee shall consist of seven Members, to be chosen by the Society of whom a majority shall be resident within a convenient distance of the City of Philadelphia.

On the death or resignation of a Member the vacancy shall be supplied by the Society.

The Committee shall be subject to the general instructions of the Society.

2d. The Committee shall at their first meeting and afterwards on the first Mondays of November and May in every year, elect by ballot a Chairman, who shall preside during the succeeding six months, & shall also perform ye duty of Secretary.

He shall be re-eligible from time to time. In case of the death, resignation or permanent absence of the Chairman, within the half-year, another shall be elected in his stead for the remainder of the term.

Duties of the Committee

A correspondence shall be opened, from time to time, with such persons in different parts of N[orth] America, as may be thought competent to the furnishing of information concerning its Antiquities.

The Committee shall occasionally report to the Society the particular objects proper to be pursued—and the means for effecting them.

The Committee shall keep three books: (viz:) A Journal of their proceedings; an Account of Receipts and Expenditures;—and a Letter book, into which all letters written or received shall be fairly transcribed: the books of Receipt, &c. shall be submitted to the inspection of the Society twice every year, that is, at each first meeting in Jan[uar]y and July, & the other books once in two months.[8]

This report was read in its entirety, amended, and a most prestigious committee was appointed: Thomas Jefferson, Charles Willson Peale, Caspar Wistar, Jonathan Williams, General James Wilkinson, Adam Seybert, and Judge George Turner. When Williams moved from the city, Nicholas Collin replaced him. The committee signed its report and published it in the *Transactions,* volume V (1802):

The Society having appointed a committee to collect information respecting the past and present state of this country, the committee during the last year addressed the following letter to such persons as were likely, in their opinion, to advance the object of the Society

[Circular][4 August 1797]

Sir, The American Philosophical Society have always considered the antiquity, changes, and present state of their own country, as primary objects of their research; and with a view to facilitate such discoveries, a permanent committee has been established among whose duties the following have been recommended as requiring particular attention.

1. To procure one or more entire skeletons of the Mammoth, so called, and of such other unknown animals as either have been, or hereafter may be discovered in America.

2. To obtain accurate plans, drawings and descriptions of whatever is interesting, (where the originals cannot be had) and especially ascertaining the materials composing them, their contents, the purposes for which they were probably designed, &c.

3. To Invite researches into the Natural History of the Earth, the changes it has undergone as to Mountains, Lakes, Rivers, Prairies, &c.

4. To inquire into the Customs, Manners, Languages and Character of the Indian nations, ancient and modern, and their migrations.

The importance of these objects will be acknowledged by every Lover of Science, and, we trust, sufficiently apologize for thus troubling you: for without the aid of gentlemen who have taste and opportunity for such researches, our means would be very confined. We therefore solicit your communications, now or in the future, on these subjects; which will be at all times thankfully received, and duly noticed in the publications of the Society.

As to the first object, the committee suggest to Gentlemen who may be in the way of inquiries of that kind, that the Great Bone lick on the Ohio, and other places where there may be mineral salt, are the most eligible spots for the purpose; because animals are known to resort to such places.

With respect to the second head, the committee are desirous that cuts in various directions may be made into many of the Tumuli, to ascertain their contents; while the diameter of the largest tree growing thereon, the number of its annulars, and the species of the tree, may tend to give some idea of their antiquity. If the works should be found to be of Masonry; the length, breadth, and height of the walls ought to be carefully measured, the form and nature of the stones described, and specimens of both the cement and stones sent to the committee.

The best methods of obtaining information on the other subjects will naturally suggest themselves to you; and we rely on a disposition favourable to our wishes. The Committee consist of the following Gentlemen, viz.

Thomas Jefferson, President of the American Philosophical Society, at Monticello in Virginia.

James Wilkinson, Commander of the Army at Head Quarters.

Dr. Caspar Wistar, Vice President of the A. P. S.

Dr. Adam Seybert, Secretary of do[sic] in Philadel. [sic]

C. W. Peale, and Jon. Williams

Your communications may be addressed to any one of the Committee, but the articles you may think proper to furnish should be sent to this place.[9]

At the same time this committee was being formed and the report on the Cabinet was being considered for publication, Caspar Wistar, William Bache, and Adam Seybert were ordered 16 February 1798 "to devise the best methods of preserving Fossil Bones," for Hugh Williamson of North Carolina wrote that someone was "ready to raise bones of the Animal Incognitum in the Western Territory who said they were liable to decay as soon as they came into contact with the atmosphere." This committee reported its work completed on 5 April 1799 and the bones, evidently, were preserved.

A committee was named on 18 January 1799 to catalogue the books and apparatus of the Society. Almost one year later, on 6 December, the "List of Apparatus belonging to the American Philosophical Society" was presented, consisting of nine items. Robert Patterson, Joseph Clay, and Thomas Peters Smith listed:

An Electrophorus

An Universal Compound Microscope

A Compound Burning-Glass

A Thirty-inch Sliding Rule

A Wheel Barometer and a Thermometer

An Electrical Machine, formerly in the possession of [member] F[rancis] Hopkinson; supposed to be now in the house of the late D[avid] Rittenhouse.

An Achromatic Telescope now in the possession of [member] A[ndrew] Ellicott.

An Eight-day Clock.

A whale-bone Hydrometer broken.

Jefferson wrote the Society on 20 January 1804 and thanked the Members for the honor of re-electing him President of the Society. He then added what surely must be the most wide-ranging and totally encompassing offer ever made to any learned body:

The renewed evidence of regard which I receive through you from the American Philosophical society, calls for my grateful acknowledgements. The suffrage of a body of men of the first order of science, associated for the purposes of enlightening the mind of man, of multiplying his physical comforts improving his moral faculties, and enlarging the boundaries of his knowledge in general, is a testimonial which I cherish among those most dear to me.

After making my just acknowledgements to the society for their favors, I add congratulations on the enlarged field of unexplored country lately opened to free research. Should the unknown regions of Louisiana attract the attentions of the friends of science, such facilities and patronage as are within the limits of it's authority will be cordially afforded by a government founding it's security best hopes in the knolege of its citizens, not in their ignorance.

I pray you to present my high respect to the society, and to accept yourself assurances of my great consideration.[10]

Throughout the first century of the Society's existence, the Secretary was often asked to do what must have been curatorial duties. For example, on 14 February 1806, the members told the Secretary to "make a listing of the donations from the year 1767 when the two Societies united...down to 1780 when the printed list of donations begins." [11] The listing was not completed by 8 August when "further time" was allowed the Secretary for this task. [12]

Generally, when curators were ordered by the members to do something, they often did precisely what was asked, but sometimes the tasks were too difficult, such as making a comprehensive list of items presented to the Society or identifying coins. medals, and bones. The curators continued to act and occasional entries in the Minutes exhibit their concern for the expanding collection. For example, the curators listed, on 6 February 1835, the collections, and the lists were used to insure the "Cabinet of Minerals and miscellaneous items" for $4,000.

On 6 May 1853 the members resolved that the curators could exchange with other societies or individuals, duplicate "or supernumerary" specimens of "coins, medals, minerals and other articles" which were "unnecessary to be retained in the Cabinet of the Society, for such other specimens, of equal value" which would augment the Cabinet. [13] When the Society began to place parts of the Cabinet in other institutions, the curators were asked to provide adequate safeguards. The first such deposit was of "fossil organic remains" which went to the Academy of Natural Sciences of Philadelphia on 6 December 1849. [14] On 18 March 1864, the curators were, once again, authorized to deposit fossils and minerals with the Academy. [15] They were told to see if the United States Mint would accept the coin collection, "for public display" and on 17 November 1876 the curators were ordered to place it with the Mint. [16] When this fell through on 15 November 1878 the curators were ordered to deposit the coin and medal collection on deposit with the Numismatic and Antiquarian Society of Philadelphia and they reported it done on 6 December 1878. Also, they reported that the American Indian collection was deposited with the Academy of Natural Sciences of Philadelphia on 6 December 1878. [17]

While the Cabinet occupied less space, the Library expanded. The curators were generally more concerned with the preservation of the portraits and busts, and the portraits were often repaired and put under glass for preservation. Then, the glass would be removed, depending on the beliefs of the various curators. Few references were made to the other items in the Cabinet. Today, the curator maintains his interest in the better preservation of existing portraits and busts, and the acquisition of additional items.

When the Society regained control of its building and the City of Philadelphia moved its legal division into the newly completed City Hall, some of the curators wished to have the Cabinet of Curiosities, except the fossils, returned, and many discussions ensued. The members stipulated that the Franklin Peale Stone Age Collection and the coin and medal collections be returned. [18]

On 22 February 1897 the curators made a comprehensive report on the Cabinet. This report was the first written evaluation, as well as a brief history, of the Cabinet. In it, the curators proposed some suggestions for the future of the collections.

The Cabinet at present contains what might be called the residium left by much good work done in the past, together with certain articles of historic value, chiefly from association with Members of the Society.

It also gives space to some objects which no doubt *were* of passing interest at the time they were deposited, but have long since become useless, in fact comparatively uninteresting from any point of view.

To correctly appreciate this condition of things, and to place a just valuation upon what remains, it will not be inopportune to recall the following facts in the formation and history of the Cabinet itself....

The Cabinet having been called into existence by the Charter of the Society, it was originally intended to preserve any object of interest in connection with useful knowledge, that possessed significance sufficient to make it worth preserving. The donations to the Society were often made under the specific heads of "Donations to the Cabinet,"...The long list of donations to the Cabinet from colonial times to the middle of this century shows the record. In not a few instances the donors appear to have acted upon the principle that any item possessing sufficient novelty even if not of much scientific value, should find its proper resting place in the Cabinet of the Philosophical Society,—and the Society received the same, with thanks.

The collection thus obtained, so varied both in kind and quality, possessed however a peculiar significance owing to that very fact. It illustrated in some degree the diversification which already began to characterize the progress of the New States. It testified to the fact that the Philosophical Society occupied a responsive and favorable position in relation to *all* branches of systematized research, as its founder intended. From this point of view the Cabinet became a potent means in fulfilling the purpose for which the Society was founded.

Later on, many of the objects collected proved of such value to specialists in various lines of work, that they were sought for by other organizations, to perfect their own collections; and the Society co-operated in a marked degree by depositing in the collections of Specialists objects taken from its own Cabinet. The Catalogue shows that the Collections of the Cabinet or Museum [the words were interchangeable] grew rapidly until 1848. From that period the feature of the depositing elsewhere became more frequent as opportunities arose, until in 1864 it assumed definite shape as a policy for the Society to adopt. At an informal Conference between Doctors [Joseph] Leidy, [James T.] Mitchell, [John L.] Le Conte and others, then held, it was agreed that objects relating to Paleontology, Mineralogy, Geology, Botany and Natural History could be better cared for and displayed at the Academy of Natural Sciences, (and those relating to Medicine at the College of Physicians) so that the Philosophical Society could make collection of objects illustrating the progress of human thought, anthropology and kindred branches of research. The records show that Loan Deposits were made in 1864 subsequently and in accordance with the views expressed at this Conference....

Again in 1878, in order to gain space for accumulated books and stock, and on account of the condition of the building, the [Joel Roberts] Poinsett and [William H.] Keating collection was deposited elsewhere, returnable on demand.

Reference may also be made to the [Franklin] Peale Collection sent to this Museum at an early date and eventually lost....

It would appear from the records that articles have in this manner been sent to the Numismatic and Antiquarian Society; Academy of Natural Sciences; Historical Society of Pennsylvania; Penn[sylvani]a Museum and School of Industrial Art, and possibly others, taking receipts therefore, and providing for return on demand.

Although there does not appear to be any record showing that the Society itself stated by resolution in direct terms, that this distribution of its collections should be considered as a definite policy to be continually acted upon by the Curators, yet such a policy has been so repeatedly and constantly embodied in acts (which speak louder than words) that there is no doubt that such was the intention. In fact at the Meeting held as late as Dec[ember] 6th, 1895, one hundred and three members being present, when the question came up as to whether certain medals and casts should be sent elsewhere, it was "Resolved, —that the Curators be authorized, in accordance with the policy heretofore adopted, to deposit at the Pennsylvania Museum and School of Industrial Arts medals" etc. etc. thus referring to this policy of the Society as an established fact.

Such being the past experience with regard to this matter, the result may be seen in the condition of the Cabinet today.

It is now evident that nearly, if not quite all the articles which could be utilized better elsewhere, have already been distributed, and such as remain derive their interest and value chiefly from historic association, associations with members of the Society, or as marking some era or stage of progress in the Society's own work....

The above statements lead naturally to considerations with regard to the future.... It is to be accepted or settled that the Society does not propose to enter into any competition, so to speak, with other Associations in the matter of Collections for a Museum. The intention is rather to retain and strengthen in every way a position much more exalted in relation to Philosophy and Science, the position in fact which has characterized its action during the last half century.

As the Nestor among learned Societies in America, its published transactions and proceedings contain the important records as to work done, and these take that position among the literature of science to which they are entitled.

From this point of view the proper production and care of the Society's own Publications, together with the care of the objects of interest illustratively of its own history, call for constant attention; the further development of the Library, and the Reading Room facilities, in the matter of exchanges, becomes essential to the welfare of the Society.

The publications of the Society and its collection of objects relating to its own history, should not be separated, unless for very urgent reasons; They complement and illustrate each other. The portraits and busts, for example, which form so salient a feature to the eye among the effects of the Society, these may be used, and are only useful, in promoting that harmony with environment which the conditions demand. The historical significance tells with a force potent for good. They are often silent witnesses to facts which have never gotten into the Proceedings and Transactions, and yet embody useful knowledge; They suggest the individual and the strength of personality; They speak of original effort, perseverance, trials, failures, successes and ultimate triumphs of those who have here worked and recorded, proceeded and transacted. Such objects of interest, taken in connection with the publications of the Society embody in no small degree, that peculiar sacred feeling which not only the members but many of the public at large have associated for generations with this venerable and honored organization.

Acting upon these considerations, the Curators present herewith a project to further carry on the work of the Society which they think will be better suited to the changed and varied conditions than heretofore, will harmonize the work as a whole, will aid in developing the Library by giving a fitting locale to the Publications of the Society, and at the same time will properly preserve the objects of historic interest in the Cabinet....

The Cabinet as a feature in the Society's work being established by the Charter, it is proposed to extend its scope and significance beyond the original Museum idea, and recognize the several acceptations of that term which may be applied.

1st.—A portion of the building set apart for the conservation of antiquities, works of art and industry, in this respect a receptacle for curiosities especially those of historic interest in connection with work done here, thereby recognizing so far as possible the original idea of the Cabinet.

2nd.—A private room in which consultation may be held, and where the Publications of the Society may be found, thereby recognizing the demands for Library extension which the growth of the Society calls for.

3rd. — A place for meetings or sessions as an ante-room in connection with public meetings and receptions.

From this point of view the Cabinet of the Society may be said to have outgrown its original limited sphere of action and use, and although curtailed in one direction, in the future its scope will be enlarged in other ways, to meet the new demands. The intention is to provide the Society with a Cabinet of greater scope and efficiency than heretofore, one that will not only meet the requirements demanded by the Charter but will further the policy of the Society in the future.

The objects of historic interest will be well placed, the Publications of the Society, its volumes of Proceedings and Transactions will receive that special recognition to which they are entitled. The two will serve together, as complementary and illustrative of each other....

The curators then outlined how the north room of Philosophical Hall was to be refinished and refurnished, and recommended that the
historical associations connected with the locality itself need not be lost sight of...it is proposed to designate the north-west corner...as [Charles Willson] Peale's alcove, and place within it such souvenirs as remain of the Artist and Member of the Society, thus preserving its association with the presence of [George] Washington, [Thomas] Jefferson, [David] Rittenhouse and C. W. Peale, the latter of whom used it for some time as a studio, and there painted not a few of his portraits of contemporaries, members of this Society.

The eastern portion of the room, with table to be considered as the Consultation Cabinet proper—in proximity to which should be placed in the cases the publications of the Society. The fire proof safe is already at that end of the room.

The South-west corner, adjacent to Peale's alcove to be considered as the Inner cabinet, where in the Curators closet is placed. The walls of the room to be furnished with cases to the height of six feet six inches....

The wall space above and between the cases, and at other points down to a lower level, to be used for the display of such portraits and illustrations as may be more appropriate in the Cabinet than in the Main Room. The tops of the cases and pedestals will furnish appropriate positions for such busts and casts, models and kindred objects as may be thus displayed.[19]

This report is the last major attempt by the curators, for many years, to arrange rooms and items for exhibition. Some of the recommendations were adopted, but the pressure of the expanding library demanded that the room be used for other purposes.
However, interest in the cabinet of curiosities did not die and the curators made a comprehensive report on 2 December 1898 on the various collections of the cabinet and their dispositions:
In accordance with the Rules of Administration our Order adopted at the last meeting of the Society, Nov. 1898, the Curators respectfully submit the following report:

With regard to the collections which have been deposited by this society elsewhere than in their own Hall, the following list gives the localities and general character of the collection.

In the Academy of Natural Sciences—Philadelphia

[Joel R.] Poinsett Collection of Mexican Antiquities.

[William H.] Keating do do[sic]

Various minerals, fossils, and other objects, as per records of the Society.

Also the following botanical collections

[Henry E.] Muhlenberg' Herbarium

[Charles W.] Short, and Louis [Meriwether Lewis] & [William]

Clarke's [sic] Collection

These being in part all the botanical collections at present belonging to this Society.

In the Smithsonian Institute [sic] Washington, D. C.:

The official French Metre.

In the Pennsylvania Museum and School of Industrial Art, Fairmount Park, Philadelphia, Memorial Hall

Coins and medals, originally deposited with the Numismatic and Antiquarian Society. At the request of the latter, and under the authority of this society, this collection was redeposited in the Penn[sylvani]a Museum & School of Industrial Art, together with other coins, medals and casts found in the Cabinet.

In addition to the above, the Curators are now making arrangements for deposit at the Wagner [Free] Institute [of Science], Philadelphia, or elsewhere, the minerals, geological specimens, fossils, casts, moulds, &c. as still remain in the Society's possession.

These objects have been labeled, also a card-catalogue prepared. In order to preserve the historic record in better form than heretofore, the Curators are now preparing a complete Catalogue of the entries upon the minutes of Donations to the Cabinet, and of the various particles which from time to time have been committed to their care.

As to the Portraits, Busts and Bas-reliefs, the following may be said:

During the summer of 1897, the North Room, second floor, was completely renovated and rearranged for the purpose of affording additional Library facilities. Up to this time many of the more valuable portraits and busts had been collected together in the main Hall, South room, second floor, where owing to their number, and the limited space upon the walls, they did not appear to so good an advantage as was desirable.

The Curators therefore, as part of the new arrangement of the Library, provided for a more satisfactory display. The collection of portraits, although not numerous, [ ] in all), is already comprehensive enough to possess much historic and artistic interest. The Curators endeavored to accentuate this historic significance in the new arrangement, to illustrate either the chronological sequence in official relations to the Society itself, or representative characteristics in professional career. This being the first effort in this direction with the collection of this Society, it is hoped that a precedent has been made here, in conformity with modern usage in collections of a similar character elsewhere. The portraits of the Presidents of the Society only, have been retained in the main Hall, together with that of Washington. The other portraits were placed in the North Room, where they have added greatly to the general effect of the new Library installation and certainly appear to greater advantage than heretofore. The busts and bas-reliefs have been placed throughout both rooms, and in the Hall, and in the Main Library—in positions which seemed appropriate. During the summer of 1898, the Society deemed it advisable to tint the walls and woodwork of the Main Hall, to bring it into conformity with the original plan of the Committee on accommodations, and the recent work of the Library extension in the North Room. The Curators again availed themselves of the opportunity offered, and had all the portraits, busts and bas-reliefs properly examined, relabeled with name and dates, and placed in best condition for future preservation. The portraits were cleaned and revarnished by experts—the marbles carefully cleaned, and plaster busts ivory-tinted. It is now hoped that these properties of the Society may not require much extra care in that respect for many years to come.

The Curators were also fortunate in accepting the proffered services of Mr. Julius F. Sachse, Mem[ber]. A[merican]. P[hilosophical]. S[ociety]., who, while the pictures were off the walls, photographed the entire collection, thus insuring additional authentic and artistic records of the originals.

In order to complete the work thus commenced, the Curators are now engaged in preparing an illustrated catalogue of these historic portraits, busts and bas-reliefs upon a more comprehensive scale than heretofore, and embracing such biographical notes and statistical data as will enable the visitor to intelligently examine the originals themselves.[20]

The curators made a comprehensive report on 2 December 1898 on the various collections of the Cabinet and their disposition:
In accordance with the Rules of Administration our Order adopted at the last meeting of the Society, Nov. 1898, the Curators respectfully submit the following report: With regard to the collections which have been deposited by this society elsewhere than in their own Hall, the following list give the localities and general character of the collection.

In the Academy of Natural Sciences — Philadelphia

Poinsett Collection of Mexican Antiquities.
Keating   do   do[sic]
Various minerals, fossils, and other objects, as per records of the Society.
Also the following botanical collections
[Gotthilf Heinrich Ernst] Muhlenberg Herbarium, [Charles W.] Short, [Meriwether] Lewis & [William] Clarke's [sic] Collection. These being in part all the botanical collections at present belonging to this society.

This last major effort of the curators also included their report of 29 November 1898:
During the past year they have been engaged continuously in the task of arranging the articles still left in the Cabinet (or Museum) of the Society, and in accordance with its policy through many years of depositing on condition of their safe conservation and return on demand of such classes of articles as can be better displayed or studied elsewhere. Thus besides the Numismatic Collections now in deposit at the Pennsylvania Museum in Fairmount Park, a number of medals &c. which have accumulated are now being prepared for deposit there: while all of the mineralogical & geological specimens have been removed to the Wagner [Free] Institute [of Science]. In this connection they regret to state that owing to the many movings and vicissitudes which these specimens have undergone many of their labels & means of identification have been hopelessly lost or destroyed so that they have become comparatively valueless. Such material as been placed at the service of

the Superintendent of the High School for use in their analytical classes - and a catalogue of the remains of our Mineralogical cabinet is now in course of preparation by Mr. Johnson of the Wagner [Free] Institute [of Science].

In this connection they also regret to have to report the almost total destruction of the set of Trilobite casts belonging to the Society, as well as the casts & moulds of Mastodon & other fossils which were made under direction of [member] Dr. [Isaac] Hays in 1831, and from which the curators were authorized to keep sets of casts for sale at $30 per set, in 1834. These moulds were especially interesting and valuable, not only from the care & skill evidenced in their construction but as having been made from the type specimens described and figured by Dr. Hays in the Transactions of the Society now deposited with many others at the Acad[emy] of Nat[ural]. Sciences [of Philadelphia]. These moulds, casts & mineral specimens were moved from place to place until at last having in the course of the alterations to the North Room they were placed in boxes & barrels in the basement, notwithstanding the protest of at least one of the Curators. The rough handling they were thus subjected to has damaged them beyond repair, but the remnants may still prove useful to those who may hereafter study mastodon fossils: and the Curators have therefore arranged for their transportation to the Acad[emy]. of Natural Sciences [of Philadelphia] where they may still be useful for comparison with & identification of the original type of specimens.

The Collection of Portraits & Busts has been maintained in excellent order and a catalogue of them prepared mainly under the direction of member Mr. [Henry] Pettit as noted in he Proceedings...and a very valuable original portrait of [member] Dr. Benjamin Rush, found amongst old papers &c. in the Library is now in process of repair. It will soon be placed on our walls. Efforts are also now making to secure additional portraits of the valued members who have distinguished themselves by their devotion to the Society and by their contributions to science....

The Franklin Peale Collection of Implements of the Stone Age has been removed in accordance with the request of the Library Committee from the North Room to the Meeting Room—and arranged in order. This in connection with other remains of Indian workmanship now there constitutes a very valuable & interesting portion of he Society's possessions to those interested in anthropological research.[21]

On 7 December 1900 the curators reported for the year:
The various collections in our charge which were on deposit in the Academy of Natural Sciences [of Philadelphia], Memorial Hall [the Pennsylvania Museum and School of Industrial Art] and the Wagner Free Institute [of Science] have from time to time been informally inspected by us, and are believed to be in good condition and well displayed; as also are those in the Hall of the Society. More definite identification of those at the Academy of Natural Sciences, with the aid of our catalogue, is now in progress. There were but few additions to the Cabinet; but they include the valuable portraits of Dr. Joseph Leidy and Former Secretary Dr. Daniel G. Brinton, and a medal of Dr. Brinton.[22]

Numismatic Collections now in deposit at the Pennsylvania Museum [and School of Industrial Art] in Fairmount Park, a number of medals &c. which have accumulated are now being prepared for deposit there: while all of the mineralogical & geological specimens have been removed to the Wagner [Free] Institute [of Science]. In this connection they regret to state that owing to the many movings and vicissitudes which these specimens have undergone, many of their labels & means of identification have been hopelessly lost or destroyed so that they have become comparatively valueless. Such material has been placed at the service of the Superintendent of the High School for use in their analytical classes—and a catalogue of the remains of our Mineralogical cabinet is now in course of preparation by Mr. Johnson of the Wagner [Free] Institute.

In this connection they also regret to have to report the almost total destruction of the set of Trilobite casts belonging to the Society, as well as the casts & moulds of Mastodon & other fossils which were made under the direction of Dr. [Isaac] Hays in 1831, and from which the curators were authorized to keep sets of casts for sale at $30 per set, in 1834. These moulds were especially interesting and valuable, not only from the care & skill evidenced in their construction but as having been made from the type specimens described and figured by Dr. Hays in the Transactions of the Society now deposited with many others at the Acad[emy] of Nat[ural] Sci[ences of Philadelphia]. These moulds, casts & mineral specimens were moved from place to place until at last having in the course of the alterations to the North Room they were placed in boxes & barrels in the basement, notwithstanding the protest of at least one of the Curators. The rough handling they were thus subjected to has damaged them beyond repair, but the remnants may still prove useful to those who may hereafter study mastodon fossils: and the curators have therefore arranged for their transportation to the Acad[emy] of Natural Sciences where they may still be useful for comparison with & identification of the original type specimens.

The Collection of Portraits & Busts has been maintained in excellent order and a catalogue of them prepared mainly under the direction of [member] Mr. [Henry] Pettit as noted in the Proceedings and a very valuable original portrait of [member] Dr. Benjamin Rush, found amongst old papers &c. in the Library is now in process of repair. It will soon be placed on our walls. Efforts are also now making to secure additional portraits of the valued members who have distinguished themselves by their devotion to the Society and by their contributions to science. In addition to the above a complete set of Records of the Donations to the Society from its foundation to the present time has been prepared from the original minutes by Mr. Oscar Hunnersdorff under the direction of the Curators, together with an Index of reference, in this are noted as far as possible the present location of each article. A card catalogue has been prepared, and descriptive cards also attached to the articles as they have been recognized. This has been a very difficult task which has occupied many of the spare hours of one of your curators during the past ten years, and which he feels happy in having now so nearly accomplished (as there remain but few objects unrecognized & unidentified) that the labors of future curators will be greatly lessened, and a possibility afforded of keeping better records in the future than there has been in the past.

The Franklin Peale Collection of Implements of the Stone Age has been removed in accordance with the request of the Library Committee from the north Room to the Meeting Room - and arranged in order. This in connection with other remains of Indian workmanship now there constitutes a very valuable & interesting portion of the Society's possessions to those interested in anthropological research.[21]

The Records of Donations to the Society are nowhere near a complete listing. A man assembled the data from only the minutes. Too many items were presented and not entered in the minutes, or were merely entered, ignoring the lists which had been prepared of the donation. Also, the correspondence often lists items presented, as does the *Transactions*, and they are not in this Records of Donations.

On 7 December 1900 the curators reported for the year:
The various collections in our charge which were on deposit in the Academy of Natural Sciences, Memorial Hall and the Wagner Free Institute have from time to time been informally been inspected by us, and are believed to be in good condition and well displayed; as also are those in the hall of the Society. More definite identification of those at the Academy of Natural Sciences, with the aid of our

catalogue, is now in progress. There were but few additions to the Cabinet; but they include the valuable portraits of [members] Dr. Joseph Leidy and Former Secretary Dr. Daniel G. Brinton, and a medal of Dr. Brinton.[22]

After this splendid outlay of energy, the subsequent curators had little to do. The Cabinet of Curiosities was effectively deposited and remained as listed above, until the late 1920s when the Native American Collection with some of the oddities (artifacts from other parts of the world, were placed in the University Museum of the University of Pennsylvania. The day of the Cabinet was now over. The constantly growing library needed additional space. The North Room was devoted to the library and the curators henceforth dealt with the objets d'art (portraits and busts) the instruments and models, and the relics of past presidents. [21]

And yet, occasionally the curators were asked to obtain lists of the Society's deposits, and some members would wish the return of the Cabinet. By 1900 the minutes, as printed in the *Proceedings*, became very brief. A researcher has to use the manuscript minutes to do adequate research. Also, on 17 May 1901, Isaac Minis Hays proposed a general meeting for all the members, rather than the usual local members attending the regular meetings, and by 1902 the general meetings of the Society, twice a year, began. The minutes then, for all practical purposes, ceased to exist, and the library records assumed the greatest importance of all.

As late as 1987 the curator was asked to get a written report from the sister institutions of the Cabinet of Curiosities items held on long-term deposit. At the meeting of 23 April 1987, the Council of the Society voted to make these deposits, with certain exceptions, gifts.[24]

Role of the Curators—References
1. Franklin, B. A Proposal for Promoting Useful Knowledge among the British Plantations in America. Philadelphia, [B. Franklin:], 14 May 1743.
2. For a concise history of the two Societies, see: [Carl Bridenbaugh,] "Propagating Useful Knowledge from Philadelphia, 1768–1771," The Transactions of the American Philosophical Society, &c. Published in the American Magazine during 1769. Memoirs of the APS, vol. 77. Philadelphia: APS: 1969.
3. Ibid., 126.
4. American Society. Minutes, 25 March, 26 Aug., 23 Sept. and 9 Dec. 1768.
5. Archives. APS. Report, 20 April 1770.
6. Ibid., 7 Sept. 1777.
7. Ibid., 2 April 1783.
8. Ibid., 4 Aug. 1797.
9. Trans., vol. 5, pp. ixxi.
10. Archives. T. Jefferson to T. H. Hewson, 20 Jan. 1804.
11. Trans., vol. 5, p. 24.
12. Ibid.
13. Proc., vol. 5, p. 329.
14. Ibid., 111–112.
15. Ibid., vol. 9, pp. 353–354.
16. Ibid., vol. 16, p. 334.
17. Ibid., 273.
18. Minutes, 16 June 1795, 18 Jan. 1799, 14 Feb. 1806, 25 Jan. 1828, etc.; Officers and Councillors. Minutes, 3 and 12 Feb. 1892, and 10 Feb. 1893; Proc., vol. 30, pp. 31112, vol. 31, pp. 1213, 13233; "Arch." R. M. Bache to W. P. Tatham, 1 Aug. 1891, R. M. Bache to H. Phillips, Jr., 4 and 14 Sept. 1892, H. Goodwin to H. Phillips, Jr., 17 March 1893, J. S. Price to J. C. Morris, 21 April 1893; Curators report, 3 Feb. 1893.
19. Archives. Curators report, 22 Feb. 1897.
20. Ibid., 2 Feb. 1898.
21. Ibid., 29 Nov. 1899.
22. Ibid., 7 Dec. 1900.
23. Minutes, 12 April, 4 Oct. 1901, 3 and 17 Jan. 1902; Proc., vol. 29, p. 220.
24. Council minutes, 23 April 1987.

Chapter 2.
Native American Antiquities

27 May 1768

"Part of an Ornament found about a dead Indian in Ac[c]omack County where an Indian Town formerly stood." It seemed to be part of a belt which surrounded the head and body of the Indian, who must have been buried "upwards of 80 years. The age of the burial was relatively exact, for there was a sawmill erected over the grave 80 years ago." It was "composed of small copper Tubes about 22' Inches long, with Deer and other Sinews passing through them, which are in parallel Lines & so connected by the Deer Sinews as to be moveable like a belt of Wampum."

Clement Biddle

1 May 1772

An Indian hatchet of stone.

Israel Jacobs

Two pairs of "Arcadian Indian" snow shoes. Dickinson wrote David Rittenhouse that they were "filled in their crossbarring with the raw Hide of a Carabooe & made by an Indian woman of that country."[1]

James Dickinson.

19 October 1787

Indian spear-stones from near the river Wye in Maryland. They had been found "lately" in the mud. Bordley sent a letter "containing various speculations & conjectures concerning" them.[2]

John Beale Bordley

3 October 1788

From Lancaster, Pennsylvania, came several gifts including "*Indian darts,* frequently found in the fields near Lancaster; Water Birch bark specimens; *Bear's gut,* when first cleaned, resembling a silk ribbon," the last used by Indians for different purposes.

Matthias Barton

2 October 1789

Some Indian pottery "lately found in a bank near Washington," Pennsylvania.

David Redick

1 October 1790

P. Pond's account of certain Indian inscriptions or writings "which have been discovered in the Bay of Naragansett [sic] and a drawing of the same." Both letter and drawing are missing from the Archives.

Ezra Stiles

19 August 1791

"A curious piece of Indian Sculpture, supposed to represent an Indian woman in labor." It was found near the Cumberland River in Virginia.[3]

Thomas Jefferson

An officer, Mr. Heart, "in the late Western Expedition," wrote Benjamin Smith Barton, "giving an account, under a great variety of particulars," of some of the antiquities of the western country. His letter was "read & referred to the Committee of Publications." Heart was killed in the defeat of General Arthur St. Clair of that year.

Benjamin Smith Barton

18 May 1792

A copy of a letter from Colonel George Morgan, written to his brother, John Morgan, from Prospect, New Jersey was received. It concerned "Ancient Fortifications" on the Mississippi and Missouri Rivers in the western country, and a drawing of the ruin opposite Scioto, Ohio, was shown. Neither of these items is in the Archives today. There is, however, a lengthy letter from Manasseh Cutler to Benjamin Smith Barton dated Ipswich, Massachusetts, 31 August 1792, about the ancient fortifications in the Ohio country. Cutler measured the trees and counted the rings, "thereby proving the age of the ruins."[4]

5 October 1792
A stone dodecahedron, found on the banks of the Ohio River. It was described as a "stone of black slate, in form of a regular dodecahedron, the side of each pentagon about one inch and a half."5 On 23 April 1897, this item was examined carefully, and it was reported that the stone had some marks on it indicating that it had belonged to an Indian medicine man. It was surmised that the stone had been used to enable the shaman to keep a better account of the lunar months.[6]

Charles Brown

16 January 1795
An idol worshipped by the natives of Hispaniola. It was of stone and represented a kneeling man with a cable-like disk on his head. The man was naked, showing the vertebrae. The ear disks were the only ornaments.[7]

Mederic L. E. Moreau de Saint Mery

5 February 1796
From Cincinnati, North west Territory, sent to David Rittenhouse, two specimens of Indian workmanship. Donor Judge George Turner wrote on 12 January 1794:

> I have in possession numerous other western rarities, at the service of the Society; and I hope to add to them from time to time. They shall be forwarded by convenient opportunities. It would afford me infinite Satisfaction to hear that the Society have taken order for the arranging and extending their cabinet. The productions, whether animal, vegetable, or mineral, of the western world—passing, as it does, through every climate, and perhaps with all the varieties of face and soil—call loudly for the notice of its inhabitants. The best way to excite that notice is, by collecting specimens of those productions, and placing them with some public body for public inspection. Thus Genius would be inticed [sic] into the fields of Research, and the knowledge of our country essentially promoted. Individuals must feel an interest in exploring the walks of Nature to gather her Materials, whenever it shall be known that a Repository is opened for them, founded—as it ought to be—on a public and permanent basis.[8]

The gifts were two pipes "of curious workmanship made of some kind of stone of a beautiful flesh color, and inlaid with pewter." They were presented through Nicholas Collin. The other gift was a present from Zenon Trudeaux, the commandant of Saint Louis, to Turner, who sent it to the Society. It was a gift of two Indian leggings of buckskin ornamented with porcupine quills and Indian hair. They came from a nation of Indians "high up the Missouri who never but once saw a white man."[9] George Turner wrote John Vaughan on the same day, 12 January 1794, that he hoped to "carry into effect my promise of furnishing at times, the philosophical Society with our Western productions." He added that they would be shipped collect "*at your expense*—for this is part of the promise." Also, he made some comments on the great increase of the white population along the Ohio:

> The rapid improvement of this country is beyond ordinary conception. Both shores of the Ohio, in most of its extent between [Cincinnati] and Pittsburgh—a distance of 500 miles, are covered with towns and detached houses. Opposite the town whence I date, on the Kentucky shore, I have in view a town that was born in my absence and christened Newport. And as to Cincinnati, tho' not yet 4 years old, the houses are now both numerous and respectable. Some are of hewn timber, others are frames, and a few are of stone: total number about 300—among which there are nearly 30 stores, and some of these capital houses of trade.

> The army is lying still. [General Anthony] Wayne has advanced a post on St. Clair's Battle Ground, and called it, not unaptly, Fort Recovery. The bones of about 300 of those slain on the fatal fourth of November have been buried with full military honours and sev[era]l pieces of the field ordnance have been recovered. The fort is garrisoned with two companies. Head Quarters remain, as before, six miles advanced of Fort Jefferson.

John Vaughan endorsed this letter to the president of the Society and noted that he was sending a box of shells that Turner had sent him, along with the letter."[10]

George Turner

19 February 1796

Some Indian antiquities with an account of them accompanied by sketches were presented through Benjamin Smith Barton by Colonel Jonathan D. Sergeant.[11] Sergeant wrote Barton on 25 November 1799 and described them as "some account of certain Articles, which were taken out of an ancient Tumulus, or Grave, in the Western Country"—Cincinnati, in fact. The grave was

> really very ancient; there were stumps of oak trees on the mount seven feet in
> diameter [on] an extensive artificial mound of earth, raised probably for the purpose
> of a burial ground...[It had] a gradual slope in the various directions, and a base of
> about 120 feet by sixty...In addition to the matters of which you have the drawing,
> were several utensils, or ornaments, lost or mislaid.[12]

Because the grave was elevated on dry land, there was almost no "Decay of the Skeleton upon being exposed to the Air," and Sergeant forwarded the big part of the thighbone to the Society.[13]

Judge Turner wished to clear up some "misconceptions concerning certain articles found in an Indian tumulus at Cincinnati" and wrote his remarks on these funeral[14] objects. Turner's article on this mound follows that of Jonathan D. Sergeant in volume IV of the *Transactions*.

Jonathan D. Sergeant

10 February 1797

A large number of artifacts, with a promise by Judge Turner to label them all. This collection was a "variety of very curious and interesting articles from different parts of the Western Country," especially from the Missouri, Mississippi and Tennessee Rivers. They tended "to throw some illustration on the Indian Antiquities of North America." This mass of items included a pair of leggings for a boy, from the Missouri area. A peace pipe, or "Calumet...elegantly ornamented with porcupine quills" from the Ausage tribe, which inhabited a branch of the Missouri River, was probably presented earlier and referred to again on this date. A conjurer's mask "formed of the scalp, &c. of a Buffalo," from the Missouri area, was followed by an arrow "neatly headed with bone" from the Saukis Indians from the upper part of the Mississippi River. Eight of the arrows generally used by the Miami Indians and the neighboring tribes and a "Stone Pestle used by the Indians formerly, for pounding corn and jerking fleash" followed. A hatchet with a head of stone which the natives formerly used and "an Indian bowl, taken out of the bed of the Tennessee River" were listed. Some sea shells and some perforated bones were presented: they had been "taken out of an ancient Indian grave on the Great Kananwa [Kanawha]." Two batches of porcupine quills were included in this gift—some were "dyed with different colors, used to ornament various works," and others were of their natural color.

A most unusual gift was the "skin of an Indian taken from the side." More to the point, however, it must have been "part of a sea-otter skin, from its flank, where the fur is shortest." This specimen was from the Pacific Coast, brought by Alexander McKenzie, who traveled across Canada and returned by the Pacific northwest coast in 1794. Originally, this specimen had been part of a blanket coat from the Pacific coast. A spear that had been used by the Indians when they fought the Americans and that had killed "Colonel Chew" in the fight on the Ohio River "about 11 miles above Fort Massac" was supposedly made from a bayonet "used under Gen. St. Clair, in the action November 4, 1791." There were, also, "various Indian Arrows from the North Western territory" and a piece of wooden Indian sculpture that resembled a beaver "from the Kaskaskian nation" brought from there by William Clark. This was used by the Indians as a "Tureen." There was a pair of Indian garters "tipped with tin and Porcupine quills, from the Wabash" and another pair from the Creek nation. Finally, there was "an Indian belt, from the Mississippi."[15] The arrows and the spear are in the Society's collection today.

George Turner

On 5 May 1797, a committee composed of George Turner, Caspar Wistar, Nicholas Collin, Richard Peters Smith, and Adam Seybert were appointed "to report a plan of collecting Information respecting American antiquities." Reports were made on 26 May and 16 June, and the latter was ordered to "lie on the table."[16] It was reconsidered on 21 July 1797. On 6 April 1798, the report was again read and was amended "by paragraphs," and a new committee was appointed consisting of Thomas Jefferson, George Turner, Caspar Wistar, Adam Seybert, Charles Willson Peale, James Wilkinson, and Jonathan Williams. The result was a circular letter, which was published in the *Transactions.*

The American Philosophical Society have always considered the antiquity, changes, and present state of their own country as primary objects of their research; and with a view to facilitate such discoveries, a permanent committee has been established, among whose duties the following have been recommended as requiring particular attention.

1. To procure one or more entire skeletons of the Mammoth, so called, and of such other unknown animals as either have been, or hereafter may be discovered in America.

2. To obtain accurate plans, drawings and descriptions of whatever is interesting, (where the originals cannot be had) and especially of ancient Fortifications, Tumuli, and other Indian works of art: ascertaining the materials composing them, their contents, the purposes for which they are probably designed, &c.

3. To invite researches into the Natural History of the Earth, the changes it has undergone as to Mountains, Lakes, Rivers, Prairies, etc.

4. To inquire into the Customs, Manners, Languages and Character of the Indian nations, ancient and modern, and their migrations.

The importance of these objects will be acknowledged by every Lover of Science, and, we trust, sufficiently apologize for thus troubling you: for without the aid of gentlemen who have taste and opportunity for such researches, our means would be very confined. We therefore solicit your communications, now or in the future, on these subjects; which will be at all times thankfully received, and duly noticed in the publications of the Society.

As to the first object, the committee suggest to Gentlemen who may be in the way of inquiries of that kind, that the Great Bone Lick on the Ohio, and other places where there may be mineral salt, are the most eligible spots for the purpose; because animals are known to resort to such places.

With respect to the second head, the committee are desirous that cuts in various directions may be made into many of the Tumuli, to ascertain their contents; while the diameter of the largest tree growing thereon, the number of its annulars and the species of the tree, may tend to give some idea of their antiquity. If the works should be found to be of Masonry; the length, breadth, and height of the walls ought to be carefully measured, form and nature of the stones described, and specimens of both the cement and stones sent to the committee.

The best methods of obtaining information on the other subjects will naturally suggest themselves to you; and we rely on a disposition favourable to our wishes....

Your communications may be addressed to any one of the Committee, but the articles you may think proper to furnish should be sent to this place [Philosophical Hall, Philadelphia, Pennsylvania].[17]

Benjamin Smith Barton, ever eager to learn more about the fascinating Native Americans, exhibited a specimen of Indian picture writing and read a paper on it on 31 March 1797.

Members heard a paper read on 19 May 1797 about two very ancient walls that had been recently discovered in North Carolina. The Reverend Samuel Spring and S. McCorkle had written about these walls. Some specimens of the cement and stone of the walls were delivered on 16 June 1797. Adam Seybert was asked to examine and report on them. Dr. Seybert showed the specimens on 16 June and promised the "analysis hereafter." On 21 July his chemical analysis was read and referred to Thomas C. James and George Turner with the original communication with a view to the publication of both at the same time,[18] Seybert's and James Woodhouse's papers on the analysis of the materials in the wall were delivered 1 June 1798, as were some letters on the subject between Woodhouse and James Hall, Jr. All of these were turned over to a committee composed of Caspar Wistar, Robert Strettell Jones, and George Turner. The committee reported 21 December 1798 that Seybert's and Woodhouse's papers contained

an ingenious analysis of the different substances in question, with very satisfactory reasons for considering the supposed Wall, as a natural, & not an artificial production—but that the principles on which the different experiments were formed being similar, the experiments much alike, & the result allmost the same, in both papers, the Committee cannot recommend the publication of both, and wish the learned Authors to write in the formation of one memoir on the subject which they are confident will be very satisfactory to all the Chemists who may read it.[18]

There is a reference in the *Transactions*, volume IV, to Judge George Turner's gift of an "oviform stone, from the Wabash." This may have been the "Quartz (from a Mound, Ohio)" as described on a curators card in the Library.

S. F. Hutchinson sent 24 November 1797 a written description of some very "singular ceremonies which he was present at among the Naudowessi Indians," an Indian nation living west of the Mississippi, "giving an account of their Music, exemplified by a Specimen of musical Notes." The ceremony he described was the *Wakam-Mantah*, or calumet dance. It was "a dance of rejoicing and expressions of peace." This [19] is a long paper of ten oversize pages. George Turner and Robert Patterson were on the committee which reported on it 1 December 1797:[20] "That in their opinion the paper bears evident marks of an intention in the writer to impose on the Society and is therefore unworthy of further notice.[21] The members asked the reasons for this negative report and, after hearing them, decided that the reasons were "satisfactory."

The Indian female idol which was presented by Thomas Jefferson was lent to Benjamin Smith Barton so he could make a drawing of it. It was receipted, and Barton promised to return it, which he did on 3 December 1802.

2 April 1802 (?)
Arrow belt with poisoned arrows, and a tube to blow them through. They came originally from Peru and the tube was 7 feet in length.[22]

Ross [Rose?] Campbell

18 November 1803
A Roman Catholic amulet "found some feet underground near Nashville, Tennessee." It is supposedly the relic of an Indian.[23]

Samuel Brown

15 June 1804
The members were shown several Mexican paintings.[24]

Benjamin Smith Barton

17 August 1804
An Indian hatchet.

Major Rivardi

17 May 1805

Some Indian beads found on a female skeleton "on the Delaware [River] shore near Easton," on the Lehigh River.[25]

Anthony Fothergill

4 October 1805

An earthernware bottle made by the Indians, found in "upper Louisiana."

Henry Peyrouse

1 November 1805

A "small earthen cup (broken in carriage)."

Samuel Brown

7 March 1806

Some "manufactured copper" which had been found in an artificial mound in Cincinnati, Ohio, in March 1804. It was taken from the same mound with the "Specimens described by Mr. Sergeant, 4th Vol[ume] of Trans[actions]." With this was a history by Daniel Drake of its discovery with "Various articles found in a Tumulus at Cincinnati." Barton read some comment on the tumulus:

> On viewing it horizontally (which we are enabled to do in consequence of large quantities of earth being taken away to firm the street) we observed several strata, which exhibit different appearances. As well as I recollect we first observed over the whole a covering of mould or soil from 9 to 12 feet thick. Immediately under that, we see a Stratum of Pebble Stones, of various sizes, with very little Earth between them. This Stratum which is from 1 to 2 feet in Depth, is somewhat arched according to the convexity of the tumulus. Directly below this, we observe a layer or bed of common Clay, from 6 to 8 feet in depth, and all below that, as far as the destruction of the Tumulus (in a vertical manner) had extended, we see nothing but a bed of sand. Throughout the whole, calcareous stones of different sizes, but none of them very large, are seen, disposed in an horizontal, oblique, or perpendicular manner. Towards the bottom of the stratum of Clay, probably six feet under the surface, the piece of Copper was found. Nearly all the finger and metacarpel [sic] Bones of the human hand were grasping in contact with it. Some of them were coloured green.
>
> Around the short axis of the internal Plates a considerable quantity of fibrous substance, not unlike the inner bark of flax, was wound or disposed in a concentric manner. In the neighbourhood of this Copper, a number of decayed human bones, shells, & other fossils have been found. The stratum of pebble stones is perfectly entire over the whole; and appears evidently to have been formed or accumulated, since those substances were deposited in the tumulus.[28]

Benjamin Smith Barton

21 March 1806

Sketches of "two supposed Mexican Monuments." The members asked the donor to furnish an account of them to the Society.

Josef Joachim de Ferrer

19 August 1808

Some "vitrifaction from ancient Fort on Paint Creek, nine miles from Chilicothe [Ohio]." This was referred to Joseph Cloud, who reported on 2 December of the same year that it was "an earthy substance, combined with a small portion of iron."[29]

Thomas Worthington

4 September 1811
The discovery of Mammoth Cave in Kentucky excited much interest, and Benjamin Smith
Barton received a letter from John D. Clifford, dated Lexington, Kentucky, 4 September
1811, which described the use the Indians made of it:

Mr. Wilkins has lately returned from the Cave. He informs me that in many parts as
far as he has explored it there are circular Collections of stones, generally about 3
feet Diameter piled up in the form of a wall & that by scraping the Earth beneath
they find Charcoal. This evinces the Cave to have been Inhabited either by a horde
of Troglodytes or else must have been the scene of the Religious Mysteries. They
have lately been removing some of the vast Rocks which are scattered in the large
Chamber into which the Entrance of the Cave leads. Underneath these masses of
stones they have found several platted shoes or moccasons made from the fiber of
the flag plant. Two of them will be sent on to Philad[elphi]a—the ensuing winter, it
is therefore unnecessary to describe them. They however discover great
ingenuity—& are totally different from any fabrick of our Indians. There were also
found a few masks of a sort made from the same materials. The knot is the same as
the one we use & the mask about the size of a shad net. The atmosphere of these
nitre caves prevents all putrifaction. Dead bodies have been found, which when
first seen, were apparently as perfect as at the period when deposited there. A Child
was lately dug up in a cave adjoining that of Mr. Wilkins wrapped up in a Cloth
described as resembling Canvas; this was again enveloped in a Deer Skin. The
corpse appeared as if newly Dead but upon exposure to the open atmosphere it in a
few hours crumbled into its native Dust. Many human bones have also been found
in the nitre caves of the Cumberland Mountains similar to that of the Child—tho'
they were wrapped up in garments made from the outer surface of the cave
intermingling with feathers. It would be a great desideration to see one of these
bodies, to delineate their features & to particularly observe whether they have that
slant of the Eyes peculiar to the Tartar natives.

I am in hope Mr. Wilkins will be able to procure the Cloth which envelloped the
Child. It will inform us whether the Aborigines wove or not. He is also
endeavouring to procure the skull which remained entire—tho' several of the other
bones moulded away.[30]

19 May 1815
A fragment of an Indian vase found three miles from the donor's house in Luzerne County,
on Buck Mountain, Pennsylvania, "in a cavity that had been entirely closed by an immense
rock, and which was lately thrown down the mountain by some unknown convulsion."
Jose F. Correa da Serra observed that from the "marks on the fragment in evidence it had
been made inside a mould of basket work after the Cherokee fashion."[31]
The communication, addressed to Thomas T. Hewson and written 10 June 1815, is a
lengthy description of the locale of the fragment and other such Indian artifacts of the area:

You appear [anxious?] of procuring for the information relative to a fragment of an
Indian Vase presented by the hands of Professor [R.] Patterson. The Vase was
discovered in a small cavity near the Indian Cave on the Buck Mountain about a
mile and a half from Conyngham. The Rocks which form the Indian cave (or Rock
Houses as they are called in this country) have been separated by some violent
convulsion of Nature at some remote period and a large fragment of rock falling
from the summit of one of the highest fell in a reclining position near the house.
This fragment has been broken this Spring and discovered a cavity in the rock in
which was discovered the Indian Vase exactly in the form you now have it. This
fragment of Rock may have been placed by Human means but certainly at some
early period.

The perpendicular sides of the Rock are from fifteen to twenty-five in height and
they were about four feet apart. They are about thirty in length and four in breadth.
Fragments of Vases are frequently found on the bank of the Susquehanna near the

towns of Mercopeck(?) and Wilkes barre. There is no doubt that the lines on the side of the Vase were made by an instrument made of slate. This Instrument has been found near Ochre beds in this Country. Jacob Cist Esqr of Wilkes Barre has in his possession a Vase smaller than the one I have the honour to present—but equally curious. He has promised me that he will present it to the Society with an account [of the] mound in which it was found.

I am informed by Judge [John B.] Gibson that he found a [small?] pot made of the same materials a few years ago in a cave near Carlisle which he called an Indian paint pot for it appeared made for that purpose of holding yellow ochre.

Within a few miles of the Indian Cave a skeleton of a man was discovered buried in an upright position in a bed of yellow ochre. The skeleton was perfect—it measured six feet in length. A stone stubbing hoe was found near about five feet under the surface. There was no hole in the centre. From the form of it the Indians must have fastened a handle by twisting it round the Centre either by means of that species of tree known by the name of leather Wood or Hickory.

Some person thro' Mischief or from some other cause has secreted this Instrument. If I am enabled to recover it I shall forward it to the Society as I considered it well worthy of notice.

Over the Skeleton there were placed [ ] Rocks one on the surface of the other. It required all the exerted strength of ten or eleven Men to remove them from their immense weight and size. These rocks evidently were placed there and I have no doubt they were taken from some distant spot by Indians.

I am informed that Dr. [David] Hosack of New York in a work lately published there has given an account of two Vases similar to those already mentioned.[32]

This was referred to a committee composed of Caspar Wistar, Peter S. Du Ponceau, and James Mease on 16 June 1815.

Redmond Conyngham

17 May 1816

Various "Articles found in a Tumulus Cincinnati." Cinders were in the Indian fort where the articles were found. Carved bones were included as one item, which may have been an ornament shaped like a raven's beak.[33]

Daniel Drake

31 August 1816

A sketch of an Indian fort located three miles southwest of Lexington, Kentucky.[34]

Charles W. Short

4 April 1817

Part of a letter from John D. Clifford of Lexington, Kentucky:
I have lately procured a curious piece of pottery found on the Cany fork of Cumberland river (Tennessee) being dug up a few feet under the surface within one of the lines of circumwallation which we usually call Indian fortifications. The vessel consists of tee distinct Tartar heads, hollow within and joined by three tubes, at the occiput to the central neck of the flagon. It holds about a quart & I think must have been used for a vessel of libation as no liquid could be poured out of more than two of the heads without turning it completely upside down. One of the faces is painted all over with red ochre, having however the deepest tinge in the cheeks. The other two are painted with broad lines of yellow ochre partly decomposed. A streak goes across the forehead & lower jaw of one head & on the other across the eyes and down the nose.

This method of painting I believe accords with the custom of the diff[eren]t gentoo Castes.[35]

Carpar Wistar

17 July 1818

Through P. S. Du Ponceau, a pair of Indian "Moxen or Mockasins & a Tobacco Pouch of like materials."[36]

John G. E. Heckewelder

John C. Calhoun notified the Society on 11 March 1819 of Stephen H. Long's expedition wherein contact with the Indian would be a primary interest. Long was to explore the vast area between the Mississippi and the southwest.[37] Robert Walsh wrote on 30 March 1819 that he and Du Ponceau, Samuel Brown, Robert M. Patterson and Thomas Cooper were appointed a committee to draw up recommendations of topics for Long to research. They did, and the recommendations were forwarded to Calhoun.[38]

21 June 1822

Two pieces of cloth from Peru, taken "from their mound or burial ground near Narca above Lima."[39] One is embroidered with a bold design of a demon, on red over blue."[40] The minutes list them as "Ancient Mexican Cloth."

S. Curson

13 October 1825

From Chambersburg, Pennsylvania, came word that the donor had collected some items when he traveled

> over the mountains. The perforated Stone was in Huntingdon County and is evidently the work of art. But for what purpose must be altogether conjecture. The opinion of the people in that country is, that it is an Indian quoit—and used by them in some game, or sport of that kind....A few fragments of their earthen manufacture, turned up by the plough, in the same county are also sent as taking up but little room.[41]

Charles Smith

16 March 1827

A stone hatchet found on the banks of the Schuylkill River.

William Lewis.[42]

20 June 1828

Models of the Aztec Calendar stone and an Aztec sacrificial stone (wood, with wax relief).

Joel Roberts Poinsett[43]

29 December 1828

Manuscripts collected in Mexico "relating to early journeys made through portions of Mexico, and to certain activities." The two volume manuscript set of explorations by Guillermo Du Paix with numerous sketches by Josef Castenada is in the library. [It is of particular interest to note that the expeditions by Du Paix, 180507, were to discover "ancient Indian artifacts and ruins." His report, replete with a volume of drawings, is extraordinarily skimpy. Evidently no one paid attention to the soil of Mexico which has delivered thousands of objects over the years. But, in 180507, very few artifacts and ruins were known and recognized. His report was reproduced twice: Viscount Kingsborough published them, with other materials, in 1831 in his *Antiquities of Mexico* and Henri Baradere, in his *Antiquities Mexicaines*. This report was already out of date when it was published. A few years later, 1828 and 1830, Poinsett was able to send hundreds of items he collected in Mexico to the Society.

Joel Roberts Poinsett

22 February 1830

Poinsett wrote John Vaughan from Cincinnati introducing an artist,
> Maximilian Franck who has been employed in Mexico under my patronage in a
> work which will I think prove highly useful. He has designed with the greatest
> fidelity all the specimens of sculpture which have as yet been collected in that capital
> and wishes to add to them those which I have sent to Philadelphia. You will be so
> good as to permit him to copy them. Fran[c]k intends to publish his work in Paris,
> and I hope he may obtain some subscribers in your city.

Poinsett added that his second collection, which he left at Tampico, was to be shipped to
New York and as soon as it arrived, he would have it shipped to the Society.[44] After the
receipt of the splendid gift of Mexican antiquities from William H. Keating and Poinsett,
the members authorized lending Mr. Franck "such of the specimens of Mexican
antiquities...to illustrate the fidelity of his drawings, now exhibited to the public." Franck
availed himself of this opportunity and his drawings showed "much fidelity and talent."
Also, it was confirmed that Franck would "make and publish drawings from the Mexican
specimens."[45]

1 April 1830

The massive collection of Mexican antiquities collected by Poinsett while serving as United
States Minister to Mexico for five years. Poinsett's objects were "Collected from the City
of Mexico, the Plains near the Pyramids of St. Juan Teotihuacan, Cholulu, Tescuco, the
Island of Sacrifices, &c. &c."[46] in. H. Keating sent a listing of this collection to John K.
Kane 6 April 1830, as Kane had requested. Poinsett's donation consisted of:

9 figures of Stone resembling the human figure in various attitudes cut in porphyry,
Verd antique, lava & other rocks.

7 masks of the human face very beautifully worked in alabaster, porphyry, verd
antique, &c.

18 masks of pottery representing the human face of natural size but very grotesque
features.

alabaster vases of very tasteful forms and neat workmanship.

Several specimens of jade, porphyry, obsidian & other rocks carved into the forms
of toads, lizards and other animals.

A great variety of specimens of ancient pottery including several hundred heads of
the human figure, nearly one hundred figures entire, many vases, pitchers, jars,
jugs, plates, cups & other domestic utensils; musical instruments, representations
of the ancient Mexican temples, and other objects the nature of which is still
uncertain.

A number of heads, rings & other toys made of obsidian &c. copper &c. Copies of
the ancient sacrificial stone, calendar stone & Goddess of War, modelled in wax
from the originals in the national museum of Mexico. Golden ornament, found in a
Grave representing an Ancient Mexican Helmet, & other ornaments of a Mexican
Warrior. [The minutes state that Poinsett presented 16 April 1830 "in addition to his
gifts of the last meeting" some examples of workmanship of pure gold which had
been "found in the tombs of the original inhabitants of Mexico."]

Paintings on maguey Paper in *heyroglphics* [sic] [The Aztec tribute roll. These last two items are entered in the hand of secretary John Vaughan.]

William H. Keating's donation, amassed "from the city of Mexico, the plains near the pyramids of San Juan Teotihuacan, and the western side of the Sierra Madre of the Cordilleras" consisted of:

11 figures of stone resembling the human form in various attitudes & of various sizes, cut in porphyry, verd antique, serpentine, clayolate talc rock, lava jade, &c. masks of the human face and of various sizes in basalt, porphyry, serpentine &c. &c. 1 fragment of a very large representation in stone of the rattlesnake of Mexico. About 1000 heads of pottery representing the human face in its natural or, deformed appearances, and exhibiting a great variety of headdresses & ornaments for the hair. A large quantity of fragments of obsidian cut into the shapes of arrowheads, knives & other domestic instruments. Several beads of porphyry, jade &c. A collection of pottery consisting of pitchers, cups, plates &c. [47]

Joel Roberts Poinsett

The donors were asked to "unite with the Curators in arranging and preparing a catalogue" of this magnificent gift.[48] Also, the curators were authorized to provide proper cases for these objects.

16 July 1830
Two sacerdotal Peruvian vases and cestus worn originally by a Virgin of the Sun at the time of the conquest of Peru by Pizarro.
   The Vases were used by the priests of the Temple of the Sun in Peru, & were taken therefrom by one of the Soldiers of Pizarro, as was the Cestus from the body of a Virgin of the Sun, at the time he sacked the Temple. They were presented to me whilst resident in Spain by D[ona] Maria Morris, born in Lima, a descendant of the Soldier, who gave me this account of them.[49]

[These items were returned to Bloomfield "through his attorney" 25 June 1846.[50]]

Joseph E. Bloomfield

5 August 1830
From New Orleans, Joseph Barabino wrote that "Our common Friend member C[harles] A. Lesueur" must have brought the news that he planned to send a Mexican idol and other items to the Society. He had not done so for the captain bringing the idol was careless, part of the face was destroyed, and "I wrote for another one."[51] A cryptic comment is recorded 3 December 1830 in the Minutes: "The Poinsett Committee reported progress."[52]

4 March 1831
Maximilian Franck took his drawings to Europe and showed them to the Societe de Geographie de Paris, and David Baillie Warden wrote a report of them. There were 81 large folio leaves that held about 600 sketches. Of these, 24 were from objects in the American Philosophical Society's cabinet. There were 148 figures; 55 heads of humans, 30 masks and busts, 20 animal figures, and, vases, ornaments, and other items. The originals were basalt, green, yellow and gray marble, vert antique, serpentine, terra-cotta, jade, and porphyry. Franck also sketched an Indian woman of the village of Ticoman, near Mexico City, "pour servir de comparaison avec les anciennes figures et demontrer leur resemblance." These sketches showed resemblances to the Egyptian, Chinese, Tartars, and Mongols. The vases were considered remarkable in their beauty of form, but the ornaments were considered more remarkable because of the richly sculpted animal forms (monkeys, alligators, tortoises).The gold ornaments showed how adept the Mexicans were in working the metal. Hieroglyphs were recognizable. Moreover, copies of the Aztec calendar stone, instruments of war, and altars for sacrifices were modeled with wax from the originals in the National Museum of Mexico. Franck also delivered letters testifying to his faithful rendering of the originals. From the Society on 28 May 1830:

Nous soussignes, officiers et membres de la Societe philosphique de Philadelphie, certifions qu'apres avoir examine les dessins executes par M. Maximilien Franck, d'apres les antiquites mexicaines appartement a la Societe, et les avoir compares avec les, nous les avons trouves parfaitement ressemblans, et executes avec une exactitude et une precision remarquables.

Poinsett wrote the Society:
Je prends la liberté de récommander particulierement a l'interet de la Societé [Philosophique Américaine] M. Franck, artiste bavaroise du plus grand mérite, qui, pendant un séjour de deux annees qu'l a fait chez moi, a Mexico, a dessiné avec une scrupuleuse fidelité les anciens restes des sculptures mexicaines, qui ont eté reuniés dans cette ville. Sa collection est extrement curieuse et peut fournier des éclairissemens importans l'histoire de ce pays.

There was a great gathering of savants at the Societe de Geographique de Paris, debating questions about the American Indian and his ruins and antiquities when Franck exhibited his drawings. From this conclave came the huge publication, edited by Henri Baradere: *Antiquites mexicaines. Relation des trois expeditions du capitaine Dupaix, ordonées en 1805, 1806, et 1807, pour la récherche des antiquités de pays...* Several outstanding scholars appended their own notes, and David Baillie Warden published therein a listing of Maximilien Franck's drawings, and appended a history of the American Indian [especially North American] and their cultures.

For some reason, Edme Francois Jomard wrote a note, casting doubt on the perfection of Franck's sketches. He thought some had been imported from Africa and China and cited a few instances of Egyptian and Chinese influence on the Mexican Indians. Franck replied in a letter dated 20 April to the president of the Societe Geographique de Paris, protesting the criticism by Jomard, and sent a copy of his letter to the American Philosophical Society. "Le temoignage des Savans les plus distingues de l'amerique a atteste mes representations." Peter Stephen Du Ponceau had found Egyptian traces in the Mexican artifacts as seen "dans l'ouvrage de M. [Baron Dominique Vivant] Denon sur l'Egypt." Luciano Castenada, the artist who travelled with Guillermo Du Paix and made sketches of Mexican Indian ruins and artifacts, agreed that the carvings at Palenque showed "une relation entre la chine et le mexique, longtemps avant la soi disant decouverte de l'amerique." Moreover, Franck averred, ancient Mexicans had knowledge of Africans before the Spaniards introduced Negro slaves.
On m'a dit aussi que Mr. Jomard cherche a persuader le public, que les objets de ma collection, ont ete introduites a mexico; je crois que on que j'ai dit suf fire pour refuter une objection, que n'est sortit que de l'imagination de Mr. Jomard, j'ajouterai seulement que j'avois expose ma collection au public americain a Philadelphie, ou on est plus a porte de connoitre les particularit es des antiquites americaines, puis que le musees de Messieurs Piles [Charles Willson Peale] a Philadelphie et New York, et la cabinet de la Societe philosophique a Philadelphie sont remplis des antiquites trouvees et deterrees en amerique. Tous les journaux de Philadelphie ont parle avec les plus grands elogues de ma collection, il n'est pas venu dansl'idee d'aucun, de jetter une doute sur son authenticite, comme Mr. Jomard ose le faire a Paris, lui qui n'a jamais traverse l'altlantique [sic]; d'ailleurs il faudroit appeles imposteurs les Directeurs du Musee de Mexico, tous les gouvernantes de la republique, Mr. le ministre [Joel Roberts] Poinsett, Mr. le baron [Alexander] de Humboldt, Mr. le commodor[e] Porter, Mr. [Peter S.] Duponfeau, Mr. le comte de Penasco, Mr. le comte de Lilaro, Mr. [William H.] Keating, et tous la reste de Savans et amateurs de I`amerique, pour contenter Mr. Jomard! [53]

In 1834, this "Rapport" was published in its entirety in Paris by Henri Baradere in his monumental edition of the travels of Du Pais with the drawings of Castenada, but the Jomard note was omitted.
Sometime around 1830 John Vaughan made a note about David Baillie Warden's report of Maximilian Franck's drawings of the Mexican antiquities: "This report

of Mr. Warden leads to no result; but it is interesting inasmuch as it contains a good description of those in our Cabinet. It should be referred to our Curators to make a complete one, to be published in our Transactions. Mr. Keating should be requested to aid."[54] By 6 May 1831, the curators had prepared a catalogue of the gifts of Mexican antiquities which had been given by Joel R. Poinsett and William H. Keating, and Keating had, indeed, aided the curators in preparing this catalogue.

20 January 1832
Richard Harlan presented from C. P. Wetherill several specimens of Indian pottery. A very large piece had been discovered at the Falls of Kentucky and one in the state of Illinois. Other jugs were from Quilca, Peru.[55] Marmaduke Burrough left with Samuel G. Morton "a very valuable and numerous collection of Huacaros, or Indian Antiquities" from ancient Peruvian cemeteries which had been collected "principally from the neighborhood anciente Truxillo in lower Peru, and from Arica and Quilca in Upper Peru."[56]

C.P. Wetherill and Marmaduke Burrough

3 February 1832

"[A] Peruvian ewer of antique form found at Huaco, Montilipo, 16 leagues from Lambayoque."[57] This may, originally, have been included in the gift of Sterne Humphrys, received on 17 February 1832, for there were some ancient pottery pieces from Huaco, Peru, in that gift and the gift was presented through Frederick Brown. Humphrys was an officer in the United States Navy on board the St. Louis while cruising the American Pacific coast.[58]

Sterne Humphrys described his gift:
The Earthern Vessels from Peru They were found in an Ancient Guaco (or tomb) near the sea coast in the province of Truxillo Monslipo 18 leagues distant from Lambayoque. It was the Custom of the Ancient Peruvians, on the deaths of their Chiefs of distinction to fill these vessels with Mayce and different kinds of fruits & place them in the tomb with the body as also his arms and trinkets. These vessels are called Guauaros. They are held in high veneration by the full blooded Indians of Peru, so much so that they will seldom part with them. This information I have from an American gentleman who has long resided in Peru. The Pipe is from the West Coast; it was procured from a vessel trading to that Coast...The Bowl, drinking Cup, and the Bow & Arrows are from the coast of California, such as are used by the Nations, a short distance in the interior.[59]

Morton wrote John Vaughan of this gift:
I will thank you to send a large Basket in the hands of a careful person, as soon as may be; for I fear they may get injured in my office. Dr. Burrough's splendid present will be accompanied by a memoir illustrative of the circumstances under which these relics were found.[60]

Frederick Brown

Baron de Beher wrote on 11 November 1833[5] that Peter Du Ponceau informed him of the Mexican antiquities in the cabinet and asked permission to examine them.[61]

16 December 1833
"A sett of Porcupine tablematts, manufactured by the Aborigines of Saint John, New Brunswick."[62]

John Howe

Joel R. Poinsett wrote John Vaughan on 25 June 1835 and introduced Bishop Anders, who wished to examine the Mexican antiquities and minerals. I am sure it will afford you great pleasure to show the Bishop the Library and collection belonging to our Society, and you will be equally pleased to make the acquaintance of this estimable and learned prelate.[63]

18 November 1835
Thomas Nuttall, naturalist on the United States Exploring Expedition, a beehive cap, or hat, made of grass and cordage, which had been worn by the Chinook Indians on the Columbia River. There was also a "Bag made of the Helonias Tenax & bark cordage" made by the Chinooks. With these was a mat which was made of strips of bark by natives of the north west coast of America, which resembled the mats from the Hawaiian Islands.[63]

Thomas Nuttall

18 August 1837
On 18 August 1837 the members authorized the purchase of "Five Mexican gold idols" for $25. John Vaughan purchased them from J. H. Gibbon on 24 August, and they were from Santa Fe de Bogota (Colombia).[64] Vaughan must have asked Gibbon to write an account of them, for on 25 August 1837 just such an account was written:

> Gen[era]l Mc Afee Charge d'Affaires of the United States at Bogota in New Granada purchased five small golden figures supposed to be idols of the aboriginal inhabitants of that country. They are found in the plain of Bogota near the falls of the river upon the site of ancient Indian village: it is said mingled with the remnants of pottery. The discoverers brought them to the owner of the land giving this account of them.

> Such articles are frequently dug up in the vicinity of Bogota and the Charge d'Affaires of France has a collection the expense in obtaining which is payed by his government but I do not recollect that any of them are so large as these bought by Gen'l McAfee.

> I happened by accident to find these images in the hands of a broker who exhibited them as a curiosity, but intending to sell them to a jeweller. I am gratified to have been the means of introducing them to the attention of the Am. Phil. Socy.[65]

John Vaughan

18 August 1837
Some boxes of Mexican antiquities, which were the property of Charles Bagley, offered for deposit on certain conditions. The members accepted the conditions and asked Keating, John K. Kane, and Isaac Hays "to carry it into execution.[66] Three cases were received 1 January 1838 and $35.05 was paid for the freight.[67]

William H. Keating

17 November 1837
An Indian pipe "curiously wrought" by Indians of California. There were the heads of a bird, a frog, and a man on it.[68]

Silvain Godon

From Wheeling, S. P. Hullihen wrote Robert Harlan on 27 September 1838 about a stone which had been "found in a tumulus at Grave Creek." This stone bore strange markings, much like runes, and Hullihen had seen a coin which bore three of these markings. He enclosed a sketch of the stone, with the markings "as near as I can draw with a pen."[69] A committee composed of Peter S. Du Ponceau, Robley Dunglison, and Isaac Lea reported on 21 June 1839 that, "having been in correspondence with Dr. [David] Townsend for the purpose of getting a correct description and figure of the inscription learned, an account of it had already been published in the Cincinnati Monthly Chronicle for Feby last, the Committee cannot recommend its publication in the Transactions."[70] The committee was then discharged.

The Society was informed on 5 October 1838 that one of the judges of the Superior Court of the Territory of Wisconsin had seen some fire-hardened bricks in a mound near Aztalan in Jefferson County:

> About 35 or 40 miles West of Milwaukee, [Wisconsin] there has been found a large quantity of Bricks, not dried in the Sun, but burnt; & that tho' they have lost their forms by age and are many of them crumbling into dust, it is easy to perceive that they have been subjected to the operation of fire. Judge Frazer intends to revisit that

place next year, & to make written communication to our Society on the subject, accompanied by some of the bricks.[72]

19 June 1840
On 16 May 1840 Redmond Conyngham wrote John Vaughan about what was commonly known as an "Indian Workshop" about seven miles from Paradise, Pennsylvania. Stone bowls were hammered out there by the aborigines, and Conyngham offered to send "a few specimens in a box," if the members so desired.[73] He sent, on 5 June 1840, a box that "contains several stones work'd by the Indians with stone hammers; they were obtain'd from the remains of the Indian Work Shop...Tradition gives no further particulars."

2 October 1840
A brick from the "Mounds on Lake St. Joseph, Louisiana." Some of the specimens were "imperfectly burnt" because of "the entire combustion of the moss used to give the mortar consistency."[75]

C. G. Forshey

Joseph E. Bloomfield wrote on 26 September 1841 reminding John Vaughan that he had loaned "three silver goblets & a cestus taken by one of [Francisco] Pizarro's soldiers from the Temple of the Sun in Peru." These objects were loaned so that Maximilian Franck could draw them at the same time he was sketching the Mexican artifacts in the cabinet. Bloomfield wanted a receipt "subject to my order." Vaughan noted on 29 September 1841 that he gave a receipt "with a request that he would not withdraw it as with what we had from Peru & Mexico they could be nowhere placed to equal advantage or be more appreciated." Bloomfield's letter was read to the members on 1 October. 1841.[76] On 11 June 1846 Henry M'Ilvaine wrote the Society recapitulating the history of this deposit and asked that the Society "direct the delivery to me, as the agent of Mr. Bloomfield, the articles I have named."[77] This was read at the 19 June meeting, and authorization for the return of the deposit was given.[78] George Ord reported on 17 July 1846 that "the two silver Peruvian vases and the cestus" had been delivered as ordered.[79]

16 June 1843
An old Indian stone relic, a discoidal stone, found in East Tennessee. None of the present-day Cherokee had any tradition of its uses. "These stones are not uncommon in East Tennessee," he wrote.[80] At the same time, Trautwine delivered an ancient Indian pipe uncovered by the action of the Hiwassee River in Polk County, East Tennessee.[81]

John C. Trautwine

Samuel George Morton wrote George Ord on 5 June 1846 that Ephraim George Squier, of Chilicothe, Ohio, who had "been engaged in opening the mounds of that section of the country" wished to examine the Poinsett collection.[82] On 26 October 1846 Samuel G. Morton wrote George Ord proposing an exchange of books for "a solitary skull, that of a Mexican, which I have figured in my Crania Americana, plate 18." Morton thought that, because the Society would never have a large collection of skulls "and as this cranium would be valuable in my series as a voucher for the accuracy of my plate and description," the skull might easily be exchanged.[83]

18 June 1847
Through Joseph Saxton, the family of the late J. Milnor Williams presented two ancient South American vases. One was from the island of Puira and the other came from the island of Payta.[84]

Family of J. Milnor Williams

Peter Arnett Browne wrote 26 April 1850 that, after making a "microscopic examination of the hair of the head & portions of the scalp from Pachacamac (the Temple of the Sun, 5 leagues from Lima), & from Arica & Pisco (Peru)", he was ready to discuss the results. He had compared his results with the present-day Indians' hair and was "prepared to demonstrate that they all belong to the same species."[85]

15 April 1853
Indian arrow from Oregon.[86]

Franklin Stewart

2 December 1859
Two golden images which had been found "lately" at Chiriqui, Central America, in Indian graves. One was in the shape of a reptile and other was a bird. These were part of the United States Mint collection. The materials were especially heavy in copper content in the gold, for the U. S. Assay Office in New York had lately melted down "a considerable quantity of these images" and "the proportion of the mass was 788 parts of gold, 190 part of copper, and only 22 parts silver." It was assumed that such images were made "to propitiate such creatures as were most likely to disturb the repose of the dead."[87]

Patterson Du Bois
Another such gold image that had been in his possession many years and "may have been obtained from the same localities."[88]

Franklin Peale

21 December 1860
"A numerous collection of Indian arrowheads flint-knives, and pottery" The donor gave a lengthy talk on such Stone Age implements. He stressed that America had a magnificent past for the ethnologist for some Indians yet used such stone implements. The pottery was coeval with the flint tools, and Peale made references to the current European authorities and their discoveries. [89]

Franklin Peale

5 April 1861
After a talk wherein the donor discussed how the aborigines affixed stone axes to handles, the donor exhibited a specimen of a Rocky Mountain stone mallet, which, except for its striking face, was covered with "tight-stretched hide sewed up along the handle."[90]

Franklin Peale
Peale also read a paper on 21 June 1861 on these implements and "illustrated it with a numerous collection of specimens from his own cabinet. [91] On 20 December 1861 he showed the members some Irish and Scandinavian stone implements which showed a "remarkable similarity with those of the North American Indians."[92] He spoke 3 January 1862 of a recent publication by the Smithsonian Institution on "a saw-like stone" and exhibited a similar item from his collection. [93] Peale exhibited on 18 April 1862 a large group of "Stone implements of the Ancient Britons" that had been dug from barrows" in the North Riding of Yorkshire" [94] On 15 April 1863 Peale displayed a "hand-hammer" which he had recently added to the Society's cabinet. It was exactly like the one Sir Charles Lyell described in *Geological Evidences of the Antiquity of Man* (page 184) from Aurignac, France, yet Peale's donation came from Monroe County, Pennsylvania. Such rounded stone hammers were not rare in the United States, and from such similarities as European and American Indian stone implements, Peale wondered whether these did not point to the unity of man's origin in the past. [95] Peale displayed a box of stone implements on 1 May 1863 that John Evans of England had removed "with his own hands, from the gravel pits of St. Acheuil, near Amiens." Peale compared these with Indian artifacts from his collection. All were made of flints of the Cretaceous formation and all were artificially shaped.[96]

On 21 June 1861 Gouverneur Emerson spoke of finding a "bed of charred human bones" on the tide waters of the Delaware "some years ago." Broken Indian pipes lay over them. One was of a different form "symmetrical and peculiar, unlike the well-known forms" discovered elsewhere. He judged "these peculiarities" to be indicative of the greater antiquity and different [ ] stirpal origin of the Indians" whose bones he had found.[97]

The curators were authorized on 20 November 1863 to exchange "the intestinal calculus in the cabinet of the Society, for certain stone implements in the museum of the University of Pennsylvania."[98]

Joseph Henry wrote on 12 December 1863 asking to borrow "the more important specimens" of American Indian ethnographic interest to make copies for the Smithsonian Institution.[99] The letter was read and the curators were authorized to reply "with power to grant the request."[100] George Auguste Matile of the Smithsonian wrote concerning casts to be taken of thirty-four pieces of Indian antiquities. This letter was read on 19 August 1864, and the casts were "to be taken for general distribution."[101]

On 4 March 1864 Joseph Leidy's letter from the Academy of Natural Sciences of Philadelphia was read, containing the proposal with the view of facilitating the study of Archaeology: Resolved that the specimens of antique art belonging to the Academy be deposited in the Museum of the Amer[ican] Philos[ophical] Soc[iety], provided that they shall be returned on demand, and that the Curators of the Society shall give a receipt for the same to the Curators of the Academy.

Although the collection was small, Joseph Liedy wrote that the Academy had received "valuable specimens" and these, with the Society's collection, "I hope soon to see a noble Archaeological Museum, which will be one of the scientific attractions of our city." Leidy would pack and send the Academy's collection with "a few rare things" of his own. "I suppose some day our friend, Mr. [Franklin] Peale will transfer his cabinet to that of the Society." This letter was referred to the curators for action.[102] Their report was read on 18 March and they felt that it was "highly expedient" that the deposit be accepted. They urged that the Society "lend their fostering countenance to this department of science, particularly as there is no institution in the city or State which has paid any attention to the subject, or afforded any facilities for its study or development." The report was accepted,[103] and yet, no further action was taken, and nothing from the Academy came to the Society.

2 December 1864

Fragments of some large Indian pottery vessels which still preserved "the impressions of the osier wickerwork baskets" that ornamented them. They came from Galena County, Illinois, "at the ancient salt springs.[104]

Franklin Peale

Thomas Conrad Porter, of Lancaster, Pennsylvania, sent a letter which was read on 7 April 1865 about Indian petroglyphs cut into rocks at Safe Harbor on the Susquehanna River. A photograph accompanied this communication. He proposed sending a set of plaster casts of them from the Linnean Society of Lancaster. Porter described the rocks at length and said that there were "upwards of 80 distinct figures." They had been sketched by Jacob Stauffer, a local artist. The figures "were made by the Aborigines, and made, at large cost of time and labor, with rude stone implements." Porter believed that this "in connection with their number and variety proves that they were not the offspring of idle fancy, or the work of idle hours, but the product of design toward some end of high importance."[105] Plates A and B at the end of the first section of volume 10 of the *Proceedings* depicts these carvings. T. C. Porter wrote on 10 July 1865 that he hoped that the making of a set of plaster casts of the carvings for the Society would commence shortly.[106] On 15 September the resolution of the Linnean Society of Lancaster to furnish these casts was read.[107] Porter's letter "announcing the transmission" of these casts was read on 15 June 1866. The casts had been received and were "distributed about the Hall of the Society" and Porter then spoke about them.[108] He gave a brief history of their discovery on an island in the Susquehanna and of the difficulty in getting the casts because of the high water of the river and because some carvings reached below the water. The thanks of the Society were returned, and a special committee was named to report on these casts.[109]

J. Peter Lesley described on 6 October 1865 some items removed from Indian graves near Wilkes Barre, and Benjamin Hornor Coates commented on the wear of the teeth, without decay, in skulls found on the West Branch of the Schuylkill River.[110]

Horatio C. Wood spoke on 3 November 1865 of some Indian implements found along the Cohansey Creek in New Jersey. A "spindle-shaped stone" was located there and it was probably a roller or a pestle of a quern, used in grinding food. The Pueblo Indians still used such a tool, and Charles B. Trego described such an implement "of greenstone trap from Bucks County, "Pennsylvania.[111]

16 February 1866
A pestle, found in Union County, Pennsylvania, in White Deer Creek. Franklin Peale commented on such a tool.[112]

Robert P. King

4 May 1866
A photograph of Indian pottery found at the Little Falls of the Potomac and some specimens of Stone Age Indian pottery obtained there.

Franklin Peale

Ferdinand V. Hayden recommended on 15 February 1867 that the Society preserve photographs of the scenery and aboriginal inhabitants of the region west of the Mississippi. He made a proposal, which was adopted, that a committee be appointed "to procure photographic portraits of North American Indians for ethnological purposes, and that an appropriation of fifty dollars be now made to carry the object into effect.[113] Hayden, Alexander Wilcocks, and Franklin Peale were named the committee, and Pliny Earle Chase was added on 1 March. Hayden exhibited on 3 May some photographs of Dakota Indians, and Charles M. Cresson proposed, and the members agreed, to appropriate fifty additional dollars for Indian photographs. On 3 April 1868 Hayden spoke of the "series of Indian photographs" procured for the Society, and the treasurer was ordered to pay for them.[116] These photographs, bound in a volume, are in the library today.

At the meeting of 19 June 1868 Franklin Peale read a lengthy paper on the manufacture and ornamentation of stone age pottery, both Native American and European. Four lithographic plates embellish this paper, which was printed in volume 10 of the *Proceedings.*[7]

4 December 1868
Nine drawings of aboriginal figures cut into rocks on the Susquehanna River near the Maryland state line. These were facsimiles "in size and character," because S. G. Boyd, of York, Pennsylvania, had applied "paper sheets to the sculptured surfaces. Some of these carvings were like concentric circles.[118]

T. C. Porter

Porter's letter of 6 January 1869 was read on 15 January, and additional information from Mr. Boyd was added. There were numerous inscriptions, unknown to the local inhabitants. Not all the carvings were copied. The carvings were in a fine state of preservation when not directly exposed to the abrading force of ice and driftwood. They occur on the sides and tops of some half-dozen rocks. "Although at first sight they might seem to have no connection with each other, I have been able to trace an arrangement in horizontal and vertical lines. The grooves are semicylindric, and in some cases have a depth of half an inch or more."[119]

19 March 1869
Four fragments of painted pottery which came from the Island of Sacrifices near Vera Cruz, Mexico. One was a doll, or image; one was a whistle, and, the other two fragments were ornamented with a bird's and "something like a calf's" head and "are very imperfect."[120]

John Marston

20 August 1869
Joseph Leidy delivered "three highly ornamented Ojibwa pipes" from Mr. Clark.[121]

[Mr.]Clark

On 12 November 1869 a letter from Peale was read. He wished the members to purchase, with extra Magellanic funds, "a certain collection of archaeological objects now in the city." A special committee was appointed to examine this collection and it reported on 19 November against the purchase because "the price [was] too large to pay for a collection so similar in most respects to the collection in the museum of the Society.[122]

19 November 1869
Some Indian relics, including parts of a skeleton. These had been uncovered from a bed of sand near his residence in Southern New Jersey. The man had been buried in a sitting position, facing the east, and stone implements were buried with him. Other Indian artifacts

came from the neighborhood and Dr. Wood supposed that a "ridge, composed chiefly of oyster shells," was the refuse of the Indians.[123]

Horatio C. Wood

On 4 March 1870 Wood stated that the Indian cranium had a breadth "which exceeded that of most European heads; and altogether the size of the cranium was much greater than that of the head of the present race of Indians." He assumed the man to have "belonged to a race which had preceded that found here by the Europeans" and the skeleton was "more than 500 years old, perhaps 1,000."[124]

18 March 1870

Some photographs of "figures of the human foot" carved in the red sandstone of the Upper Cretaceous, near Topeka, Kansas. The westerners thought these were fossils, but Cope showed that they were manmade by the aborigines. "A discussion of the use of the foot in aboriginal picture writing followed."[125]

Edward D. Cope

On 15 July 1870 a communication respecting Frankin Peale's "Cabinet of Antiquities" was presented.[126] A memoir, read on 16 December 1870 by Robert Patterson, stated:

For some years before his death, Mr. Peale was greatly interested in that branch of Archaeology which relates to the so-called Stone Age. He determined to make a collection of implements illustrating that age, and by energy and patience succeeded in accumulating over twelve hundred specimens, many of them very choice. The most of these were gathered by himself at the ancient homes of the Shawnees and Delawares, around the Water Gap [of the Delaware River], where he spent many autumns, others were secured by exchange or purchase. These have all been arranged for easy examination on a plan devise by himself, and full of his characteristic ingenuity and taste, and he has left behind a manuscript catalogue with an introduction and full descriptive details which leave nothing further to be desired. It affords me great satisfaction to add that this valuable collection, the latest labor of Mr. Peale, is to be presented to this Society.[127]

Mrs. Peale had a small number of volumes printed, illustrated by photographs, of the collection. Because the collection was presented to the Society, she did not feel that a copy of the volume would be needed. (There is, at present, a copy of the volume in the Free Library of Philadelphia. It consists of a few printed pages, Franklin Peale's articles on the artifacts, published by the Society, and photographs of the items.)

7 October 1870

"Cap worn by the natives of *[Chiriqui]* was made of the "sheath of the Coible Galen nut." J. A. McNeill was introduced and spoke of his Central American explorations and of his plans to explore the ruins of cities on the river flowing into the Chiriqui lagoon. J. Blodget Brittan said this was unexplored territory and no stone monuments were known so far south. They were valuable as furnishing a possible key to the connection between the Mexican, Central American, and Peruvian stone monuments.[128]

A description of some Indian sculpture on a rock which had been found on the banks of the Monongahela River was delivered 20 January 1871 by Edward D. Cope. It had been found by Joseph D. Reid, and a drawing accompanied the description.[129]

Charles H. Stubbs, M. D., of Wakefield in Lancaster County, Pennsylvania, wrote on 8 July 1872 that he could sell the Society a set of photographs of "Picture Rocks (Evidently made by a race existing at an Early period)" on the Susquehanna River. Secretary J. Peter Lesley wrote for these 7 March 1874. These carvings were on a rock in the Susquehanna River near Bald Friar, Maryland. Over one hundred such carvings (characters, diagrams, and figures) were carved there by the Indians. The photographs were made in July 1871, and sets were in the Maryland Academy of Sciences, the Academy of Natural Sciences of Philadelphia and the Linnean Society of Lancaster.[130]

Persifor Frazer exhibited on 18 April 1873 two specimens of wood carvings found in a ruined aboriginal temple near Santa Fe, New Mexico, on the Pecos River. They were not Aztec, although Harrison Allen believed that they had been carved under Aztec influence.[131]

On 5 December 1873 John L. Le Conte was granted permission to borrow a few small Mexican pottery articles.[132]

Robert Patterson asked the members on 1 May 1874 to examine his copy of the published catalogue of the Franklin Peale Collection. Mrs. E. Girard Haslam Peale, the widow, had twenty-five copies printed for private distribution. It contained 81 plates of 1,153 specimens of European and American artifacts.134 An extract of the will of Mrs. Peale, dated 12 October 1874, was received.

I give to the American Philosophical Society held at Philadelphia, for promoting useful knowledge, the collection of relics illustrative of the Stone Age, with the descriptive Catalogue thereof, made by my beloved husband Franklin Peale, in trust to preserve the same as a separate collection, within the Hall Building of the Society, or in some suitable place, and open to the inspection of all visitors, under such regulations as may be proper for the security thereof: the collection to be designated so as to distinguish the object and name of the collection as follows:

• Implements of the Stone Age from various parts of America, Europe, Great Britain and the British Isles, collected and arranged as impressively confirming the unity of the human race, by Franklin Peale."

• Provided, that said collection shall not be placed within the building of said Society until the same shall be fire proof .[134]

This was read 5 November 1875, and a committee was appointed to consider the bequest. Its report of 19 November recommended acceptance, and the members resolved to deposit the collection in the Philadelphia Savings Fund Society "and the curators be authorized to make arrangements with the said Society for its safe keeping."[135]

Charles M. Cresson recommended on 12 May 1876 that the Board of Officers and Council of the Society notify the Academy of Natural sciences that it could receive, on deposit, the "Cabinet of antiquities...on condition that the said Cabinet shall be returned to the Hall of the Society upon demand of the curators."[36]

George A. Matile wrote P. E. Chase on 22 July 1876 asking for the loan of certain Indian items from the Poinsett collection. He wished to make plaster copies for the Princeton Museum.[137] The members authorized this loan on 18 August to Matile and Arnold Henry Guyot provided the curators took "the usual guarantees for their safe return."[138] Guyot wrote that the Museum of Geology and Archaeology of Princeton would be responsible for all expenses and would offer "in compensation, free of charge, copies of such of our specimens which might be wanting in your collections."[139] On 6 October 1876 Guyot wrote that Matile had finished, and the Mexican antiquities were being returned.[140] Matile and Guyot presented on 20 October 1876 some copies of such antiquities in the Princeton Museum: "snakes, tortoises, and other bizarre figures, found in Puerto Rico." They also suggested an exchange of duplicates between the two institutions, and Matile selected such duplicates and discussed some of the items that might be exchanged. A committee reported favorably on 3 November 1876.[141] Guyot wrote on 8 November thanking the Society for this exchange: "I trust transactions of that kind will always be found profitable to both institutions."[142]

He wrote on 13 December that Matile would arrive in Philadelphia "with the loaned specimens of Mexican Antiquities & ten more copies of our own destined for your museum." He would at that time obtain the duplicate items.[143] Matile wrote on 13 July 1877 thanking the Society for the cooperation and enclosed a letter of thanks from Guyot.[144] On 21 June 1878 "a set of 21 colored plaster casts" was displayed as "imitations of original Archaeological Specimens" that came from the Princeton Museum.

16 February 1877
Some drawings of scratched figures found on coal shales near Davenport, Iowa, in an Indian mound. One drawing was a zodiac "of such unusual excellence of design and the accompanying symbols and letters have so Indo-germanic an aspect" that several members doubted their being genuine.[146]

Edward D. Cope

William S. in Ruschenberger proposed on 21 September 1877, and the members agreed, that the Franklin Peale Collection of Stone Age implements be deposited in the Academy of Natural Sciences of Philadelphia.[147] The executor of Mrs. Peale's estate, Robert Patterson, wrote on 2 October 1877:

> Mrs. Peale's bequest is conditioned on the collection being lodged in a fire proof building, and it now lies in the building of the Phil[delphia] Sav[ings] Fund Society, but is boxed up so as to be unavailable for examination. This disposal of the collection, while technically in compliance with the will, does not carry out what I know to have been the wishes of the testatrix. I would respectfully suggest that an arrangement could probably be made with the Academy of Natural Sciences to receive the collection as a deposit by the Society. If that can be done, I would cheerfully bear the necessary expense of making the transfer, and setting the relics in the Cases.[148]

The curators reported on 5 October 1877 that Robert Patterson agreed with placing the collection in the Academy and read the above letter. The members then resolved that the deposit be made.[149]

Members and curators Hector Tyndale and Charles M. Cresson authorized the removal of the Peale Collection from the vaults of the bank on 18 October, and later in October William S. Ruschenberger, as president of the Academy of Natural Sciences, authorized the bank to deliver the collection to Joseph Leidy for the Academy.[150] A receipt for "a collection of Specimens of the Stone age of the Human Race, as collected and arranged by Franklin Peale'" was received on 16 November 1877.[151]

C. M. Cresson offered a resolution on 16 November 1877 "That the Curators be directed to make arrangements for the deposit of the collection of Mexican, Peruvian and other Relics belonging to the Society in the Academy of Natural Sciences, under agreement that the said collections shall be returned on demand." The members agreed to this resolution.[152] The curator of the Academy asked if he could get the American Indian collection on 20 November[153] and Ruschenberger wrote on 30 November asking that "all those collections of Mexican, Peruvian and other relics and specimens" be delivered to Charles F. Parker, curator of the Academy.[154] On 6 December the curators reported that the corpus of the "Cabinet of Antiquities" was now in the Academy of Natural Sciences. By agreement, it was to be "properly guarded, cared for, exhibited, and restored to the custody of the Society on demand.[155]

Samuel S. Haldeman wrote an article and made drawings of prehistoric remains found in a cave near Chiques Rock, Lancaster County, Pennsylvania. He had reported finding these artifacts 7 March 1876. The area was quite small, only 12 feet by 10 feet, "in an anticlinal axis" near his home. From the evidence, it had been a place of Indian residence. He located "200 pieces of pottery, 150 arrowheads, many flake knives, about a dozen of chisels, bones, hatchets, etc." He estimated, from the depth of some items, that the area had been occupied for "at least 2,000 years.[156] The artist Edward J. Nolan examined "the stone implements to be drawn" illustrating the paper and wrote his estimate of expense for making plates 11 February 1880.[157] On 3 December 1880 Mrs. Haldeman asked about her late husband's memoir and the relics for illustration. The members authorized the deposit of the "cards on which these relics are arranged .... and to take a receipt for the same, as in the case of other curiosities belonging to this Society there deposited. [158]

23 January 1879
A photograph of a Mayan inscribed stone from Palenque. The stone had been sent to the Smithsonian institution in 1842 and was inserted into a wall of the building.

Albert Samuel Gatschet

A Mrs. Haldeman shipped an additional box of Indian artifacts in care of the Academy of Natural Sciences for the Society. The members voted on 1 April 1881 to deposit this gift with the others in the Academy of Natural Sciences and had the list verified by George Horn.[160]

18 May 1881

Three pieces of Aztec jewelry and one silver spoon, the property of the Society, were received by Dalton Dorr for the Pennsylvania Museum and School of Industrial Art.[161]

On 27 April 1882 Milton T. Cresson wrote Henry S. Phillips, Jr., of the archaeological collections in the Academy of Natural Sciences: the Poinsett Collection of Mexican antiquities (APS); the Haldeman collection; the Peale Collection 'formed by Franklin Peale of Philadelphia, & was presented to the Academys [sic] museum by his widow in 1878 [incorrect];' the Ruschenberger collection of Peruvian pottery; and, the Vaux collection. The Haldeman collection was immense, approximately 10,000 items; the Poinsett collection had 2800 items and the Peale Collection 1800. "The especial features are the specimens of pottery in the Vaux, Ruschenberger, Poinsett and Haldeman collections, together with a fine collection of Mexican Antiquities, unique in the United States, in the Poinsett collection, consisting of terracottas, objects of glass, gold & silver, beads, sculptures, manuscripts &c. &c. The collection was in process of being catalogued and the location (where known) was given where each specimen was found.[162] This information was used by Henry Phillips, Jr., in his speech before the Society later on.[163] Ownership of the collections was becoming confused already.

Mr. Cresson on 16 March 1883 borrowed the Mexican flutes, still in Philosophical Hall, so that Mr. Cox could examine them. By 6 April Cox "had obtained from them a diatonic scale of an octave and a quarter in extent."[164]

Henry Phillips, Jr., read on 4 May 1883 "A brief account of the more important public collections of American archaeology in the United States," and the Society's collection was discussed therein, as were the collections in the Academy of Natural Sciences.[165]

On 4 January 1884, Daniel Garrison Brinton, Henry Phillips, Jr., and J. P. Lesley were appointed a "committee to examine the Mexican MSS. belonging to the Society now on deposit with the Academy of Natural Sciences." The committee was to then report on "the propriety of preparing any of them for publication." These fragments of Aztec writing were among the great gift of Mexican artifacts which Poinsett had presented to the Society and by 1 February 1884 the committee had collected the fragments from the Academy. The president thought a "complete inventory" of the Poinsett collection was needed and Henry Phillips, Jr., said that Milton T. Cresson had written "a preliminary synopsis of the Collection." The committee reported "progress" twice (15 February, 21 March) and by 16 November 1888 Brinton reported on "the desirability of reproducing the MSS. of the Aztec Tribute Roll." The members agreed and Brinton, Phillips and J. Cheston Morris were appointed a committee and reported several times (7, 21 December 1888; 4, 18 January; 1, 15 February; 1, 15 March 1889) and on 5 April 1889 it reported the Codex Poinsett should be published at the cost of $700. The same committee was authorized to "prepare the necessary letter press and to supervise the issuing the work."

On 14 and 21 November 1884 the board of officers resolved to spend $50 for a copy of the "Indian picture rock" to pay for "its purchase, preparation and transportation to Philadelphia." The board of officers recommended on 14 November 1884 that a circular letter be "sent to our correspondents urging them to preserve the monuments of antiquity" in their localities.[167]

George H. Horn wrote Henry Phillips on 23 January 1888 that the Academy of Natural Sciences did not give, nor was it asked to give, a receipt to the Society for the deposit of the American Indian antiquities.[168] He wrote the next day to say that some items were deposited in the Academy as early as 1852.[169]

Mrs. Ellen Russell Emerson requested on 15 July 1889 photographs of "grotesque Mexican masks" which she wished to include in her collection of masks. These were "of great ethnological interest" to her: "If your collection comprises different classes, for instance, masks of the sun-diety—or other divinities, animal, architectural, and others, one picture of each class would be sufficient".[170] She followed this request 18 December 1889 by asking for all historical data pertaining to them. "Will you kindly give me such information as you may find, either by sending me the Catalogue, or by copy of records— if there is not more matter than is convenient. Should the items prove important I am prepared to renumerate a copyist to the amount you deem proper.[171] Phillips replied 20 December that she should consult the Massachusetts Historical Society for information about the masks she indicated, for the Society had no records which would answer her queries. Years ago this Society owned a valuable collection of Mexican Antiquities presented by Joel R. Poinsett which it placed for safekeeping in the fireproof building of the Academy of Natural Sciences and which is under the protection of its Trustees. The Academy's officials...never furnished us with a catalogue receipt of objects so deposited.[172]

Robert Patterson wrote in reference to the Franklin Peale Collection of Stone Age implements and the letter was referred to the curators 5 December 1890. Patterson reported 27 July 1891 that the Peale Collection was in two cases in the Academy of Natural Sciences and appeared "to be in good order."[174] He wrote curator J. Cheston Morris 6 November that should a resolution be needed to bring these artifacts back to Philosophical Hall, he would propose the resolution at a later meeting. [175] Philosophical Hall was now judged fireproof and thereby complied with the terms of the donor of the gift.

By the end of the year Isaac Minis Hays wrote some notes on the disposition of some of the Society's collections. Because the north room of Philosophical Hall was to be used as a museum area, "the curators find it impossible to arrange without knowing *what we have to arrange.*" Hays also noted that it was unfair to let the Academy of Natural Science construct additional space if the Society intended to reclaim its collections. The Poinsett and Keating collections and the Peale collection were of great value and the Society would never "part with title to them." They would be accessible for study, with reference books in the Library, in Philosophical Hall. He stressed the importance of these objects "*showing the progress of human thought & invention*" and urged that they be preserved in the Hall.[176]

On 6 November 1891 J. C. Morris commented on the Peale Collection and referred to a note by Robert Patterson, trustee of the Peale estate. Morris moved that the curators get the collection from the Academy of Natural Sciences and exhibit it in the Hall. The president spoke of the terms of the donation and a lively discussion ensued. It was decided that the curators were to "examine into the facts and report upon the same at the next meeting." On 13 November Patterson sent Morrisan extract from the will of Mrs. Peale and added that "the Society accepted this bequest, and by resolution deposited the collection" with the Academy of Natura lSciences.[177] The curators reported, and proposed 4 December 1891, the resolution: "That the return of the Peale Stone Age Collection from its temporary place of deposit, the Academy of Natural Sciences, be now requested."[178] On 19 February the curators reported the collection was "in the Society's museum, and that all expenses connected with the transfer of the same had been borne by Mr. Robert Patterson, to whom the thanks of the' Society were tendered."[179] Patterson lent his published copy of the catalogue to Morris 25 February 1892.[180] At a curators meeting, 23 October 1897, the bill for the new cases for the Peale Collection was authorized to be paid[181] and on 8 November 1899 the expenses to the curators for the Peale Collection was listed as about $148.[182]

Curator J. Cheston Morris proposed 18 December 1891 that the Poinsett collection be returned to the Society from the Academy of Natural Sciences. After some discussion, the motion was withdrawn by Morris. He spoke to Angelo Heilprin of the Academy and Heilprin wrote that he was not certain that the Academy gave the Society a receipt for the collection, but he thought Dr. Leidy signed one.[184]

The curators, now that the Society was in possession of most of Philosophical Hall, were asked to report on all collections on deposit and on 6 May 1892 the report was made. Also, the curators were to propose what space in the Hall might be needed to properly display them.

First, coins at Memorial Hall, deposited about 1878. The collection is small, probably not five hundred pieces. These could easily [be] displayed in a case such as that now at the southwest corner of this meeting-room. There is, however, a fine oak cabinet belonging to the Society, at present in charge of the Numismatic Society, which is of ample capacity, and could be utilized if necessary.

Second, the Poinsett and Keating collections of Mexican and other objects. These comprise about twenty-eight hundred objects of archaeological interest. The combined collection is perhaps unique in some respects, and was deposited at the Academy of Natural Sciences in 1878. We believe that this collection could be displayed fairly well in such space as that now occupied by the cases on the north wall of this meeting-room, west of the door.

Third, various paleontological specimens deposited at the Academy of Natural Sciences in 1864.

Fourth, the French metre, loaned to the Coast Survey some forty or fifty years ago, and in use by them as a standard.

Fifth, a stone cannonball fired at Queen Mary [of Scotland] and [Henry Stewart, Lord] Darnley as they were escaping from Loch Leven Castle. Loaned to the Historical Society March 31, 1874.[185]

Talcott Williams proposed a resolution 16 December 1892 which was adopted:
Resolved, That the Curators of the Society be requested to report upon the cost of placing the Poinsett and Keating collection in this Museum and caring for it, and upon other collections or institutions in this city, if any, with which this collection could be deposited with advantage to the cause of science and the study of this collection, and upon some plan for arranging the collections of the Society in its Museum in accordance with the wishes, if any, of the donors of different collections.[186]

A letter from the Academy of Natural Sciences of 30 December 1892 about the "Poinsett-Keating Collection of Aztec objects" was read and referred to the curators.[187] The Academy wrote on 19 January 1893 about the retention of this collection in their hands:
Although all the specimens of the Poinsett Collection are artificial and therefore not absolutely within the scope of the Academy's chief purpose, which is the study of natural objects, it is considered desirable that the Academy shall still retain said collection as a loan on the conditions stipulated at the time of its deposit.

The American Philosophical Society may be assured that the Poinsett collection while in custody of the Academy will be carefully preserved; and that as soon as the perfectly fireproof addition to the Academy's building now in course of construction under contract to be completed next June, is finished, there will be ample room for a satisfactory display of it as well as of similar collections. As the museum of the Academy is freely open to the public from eight to ten hours every day, except Sunday through the year, it is confidently conjectured that the Poinsett collection will be visited and studied here by a greater number of persons than it would be in any other place of exhibition in the city.[188]

This letter was turned over to the curators 20 January 1893.[189]
At the meeting of 3 February 1893 Daniel G. Brinton moved "that the Society would prefer" having all of its collections "displayed by such other educational institutions of Philadelphia as would offer the greatest security and usefulness" of the collections. He then read a letter from Sara Y. Stevenson, secretary pro tem of the board of

managers of the Department of Archaeology and Paleontology of the University of Pennsylvania. The board wished the Poinsett collection "to be deposited at the Museum of the University of Pennsylvania" due to the following reasons:

The Museum of Archaeology & Paleontology of the University was founded for the precise purpose of advancing, in this city, the sciences, the names of which appear in its title, and already possesses large and valuable collections, illustrative of the development of man and civilization.

It, moreover, disposes of the services of a competent staff of special scholars, fully qualified to scientifically classify, properly label, and thoroughly "work up" such collections, and to display them to the very best advantage for the use of students.

An isolated collection, containing specimens of the arts and industries of man, as founded upon a few disconnected points—such as the one now at the disposal of the Philosophical Society—however valuable it may be, is practically of very limited use to science. But made to fill an important place in a large ethnographical series—where the story it tells forms an interesting chapter of scientific research in the history of mankind—it becomes of priceless value to scholars, and is a link in the long chain of human evolution.

In respectfully submitting the above to the consideration of the Philosophical Society, the Dep[artmen]t of Archaeology & Paleontology of the University of P[ennsylvani]a pledges itself—if its earnest request be granted—to give the collection the very best accommodation; to provide suitable cases; to display, classify & label it with the most conscientious care, and to spare no pains to insure its preservation, & to make it of the highest possible value to scholars and to the general public. [190]

This proposal provoked some discussion, and the question was referred to the council of the Society.[191]

The managers of the Chicago Exposition asked the Society for the loan of some items and on 3 February 1893 the curators reported that the items could be lent. However, the members

Resolved, That the Society while being desirous of doing everything to gratify the wishes of the Committee of Councils on the World's Columbian Exposition, feels that it cannot allow the articles mentioned in the request of the Committee, to be taken away at this time, as it intends to have a sesquicentennial exhibition in its own rooms during the latter part of May, 1893, and will need them here.[192]

On 5 April the Pennsylvania office of the Board of World's Fair Managers wrote and asked to borrow the Haldeman collection of Indian relics for exhibition. The Society was asked whether this collection can be had, and under what circumstances and conditions. Is it labeled, arranged and ac[ce]s[sione]d? If so, can the cases in which it now is to be had in which to exhibit it at Chicago? Is it so distinctly labeled and arranged that a bright intelligent person will be able to install it there, or will it be necessary to send an expert? Victor M. Haldeman had written that this collection "represents several thousand specimens, all taken from one locality, namely a cave in our yard and Chickies." It represented "the entire art of arrow-making, from the round pebble to the artistically finished dart."[193] Frederick Fraley moved 5 May 1893 that this request be referred to the curators for answer and a discussion ensued. "The Chairman observed that no objects should be loaned, according to a Bylaw of the Society except for the purpose of study."[194]

7 December 1894

Photographs of the Aztec calendar stone and the sacrificial stone.[195]

Charles A. Rutter

The curators decided 15 January 1897 to have casts made of the Indian petroglyphs on the Susquehanna River.

Robert Patterson authorized the loan from the Library Company of Philadelphia to the Society on 16 March 1897 of his copy of the Franklin Peale stone age collection, and it was to be photographed in the Society's rooms. He stressed the value and scarcity of the item and insisted that it be "carefully handled."[197] A postal card was dispatched on 8 October 1897 to J. Cheston Morris to find the location of the catalogue[198] and at the curators meeting of 31 March 1898 Morris was authorized to visit the Library Company of Philadelphia and get it.[199] The special committee on the library reported 2 April 1897 that the "Peale Collection be maintained in the North Room for the present[200] and on 15 April 1898 letters from Robert Patterson were read whereby he presented "a volume of photographs of the Peale collection of Indian relics" to the Society. The members resolved that their "best thanks" be returned to Patterson for this gift.[201]

By 20 October 1899 shelf room was needed for the constantly expanding library, so it was proposed that the Franklin Peale Collection be moved "into cases in the meeting room."

J. Cheston Morris borrowed the "Pentagonal Dodecahedron" to study its "character and nature more thoroughly." On 23 April 1897 he read a paper on it, pointing out that, although it had been presented a century earlier, he had determined that it had been used by a medicine man, possibly to keep a record of the lunar months.

Henry Pettit wrote Morris 13 September 1897 that the new case for the Peale Collection had arrived and Morris and Benjamin S. Lyman should supervise the transfer of the collection into the new case. The casts of the Indian carvings on rocks in the Susquehanna River were authorized to be loaned to J. Cheston Morris on 3 December 1897. Some pages of the Montezuma Tribute Roll had come to the Society with the Poinsett collection and the Society had treasured the writings aid reproduced them in the Transactions, vol. 17, pp. 5061. A gift from the Mexican government arrived on 6 December 1898 and Joseph G. Rosengarten proposed that these pages be presented to the Mexican government, if, "after an examination by experts, to be appointed by the Society, it is ascertained that these are originals needed to complete the collections in Mexico." Throughout its history, the various collections of the Society were used, although their organization was quite often misunderstood. Curator Benjamin S. Lyman wrote 24 February 1899 about the "man who inquired about Leyden jars in the Poinsett & Keating collections."[204]

A collection of reference volumes was received from Charles Robert Hildeburn in 1900 and the library committee asked if the curators could move "the Peale Collection in the meeting room" thereby providing enough room to accommodate the Hildeburn gift.

Toward 1900 the Academy of Natural Sciences began a new record of accessions. Evidently there were lapses in the keeping of the items for a note reads:

The Mexicana belonging to the American Philosophical Society, deposited here in 1879, long lay in open boxes & on shelves in a dark room & much of the data was lost. Comparison with photographs and descriptive reference to originals indicates that all this material belonged to the mass of objects brought back by Poinsett and Keating.[205]

The record was immense and the Society entries were marked, where known. Many of them were identifiable by donor or description. A huge number were not identified. The Poinsett-Keating entries ran from 11493 through 12835 with a few other entries included.

Witmer Stone, assistant curator of the Academy of Natural Sciences sent a listing of the Society's property in the Academy. The following are the Indian items he listed:
3 Alabaster Vases
2 wax models of "Calendar Stone"
String of beads
4 Aztec "Charms"
7 Obsidian skin knives (Keating Coll.)
16   "   "

19 " arrow points
1 Tray of Beads and Rings of Obsidian (Poinsett)
1 " " Stone Beads
1 " " Beads and Ornaments
1 " " Shell Beads
9 Clay Flutes and 4 Fragments.
Fragment of Sculptured Pottery
18 Clay Whistles
20 trays containing several hundred Clay heads and Images....
Discoidal Stone (Tennessee Indians)
3 "pestels [pestles]" (N[orth] A[merican] Indians)...
Mummy Cloth (Peru)
Specimens associated with the Mexican material of previous list and in all probability
    Amer[ican] Phil[osophical] Soc[iety] but without original labels to that effect.
38 Mexican Face Masks.
1.3Stone Images (large)
5 small pieces of carved stone, two of them Images.
1 small Image of Green stone.
4 stone Images.
3 carved Stone Faces
11 Casts of Mexican Stone Images (painted Black)
1 tray of 10 small Images.
1 Obsidian (?) Frog.
3 Lava Images (in tray)
8 Smooth Stones "
1 tray of Obsidian Fragments.
19 Clay Cups with two cavities (games?)
6 " Rattles.
7 Fragments of Pottery.
11 Trays of small Clay heads and Images. [206]

      Arthur Willis Goodspeed sent Curator J. Cheston Morris 22 October 1901 a list of the Society's deposits in the Academy of Natural Sciences and at the same time he forwarded a list of the Society's deposits in the Wagner Free Institute of Science.[207]

      The following Indian artifacts were in Philosophical Hall as late as the turn of the century:
Basket with feather ornaments presented by Titian Ramsay Peale (western North America)
Beads from Mexico, presented by Jonathan D. Sergeant
Stone chisels; ear ornaments from Lewis and Clark (?)
Earthern vessel (from Alaska?)
Eskimo fishhook (Irigut, Greenland), presented by Lieutenant W. A. Mintzer
An Indian lance from Long Island.[208]
These were, most probably, deposited in the University Museum of the University of Pennsylvania.

      Meanwhile, the Academy of Natural Sciences dismounted its Archaeological Department and the American Indian antiquities went into storage where they were, in essence, forgotten. However, on 7 November 1930 the curator reported that the Poinsett collection "and such other specimens belonging to" the Society had been stored in the old Museum Hall. Permission was granted to remove them and place them in the University Museum of the University of Pennsylvania where they remain. In 1933 the Franklin Peale Collection of stone age implements were deposited at the University Museum.

      Registrar Geraldine Bruchner of the University Museum sent Edwin Grant Conklin 11 April 1942 a listing of the Poinsett collection in the Museum. Some items, "originally part of the Poinsett Collection...were not turned over to us by the Academy of Natural Sciences."[209] The registrar sent 23 December 1949 a far more detailed listing of the Society's artifacts in the University Museum, which included various American Indian artifacts (the Poinsett collection, etc.), Oceanic and African artifacts.[210]

And yet, some items have been overlooked and still remain in the Society's buildings. They include the dodecahedron of black slate, perhaps an Indian shaman's prized possession for keeping track of the lunar months, presented by Charles Brown in 1792; Mexican artifacts (?) mounted on a board and a Mexican goddess of war (?)from the Poinsett-Keating collections (?); Indian earthern bottle or vase found in upper Louisiana and presented by Mr. Peyrouse, 20 September 1805; and, the spear which slew Colonel Chew, with some Indian arrows, presented by Judge George Turner on 10 February 1797. Also, with the gift of the Frank Gouldsmith Speck papers in 1950 came an Indian-painted gourd and a beaded Montagnais-Naskapi knife case, with knife.

The interest in the American Indian continues. Peter Stephen Du Ponceau and Thomas Jefferson were fascinated with the linguistics of the aborigines and gave many manuscripts and books to the library. That interest continues to this day and in 1966 *A Guide to Manuscripts Relating to the American Indian in the Libraryof the American Philosophical Society* by John F. Freeman and Murphy D. Smith was published. A supplement was published in 1982 by Daythal Kendall.

NATIVE AMERICAN ANTIQUITIES—References
1. Curators Cards; *Archives* J. Dickinson to D. Rittenhouse, 1 May 1772.
2. *Trans.*, vol. 3.
3. *Ibid.*
4. *MS. Corn.* M. Cutler to B. S. Barton, 31 Aug. 1792.
5. *Trans.*, vol. 3.
6. *Proc.*, vol. 3, pp. 179–192.
7. *American Anthropology*, 1909, pp. 349–358.
8. *Archives* G. Turner to D. Rittenhouse, 12 Jan. 1794.
9. *Trans.*, vol. 4.
10. *Archives* G. Turner to D. Rittenhouse, 12 Jan. 1794.
11. *Ibid.*, J. Sergeant to APS, 1796.
12. *Trans.*, vol. 4, pp. 177-78.
13. *Archives* J. Sergeant to B. S. Barton, 19 Feb. 1796.
14. *Ibid.* APS. Report, 20 Dec. 1799.
15. *Ibid.* APS. List, Feb. 1797; *Trans.*, vol. 4.
16. *Ibid.* APS. Report, [16 June 1797].
17. *Trans.*, vol. 5, pp. ix-xi.
18. Cur. Rec.
19. MS. Com. S. F. Hutchison to C. W. Peale, 25 May 1797.
20. Cur. Rec.
21. *Archives* APS. Report, 1 Dec. 1797.
22. *Trans.*, vol. 6.
23. *Ibid.*
24. *Ibid.*
25. *Ibid.*
26. *Ibid.*
27. *Ibid.*, n. s., vol. 1.
28. *Archives* Verbal communications.
29. *Archives* APS. Report, 2 Dec. 1808; *Trans.*, vol. 6.
30. MS Com. J. D. Clifford to B. S. Barton, 4 Sept. 1811.
31. *Donation Book;* *Trans.*, n. s., vol. 1; Com. Rec., vol. 2.
32. *Archives* R. Conyngham to T. T. Hewson, 10 June 1815.
33. *Donation Book;* *Trans.*, n. s., vol. 1.
34. *Archives* C. W. Short. Sketch, 31 Aug. 1816.
35. *Ibid.*, Verbal communication.
36. *Trans.*, n. s., vol. 2.
37. MS. Com. J. C. Calhoun to R. Walsh, 11 March 1819; J. C Calhoun to S. H. Long, 8 March. 1819.
38. *Ibid.*, R. Walsh to J. C. Calhoun, 30 March 1819.
39. *Donation Book;* *Trans.*, n. s., vol. 2.
40. *Curators Cards.*
41. *Archives* C. Smith to P. S. Du Ponceau, 13 Oct. 1825.
42. *Donation Book;* *Trans.*, n. s., vol. 3.
43. University Museum, University of Pennsylvania. Accession cards.
44. *Archives* J. R. Poinsett to J. Vaughan, 22 Feb. 1830.
45. *Trans.*, n. s., vol. 3.
46. *Donation Book;* *Trans.*, n. s., vol. 3.
47. *Archives* W. H. Keating to J. K. Kane, 6 April 1830; *Donation Book;* *Trans.*, n. s., vol. 3.
48. Com. Rec., vol. 2; Donations to the Cabinet, pp. 11-12.
49. *Donation Book;* *Trans.*, n. s., vol. 4; "Arch." J. E. Bloomfield to J. Vaughan, 9 July 1830.
50. *Donation Book*, 16 July 1830.
51. *Archives* J. Barabino to J. Vaughan, 5 Aug. 1830.
52. *Extrait du Bulletin de la Society de Geographie.* D. B. Warden. Rapport... Sur la Collection de dessins d'Antiquites Mexicaines executes par M. Franck, 4 March 1831.
53. Misc. MS. Col. M. Franck to the president of the Societe Geographique de Paris, 20 April 1831.
54. *Archives* J. Vaughan. Concerning the Mexican antiquities, 1831.
55. *Archives Trans.*, n. s., vol. 4.
56. *Ibid.*

57. *Trans.*, n. s., vol. 4.
58. *Ibid.*
59. *Archives* 5. Humphrys to J. K. Kane, 15 Feb. 1832.
60. *Ibid.* S. G. Morton to J. Vaughan, 24 April 1832; Com. Rec., 20 July 1832.
61. *Ibid.* Baron de Beher to ----, 11 Nov. 1833.
62. *Ibid.* John Howe to J. Vaughan, 16 Dec. 1833.
63. *Donation Book;* Gift of T. Nuttall, 18 Nov. 1836; *Trans.*, n. s., vol. 5.
64. *Archives* J. H. Gibbon. Receipt, 24 Aug. 1837.
65. *Ibid.* J. H. Gibbon to J. Vaughan, 25 Aug. 1837.
66. *Donation Book; Trans.*, n. s., vol. 6.
67. *Archives* J. Snider, Jr. Receipt, 1 Jan. 1838.
68. *Ibid.* APS. Report, 21 June 1839.
69. *Proc.*, vol. 1, pp. 46, 104.
70. *Archives* APS. Report, 21 June 1839.
71. *Proc.*, vol. 1, pp. 46, 104.
72. *Archives* P. S. Du Ponceau. Concerning..., 5 Oct. 1838.
73. *Ibid.* R. Conyngham to J. Vaughan, 16 May 1840.
74. *Ibid.*, 5 June 1840.
75. *Ibid.* C. G. Forshey to J. Vaughan, 3 Sept. 1840; *Proc.*, vol. 1. p. 279.
76. *Ibid.* J. Bloomfield to J. Vaughan, 26 Sept. 1841; *Proc.*, vol. 2, p. 99.
77. *Ibid.* H. M'Ilvaine to APS, 11 June 1846.
78. *Proc.*, vol. 4, p. 256.
79. *Ibid.*, p. 274.
80. *Ibid.*, p. 3; *Donation Book; Trans.*, vol. 9; Curator Cards.
81. *Donation Book; Trans.*, vol. 9.
82. *Archives* S. G. Morton to G. Ord, 5 June 1846.
83. *Ibid.* 26 Oct. 1846; *Proc.*, vol. 4, p. 286.
84. *Proc.*, vol. 4, p. 338; Don. Book.
85. *Archives* P. A. Browne to APS, 26 April 1850.
86. *Proc.*, vol. 5, p. 535; Don. Book.
87. *Ibid.*, vol. 7, pp. 162-63.
88. *Ibid.*, p. 164.
89. *Ibid.*, pp. 411–416.
90. *Ibid.*, vol. 8, p. 258.
91. *Ibid.*, pp. 265–272.
92. *Ibid.*, p. 394.
93. *Ibid.*, vol. 9, pp. 21-23.
94. *Ibid.*, p. 261.
95. *Ibid.*, pp. 371, 401-03.
96. *Ibid.*, p. 224.
97. *Ibid.*, vol. 8, p. 272.
98. *Ibid.*, vol. 9, p. 277.
99. *Archives* J. Henry to APS, 12 Dec, 1863; *Proc.*, vol. 9, p. 281.
100. *Proc.*, vol. 9, p. 281.
101. *Archives* p. 412.
102. *Archives* J. Leidy to J. P. Leslie, 23 Feb. 1864; *Proc.*, vol. 9, p. 344; Com, Recs.
103. *Proc.*, vol. 9, pp. 353–354.
104. *Ibid.*, p. 460.
105. *Ibid.*, vol. 10, pp. 30-32.
106. *Archives* T. C. Porter to J. P. Lesley, 10 July 1865.
107. *Proc.*, vol. 10, p. 149.
108. Com. Rec.
109. *Proc.*, vol. 10, p. [255]; Don. Book.
110. *Ibid.*, p. 151.
111. *Ibid.*, p. 168.
112. *Ibid.*, pp. 243-44.
113. *Ibid.*, pp. 321-22.
114. *Ibid.*, pp. 321, 330.
115. *Ibid.*, p. 338.
116. *Ibid.*, p. 388.
117. *Ibid.*, pp. 430–435.
118. *Ibid.*, p. 522.
119. *Ibid.*, vol. 11, pp. 3-4.
120. *Ibid.*, pp. 83-84.
121. *Ibid.*, p. 192.
122. Officers and Council. Minutes.
123. *Proc.*, vol. 11, pp. 213-14.
124. *Ibid.*, p. 283.
125. *Ibid.*, p. 311.
126. *Ibid.*, p. 447.
127. Robert Patterson. Obituary notice; *Proc.*, vol. 11, p. 603.
128. *Proc.*, vol. 11, pp. 514–515.
129. *Ibid.*, vol. 12, pp. 11–13, plate I, p. 14.
130. *Proc.*, vol. 13, p. 210.
131. *Proc.*, vol. 13, p. 210.
132. *Ibid.*, p. 269.
133. *Ibid.*, vol. 14, p. 174.
134. *Archives.* Will of Mrs. Caroline Peale, 12 Oct. 1875; R. Patterson to G. B. Wood, 30 Oct. 1875.
135. Ibid. APS. Resolution, 19 Nov. 1875; *Proc.*, vol. 14, pp. 649-50.
136. Officers and Council. Minutes.
137. *Archives.* G. A. Matile to P. E. Chase, 22 July 1876; A. H. Guyot to APS and Academy of Natural Sciences, 1876; *Proc.*, vol. 16, p. 282.
138. *Proc.*, vol. 16, p. 283.
139. *Archives.* A. H. Guyot to APS, [1876].
140. *Ibid.* A. H. Guyot to P. E. Chase, 6 Oct. 1876.

141. *Ibid.* APS. Curators report, 3 Nov. 1876; Proc., vol. 16, p. 290.
142. *Ibid.* A. H. Guyot to J. P. Lesley, 8 Nov. 1876.
143. *Ibid.,* 13 Dec. 1876.
144. *Ibid.* G. A. Matile to APS, 13 July 1877; A. H. Guyot to P. E. Chase, [1876].
145. *Proc.,* vol. 17, p. 727.
146. *Ibid.* vol. 16, p. 391.
147. *Ibid.,* vol. 17, p. 13.
148. *Archives.* R. Patterson to H. Tyndale, 2 Oct. 1877.
149. *Proc.,* vol. 17, pp. 14-15.
150. Academy of Natural Sciences of Philadelphia. *Archives.* Collection 177; *Archives.* Academy of Natural Sciences to H. Tyndale, 25 Oct. 1877; *Proc..,* vol. 17, p. 272.
151. *Archives.* Academy of Natural Sciences. Receipt, 13 Nov. 1877; *Proc.,* vol. 17, p. 273.
152. *Proc.,* vol. 17, p. 273.
153. *Archives.* Academy of Natural Sciences to J. P. Lesley, 20 Nov. 1878.
154. *Ibid.* 30 Nov. 1878.
155. *Proc.,* vol. 18, pp. 86-87.
156. Academy of Natural Sciences. *Archives.* Minutes, vol. 12.
157. *Archives.* E. J. Nolan to J. L. Le Conte, 11 Feb. 1880.
158. *Proc.,* vol. 19, p. 194.
159. *Archives.* A. S. Gatschet to APS, 23 Jan. 1879.
160. *Proc.,* vol. 19, pp. 348-49; Curators Cards.
161. *Archives.* Pennsylvania Museum.., Receipt, 18 May 1881.
162. *Ibid.* M. T. Cresson to H. S. Phillips, Jr., 27 April 1882.
163. *Proc.,* vol. 21, pp. 111-12.
164. *Ibid.* vol. 20, pp. 648-49.
165. *Ibid.* vol. 21, pp. 111-19.
166. *Officers and Council.* Minutes.
167. *Ibid.*
168. *Archives.* G. H. Horn to H. Phillips Jr., 23 Jan. 1888.
169. *Ibid.* 24 Jan. 1888.
170. *Ibid.* E. R. Emerson to APS, 15 July 1889.
171. *Ibid.* E. R. Emerson to H. Phillips Jr., 18 Dec. 1889.
172. *Ibid.* H. Phillips, Jr., to E. R. Emerson, 20 Dec. 1889.
173. *Ibid.* R. Patterson to F. Fraley, 5 Dec. 1890; *Proc.,* vol. 28, p. 260.
174. *Ibid.* R. Patterson to J. C. Morris, 27 July 1891.
175. *Ibid.* 6 Nov. 1891.
176. *Ibid.* I. M. Hays. Notes, 1898?
177. *Ibid.* R. Patterson to J. C. Morris, 13 Nov. 1891.
178. *Proc.,* vol. 29, p. 165
179. *Ibid.,* vol. 30, p. 116.
180. *Archives.* R. Patterson to J. C. Morris, 25 Feb. 1892.
181. *Curators.* Minutes, 23 Oct. 1892.
182. *Ibid.,* 8 Nov. 1899.
183. *Proc.,* vol. 29, pp. 220-21.
184. *Archives.* A. Heilprin to H. Phillips, Jr., 27 April 1892.
185. *Ibid.* Curators. Report, 6 May 1892; Proc., vol. 30, p. 262.
186. *Ibid.* 16 Dec. 1892; Proc., vol. 30, p. 316.
187. *Proc.,* vol. 31, p. 2.
188. *Archives.* Academy of Natural Sciences to H. Phillips, Jr., 19 Jan. 1893.
189. *Proc.,* vol. 31, pp. 5-6.
190. *Archives.* University Museum of the University of Pennsylvania to D G. Brinton, 1 Jan., 1893; Proc., vol. 31, p. 31.
191. *Proc.,* vol. 31, p. 14.
192. *Ibid.* p. 12.
193. *Archives.* Pennsylvania Board of World's Fair Managers to F. Fraley, 5 April 1893.
194. *Ibid.,* F. Fraley to H. Phillips, Jr., 16 March 1893; Proc., vol. 31, p. 227.
195. *Proc.,* vol. 33, p. 368.
196. *Archives.* Curators. Minutes, 15 Jan. 1897.
197. *Ibid.* R. Patterson to J. C. Morris, 16 March 1897.
198. *Ibid.* E. M. Morison to J. C. Morris, 8 Oct. 1897.
199. *Ibid.* Curators. Minutes, 31 March 1898.
200. *Proc.,* vol. 36, p. 175.
201. *Archives.* R. Patterson to J. C. Morris, 13 April 1898; R. Patterson to F. Fraley, 13 April 1898; Proc., vol. 37, p. 142.
202. See chapter on Mineralogy; *Proc.,* vol. 36, pp. 178-92.
203. *Archives.* H. Pettit to B. S. Lyman, 13 Sept. 1897.
204. *Ibid.* B. S. Lyman to E. M. Morison, 24 Feb. 1899.
205. Academy of Natural Sciences. Collection 141, IIc, p. 72.
206. *Archives.* Academy of Natural Sciences to APS, 3 June 1901; Academy of Natural Sciences. List, 3 June 1901.
207. *Ibid.,* A. W Goodspeed to J. C. Morris, 22 Oct. 1901.
208. *Curators Cards*
209. *Conklin Papers.* G. Bruckner to E. G. Conlin, 11 April 1942.
210. *Eisenhart Papers.* G. Buckner to L. P. Eisenhart, 23 Dec. 1949.

Chapter 3.
Botanical Specimens

Botany, more than any other subject, was what first interested European scientists in America. John Bartram, though corresponding with European savants, however, was not very active in the Society, nor was his son, William. Publications on botany arrived for the Society, as did some specimens, but, unfortunately, there was no resident American botanist. Founder-member Benjamin Franklin's "Proposal" which founded the Society, stated that the Society would be interested in "All new discovered Plants, Herbs, Trees, Roots, &c., their Virtues, Uses, &c. Methods of Propagating them...Improvement of vegetables Juices, as Cyders, Wines ... "

Members, including Charles Thomson, thought that the Society must support mankind at large, and agriculture, manufactures, and commerce were important, but that agriculture was the first in importance and should be concentrated on the most. Members looked forward to helping develop viticulture in the United States through agriculture, and envisioned better ships and maritime trade through the use of forests and agricultural products.

Several utilitarian projects based on botany were encouraged by the Society in the early period: the production of wine, the distillation of persimmons, and the extraction of oil from sunflower seeds. Early members wished also to help eradicate, or lessen, the loss of wheat caused by the Hessian fly. They sought a method of removing wild garlic from cultivated fields and were concerned with ploughs and other farming implements. In addition, there was an interest in developing a native silk industry and there remain many publications in the Library on the raising of silk worms, mulberry trees, and the manufacture of silk—carefully integrated with the desire to develop further the agriculture of the United States.

The understanding and development of medicinal plants were ignored, and the Society's interest in the purely medicinal aspect of botany was practically nonexistent. The Pennsylvania Hospital had a garden where herbs and other medicinal plants were raised and the physicians in the University of Pennsylvania Medical School lectured on *materia medica.* Some plants and descriptions did come to the Society and were discussed, but little else occurred in this field.

Following the successful conclusion of the Revolution, many new organizations were formed in America and two which removed many botanical and agricultural communications and donations from the province of the Society were the Philadelphia Society for Promoting Agriculture, which continues to exist, albeit in a drastically altered form, and later, the Academy of Natural Sciences of Philadelphia was formed, which consequently became the most important organization in the city for the study of natural sciences.

For many years, however, items of major botanical interest came to the Society. A premium was offered at the end of the eighteenth century for the best method for preventing the premature decay of peach trees. Nevertheless, the foremost American botanists, John and William Bartram, Gotthilf Heinrich Ernest Muhlenberg, and Humphry Marshall, as well as naturalists, such as Thomas Jefferson and Charles Willson Peale, felt that the Society was the proper organization to receive the reports of their accomplishments. Charles Thomson viewed Thomas Jefferson's Notes on Virginia "a most excellent natural history not, merely of Virginia, but of North America."

Both the American Society and the American Philosophical Society, before their union, encouraged the publication of information long before the *Transactions* began in 1771. They utilized the local newspapers, the *Pennsylvania Gazette,* and the *Pennsylvania Chronicle,* and the American Society not only gave public thanks for gifts received on 18 March 1768, but asked for public help for more gifts:

The Society returns thanks to the Several Gentlemen who have sent them specimens of the Silk Cotton, Labrador Tea & American Bole an account of which is duly entered upon their Minutes & proper measure will be taken to inquire into & inform the public of what use these particlars may prove to the Community.

A very acceptable present of a Curious Collection of Fishes from a Gentleman of taste & public Spirit in this City is received for which the Society make him their grateful acknowledgements.

They doubt not but these instances of public Spirit will encourage other persons who have it in their power, to make similar presents, or to Communicate whatever is curious or useful, to the Society.[1]

Members who owned farms experimented on various means of production and there were several botanical gardens in the environs of Philadelphia, among which was John Bartram's where he sold seeds, cuttings, plants, and roots. The splendid garden of William Hamilton at The Woodlands was beautiful, but his interest lay chiefly in plants which beautified the grounds. There were private arboreta later, and some few yet exist, for example, Tyler, Morris, Longwood, Winterthur, among others.

The first six volumes of the *Transactions* contain many articles pertaining to agriculture, manufactures and botany. By the time Volume I appeared in the New Series in 1818, practically nothing pertaining to general agriculture was published, and what did appear resembled more closely what we would call botany today. Even before the publication of the *Transactions* began, articles on the sowing of pease, the destruction of wild garlic in grain fields, and aspects of *materia medica* (plants for the use of helping cure diarrhea and intermittent fevers) appeared under the aegis of the Society in the *American Magazine* of 1769. In the first volume of the *Transactions,* other articles on the preservation of pease, the destruction of wild garlic in grain fields, and extracts from John Ellis's writings on how to ship seeds and plants were published, two articles on the grape and the care of vines appeared, as well as articles on the curing of figs, and an article on the strammonium (thorn apple), as well as a general essay on climate and vegetable productions. The sole entry in Volume II pertaining to botany was how to dry parsnips for preservation.

The third volume of the *Transactions* contained two articles concerning agriculture: the sugar maple and how to get sugar from the sap; and, how over used, or poor, soil could be enriched by using a plant, the cassia chaecrista. There were four articles which were, more properly, botanical studies. G. H. E. Muhlenberg's "Index Flora Lancasterensis," Karl Peter Thunberg's description of "the Podophyllum Diphyllum" (a genus of Ranunculeae), Baron Ambroise Marie Francois Joseph Palisot de Beauvois's observations on the "crytogamick" plants, and James Greenway's study of a poisonous plant which was "growing spontaneously in the southern part of Virginia."

Heinrich Muhlenberg supplemented his index in Volume IV of the *Transactions* and Baron Ambroise Palisot de Beauvois wrote of a new Pennsylvania plant. Benjamin Smith Barton reported on "the Stimulant Effects of Camphor upon Vegetables."

The Society advertised in 1797 a Magellanic Premium for the best method of preserving peach trees and several entries were received through 1800. Two of these were published in Volume V of the Transactions. Also a report of a new underground vegetable appeared therein, as well as a study on vegetables, polyps and insects by Pierre S. Du Pont (de Nemours). In addition to these articles and studies, many publications on botany and agriculture were received—most of them are in the library, which also has papers and reports on botanical items not listed above. Some are described in the Minutes.

On 24 October 1766 "An Indian Remedy for a green wound" was read before the American Society. Owen Biddle had the recipe (the root of the wild indigo plant was boiled and pressed, and the liquor applied to the wound) from Colonel Asher Clayton who had seen an Indian cure his wound. The Indian had struck the hatchet end of a tomahawk through the calf of his leg but missed the bone.

The wound was large enough to admit 3 fingers; and in drawing the Tomahawk out of the wound it tore the flesh considerably by reason of its shape. When the hatchet was taken out the blood followed in a Stream as large as a man's finger. They immediately tyed a bandage round the Leg to stop the bleeding until they prepared the above Liquor w[hi]ch they applied. On the third day he saw the man walking about and in a few days was well enough to go a hunting. It prevents Inflammation and makes the wound suppurate kindly.[2]

Isaac Bartram produced a dissertation on 13 March 1767 on the "Many and great Advantages that would accrue" to Pennsylvania by the raising and use of the persimmon tree. He was authorized to distill the liquor by the members in 1767 and "produced some Spirit of an Excellent Flavour Drawn from the fruit of the said tree by Distillation which when Meliorated by age Will be equal to, and answer all the purposes of the Common West India Rum." His paper, published in the *American Magazine* in 1769, concluded that the cultivation of the persimmon, "is an object worthy of the Attention of our farmers, as it promises great profit to themselves and a still greater advantage to the community in general." [3]

The year 1768 was productive for botanists; the Society received several offerings. George Glentworth, for example, gave John Morgan some samples of Labrador tea and Morgan presented them to the American Society on 11 March 1768. Isaac Bartram and James Alexander[4] examined them and said they were from a species of the *Ilex vomitoria,* or the Cassina. Alexander later in the month, on 25 March, presented some leaves of the same plant, "from Carolina."[5] On 18 March 1768 Alexander exhibited before the Society "the Leaves of several plants Anatomised." He had soaked them in water until the skin was slightly rotted and then he peeled the skin off "and the Paranchyma may be easily washed out.[6] Also in March, on the 25th, Richard Wells gave the American Society a large collection of "curiously preserved" English plants. The Society decided that they might be of use in determining species "of such Plants as are or may be found in America of the same kinds."[7] John Hood exhibited on 1 April 1768 some vegetable bark which had been lately gathered, and "with no other Preparation than being rub'd between the Hands" seemed to become soft and strong hemp. He promised to deliver the root of the plant to a member for further enquiry.[8] On 1 July and 19 August 1768 a root of the "Rubia, a plant used by the Indians for dyeing their porcupine Quils, Deer's Hair &c. of a Red Colour" was received from James Bartram with a statement as to the preparation for dyeing:

Take the Root and carefully boil it in a brass Kettle; of Crab Apples take a
proportional Quantity and boil them in another Kettle; the matter intended to be dyed
is first infused into the liquid made of the Rubia, and then into the Crab Apple juice,
which firmly fixes the Colour.[9]

Also on 1 July 1768 Humphry Marshall's letter on "several natural productions" was received.

20 September 1768
A specimen of the fruit from a "Cucumber tree, aromatic & resembling Cucumbers for Pickling." (The Magnolia acuminata and other American species have fruits which resemble small cucumbers.)

James Wright

A specimen of American rhubarb from the seeds of the Russian variety. *Edward Anthill*
"The seeds of the Rose Apple" (Eugenia malaccensis).[10] These were turned over to the Medical Committee for reports.

Captain Reddle

15 November 1768
"The seed of the Black Alder of Jamaica [Prinos verticillatus], used instead of Black Pepper in that island, with an agreeable mixture of the flavor of ginger and Pepper." It was thought diet and medicine possibly could make great use of the seed.[11]

Thomas Bond for Mr. Law

9 December 1768
A sample of lentils and pease. After thanking the donor, members of the American Society wished him to write an account of the manner of cultivating the "Millet & Lentils."[12] The article was written and published in the *American Magazine* in 1769.
John Peter Miller

16 January 1769
Some Chinese vetches. The committee requested on 3 March 1769 that the donor be thanked, "especially for his ingenious account of the Chinese vetches" and the vetches "be distributed to Pemberton, John and Isaac Bartram, John Morgan, John Rhea, Abel James, Thomas Clifford, John Gibson & George Roberts." If the vetch lived, and if the reports were made, they have all disappeared.
Samuel Bowen

20 May 1769
A bag of berry seed which "produces an oyl equal in quality to Florence oyl, some say preferable." Florence oil was a superior kind of olive oil. Maris claimed that the produce was "amazingly great" from these berries. The seeds were to be planted ten seeds to a hole, three feet apart, with only three or four allowed to grow per hole. The berries grew in pods and were gathered full grown and dry. "Isaac Bartram to experiment with some, & the rest to be distributed among the members to plant." There is no report on the outcome of this experiment.
Jesse Maris

19 December 1771
Some Siberian barley and a broadside praising it. "It thrives in our climate. A Gentleman who has sown it in clay, in sand, and in a mixture of both, has observed that it yields a better crop on each of these soils than any of the common Barley in the neighbourhood. "High praise was heaped on the yield, the beer and ale made from it, and the bread. We may conclude from the saving in the seed of the Siberian Barley, from its superior weight, from the goodness of the bread made of it, and from the much superior quality of the malt made of it, that this Barley may turn out one of the greatest acquisitions this kingdom has made for ages.[13]
Isaac Bartram
        John Claudius Loudon wrote in 1857 in his *Encyclopaedia Agriculture* that Siberian barley was introduced into England in 1768 but by his date it was either lost or had become merged with the parent species.

21 February 1772
Some seeds and dried flowers of the "*Somo Skimi* & some branches of the *Emetic Bear*" were received from a member in Pensacola, Florida. These were in Hugh Williamson's possession, and were referred to the committee of natural history and chemistry.
John Lorimer

27 December 1772
Some moss, used for dyeing purple. The donor wrote: "I cannot inform you of the Method of using it tho I have used the utmost diligence in Enquiring. The only person viz Martha Moore who used it being Dead. However I will if possible inform my Self & ... will not fail Communicating it to your Society."[14]
Rednap Howell
        John Leacock wrote the Society on 29 December 1772 that he had successfully established a vineyard but needed additional funds to acquire additional cuttings and plants:
    The subscriber, having been employed in the undertaking, Solely, and without any
    assistance from Public Bodies of Men, or Private Persons, notwithstanding his
    meeting with many discouraging difficulties natural Concomitants, in the beginning
    of such undertakings has, by dint of Industry, Perseverance & great expence,
    brought about a pleasing Prosepct of its being practicable & promises future
    Success.

Leacock asked the members to subscribe to the venture, "as Adventurers."[15] This proposal for establishing a public vineyard by lottery was read on 1 January 1773, and members decided that the secretaries were to write, informing Leacock "that they approve encouraging the culture of Vines & wish him the greatest Success, but, as Lotteries are contrary to the Laws of the Province, they cannot countenance his Undertaking."

Francis Alison wrote on 2 April 1773 recommending that the Society instruct American farmers how to preserve the fertility of the soil, the best crops for the particular area, encourage viticulture, give premiums, etc.[16] Bernard Romans spoke of his botanical trip in Florida and promised at the meeting of 20 August 1773 to leave drawings of "two nondescript plants, natives of Florida" which he had named *Kalmia Floridiana* and *Lupinus Emiticus seu L. foliisternatis*. True to his word, on 18 February 1774, he sent Owen Biddle two sketches: one of a new species of Florida Kalmia "& a figure & description of the Semen Badiananisam Stellatu, or Illicium Floridianum." He wrote publishers William and Thomas Bradford on 28 February 1774, that he would like "to know, whether the Drawings I sent to Mr. Owen Biddle in November last for the use of the American Society came to hand or not."[17] Romans published in New York in 1775 his *Concise History of East and West Florida*. but the plants mentioned above are not depicted in this publication.

4 November 1782
Report of a "Tea Plant or herb of such Quality" that the donors thought, with encouragement from the members, they could shortly produce "Ten Tons or more of it" yearly. A sample of this tea "equal in Flavor and Taste to the East India Bohea Tea" was sent. The communication was endorsed: "respecting a supposed discovery of Tea."[18]

George and Jacob Stonemetz

16 January 1784
"A collection of specimens of the several woods growing in the island of Jamaica."

Samuel Filsted[19]

16 June 1786
"Red root, or Indian paint, used as a dye," along with several items, but the root of the rubia was deemed "most worthy of note." This was delivered through Benjamin Franklin. The "red root" is a native of New Jersey and is called also the New Jersey tea.

John Bartram

3 October 1788
"Water birch bark." This may have been intended as an American Indian artifact.

Matthias Barton

2 October 1789
Specimens of the papyrus of Syracuse.[20]

Benjamin Franklin

19 December 1789
Sundry "Philosophical" curiosities:

2. West Indian Quinquine [chinchona, or Jesuit's bark, used for quinine]. I have given to [members] Doctors [Benjamin] Rush & [Caspar] Wistar of the Society a considerable quantity of it, to try as a Medicine. They no doubt will inform the Society of its qualities. Its character in St. Domingo is that of a very strong bitter; but is not considered as so good a Remedy in Fevers as the Red Bark.

3. A Specimen of Cinnamon the growth of Jamaica. Its spice is as strong as that obtained from the East Indies.

4. A Species of the Bread Fruit, known by the Names of *Pain de Singe & Jack Bread Fruit* in the West Indies, & obtained but lately from the Isle of France. I have sent the Shell, some of the seeds clear of the Pulp, & some others covered with the Pulp. The Shell was filled with Seeds, each of them covered with the Pulp. It is a Luxury & not a necessity. [21]

Samuel Vaughan, Jr

30 September 1790
"A branch of Radish incorporated with a red beet, the two growing together, must understandably have caused it.". The donor wrote that many large radishes grew in the same bed "some 13 inches round" and this radish was about four inches from the beet. [22]

William Bradford

A cryptic comment was entered 15 January 1790: Andrew Ellicott "displayed articles of Natural History from the Western Territory. Referred to Dr. Benjamin S. Barton to examine and report." Nothing else is known of this subject.

Andre Michaux proposed on 29 April 1793 to explore the trans-Mississippi west for natural history objects and various members of the Society, including Thomas Jefferson, were active in raising funds to underwrite the expedition.[23] Though it was never made, Jefferson wrote some instructions on what should be sought. These were valuable thoughts when he sent Meriwether Lewis and William Clark on their epic expedition.

William Roxburgh was the botanist to the East India Company and he sent on 30 May 1794 "sundry Asiatic plants" and they were left with William Hamilton of the Woodlands to be delivered to the Society on demand:

Altho totally unknown to you, yet I take the liberty of sending you, for the benefit of mankind (& that is my chief view) a box containing several of our most valuable East India, & China plants, their' Linnaean names, at least all of them that I know, are mentioned on the accompanying slip of paper.

Mr. Pringle, the Gentleman who has charge of them, hath another, tho smaller box, which varies in its contents very little. This I have given him with the same view, and to induce him to bring, or send us to India, such of your useful Plants and seeds as may be deemed most likely to add to our comforts.

I do not know myself whether the peaches, nectarines, apricots, Goos[e]berrys, currants, strawberries, apples, &c. of America are better than in England, yet as your climate must come nearer ours, they may succeed better here than the plants we receive from England.[24]

These plants were deposited with Hamilton on 19 April 1794 and John Vaughan acknowledged the letter. Also, Vaughan also made a listing of the plants in the large box:
6 Lanquuat
6 Leechee [Nephelium litchi]
6 Wampee [Clausena wampi] China fruit trees
6 mango
6 Betle [Betel nut]
6 Jack [bread fruit]
1 Eugenae malaccensis [Eugeniae is a species of tropical trees
1 do fran patria) found in America and the West Indies]
2 annastun, a malay fruit Tree
6 Teak
2 Instae a picta
4 of Ebony
3 of the Toon Tree a new [ ] [This is a form of mahogany]
3 Croatan sobiferum with cuttings of various other plants.[25]

The curators' book notes on 17 March 1797 without realizing John Vaughan's acknowledgment of the gift of these foreign plants: "William Barton and Dr. Barton: to enquire whether any acknowledgement was made of a Letter & some asiatic Plants rec[eive]d from Mr. Roxburgh of Calcutta."[26]

16 January 1795
A piece of ebony wood from Hispaniola, a coconut and the fruit of a courberil tree. The latter is a West Indian locust tree with very hard, tough wood. From the resin, the Indians made courberil copal. [27]

Mederic Louis Elie Moreau de Saint-Mery

17 July 1795
"Samples of East Indian areca nuts; some of which were given to Bartram's garden & some planted by [member] Dr. [Nicholas] Collin in his own."[28] The areca nut is the betel nut.
James Anderson

7 April 1797
The publication of Jean Francois Durande. Durande created an immense "Carte Botanique" which is in the Library today. With this, Durande published a volume: *Notions Elementaires de Botanique, avec l'explication d'une Carte composee servir aux cours publics de l'Academie de Dijon* (Dijon: 1781). Secretary William Barton wrote Grassi the thanks of the Society on 22 April 1797.[29]
Candide Frederic Antoine Grassi

6 February 1801
An article on a "New species of Vallisneria" (an aquatic plant with ribbon-like leaves) which he found growing near Philadelphia. He named it V. Americaa, and enclosed a sketch of the plant. The members referred it to Benjamin Henry Latrobe who reported 17 April "that the paper is well worthy of publication in the Transactions of the Society."[30] Nevertheless, the paper was not published.
Benjamin Smith Barton

16 October 1801
Some seeds of the sugar beet, the "disette" (Betterave champetre) along with this he included D. Commerell's memoir on its culture and use.
Louis Valentin

21 May 1802
Exotic seeds of the "Sago Tree [a palm tree from the pith of which a starchy food is prepared], of the edible Canarie Tree, of the Oil Canarie Tree from Amboyna" were received. Some were then sent to General Charles C. Pinckney in South Carolina and others were delivered to William Hamilton for cultivation.31
[UNKNOWN]

The Council of the Interior of the Batavian Republic presented several numbers of the *Flora Batavia* which had begun being printed in 1800 and continues to be presented, and asked the members on 21 October 1802 to forward some seeds and plants to them.[32] The Society ordered on 15 July 1803 that the secretary "assure the Council that the A[merican] P[hilosophical] S[ociety] will take measures to carry their wishes into effect." The members resolved that:

> the Treasurer be directed to apply to W[illia]m Hamilton Esqr on the part of the Society, with a request on their part, that he will undertake to see the order of the Council of the Batavian Republic executed, it being of importance to cultivate the correspondence thus invited by the Dutch Government & that the Treasurer be directed to furnish the necessary funds.33

The treasurer wrote Hamilton:

> You have annexed an abstract of a request of the Dutch Govern[men]t, also a list of what is wanted & a resolve of the Am[erican] Ph[ilosophical] Soc[iet]y. Permit me Sir to request your kind attention to the object. It is well suited to the public spirit you have so frequently shown on this Subject, & afford an opening to secure a Valuable Correspondence to yourself & the means of procuring in the surest manner of any thing you may want which the Batav[ian] Gov[ernmen]t can procure of you any expense I will reimburse.[34]

Hamilton refused, so Barton was requested on 19 August 1803 to forward the items, "the Treasurer to advance funds to be repaid by the Council of the Hague." On 8 December 1804 John Vaughan, as treasurer of the Society, paid Bernard McMachon $100 for 44 specific seeds and specimens for the Batavian government. The list of the items of this shipment is in the library.[35] Almost one year later, on 6 September 1805, Benjamin Waterhouse wrote Caspar Wistar asking for a listing of the seeds and plants the Society had sent the "Botanical Society of Holland." The American Academy of Arts and Sciences had been asked "that we would send them plants & seeds of our country," and he did not wish to duplicate the items.[36]

Peter Custis wrote Benjamin S. Barton on 20 May 1804 from Accomac, Virginia, about the "*Maggoty* Bean" and sent specimens. This gift and plant was described in June 1804, for "its vegetation is yet backward." It grew to a height of two or three feet and was so very branched as to shade the earth all winter.

In what manner it acts as a manure, I have not been able to learn, but from what I have seen, am inclined to believe its fertilizing property depends on the same as that of other vegetable substances, & probably the reason why it is better adapted as a manure is because it more completely defends the Soil from he scorching influence of the Sun. It happens to be suited to Clayey Cohesive Soils, which it renders more light and porous.[37]

Jonathan Bayard Smith wrote John Vaughan on 20 July 1804 an "account of the moss now exhibited to this Society" from the Reverend Mr. Tennant:

A Lady who had a temporary residence in Mr. Tennants family at Abingdon, Montgomery County [Pennsylvania] in one of her excursions through the grounds of Mr. T[ennant] had her attention taken by the singular & handsome appearance of this moss, & took home the piece now before you. Wishing to preserve it she occasionally watered it. For about 18 days or a fortnight she observed it to assume a new and handsome appearance, the whole plant appeared covered with lucid drops which soon acquired the consistence of particles of salt, & which were successively produced till the Lady's absence from the house left the plant to perish. Mr. T[ennant] states that a spoonful of the salt might be obtained daily as he thought & that the moss was kept in her own chamber not subject to interference by any person besides herself. He has promised with the assistance of the Lady to send me some of the same plant fresh from the ground as soon as it can be had. On receipt of further information I will communicate it.[38]

July 12, 1805
A "Specimen of a variety of grass (Peruvian grass). [39]

A. Fisher

19 July 1805
Some wild indigo.

Anthony Fothergill

Thomas Jefferson forwarded on 19 October 1805 a small box of seeds "with minerals for the Phil[osophica]l society to be presented in cap[tai]n [Meriwether] Lewis's name."[40] This was the first deposit of the great Lewis and Clark Expedition. Jefferson wanted the seeds sent to William Hamilton and the Society asked "Mr. Hamilton to plant the seeds and report the results with descriptions and specimens."[41] Benjamin S. Barton was asked on 15 November 1805 to examine and report on the "Hortus siccus" [42] (dried plants). John Vaughan wrote a list, insofar as he was able, of these donations on 20 December 1805. The list is in the library and was published by Reuben Gold Thwaites: *Original Journals of the Lewis and Clark Expedition 1804—1806*. William Trelease provided further identification for some of the items, but many were unidentified.[43] Barton noted in his *Philadelphia Medical Journal* that this donation had arrived in Philadelphia. The collection was made by Lewis from a "different part of the country that is watered by the river Missouri, and its branches." Barton hoped that these "specimens, with others which we may hope to receive from Captain Lewis, will serve as a beginning of a *Flora Missourica*." "[44]

19 September 1806
Some guaco juice made from the "bee plant," a tropical American vine (*Mikania guaco*) or a birthwort (*Aristolochia maxima*), "said to be a cure for snakebites" was received.

[DONOR UNKNOWN]

Captain Meriwether Lewis borrowed some specimens of natural history from the cabinet on 17 June 1807.

7 December 1810

A piece of bark used to create a yellow dye came from "Carracas."[45]

Thomas Davy

William Dandridge Peck asked the Society for seeds and he wrote his letter of thanks for them on 10 June 1811:

Herewith I transmit the name of some of them. Some of them I knew. I have had time to dissect only a few others, of others I have conjectured as well as I could judge; the latter are marked with a note of doubt. I shall commit a part of all these seeds to the gardener & hope he will succeed in putting it into my power to add more names & to correct any mistakes in this list.[46]

Fifty-two names are listed. John Vaughan endorsed this letter: "Vide Minutes," but no such entry was found in the minutes.

Francois Andre Michaux asked John Vaughan on 11 December 1811 to procure the seeds of the mango, avocado, colonial apricot, Mexican vanilla, and others, from his brother in Jamaica. Michaux wanted them for a friend who was a "grand amateur des plantes.[47]

7 February 1812

A gift of *Urtica canadensis (?) Linn.* was received. This nettle "which affords hemp," was presented by, an inventor "who had obtained a patent for his discovery, & receive great encouragement at Washington.[48]

Mr. Whitlow

3 April 1812

"Tableau Botanique des Genres Observes en Russie et Desposes selon la methode Naturelle" by Joseph Liboschitz was "de l'Imprimerie de Pluchart et Comp." It is a huge broadside in six sheets.[49]

John Morris

15 July 1814

A specimen of carbonized wood.

Solomon W. Conrad

William Paul Crillon Barton read a paper on an orchid which he discovered in the vicinity of Philadelphia in June, and which he named *Malaxis Correana* (Malaxis is the name of a genus of terrestrial orchids), on 16 June 1815. This paper also contained a drawing; a committee was formed of Jose Francesco Correa da Serra, Zaccheus Collins and David Hosack for a report.[50] The report, delivered on 10 August 1815, praised William P. C. Barton's work and verified the plant as a new species:

To the diligent researches of Dr. [Benjamin S.] Barton, jun[io]r our American Catalogue is indebted for a Malaxis unknown to it before, but as the species has long since been described and figured, the Committee are of opinion the communication need not form a part of the Society's volume.[51]

16 May 1816

A specimen of Morus Papyrifera (mulberry tree), five years old.[52]

Mr. Fisher

Benjamin S. Barton delivered on 15 December 1815 an article on the newly discovered plant, *Bartonia,* which Thomas Nuttall had identified and named.[53] The committee did not recommend publication, for it felt that "the author's usual powers of Judgment" had been diminished by his terminal illness."54 This plant is of western American herbs or undershrubs which is named also *Mentzelia* for Cristian Mentzel.

21 June 1816

A small collection of dried plants from South Carolina.[55]

John Izard Middleton

17 January 1817
A specimen of wild oats, both parched and natural, from the Michigan Territory was received. Caspar Wistar delivered the donation.[56]

Dr. Henning.

21 November 1817
The "Stem of the Moritche Tree of the Desacts Gugane Mauritia of Linne.[57]

Jose F. Correa da Serra

20 February 1818
The herbarium of G. H. E. Muhlenberg was received as a donation from Zaccheus Collins, Nathaniel Chapman, John Syng Dorsey, George Pollock, Thomas Chalkley James, William Short, William Tilghman, John Vaughan and Caspar Wistar. It was acquired from the son, Frederick Augustus Muhlenberg, for only $500, for the son wished it "to be retained in the U. S., and become the property of the A. P. S., of which his father had been a member, favoured the Society in fixing the Price." Therefore, he charged less "than he would have done had an individual applied." John Vaughan noted that this herbarium was "invaluable, from the high reputation of Mr. Muhlenberg both in Europe and America, [and] for his superior botanical Knowledge.[58] The donors subjected this gift to regulations "with a view to insure its preservation & utility."[59] At the same time certain manuscripts were probably received, among which was the letter of Palisot de Beauvois to H. Muhlenberg of 17 November 1811 on mosses and botanical matters.'[60]

19 September 1817
"A collection of dried Specimens of plants Collected in the Mountains of Jamaica."[61]

Samuel Betton

5 March 1819
A collection of eighteen specimens, dried, of sedges, of the genus *Rhynchospora*.[62] With this was a communication and the committee reported on 21 May 1819 that the article on "Cyperus" (a kind of rush, such as papyrus), as "meriting publication.[63]

William Baldwin

17 September 1819
Two South American medicines made from plants. One was "strongly recommended in Brazil for pulmonary complaints and particularly to those who hurt themselves by accident." It was made from a parasitic plant, Cepo de Chumbo. The other was Resina de Catalas, supposedly an excellent purgative.[64] Nathaniel Chapman and Philip Syng Physick were asked to test these and then report. This committee was continued 18 February 1820 and reported 15 September 1820 that the purgative was "analogous to Jallup [jalap]" but there was not enough in the sample to test its value.

F. Schmidt

On 14 April 1820 "A. S." wrote John Redmond Coxe of his discovery of a new varnish from a native American plant and asked if he would communicate it to the Society.[65] It was read 5 May and John Vaughan wrote 6 May inviting him to forward the information to the Society. "A Memoir on the Resin obtained from the Lombardy Poplar; and Its use in the Arts" was written 6 October 1820.[66] "A. S." wrote on 19 September 1820 to John Vaughan stating that this memoir "has never been published, nor have I been rewarded for the discovery, either by a patent or otherwise." With the memoir he sent a box of samples, with a "Key to the specimens" which "must be examined by daylight."[67] Zaccheus Collins and William Hembel reported as a committee 15 December 1820 on this varnish: "a beautiful pigment, perfectly resembling gold" according to the author.[68] This varnish was made from the dried buds of the Lombardy poplar macerated "in alkohol." Although varnish could be made from poplars, the committee reported:

The memoir is well written and evinces a spirit of industry and research highly creditable to the author, but under the present views of the Committee they do not feel warranted in recommending it for the Society's premium.

Still, however, if the author is pursuing his object, and suffering his memoir to remain with the Society, would, with the aid of a practical artist, test the utility of his varnish, it would afford the committee pleasure to find themselves mistaken and report accordingly.[69]

5 May 1820
Jose F. Correa da Serra delivered an unusual stalk of corn from Virginia, presented by "A Flag of Corn turned into as many ears as it had branches."[70]

Dr. Le Baron (?)

16 April 1824
Some Egyptian cotton sent from Liverpool to be compared with American cotton.[71]

Allen Armstrong

20 April 1827
From Mexico, Joel Roberts Poinsett sent John Vaughan:

a cord brought to me from Oaxaca. It is the exact measure of the circumference of a Cypress tree growing in the vicinity of that city. This tree *(cupressus distichae)* is perfectly sound and of a stupendous height. The person who measured the tree is one whose word may be relied on and he assured me that he stretched the cord on tight as it could be drawn round the body of the tree. [72]

This cord was received on 15 June 1827[73] and Vaughan's reply expressed little belief of the true size of the tree. Poinsett replied 6 September 1827, enclosing a letter "from an English gentleman" who had just been to Oaxaca. "You can compare the two measurements. I did not measure the twine I sent you. Should I visit Oaxaca before I return to the U[nited] S[tates] I will certainly measure this tree and bring you a description of it certified by the public authority of the place."[74]

18 July 1828
Some vegetable remains from the deep cut of the Delaware and Chesapeake Canal. This was the deepest earth excavation to date, and such gifts were of great interest to the philosophers.

John Kintzing Kane

19 June 1829
"[A] tropical seed, found on the coast of Iceland." [75]

Peder Pedersen

Joseph Barabino wrote John Vaughan 5 August 1830 that "Our common Friend" Charles Alexandre Lesueur of New Harmony, Indiana, had probably informed him that Barabino planned to ship some plants to the Society from New Orleans, but he lacked cork to line the bottom of the cases and he wished to ship several insects, etc., at the same time. The cork was essential for safe shipment."[76]

A "curious vegetable production" was received 9 August 1830 from A. A. McGinley, of Fannettsburg, Pennsylvania, through Peter Stephen Du Ponceau:

I herewith transmit for your inspection a specimen of curious vegetable production which in my opinion has hitherto evaded the scrutinizing eye of the naturalist, and which has never been subjected to a philosophical analysis. It was ploughed up sometime in the month of June last, in a piece of low marshy, or bottom land, bordering on a stream of water of considerable size. Unfortunately it had been cleft by the sharp edge of the plough share prior to discovery. When presented to me, which was about four days after it had been taken from the ground, it was as soft to the touch as a raw potatoe, and of a perfectly white appearance. It had neither taste nor smell that could be perceived. Near to this one, was another found, apparently of the same nature, and species, but considerably larger measuring about eighteen inches in circumference. One trait in the outward character of these vegetables arrested my attention as singular; there was no appearance of either stock or root having ever been attached to them. They lay altogether detached. I have heretofore considered the root as altogether necessary to have existence of the plant, as it is through its elementary tubes it imbibes nourishment, (Seaweeds only afford an exception to this they being nourished by their surface). If upon examination this should be found a specimen of a rare, & strange production (and there is no question of their novelty in this section of the country) I should be much gratified by seeing some notice of their nature & use from the pen of some member of your respectable society.[77]

21 June 1833
A collection of Philippine Islands materials. Hemp and items manufactured from hemp were included, as was croton oil, camphor, etc.[78]

Francis Dwight and Marmaduke Burrough

18 October 1833
An unusual ear of corn. "Each grain was separate as in the other cerelia." The committee to report on this oddity made a verbal report on 4 April 1834 and was continued. It was discharged on 16 May 1834.

Daniel B. Smith

Charles Wilkens Short, of Lexington, Kentucky, offered a collection of the botany of his area and the members accepted the offer on 17 January 1834. Short, on 19 January, wrote that he was "distributing a considerable collection" to several people, and sent "a box to the Society, containing about 535 Specimens of 295 genera. These are exclusive entirely of Cryptogamous plants—grasses—carices—asters and some other extensive tribes, of which I have on hand a considerable collection, a part of which is also at the Society's service, if desired.[79]

Short also asked to be informed of corrections or alterations of nomenclature by the members "especially of such as I may have incorrectly labelled."[80] The committee on natural history was asked on 21 March 1834 to organize and this collection was referred to it. On 18 April 1834 three additional boxes of plants of "Exotic and Cryptomous plants" supplemented this gift.[81] These, also, were referred to the committee immediately for examination and report.[82] The committee, (Robert Eglesfeld Griffith, Charles Pickering and Richard Harlan) reported on 21 November that they "beg[ged] leave to report that they have attended to the duties assigned them, and would state that this collection is a valuable addition to the Herbarium of the Society, not only as regards the variety of many of the specimens, but also for their excellent state of preservation."[83]

On 15 May 1835 additions to the Short herbarium were received.[84] Another collection of plants arrived for the Society soon after Short's first donation. Daniel Parker, executor for the estate of Zaccheus Collins, wrote on 21 March 1834 that he had received no offer to purchase "the Herbarium of American [Mexican] Plants, prepared and arranged by Mr. Collins himself." Therefore, he offered it to the Society "on *Deposit to be reclaimed*" by the executor and/or heirs. "If you should think the Herbarium, on these terms, acceptable" he needed a communication from the Society so it could "dispose of the plants as you shall deem most proper." [85] Parker wrote 18 April 1837 requesting "you to do me the favor to obtain the permission of the Society to withdraw the deposit." He asked that the herbarium be delivered to Constantine Samuel Rafinesque-Schmaltz[86] who signed a receipt for "the Herbarium and the boxes" on 4 May 1837.[87]

William Cobb Harry wrote from Calcutta on 6 April 1834 forwarding a bottle of Prangia seed for the "agricultural society." He wrote that:

it is the first ever left India, and if it proves half so valuable as we have reason to believe it will prove as great an acquisition for Europe and America as the Potatoe. You may recollect that [William] Moorcroft the traveller first described this grass and said that it yielded a most excellent fodder for cattle on the coldest and most barren mountains of Thibet. His account awakened great interest amongst the Agri[cultura]l Societies of Europe, but from the jealousy of the native Governments & the consequent difficulty of communications, it was found impossible to procure seed, till at last through the interference of Gen[era]l Allard who is in the service of Ranjeet Singh, a quantity was sent down a few days ago to our Agri[cultural] Society here. Some of it has been sown in the Botanic gardens, where it has vegetated, which proves the seed to be fresh, so that 1 am in hopes it will arrive with you in time to be productive ... I request you will interest yourself about it & when it is explained to the [American Philosophical Society], that this is the first ever procured, and that it is so very highly thought of in France & England, I am sure they will not only do their best to preserve it, but also forward seeds (in case of necessity) to Europe, as what we are about to send them there may perhaps not arrive in equally good condition.[88]

6 February 1835
A branch of the lace tree of Cuba, Daguila (*Lagetta lintearia*) "showing its natural State and when developed appears like lace."[89]

Madame Carrera

19 June 1835
"[A] large Collection of Specimens of the different Woods of Cuba."[90]

Ramon de Sangra

4 December 1835
An "interesting Collecion [sic] of Seeds from the Botanical Garden" from Calcutta.[91]

Nathaniel Wallich

John Bell, secretary of the Agricultural and Horticultural Society of Calcutta wrote 16 April 1836 proposing an exchange of "a great variety of Seeds.[92]

17 November 1837
A specimen of "Lycopodium Pattescens," the leaves of which were capable of "relaxing and expanding when wet & again contracting" when dried. This was a specimen of the family of *Lycopodiceae,* erect or creeping plants, such as club moss, ground fir.[93]

W. S. Drayton

26 December 1837
Specimens of the agave sisalana. One leaf was dressed and two were dyed.94 The strong white sisal hemp made from this plant was used for twine.

Dr. H. Perrine

3 September 1840
A "Specimen of the Spanish Moss, Tillandsia Usneoides, from Natchez, Mississippi." It was received 2 October 1840. With this was a:

specimen of Lignite, and the laminated Gympsum which enveloped it, in the form of a concretion. From the base of the Natchez Bluff, 170 feet below the surface. When obtained, the specimen was rotten wood, so decayed as to be easily crushed between the fingers. The ligneous fibre was very palpable, and showed it to be oak. After twenty days exposure, it was covered with a fine frost of Copperas, (Sulph. Iron,) and was transformed into beautiful lignite.[95]

Charles Goldsmith Forshey

18 June 1841
"[Q]uite a large collection of Western & Southern plants for the Herbarium."[96,97] The donor sent on 25 May 1842 "some species which I believe are not included in any of my previous parcels" of Kentucky plants.[98] This gift of additional plants was received 15 July 1842.[99]

Charles W. Short

6 May 1842
Specimens of wood which had been removed from a beam of a ruined Mayan building at Uxmal on the Yucatan peninsula, Mexico. The wood was from the zapodillo tree, and the natives claimed it was "insusceptible of decay."[100] The Achras sapota is a large evergreen tropical tree with durable wood and edible fruit.

James M'Kennon

Isaac Hays wrote George Ord 9 on April 1844 that there was "a Mr. Sullivan in town who seems to be a zealous Botanist." Hays asked Ord to let Sullivan examine the Muhlenberg herbarium which he "desires to see."[101] The Reverend Moses Ashley Curtis, of North Carolina, was a "distinguished Botanist," and William Darlington asked George Ord to let him visit Philosophical Hall so he could examine the Muhlenberg herbarium. Mr. Curtis "wishes much for an opportunity to verify a doubtful plant, by comparison with one in Muhlenberg's Herbarium. I told him I thought you would indulge him with a sight of Muhlenberg's plant."[102]

A parcel of dried plants came to George Ord from Gaetano Savi, of the University of Pisa. Ord asked William Darlington to examine them and decide the disposition of the parcel. William Darlington agreed to examine them on 26 July 1847. "As to the *ultimate destination* of the Parcel, & the accompanying Letter, etc., I can think of none more appropriate than [member] Prof. Asa Gray, of Cambridge, Mass[achusetts].[103] This parcel, George Ord thought, should be examined in Philosophical Hall, so Darlington wrote on 11 August 1847:

> I should have been pleased with an opportunity to look over the parcel of Botanical Specimens from Italy and still more, with the privilege of appropriating, for our Herbarium, any new or rare species provided there were duplicates of any such in the collection. But, as all this is a matter of secondary importance, and as it is morally certain that Dr. Gray will be able to make the best use of any thing, in the parcel, which may be interesting to be known in this country, I would respectfully recommend that the whole remittance from Prof. Savi be forwarded to Dr. G[ray] by the first suitable opportunity. I could not examine the collection with any satisfaction, unless I had permission to bring it home with me, & look it over at my leisure. Hence my opinion, that the whole affair had better be handed over to that first of American Botanists, Prof. Gray, of Cambridge.[104]

On 2 April 1852 George M. Justice gave a description of Arctic algae which Elisha Kent Kane brought to Philadelphia from his Arctic tour in search of Sir John Franklin. The *Protococcus Navilis* was red, not green, and Justice gave the tiny dimensions of these unicellular organisms. "The plant, when perfect, greatly resembles the red currant of our gardens.[105] Elisha K. Kane spoke on 7 May 1852 when he exhibited some vegetable specimens "found by him on the ice-plains of the polar sea." As the ice-locked ship moved with the ice masses, land was from 40 to 76 miles distant, yet two specimens of moss, a heath, lichens and "the capsule of a saxifrage were gathered." He stated that the red snow of the Arctic could be found only on snow which contained vegetable matter.[106]

November 1852
Some fiber of the coutehouc tree, used by the Choes Indians of South America.[107]
John C. Trautwine
Elias Durand spoke on 18 April 1856 of the plants Elisha K. Kane brought from the Arctic on his second expedition. There were "148 species—77 of which are dicotyledonous; 29 monocotyledonous, and 42 cryptogamous plants: all from the western coast of Greenland, between the 64th and 80th north parallels." These represented one of the richest collections ever made of Arctic plants. A study of them indicated that "the polar zone cannot, properly, be compared with the alpine regions of the more temperate climates." E. K. Kane added that the most northern "point visited by him produced plants as abundant in number as those of the botanical region of Lancaster sound."[108]

On 3 October 1856 Mr. Justice displayed a dried fungus which came from Juliustown, New Jersey. The "radii of the volva" was firmly closed over the "capitulum." When moisture was applied, however, the rays opened widely and closed again, gradually, as the plant dried—"and this may be repeated a great number of times." Justice said the plant "agrees very nearly with the description of *Gaestrum hygrometricul*" of Christian Hendrik Persoon, or the *"Lycoperdon volvam recolligens* of Schmidel."[109] John Lawrence Le Conte showed a similar dried fungus which expanded considerably when moistened also. This was the "Rose of Jericho (Anastatica Hierochontia)," of the genus of Arabian herbs, Cruciferae, and a native of Syria. Titian Ramsay Peale then observed that dried vegetables used on long sea voyages "when immersed in warm water nearly resumed their original forms and properties.[110]

Gouverneur Emerson spoke on 15 January 1858 on Chinese sugar cane as grown and refined in the United States. It was now as simple to refine as it had been difficult heretofore. Specimens of sugar, produced from the Chinese sugar cane, were exhibited; John Chapman Cresson said that "the fibrous substance of the Sorghum is well adapted to the manufacture of paper." Emerson added that the scum from the juice being processed, "as well as the leaves from the stalks, afford[s] a grateful and nourishing food for many animals. [111] Dr. Le Conte on 5 February 1858 exhibited some ground moss [*Lycopodium*] from Honduras. When dry, it was "contracted in the form of a ball; but when placed in water again, expands."[112]

On 20 April 1858 Elias Durand wrote asking permission for Thomas Potts James "to take to his house, for study, Dr. Muhlenberg's Collection of Cryptogamous plants."[113] An entry was made for this, or a similar, loan to James 17 September 1869.[114] On 17 January 1862 Samuel Powel spoke about a stalk of Asclepias which he exhibited "to show the strength of its fibre. Samuel Stehman Haldeman referred to thread spun from nettle fiber.[115] This is a North American perennial herb, such as the butterfly weed or milkweed.

Dr. Emerson stated on 17 October 1862 that a recently published pamphlet concerned the grown of cotton in the "Middle States." He, himself, raised cotton in Delaware that year and presented some bolls from his crop.[116] A box of "phantom leaves dissected entirely by insects, and in a very perfect manner" was exhibited by William P. Foulke on 16 February 1863.[117] Some specimens of the fungus, *Geastrum hygrometricum,* both living and dried, were exhibited on 16 October 1863 by T. R. Peale. He described the habits and the growth of the plants. He also "exhibited minute cryptogams resembling birds nests and eggs.[118] "A specimen ball of sea-grass" was presented by J. Peter Lesley on 18 March 1864. He described how multitudes of similar balls of all sizes were created by waves upon the shores at Nice.[119] W. P. Foulke exhibited on 20 May 1864 "a curious specimen of a triple orange."[120]

Ferdinand Vandiveer Hayden exhibited on 1 February 1867 a photograph from New Iberia, Louisiana, showing matting found in the salt deposits near that place. He spoke at the meeting of the geographical distribution of plants and animals indigenous to the regions west of the Mississippi. [121] On 15 May 1868 a specimen of an alga (conferva) from a warm spring in Virginia was exhibited by T. R. Peale. John L. Le Conte and others spoke of this variety of botanical growth of filamentous algae.[122]

Chester Dewey's report on carices, a sedge, based on travel with the Yellowstone and Missouri Expedition under the command of Topographical Engineer W. F. Raymond, was turned over to a committee on 7 May 1869. The committee agreed on 21 May that it should be published, but a note on the manuscript in the library is: "Not published." There are five beautifully drawn sketches by A. Hochstein with this paper. Ferdinand V. Hayden presented this as an appendix to his report on 7 May 1869.[123]

A posthumous work by the bryologist Eugene Amadeus Schwarz, was discussed in a letter to William Starling Sullivant by [Thomas P.] James on 17 September 1869. James wished to borrow certain mosses from the Muhlenberg herbarium to compare with "Schwarz's determination."[124] Permission was granted, provided that the mosses were returned on 6 May 1870.[125] John Sergeant Price exhibited on 21 January 1876 a piece of very light and dry wood from a well dug at the corner of Broad and Walnut Streets in Philadelphia. The wood was not mineralized at all.[126]

Joseph T. Rothrock wrote 20 December 1881 to Eli Kirk Price asking that some Muhlenberg herbarium materials be shipped to Cambridge, Massachusetts, where Asa Gray could make use of them. Gray was "at work on a book: the crowning one of his busy life, and needs to compare the Asters and Solidagoes." Such loans had been "freely accorded to him by all other institutions in the world." Rothrock urged that the members vote that at least ten dollars be granted so that:

> when in Cambridge Dr. Gray may have these plants, labels and his notes properly
> affixed to sheets so that in the future no mixing could occur and so that for all time
> these plants should bear the relation to American botany that the herbarium of
> Linnaeus does to that of the world.[127]

This letter was read 20 January 1882 and the members promptly

> *Resolved,* That the Secretary be authorized to deliver to the order of Dr. Gray, the
> Muhlenberg herbarium, in whole or in part, on the receipt of his agent to return the
> same.

Resolved, That ten dollars be appropriated for the payment of the expenses of labelling the Herbarium, in accordance with Dr. Gray's forthcoming work.[128]

Asa Gray wrote his thanks to the Society on 25 January 1882. "A brief glance which I took last week at the portion which concerns my present study suffices for the moment, But I may at no distant period have occasion to avail myself of the permission accorded to me."[129] This letter concerning Gray's Flora of North America was read 3 February 1882.[130]

Angelo Heilprin wrote on 27 April 1892 that his memory was "vague" on the subject of a receipt for specimens deposited at the Academy of Natural Sciences of Philadelphia by the Society. He could not remember if Joseph Leidy had given a receipt or not.[131]

Samuel Gibson Dixon wrote Henry Phillips, Jr. on 2 November 1893, asking permission for Stewardson Brown to examine Muhlenberg's herbarium, which was in the Academy of Natural Sciences.[132]

On 17 January 1896 Thomas Meehan's letter was read wherein he offered to label and arrange "the South American plants from Dr. [Benjamin S.] Barton `s collection belonging to the Society." Meehan also suggested that this collection be placed on deposit in the Academy of Natural Sciences.[133] This was referred to the curators at the same meeting.[134] The curators reported on 7 February 1896 that they recommended the deposit of the Society's botanical collections (Heinrich Ernest Muhlenberg, Meriwether Lewis and William Clark, Benjamin S. Barton, Charles W. Short, etc.) be made in the Academy of Natural Sciences. Thomas Meehan, after examining them, refused them as a deposit and wanted them as a gift. Should the Society wish to preserve these as a basis for an expanded herbarium, he said, the Academy "would gladly contribute some of its duplicates."[135]

On the same subject, the special committee on the library reported on 2 April 1897: "That the collections of plants be transferred in trust as a deposit, subject to recall, to such institution as may be ordered by the Society."[136] On 7 April 1897 the Academy of Natural Sciences of Philadelphia asked to "receive on deposit the 'Lewis and Clarke' [sic] and the 'Muhlenberg' collections of plants, to be positioned, labeled, and kept as a separate collection to the great Herbarium of this Society."[137] Curators and Benjamin Smith Lyman and James Cheston Morris recommended on 13 April 1897 that not only the Lewis and Clark and Muhlenberg collections but all other botanical collections be deposited "and take receipt" for them from the Academy. They were to be kept as "separate collections in the Herbarium of the Academy."[138] Stewardson Brown, conservator for the Academy, signed a receipt 21 June 1897 for this deposit:

Received from the Curators of the Am[erican] Philo[sophical] Society in accordance with Resolution passed May 14th 1897, on receipt of letter from the Academy of Natural Sciences, the following articles—viz—

30 boxes of the Muhlenberg Collection—phanerogamia

9 bundles " " "

6 boxes " " cryptogamia

7 packages " " "

18 bundles of the [Benjamin S.] Barton collection

13 bundles " " Lewis & Clarke [sic] collection (supposed)

4 bundles " " Cha[rle]s W. Short

1 " Specimens [Frederick] Pursh

2 " Dr. William Baldwin

1 box Seeds "

3 volumes of Herbarium Britannicum by G. Dunn

2 " " " Americanum 1795?

1 " " " Mary Forest.

To be kept as separate collections in the Herbarium of the Academy of Natural Sciences, and returned on demand.[139]

Thomas Meehan wrote on 6 August 1897 that the "Lewis & Clark's plants *were*" received. He had been working them over and would "soon have them all identified." He commented that:
Pursh in his Flora says there were 150 kinds in the package, and he refers to 119 of them in his work; but a large number of those he describes are not there. He took them to England with him, and they seem to have been left with [Aylmer Bourke] Lambert. Strange to say Lambert seems to have given [Lewis David von] Schweinitz plants, and some of the missing ones of this collection, are with those Lambert gave....The Lewis & Clark plants are all collections made on the *return* from the Pacific in 1806.

I note in the Minutes of the Society that a collection was received in 1805 in that year and turned over to Dr. [Benjamin S.] Barton for examination. If we could find those it would be a lucky find, as Pursh took all the cream of those 1806 ones.[140]

On 13 August 1897 Meehan wrote J. Cheston Morris of his work on the Barton herbarium:
Just as I was about giving up, I found in the last lot I handled, the package of Lewis & Clark referred to in the Society's minutes. It was the explorers' collection of 1804. The other was of 1806. The 1805, it is known, was lost by the explorers themselves. You have in the cause of botanical Science builded better than you knew, or 1 anticipated, in turning these plants over to us.[141]

Benjamin S. Lyman wrote Morris on 1 June 1898 that the outstanding bryologist, Mrs. Britton, wished the Muhlenberg collection to be sent to her at Columbia University. She would arrange it properly. The curators of the Academy were asked first and Lyman thought it was:
an excellent opportunity to have the Collection greatly improved in value at no expense to the A[merican] P[hilosophical] S[ociety], and made much more useful to botanists. The plan is to send the Collection by express at a high declared evaluation. The small appropriation she desires for the expenses of mounting paper and the like would be provided by the Botanical Section of the A[cademy] [of] N[atural] S[ciences].[142]

During the latter part of the 1890s the curators had hired someone to identify and label the various artifacts in Philosophical Hall. The following items were identified, undated, and the information on the labels is reproduced in its entirety:
Dycotyle Depressifrous from Mr. Snyder, Galena, Ill. Gum from S[outh] America.
Part of the Tucahoe Tuber (dried)
Specimen of the bark of the Blue Oak
Specimens of Fustic Extract of Logwood. From the King of Belgium.
Specimens of seeds and dried fruits.[143]
On 3 June 1901 Witmer Stone, assistant curator of the Academy of Natural Sciences of Philadelphia, sent a listing of the Society's property in the Academy. "The

Lewis & Clark Herbarium, The Muhlenberg Herbarium, The Barton Herbarium, 1 pkg. of Short's Plants" and, "Parker Collection of Plants" are on this list.[144]

Evidently there was additional botanical material in Philosophical Hall, for Isaac Minis Hays recommended on 6 May 1904 that the curators be directed to deposit four volumes of the Muhlenberg herbarium with the Academy. The curators were to take a receipt for them "on the same terms and conditions as the other portions of the Herbarium previously deposited there."[145] Samuel G. Dixon, also president of the Academy, signed a receipt on 22 November 1904 for "four additional packages of Mosses belonging to the Muhlenberg Herbarium."[146]

There is not one botanical specimen at present in the collections of the American Philosophical Society. It would seem that only the herbaria were preserved. Many gifts were received, and the seeds, and so forth were sent out to be grown; many things were fragile and disappeared; and many items were exhibited to the members and perhaps never presented, as gifts.

BOTANY—References
1. American Society. *Minutes.*
2. *Ibid.*, 24 Oct. 1766.
3. *Ibid.*, 13 March 1767.
4. *Ibid.*, 11 March 1768.
5. *Ibid.*, 25 March 1768.
6. *Ibid.*, 18 March 1768.
7. *Ibid.*, 25 March 1768.
8. *Ibid.*, 1 April 1768.
9. *Ibid.*, 1 July, 19 Aug. 1768.
10. *Ibid.*, 20 Sept. 1768.
11. *Ibid.*, 15 Nov. 1768.
12. *Ibid.*, 9 Sept. 1768.
13. Bartram, I. *An Account of Siberian Barley*, 19 July 1771. Broadside.
14. *Archives.* R. Howell to APS, 27 Dec. 1772.
15. *Ibid.*, J. Leacock to APS, 29 Dec. 1772.
16. *Ibid.*, F. Alison. Hints..., 2 April 1773.
17. Misc. MS. Col. B. Romans to W. and T. Bradford, 28 Feb. 1774.
18. *Archives.* G. and J. Stonemetz to T. Bond, 4 Nov. 1782.
19. *Trans.*, vol. 2.
20. *Ibid.*, vol. 3.
21. *Archives.* S. Vaughan, Jr., to J. Vaughan, n. d., and J. Vaughan to B. Franklin, 18 Dec. 1789.
22. *Ibid.* W. Bradford to ----, 30 Sept. 1790.
23. *Ibid.* A. Michaux. Expositions des Motifs..., 29 April 1793.
24. *Ibid.* W. Roxburgh to J. Vaughan, 26 Dec. 1793; *Trans.*, vol. 4.
25. *Ibid.* J. Vaughan. List..., 19 April 1794. (See under date and description of footnote 23 above.)
26. Com. Rec., vol. 1.
27. *Trans.*, vol. 4.
28. *Ibid.*
29. *Archives.* W. Barton to C. F. A. Grassi, 22 April 1797; *Trans.*, vol. 4.
30. *Ibid.* APS. Report, 20 Feb. 1801.
31. Com. Rec., vol. 1.
32. *Archives.* Council ofd the Interior of Batavia to the APS, 21 Oct. 1802.
33. *Ibid.* APS. Resolution, 15 July 1803.
34. *Ibid.*
35. *Ibid.* APS to B. McMahon, 8 Dec. 1804.
36. *Ibid.* B. Waterhouse to C. Wistar, 6 Sept. 1805.
37. *Ibid.* Verbal communications, 15 June 1804.
38. J. B. Smith to J. Vaughan, 20 July 1804.
39. Curators Cards.
40. *Archives.* T. Jefferson to C. W. Peale, 20 Oct. 1805.
41. Com. Recs, vol. 21
42. *Trans.*, vol. 6.
43. *Lewis and Clark Journals*, vol. IX; *Donation Book.*
44. Philadelphia...Medical Journal, vol. 2, p. 176.
45. Curators Cards.
46. *Archives.* W. D. Peck to J. Vaughan, 10 June 1811.
47. *Ibid.* F. A. Michaux to J. Vaughan, 11 Dec. 1811.
48. *Ibid.* APS. Report...papers to be published, 6 Nov. 1812.
49. *Donation Book.*
50. *Ibid.*
51. Com. Recs., vol. 2.
52. *Archives.* APS. Report, 10 Aug. 1815.
53. Curators Cards.
54. *Archives.* B. S. Barton. Concerning, 15 Dec. 1815.
55. *Ibid.* APS. Report, 15 March 1816.
56. *Donation Book; Trans.*, n. s., vol. 1.
57. *Ibid.*
58. *Ibid.;* Curators Donation Book, 18 Nov. 1831; *Trans.*, n. s., vol. 1.
59. Subscription Book.
60. *Archives.* A. M. F J. Baron de Palisot de Beauvois to H. Muhlenberg, 17 Nov. 1811.
61. *Donation Book; Trans.*, n. s., vol. 1.
62. *Ibid.;* Curators Donation Book; Curators Cards; *Trans.*, n. s., vol. 2.
63. *Archives.* APS. Report, 21 May 1819.
64. *Ibid.* F. Schmidt to APS, 18 Aug. 1819.
65. *Ibid.* A. S. to J. R. Coxe, 14 April 1820.
66. Com. Recs., vol. 2.
67. *"Arch."* A. S. to J. Vaughan, 19 Sept. 1820.
68. Com. Recs., vol. 2.
69. *"Arch."* APS. Report, 15 Dec. 1820.
70. Donation Book; Curators Cards.
71. Donation Book.
72. *Archives.* J. R. Poinsett to J. Vaughan, 20 April 1827. See also: Murphy D. D. Smith, "Of Philadelphia Philosophers and a Mexican Tree," Manuscripts, vol. 42, pp. 287–292.
73. Donation Book.
74. *Archives.* J. R. Poinsett to J. Vaughan, 6 Sept. 1827. (see also Murphy D. Smith, as in footnote 72.)
75. Curators Donation Book.
76. *Archives.* J. Barabino to J. Vaughan, 5 Aug. 1830.
77. *Ibid.* A. A. McGinley to P. S. Du Ponceau, 9 Aug. 1830.
78. Donation Book; *Trans.*, n. s., vol. 4.
79. *Archives.* C. W. Short to J. Vaughan, 19 Jan. 1834.
80. *Ibid.;* Donation Book, 21 March 1834; *Trans.*, n. s., vol. 5.
81. Donation Book.
82. Com. Recs., vol. 2.
83. *Archives.* APS. Report, 21 Nov. 1834.

84. Donation Book; Corn. Recs., vol. 2.
85. *Archives.* D. Parker to J. Vaughan, 21 March 1834; Donation Book.
86. *Ibid.,* 18 April 1837.
87. *Ibid.,* April 1837; Donation Book, 21 March 1834.
88. *Ibid.* W. C. Harry to M. Burrough, 6 April 1834; Donation Book, "pres by M. Burrough, 3 Oct. 1834"; Trans., n. s., vol. 5.
89. *Donation Book; Trans.,* n. s., vol. 5.
90. *Ibid.*
91. *Ibid.*
92. *Archives.* Agricultural and Horticultural Society of Calcutta to the APS, 16 April 1836.
93. *Donation Book; Trans.,* n. s., vol. 6.
94. Curators Cards.
95. *Archives.* C. G. Forshey to J. Vaughan, 3 Sept. 1840; Proc., vol. 1, pp. 278–279.
96. *Ibid.* C. W. Short to J. Vaughan, 10 May 1841; Trans., n. s., vol. 8.
97. *Donation Book; Proc.,* vol. 4, p. 74.
98. *Archives.* C. W. Short to G. Ord, 25 May 1842.
99. *Donation Book; Proc.,* vol. 2, pp. 198, 200; Trans., n. s., vol. 8.
100. *Ibid.; Proc.,* vol. 2, p. 175; Trans., n. s., vol. 8.
101. *Archives.* I. Hays to G. Ord, 9 April 1844.
102. *Ibid.* W. Darlington To G. Ord, 17 Oct. 1844.
103. *Ibid.,* 26 July 1847.
104. *Ibid.,* 11 Aug. 1847.
105. *Proc.,* vol. 5, p. 262.
106. *Ibid.,* pp. 26–267.
107. Curators Cards.
108. *Proc.,* vol. 6, pp. 186-187. Kane presented his collection to the Academy of Natural Sciences of Philadelphia.
109. *Ibid.,* p. 213.
110. *Ibid.,* p. 219.
111. *Ibid.,* pp. 283-84.
112. *Ibid.,* p. 287.
113. *Archives.* E. Durand to C. B. Trego, 20 April 1858.
114. Corn. Recs., vol. 2.
115. *Proc.,* vol. 9, p. 7.
116. *Ibid.,* pp. 90–91.
117. *Ibid.,* p. 139.
118. *Ibid.,* p. 275.
119. *Ibid.,* p. 350.
120. *Ibid.,* p. 388.
121. *Ibid.,* vol. 10, pp. 310–320.
122. *Archives.* C. Dewey. Report, 7 May 1869; Proc.., vol. II, p. 115.
123. *Proc.,* vol. 11, pp. 112-13.
124. *Ibid.,* p. 194.
125. *Ibid.,* p. 370.
126. *Ibid.,* vol. 16, p. 180.
127. *Archives.* J. T. Rothrock to E. K. Price, 20 Dec. 1881.
128. *Ibid.* APS. Extract of minutes, 20 Jan. 1882; Proc., vol. 20, pp. 203-04.
129. *Ibid.* A. Gray to APS, 25 Jan. 1882.
130. *Proc.,* vol. 20, p. 204.
131. *Archives.* A. Heilprin to H. Phillips, Jr., 27 April 1892.
132. *Ibid.* Academy of Natural Sciences of Philadelphia to H. Phillips, Jr., 2 Nov. 1893.
133. *Proc.,* vol. 35, p. 3.
134. *Ibid.,* p. 5.
135. *Ibid.,* pp. 10–11.
136. *Ibid.,* vol. 36, p. 175.
137. *Archives.* Academy of Natural Sciences of Philadelphia to APS, 7 April 1897. See also: *Ibid.,* List, 1897-1950.
138. *Ibid.* Cur. Recs. Report, 13 April 1897; Proc., vol. 36, p. 216.
139. *Ibid.* Academy of Natural Sciences of Philadelphia. Receipt; 21 June 1897.
140. *Ibid.* T. Meehan to J. C. Morris, 6 Aug. 1897.
141. *Ibid.* APS. Curators Report, 13 Aug. 1897.
142. *Ibid.,* B. S. Lyman to J. C. Morris, 1 June 1898.
143. Curators Cards.
144. See Footnote 137 above.
145. Cur. Recs. Academy of Natural Sciences of Philadelphia. Receipt, 22 Nov. 1904.

Chapter 5
Coins and medals

Every Cabinet of Curiosities had a collection of coins and medals to admire and study. Historians learned much from studying them. Edward Gibbon himself pored over Roman coins and medals while preparing his *Decline and Fall of the Roman Empire.* The esthetic beauty and the rare metals used in such artifacts appeal to all. Few coins and medals are in the possession of the Society today: none are preserved from the earliest period of the Society's history. Indeed, nothing was published by the Society about coins and medals in the early *Transactions.*

Very few gifts of this category came to the Society in the early days, although Thomas Brown gave a "box of medals" as early as 15 November 1768. No other reference to this gift exists. The box and the contents must have vanished during the Revolution. Fifteen years later, on 1 April 1783, J. M. Guthe sent a silver medal honoring the mathematician and physicist, Christian Meyer, a professor at the University of Heidelberg, astronomer to the Elector Palatine, and a Fellow of the Royal Society of London.[1]

In 1786 John de Magellan, a descendant of Ferdinand Magellan, presented 200 guineas for a premium which was to be awarded from time to time "to the author of the best discovery or the most useful invention relating to navigation, astronomy or natural philosophy (mere natural history only excepted)." Over the years the Society has presented this premium, sometimes in the form of a medal, to recipients of the award, and continues to do so. One medal, presented to Lewis Muhlenberg Haupt for his work on harbors is now in the possession of the Society.

Mederic Louis Elie Moreau de Saint Mery presented two medals on 16 January 1795. They commemorated two French events which held a direct interest for Americans: the convening of the French National Assembly by Louis XVI, and the Louis XV medal on the Peace of Paris of 1763 which ended the French and Indian War. Two outstanding Revolutionary War heroes delivered the last two coins presented in the eighteenth century: General Tadeusz Koscuisko presented 24 November 1797 a large square plate of a Swedish copper coin marked "4 daler selemyset [sivermynt]" through Thomas Jefferson, and it was received 19 January 17982. Count Julius Ursin Niemcewitz forwarded on 18 May 1798 a gold coin of Poland which had been minted during the last year of its independence.[3]

John Vaughan presented on 15 May 1801 thirty-two copper coins or medallions, "Struck at the Soho Mint near Birmingham, established by Tho[ma]s Bolton." The coins were of the "now current British coinage of two penny piece, one penny piece, half penny piece and farthing." Vaughan also presented a listing of the coins and described "the principles" of the minting.[4]

On 3 December 1802 Benjamin Smith Barton presented the medal "struck by Congress in Commemoration of the surrender of Burgoyne." (Today there are in the Library sketches and matrices by the artist, Augustin Dupre, for this medal, and others for American medals by the same artist. See: APS: Proceedings., vol. 101, pp. 530 ff.) Members then authorized the treasurer to acquire a container "to keep this and other medals of the Society" for preservation.

Caspar Wistar gave on 18 November 1803 an account of some coins, with a drawing of one, which were found in a field near Reading, Pennsylvania. The field was about five miles southeast of Reading. "Sixty-five years ago this area was forested and a poor Irish settler occupied it until it was purchased by the present family of Mr. Levin." Although the area was cleared and ploughed forty-eight years before, the following eighteen years saw pieces of old silver coin being found whenever the field was ploughed. "Their number was not ascertained, altho' it appears to be considerable, for many Children & Servants, of the Neighbours as well as the family" picked them up. Many bore the imperial double-headed Hapsburg eagle of the Holy Roman Empire. A drawing preserved in the library today of one side of the coin shows it to be "Spanish or Flemish of the Sixteenth Century & probably of Philip 2d." Dr. Wistar added:

The question of how they came there has not yet been resolved. Mr. Levin's father was unable to suggest any explanation of the circumstance for neither his family, nor those of the Neighbourhood, nor the first occupant, the poor Irishman, would have fixed money or any other valuable article under ground; & it is not easy to determine whether the different pieces had been buried together or not, for some of them were found thirty feet distant from the other, & they seldom discovered many at one time. The curious people of that day supposed they had been brought there by the Buccaneers, but is there any reason to suppose that the Buccaneers ever were in that part of the Country—or admitting them to have been there, is it probable they would have left money in a plain so distant from their usual haunts, & to them so difficult of access.[6]

Nicholas Collin was awarded a Magellanic premium for his "Paper on an Elevator" on 20 December 1794 and John Vaughan was asked to have the medal executed on 20 January 1807.[7]

Thomas Jefferson wrote 3 May 1805 that N. H. Weenweck, the secretary of the Royal Society of Heraldry and Genealogy in Denmark, sent 150 Roman bronze coins to him. They ranged from the time of Augustus to that of Theodosius. "He deposits them with the A. P. S. believing them well worthy of its acceptance." They were received 19 July and the minutes state "The medals" had been received from Jefferson and the librarian was authorized on 19 July 1805 to arrange them and label them, "when wanting, calling any member to his assistance." Caspar Wistar was asked to thank Jefferson for the gift.[8] By 6 December John Vaughan had made a catalogue of the gift and was ordered to deposit it with the medals.[9]

Caspar Wistar received the announcement of a donation of coins from Jefferson in a letter dated 20 June 1806:

While visiting some parts of Europe, I thought it might be useful to bring home some specimens of the different coins I met with, some of copper, some of silver, & others of a mixture of both called billion. Having then a mint to be established I supposed they might furnish subjects for consideration, & sometimes imitation. To these have been since added some other coins & some medals which have occasionally come to my hands. Knowing no place where they may more probably become useful, by being open to examination, then [sic] in the deposit of the A[merican]. Philosophical [S]ociety, I beg leave to present them for their acceptance. They may form a part of the series which future acquisitions may enlarge.[10]

These were received 18 July 1806.[11]

On 19 September 1806 Mr. Du Brouchaille presented a "Medal of Homer from a Bust" that had been found in Egypt and brought to France "by Bonaparte." This gift came through Peter Stephen Du Ponceau.[12]

Joseph Sansom presented on 7 November 1806 two silver medals of George Washington: one as commander-in-chief and the other as president. Later in the year, on 5 December, Peter S. Du Ponceau brought a gift of P. Du Brouchaille. It was a medal of the famous Chouan, Georges Cadoudal. The Chouans were the French in the Vendee region in Brittany and Normandy who fought against the revolutionary government in Paris during the French Revolution.

The Secretary of the Navy, Robert Smith, presented on 18 December 1807 a bronze medal in honor of Commodore Edward Preble. The medal was made by John Reich; its reverse depicts the American fleet bombarding the towns and forts of Tripoli. This medal was struck in 1804.[14]

Joseph Sansom designed and had John Reich engrave three silver medals which were "illustrative of the History of the American Revolution." They were presented on 6 April 1810.[15]

An extraordinary gift was delivered by Benjamin Smith Barton. He received from C. W. Lewis, in a letter of 17 April 1810, the impression of a coin which was found in Louisville, Kentucky. It is "supposed to be of Asiatic manufacture." Mr. Brooks, a "respectable Gentleman... assured me it was discovered 18 inches under ground in digging the foundation of a House." He thought the philosophers might find pleasure in considering it and he hoped "it may be serviceable to our country inasmuch as it may throw some light on its history."[16]

A bronze medal honoring vaccination was presented by John Syng Dorsey on 3 March 1815. It was ordered struck by Napoleon with his head and "Empereur et Roi" on the obverse. The reverse depicted Asclepius with a figure of Hygieia holding a bow and lancet, and the name Denon.[17]

On 21 June 1816 David Parish deposited "for safe keeping, subject to his order," as he instructed librarian John Vaughan, "a valuable collection of *Ancient Medals* and coins.[18] The members directed the secretary 6 February 1852 to write George Parish about this deposit, because David Parish had died. The question now was "whether there is any legal representative of the late Mr. David Parish.[19] George Parish answered on 24 March and his letter was read 2 April.[20] The secretary was directed to write Richard Parish, the executor, to see if any particular disposition of these coins and medals had been made, "or whether the executors wished to withdraw them."[21] George Parish replied on 21 January 1853 that no disposition had been made, but Richard Parish wished them to remain in the Society, except for two: "1) a medal of J. Parish amongst the No. 2 of the collection 2) medal of the Admiralty Hamburg 1723—No. 30 of this collection."[22] The letter was read on 4 February and the members ordered the thanks of the society, as well as the two medals, be sent to Mr. George Parish "for the liberality of his family."[23] The receipt of the medals was delivered on 8 February.[24]

Forty-two "Silver Medals or Roman Coins" were presented on 7 March 1817 by Peter S. Du Ponceau. Among the emperors depicted on the coins were Nerva, Vespasian, Antoninus, Domitian, Trajan, Decius, Posthumus, Gordianus, Philip, Gallienus, Valerianus, among others.[25]

Jacob Cist of Wilkes-Barre, Pennsylvania wrote John Vaughan on 17 August 1818 and sent a medal which had been dug from the ruins of "an ancient fortification" north of "this village." He described it thus:

This Medal bears the bust of George I with the inscription "George king of Great Britain;" on the shoulder will be perceived the date 17.1 On the reverse is the figure of an indian drawing his bow at a deer, and above is the representation of the sun, signifying that their Great Father the English king wishes his indian children fine weather and good hunting. It is in a high state of preservation and strongly exemplifies the decided advantage the Medal possesses over every other mode of perpetuating the memory of events. Scarcely have an hundred years elapsed and the fortification in which it was found is so completely levelled with the ground that the form of it can scarcely be ascertained; nor is any information respecting it to be obtained from the oldest inhabitants here.[26]

18 September 1818

A medal struck in 1813 from the Rio de la Plata region to honor "Liberdad." It was struck to commemorate, the Declaration of independence, by the Republick of Chili, in South America...Tho' the art of printing has diminished, in some measure, the advantages arising from the useful preservation of medals, they yet possess a portion of the usefulness ascribed to them.[28]

Caesar Augustus Rodney

18 September 1818

"Several old English and American Coins", among which were the coinages of William and Mary, Elizabeth, Charles II, and the province of Massachusetts, among others.

George Ord

On 5 February 1819 Joseph Sansom delivered medals of George III, French coins, a Benjamin Franklin 1783 medal, "one Penny Virginia," and others. Sansom wished to create a "Medallic History of the U. States" and he designed, and Reich engraved the dies, for three silver medals which Sansom presented: one was of Benjamin Franklin for 1776; one for George Washington for 1797; and, one was of Franklin and Washington for 1783.[30]

A medal of Matthew Bolton, Soho, England, designed by F. Pidgeon, was presented 15 June 1821 by his son, Robert Bolton, through the hands of Robert Patterson of the U. S. Mint.

Peter S. Du Ponceau proposed to William Tilghman on 1 August 1821 that a specific medal be struck for use by the Society for an American Academy of Language & Belles Lettres.[32]

William Short wrote on 20 October 1824 that he was sending "the first impressions of a few of the medals executed in Paris by order of Congress, which happen to be in my hands." He could not remember how one medal "of one side only" was acquired with them, but this odd medal honored "M. de Leeffrein, the French Admiral who so much distinguished himself in the East Indies during the revolutionary war.[33] These were received on 5 November 1824 and with them were impressions in plaster of:

James Madison, President of the U. S. A. D. 1809.

James Madison, President of the U. S. from 1809 to 1817.

James Monroe President of the U. S. A. from 1817 (3 impressions)

Thomas Macdonough Stagno Champlain Clas Reg Brit Superavit

The Congress of the U. S. to Captn James Biddle. For his Gallentry[sic] good conduct and services.

Gen [member] Alex[ander] Hamilton Sec. Treas. Unit. Sta.

Philadelphia Saving Fund Society Crescit Eundo () A Penny Saved is a Penny Earned. To Public Credit 1795.[34]

When the Corporation of the City of New York celebrated the opening of the Erie Canal, a medal was struck for the occasion. One of these medals was sent to the Society by the Corporation through Recorder R. Roker. It was received on 18 August 1826.[35]

John Bacon donated the Franklin Institute's "Prize Medal" in silver on 3 November 1826. This medal displayed the head of Benjamin Franklin and it was to be given as a premium. The legend is: "Franklin Institute of the State of Pennsylvania 1824 [ ] Reward of Skill and Ingenuity." [36]

4 January 1828

The "Centennial Medal of the Imperial Academy of Russia" was received. It was designed by academician Kohler and engraved by Count Peter AlexandrovichTolstoi. On one side was the bust of Tsar Nicholas I with the legend (in Russian): "Nicholas I by the Grace of God Emp[ero]r & Autocrat of all the Russias." On the reverse Minerva, with her attributes, was depicted crowning the busts of Peter I and Alexander: the legend here, also, was in Russian.[37]

[DONOR UNKNOWN]

6 February 1829

A "single small Russian Coin made of Platina. As perfectly new in this country it may perhaps be deemed acceptable by the Society, and if so please present it in my behalf, & let it be placed in the Collection of coins & medals." [38]

Peder Pedersen

The Royal Society of Edinburgh's Keith Bicentennial Medal was discussed in a letter from that Society on 20 March 1829. The communication was referred to a committee of John Vaughan, Alexander Dallas Bache, and John Kintzing Kane "with power to take order."

1 April 1830

Two modern gold medals and a copper one from Mexico that were almost lost in the great mass of pre-Columbian Mexican artifacts.[39]

Joel Roberts Poinsett

Henry Middleton wrote John Vaughan from Charleston, South Carolina, on 13 April 1831 that he had "the pleasure of enclosing [for] you 3 Sets of the new Russian coinage in *platinum*. You will have the goodness to present 2 pieces with my best respects to Mr. Duponceau. [sic]" [40] One coin, struck in 1829, was of three rubles denomination, and the other, struck in 1830, was worth six rubles.[41]

The elderly Nicholas Collin presented on 28 June 1831 a prized possession.

I have requested Mr. [Severin] Lorich to hand to you herewith a gold medal in honor of the great [Carolus] Linnaeus, given to me by the Swedish Academy of Sciences; which medal I beg the Philosophical Society to accept from me as a token of my respect. [42]

During this period, thieves had been active in stealing treasured medallions and coins. News of the extensive robbery of medals from the king's library in Paris on 5 or 6 November 1831 was communicated to the Society by the French consul in Philadelphia, General Dannery. He asked the cooperation of the Society in the recovery of these treasures. A list of the stolen items was given to the Society.[43]

On 6 July 1832 Peter S. Du Ponceau sent the Society a gift from John d'Homorgue of a copper coin of the United States, dated 1791, bearing the likeness of George Washington. The mint was not established until 1792 and Du Ponceau wrote:

I remember well the time when a few of these coins appeared, but was not informed by whom they were ordered to be executed. I presume it was done by some of the leading men of that day, with a view to serve as a model for the coins to be struck at the mint which was then contemplated to be established; a few of them only were struck & such pieces are now very rare. It was certainly said at that time that Genl. Washington disapproved of the plan....

Conceiving that this rare piece deserves a place in the Cabinet among the medals of the Society.... [44]

Joshua Francis Fisher asked permission to describe the American medals in the Society's collection; this was granted on 7 December 1832.

Hungarian Karoly Nagy presented a medal on 15 November 1833. It was turned over to the president for a report. On the same date a collection of Turkish, Roman, Hungarian, and German coins and medals was received from Nagy.[45] The president reported on 7 March 1834.[46]

Manuel Naxara

Three medals which had been struck to commemorate the coronation of Iturbide in Mexico in 1822. One showed the head of Iturbide with the inscription: "Augustin Proclamation La Cathedrale de Guadalajara 1822." The second displayed an eagle with a crown on its head on the obverse: on the reverse was "Inauguration de Augustin Imperador de Mexico." On the reverse of the third was the legend: "Proclamado por el Ayantamiento de Aguas Calientes, de 12 Deciembre de 1822."[47]

Manuel Naxara

James J. Barclay wrote Clement Cornell Biddle on 1 July 1834:

Captain David S. Geisinger, during his late cruise in the United States Ship Peacock, made a small collection of Silver and Copper coins, which you will receive with this note, and which I beg you to present, on behalf of Capt. Geisinger, to the American Philosophical Society.48

This collection of 82 coins was received 18 July 1834. It consisted of:
No. 1 A Cochin-chinese Dollar, of the reign of the present Emperor. Stamped in Chinese characters ming ming tung paou current coin of Ming-ming.
No. 2 Three Brazilian copper Coins. One of 80 reis, date 1828. One of 40 reis date 1829. One of 20 reis, date 1820.
No. 3 An Austrian Silver Dollar of Maria Theresa, Date 1780.
No. 4 Three pieces of Silver Coin, viz: one old Persian rupee, One new d[itt]o one half d[itt]o.

No. 5 A large, thick, solid, oblong, Square Silver Coin of Cochin-china, Stamped on both sides, in Cochin-chinese characters. On the one side, Government Silver, one tael. On the other In Mingming's reign. A much smaller piece of silver of the same form & Stamp, with this difference that on the reverse is written One mau, instead of one tael.

No.6 A thick solid, oblong piece of Silver, rounded at the ends and Stamped, being a coin of Lao, name & value unknown.

No. 7 One large piece of Copper coin of the Kingdom of Siam, bored in the middle.

No. 8 Two copper coins of Buenos Ayres; dates 1823, 1827.

No. 9 A Canton chopped quarter of a Dollar, Silver.

No. 10 Three base metal coins of Cochinchina.

No. 11 Four small silver coins of Camboge, current in Cochin-china.

No. 12 One base metal coin of Siam.

No. 13 Three copper coins of the English East Indian Company.

No. 14 One Dutch guilder from Bencoolen (Silver) Date 1792.

No. 15 Two half Sieca rupees (Silver) from Batavia, one Dutch on one side the crowned Lion of Holland, & the value 25 c., on the other the crowned W for William, & the date 1825. The other piece is in Persian characters on both sides.

No. 16 Two Madras Silver Fenams value 8 cents.

No. 17 A copper coin of the East Indian Company, current at Muscat, and called a Quarter Anna, Date 1830.

No. 18 A copper coin of Singapore, value 2' cent.

No. 19 One Bombay half rupee (Silver) value 20 cents.

No. 20 A Copper coin of Cochinchina, bored in the middle. This coin is of the reign of Kwang-trong, the youngest of the three rebellious brothers called the Tay-Suns. He reigned only a few Years, beginning in 1778.

No. 21 A double Fennam of Bengal. (Silver)

No. 22 One Silver Sicca rupee of the East Indies, value 45 cents.

No. 23 One Brass coin of Bengal (East Indian Company) Date 1804.

No. 24 One Portuguese copper coined at Goa, in the East Indies, value 15 reis. On one Side the arms of Portugal. On the other the figures 15, and the date of the coinage, 1760.

No. 25 A Portuguese Copper coin, date 1820—value 40 reis.

No. 26 Six solid pieces of Silver, being money of the Kingdom of Siam, of the following denominations & value, as stated by the donor

    1. A Catty value 80 Ticals or $49.23, at the ordinary value of 6 2' Silungs pr Dollar, not coined.

    2. A Tical, value 4 silungs, coined.

    3. Half Tical, value 2 Silungs. Coined.

    4. A Silung, value 2 Fuangs. Coined.

    5. A Fuang, [value] 2 half fuangs, coined.

    6. A half Fuang. Coined.

Note, The gold coins are of the same denomination from half fuangs to Tical, inclusive, and are from 14 to 18 times the value of the Silver, according to the greater or less purity of the gold.

A Siamese Pecul or Catty is double the weight of a Chinese.

No. 27 34 small copper coins of Mocha called Commassee. value, 380 of them equal to a Dollar.

No. 28 A leaden coin of Siam, bored in the middle, value unknown.

No. 29 A Bank note of Rio de la plata of 17 Dollars, date illegible, supposed 1827 or 1829. [49]

    These coins were referred to a committee and it was continued on 15 August. By 19 September the members requested it to report, not only on the Ceisinger gift, but also on the "ancient coins which the president [Jefferson] had presented to the Society."

A few copper coins from Assam, Bengal and China were sent to the Society by Marmaduke Burrough on 2 October 1834.[50] This gift was listed in the *Transactions* as a

"Collection of Copper Coins, chiefly from Thibet"[51] but was listed as "Chiefly from India" in the Donation Book:

No. 1 Three British Copper Coins, Ceo 2d 1734, 1750—Ceo 3d 1797.

No. 2 One old Spanish copper Coin. Date unknown.

No. 3 A copper Coin of the State of Connecticut Struck in 1788. On one side a head crowned with Laurel, on the other the genius of the State, with the legend INDETLIB. (Independence and Liberties)

No. 4 A copper Coin of Buenos Ayres, Date 1830

No. 5 Two Copper Coins of the British East India Company, Date 1808

No. 6 Three East India Copper Coins (Native)

No. 7 Two Copper pieces that were once Coins, but now entirely defaced. [52]

15 August 1834

Two English coins from the reign of James I.[53]

Auguste Henri Parmentier

Joseph Francis Fisher sent on 17 October 1834 a collection of forty-four silver and ninety-nine copper coins, of which seven were American and were coined before the Revolution, four were Roman, and the others were from various European countries.[54] Peter S. Du Ponceau and Samuel Moore, as a committee, were asked to describe this collection on the same date and it was continued 6 March 1835. A listing by the committee was accepted 20 March 1835 and the committee was discharged 15 May 1835 and, interestingly enough, there are three lists of this gift; preserved in the Archives:

No. 1 One false English guinea.

No. 2 Fourteen English pence, half pence & farthings and one two penny piece. 14 pieces.

No. 3 Nine English penny & half penny brass tokens. 9 pieces.

No. 4 An English naval half penny, with Lord Nelson's head on one side, & on the other, England expects every man to do his duty. I piece.

No. 5 Five English medals, Struck on various occasions, one of them curious: on one side a head, supposed of George III with the Legend: Gregory III, Pon on the other the figure of Britannia with the legend *"Britain rules."* 5 pieces.

No. 6 One Irish penny, half penny & farthing. 3 pieces.

No. 7 One Halifax Nova Scotia half penny. 1 piece.

No. 8 Fourteen French brass coins of Louis XVth & XVIth. & of the Republic, & some Struck for the Colonies. 14 pieces.

No. 9 One Centime of [Henri] Christophe, President of Hayti with his effigy. 1 piece.

No. 10 Nine Portuguese brass coins. 9 pieces.

No. 11 Three Russian brass coins, one of 5 Kopeks, of the reign of Catherine II, one of one kopek, of the reign of Paul and one of two Kopeks, of the reign 0f Alexander 1811. 3 pieces.

No. 12 One Turkish brass coin one Spanish d[itt]o one Danish d[itt]o one Swedish d[itt]o one Dutch d[itt]o (Province of Zealand) one d[itt]o d[itt]o (King William, 1825) one Austrian (Lombardo Venetian Kingdom) one of the State of Carthagena one brass token struck at Gibraltar, 1813. Value one quarto. 9 pieces.

No. 13 Nineteen pieces defaced or unknown. 9 pieces.

No. 14 Twelve brass counters. 12 pieces. Total number 101 pieces.[55]

Another list concerns some Roman and American coins:

No. 1 A Silver Coin of the Emperor Gudian (Roman) Note: the Society possesses several silver Coins of the Same Emperor. See Coins presented by P[eter] S. DuPonceau.

No. 2 Three Silver Coins, viz; one of Elizabeth (English) 1561. One of Maria Theresa Queen of Hungary, 1742. One of Francis II Emperor of Germany, 1797.

No. 3 Three brass coins of the Roman Emperors. One of Augustus. One of Antonius. One of Philippus. Note, the Society possesses Silver Coins of the two last—See as above.

No. 4 One Copper Coin of the Island of Barbadoes—On one side a Crow and Negroe's head; on the other a pine apple, with the legend: "Barbadoe's penny." 1788.

No. 5 Five brass American Coins, Struck before the establishment of the United States mint. One of the Commonwealth of Massachusetts, 1788. Four Cents, bearing devices and mottoes Similar to those on the old paper Continental money—Places where Struck unknown; Dates not always legible. [56]

The final list was of:

"41 Silver pieces:

"No. 1. Four English Bank tokens, one of 5 Shillings 1804, one of 3 Shillings, 1813, two of ten pence Irish 1805.

An English Six pence , 1816, bored thro'.

A light English Shilling.

A groat of the reign of Queen Anne, 1710.

A med[al] struck in honor of Geo. 3. on his competing the 50th Year of his reign. 8 pieces.

No. 2. Three Turkish Coins, value unknown. 3 pieces.

No. 3. A piece of 2 livres of the Kingdom of Italy under Napoleon, 1811. One piece.

No. 4. A piece of 24 Sols of the reign of Louis XIV. 1711. One piece.

No. 5. Seven pieces of Danish West India money. Seven pieces.

No. 6. A twelve Sols piece of the French Windward Islands, 1731 One piece.

No. 7. A Russian piece of two Kopeks, 1804. One piece.

No. 8. A piece of Papal money, 1729, on one side are the Papal Arms, with the legend *Sede vacante* & the date; on the other a dove with a halo round it, Legend: Veni Sante Spiritus. One piece.

No. 9. Six Danish coins of various dates. Six pieces.

No. 10. Two pieces of Hayti, one of [Alexander] Petion, one of [Jean Pierre] Boyer, with their effigies. Two pieces.

No. 11. One Shilling of Mecklenburg Schwerin, 1767. One piece.

No. 12. Two pieces of the United Netherlands, partly defaced. Two pieces.

No. 13. A Spanish quartillo, or one rial piece. One piece.

No. 14. Four pieces of German Coin of different Principalities, cannot well be specific. Four pieces.

No. 15. Two pieces so defaced, as not to be identified.

Total 41 pieces. [57]

On 17 April 1835 the gift of William Brown Hodgson of some "Turkish, Egyptian and Greek coins" was received. Hodgson wrote Peter S. Du Ponceau on 10 April 1835 from Washington that

Had I known, during my late extensive travels in the East, that your Society, to which I owe sensible obligations, would receive such contributions, I would have made complete collections of the modern coins of all the countries, which I visited.[59]

With this letter Hodgson sent a listing of his gift:

1. A Greek silver coin, issued under the Presidency of the Count [Ioannes Antonios] Capodistrias, in the year 1828. Its value is 16-2/3 cents, or the sixth part of a dollar. On the face or obverse, is the inscription in Greek...J. A. Kaposikstrias, President. In the field or area is the word Phoenix. On the reverse, is a Phoenix rising from its pyre, under the influence of the Cross which is suspended above it, with the legend..greek commonwealth. The Exergue bears the date of the coin in alphabetic numerals.
2. An austrian gold ducat, of the year 1818. Its value is nine shillings sterling, rather more than two dollars. On the face is the inscription *Franciscus primus, Dei gratia, Austriae imperator,* and on the reverse: Hungariae, Bohemia, Lombardiae & Venetiarum, Galiciae, Lodomiriae, Illyriae Rex. A. S.
3. A Belgian gold ducat, of the year 1831; value 9 shillings Sterling. On the obverse, is the inscription, *Moneta aurea regni Belgii, ad legem imperii,* and on the reverse, *concordia, res parvae crescunt.*
4. A Turkish gold coin, called a *Yirmilick,* or piece of twenty piastres: value, about one Spanish dollar. In the area of the face is found, as in all Turkish coins, the Toghra or seal of the reigning Sultan. The legend of both sides is *Sultan Mahoud, conqueror.* In

the area of the reverse, is the inscription, *struck at Constantinople, in the year of the Hegira, 1223*. This year corresponds with 1808 of the Christian era, when Sultan Mahmoud ascended the throne.

5. A Turkish gold coin, called a Roub, of the value of three piastres or 15 cents.
6. A Turkish silver coin, termed *Grouseh,* or piastre of the nominal value of 5 cents. A piastre contains 40 paras.
7. A Turkish *Utchlick* or piece of three piastres. On the face, is the inscription of *Sultan of two lands*, and Hachan of two seas; Sultan son of a Sultan. The reverse bears the legend, *Sultan Mahmoud Chan, son of Ab-dul-Hamid Chan; may his empire be perpetual!*
8 Two silver *Yirsni—paralicks* or pieces of twenty paras.
9. A *beshparalick* or piece of five paras coined in Egypt.
10. Two very small coins called paras. This coin in Turkey, is the unit of value. There are forty to the piastre, and thirty years ago there were 120 to the dollar. Since then, the Turkish piastre has become so much deteriorated, that twenty are reckoned to the dollar, and consequently 800 paras.[60]

16 December 1836
"[A] specimen of the new coinage of the American Dollar," with a description of the devises thereon. With this was "a specimen of medal ruling by Asa Spencer."

Robert Maskell Patterson

Also from the United States Mint, Robert M. Patterson on 17 March 1837 delivered a "Coin which had been expanded to an extraordinary degree under the press in consequence or the surface of the planchet being slightly covered with oil." He then explained how this expansion occurred. William Hypolitus Keating, Joshua F. Fisher, Isaac I. Hayes, and John K. Kane were named a committee on 18 August 1837 to "arrange the Medals, coins, &c." The committee was discharged 1 January 1841.[61]

16 February 1838
A collection of copper coins from South America.[62]

Condy Raguet

21 August 1838
A medal commemorating the independence of Chile.[63]

Caesar Rodney

Michael Nesbit wrote Franklin Bache on 2 October 1838 concerning the gold Copley Medal of the Royal Society of London which had been awarded to Benjamin Franklin. His letter was read on 2 November 1838 to the members "after the adjournment of the meeting."

The Copley Medal to Benj[ami]n Franklin has been put on sale by chances, several patriotic citizens object ot this mode; as it may put it in the possession of someperson, who would send it out of this country—a circumstance to be avoided if possible.

The same gentlemen propose, to have the matter submitted to the Philosophical Society, & engage the members to purchase it by private subscription, & place it amongst the archives of the Society.

Six Hundred Dollars (the price at which it is held) has been offered by one Society in this city but refused because no definite period could be fixed upon for payment.

I now offer it for Five Hundred dollars, to your Society—the one hundred dollars less than offered for its purchase, may be considered as a reduction in its price, or as my personal subscription towards its purchase—for your Society—whichever you may deem proper.[64]

The Society did not purchase the medal and it brought $1,000. Then, the owner, Edmund Rouvert, on 27 June 1840, offered it to the Society for that amount.

Having been told by several gentlemen from Phil[a]d[elphia] that the American Philosopohical Society much regretted that the Golden Medal presented to Benjamin Franklin by the Royal Society of London had passed into other hands than the Society

Having been the possessor of the Medal since November 1838 & having caused to be made casts of the medal which I sent to Asa Spencer, Esqr of Phil[a]d[elphia] the celebrated ruler of medallic matters who most generously ruled me a plate of the Franklin Medal in a most elegant style without making any charge

Ruled engraving of the medal will appear in the Second Edition & in all future Editions of the Works of Franklin which will enhance the celebrity of the medal. I have come to the conclusion that the medal should no longer remain in the hands of any individual however prudent a rapid fire might cause the medal to be destroyed & sudden death might cause the medal to go into foreign hands.

Therefore I propose to the American Philosophical Society to pass to them the Franklin Medal for the sum that the subscription in November 1838 which according to the letter sent me by my agent in Phil[a]d[elphia] regarding the medal & the enclosed written communication of Michael Nisbet Esqr sent to my agent that from the generous amount subscribed by the five first members would have made the subscription amount to about One thousand Dollars.[65]

Evidently, nothing was done and the medal never came to the Society.

5 October 1838
Three hundred copper coins,medals, and tokens. "This collection had been amassed by [the donor's] grandfather."[66] A committee was named to examine this collection and it reported and was discharged 18 January 1839.

Lynah James

3 May 1839
A "Turkish Medal Struck on the occasion of the Campaign of the Sultan's troops against those of the Pasha of Egypt." The donor, Dragoman to the American legation in Constantinople, sent the medal from Constantinople.

John Porter Brown

Several copies of medals arrived on 6 February 1840 from Joseph Saxton.They were produced "by the galvanic process of Prof [essor Moritz Hermann] Jacobi,of St. Petersburg," Russia. A fusible metal matrix was used and removed when the desired form was obtained. Additional medals were exhibited on 6 March 1840 made by the same process. Saxton also included pieces of charcoal and anthracite, which he had used as substitutes for the forms of fusible metal ordinarily employed. These were perfectly coated with copper, a fact which shows it to be but necessary, that the substance at the negative electrode should be a conductor of electricity.[70]

20 March 1840
Medals made by Jacobi's method.

Franklin Peale

Peale reported that Jacob Reese Eckfeldt
  of the [United States] Mint, had found the specific gravity of copper, thus procured, to be as high as that of rolled copper; that is, 8.95.

Mr. Peale also exhibited a diaphram of parchment, which had been used in the battery employed in the process; and upon which metallic copper had been precipitated. He further exhibited specimens of Metallic Silver, reduced, by a similar process, from the chloride of silver; but remarked, that it was not likely to lead to any useful analogous result, owing to the silver being deposited in a granular state. [71]

John P. Brown wrote on 10 April 1840 that he had been trying to form a complete set of coins of the Ottoman sultans of Turkey (the dynasty ruling at that time). He believed the collection was

now as perfect as I can hope to make it, for I dispair of obtaining a coin of Othman from the exteme rarity of his coins & it is generally believed that Othman had none struck among his precarious reign. I am at present drawing up a few remarks on this collection & will when finished, send them to you. Permit me to present this little collection of coins to the soc[iet]y over which you preside, as a small token of my respect for the society & the deep sense of gratitude...for your kindness to me.

Brown filled the box with some miscellaneous coins of the Near East:

No. 1. A square coin of one of the Moorish kings of Granada bearing one side the Musselman creed, "there is no God but Allah & Mahomed is the prophet of Allah" & on the reverse "struck in the city of Granada."
No. 2. A Coin of Kach Hasser as Seljuikide prince in the old Kufic Character.
3. A Coin of Kach Ahad.
4. A coin of some of the Caliphs in Kufic.
5. [   ]
6. [A] Coin of Shalim Geruz Khan of the Crimea struck at Buk the Serey.
7. A coin of a persian prince Hussuin Shah struck in Tif lis.
8. [A] Coin of a Caliph.
9. Thufishes Empire of the east.
10. [   ]of one of the Ptolomies of Egypt.
11. 12. Coins of the lower Empire.[72]
These were received 21 August 1840.[73]

At some point before 1841, two Austrian silver medals were received from Isaac Lowenstern: the coronation thaler of Franz I and another Franz I thaler. with this gift was a copper coronation medal of King William IV of Great Britain.[74]

The chief coiner of the United States Mint, Franklin Peale, submitted a complete series of United States coinage for the members to inspect on 1 January 1841.[75] From London, William Vaughan sent his brother, John Vaughan, for the Society, "a cast of a Medal of Gen[era]l Washington struck in 1805."[76]

5 November 1841
Gold medals which had been awarded to Dufoy and Bachon.[77]

David Baillie Warden

Sometime before his death in 1840 John Vaughan presented ten ancient brass coins:

1. Three Coins of the Greek Empire, on two of them nothing can be read but Basileus Romaion (Emperor of the Romans) in the Greeks language, but in Roman, with some Greeks character thus: BASILEVS ROMAIWN (w for omega). The other is legible and is a Coin of Basil & Constantine who reigned together in the tenth Century.
2. Two coins of Maxentius, who was defeated by Constantine the great under the standard of Christ.
3. Four Coins of Roman Emperor after the Caesars & the Antoninus, viz: two of Licinius, one of Carus, and one the name of which could not be made out.
In all 19 pieces. [78]

18 February 1842
Oriental copper coins, twenty-one in number.[79]

Dr. Diver

John P. Brown had received no notice of the receipt of his gift of coins by 15 July 1842. The members then "resolved that a duplicate of the usual letter of thanks" be sent him.[80] On 7 October 1842 Franklin Peale asked that George M. Justice be permitted to "have casts made from certain medals" under the supervision of the curators.[81]

Jesse Duncan Elliott sent "four ancient coins" to William H. Dillingham on 4 November 1842. One was clear, "the remaining three will my old friend Mr.[John] Vaughan here might possibly decipher in the dark. I pray not to remove therust with which they are encrusted." He stressed this, by adding that "To an antiquarian delicu(?) marks in the world."[82]

3 January 1844
A copy of a Jewish shekel, in type metal. At the same time, he gave a copy of "a Persian Daric, now in the U[nited] S[tates] Mint."[83]

George M. Justice

Robert M. Patterson, on 21 February 1845, exhibited a British sovereign, counterfeit, dated 1824, with the head of George IV on it. The copy was so perfect "as to elude detection by any of the sensible or mechanical tests in common use, singly or combined." He gave the particulars of the coin—weight, thickness, color, and mechanical execution. "The only process, short of actual assay by which it can be detected, is a trial of its specific gravity." One of these counterfeits had been assayed and was found to have a value of $4.26. A true coin was worth $4.86, so the counterfeiters made a profit of sixty cents on each coin.

> Counterfeiters are rarely contented with so small a gain, and their fraud is therefore more easily detected. In the present case, the smallness of the profit in the individual piece, gives reason to apprehend that the roguery is to be made by a grand operation, and that many such counterfeits may be already abroad.[84]

On 20 June 1845 Robert M. Patterson exhibited a counterfeit of a Belgian coin of 1648. Called a "curious coin." it had been found twenty feet below the surface of the ground in a marl pit in New Jersey.[85] Specimens of dollars which had been found in the wreck of the *San Pedro* were exhibited by Robert M. Patterson 17 October 1845. The *San Pedro* had been destroyed by fire off the coast of Venezuela in 1815.[86]

20 November 1846
Two medals, one of bronze and one of silver from the Akademie der Wissenschaften zu Berlin. They were struck in commemoration of its first president, Gottfried Wilhelm Leibniz.[87]

[DONOR UNKNOWN]

A bronze medal of President James Knox Polk was exhibited by Robert M. Patterson on 18 December 1846. The model was a large wax medallion taken from life. Thewax had been covered with metal die powder and

> by the electrotype process and a subsequent transfer in sand, made to form a mould, from which a new medallion is cast in fine iron. The iron medallion is then placed under the action of a portrait lathe propelled by steam, and by the continued action of the lathe, a die is cut of the desired size, and of softened steel. The die is then slightly retouched, and being afterwards hardened, is applied in the ordinary manner of striking medals. This medal is beautifully finished, and bears a comparison with those made by the direct action of the die-sinker.[88]

The secretary of the Royal Society of Edinburgh, James David Forbes, sent on 1 July 1848 a medal "bearing the effigy of [John] Napier of Murchison, the Inventor of

Logarithms." The likeness was taken from "an authentic picture." It was received 1 November 1850.[89]

Charles B. Trego read a paper from the huge collection of Benjamin Franklin Papers in the library on 5 April 1850. On 2 March 1778 a grayish metal was enclosed "proposed for coinage, as being impossible to be counterfeited." The members asked John Fries Frazer to analyze the specimen.[90] Frazer announced on 3 May 1850 that the composition of the metal presented by Montecot was: copper, 81; silver 15.87; iron .39; antimony .94; and, a trace of arsenic.[91]

On 10 October 1850 the Royal Swedish Academy [K. Svenska Vetenskaps Akademien,Stockholm] sent a medal which it had caused to be struck in memory of Johan Jakob Berzelius. It was received on 5 December 1851.[92]

A rare coin, known as the Washington half-dollar, was exhibited 6 December 1850: The history of the coin is not exactly known, but tradition states that a few were struck and submitted to the government as samples, when the project for establishing a mint was first entertained. Orders were immediately issued for the cessation of the issue, and for breaking the dies. The coin bears the effigy of Washington with the legend, "G. Washington President I. 1792." On the reverse was an eagle with spread wings, bearing the shield of the United States, with the olive branch and arrows, its head surrounded by the 13 stars, and the legend, "United Statesof America. "[93]

Peter S. Du Ponceau had presented a copper coin on 6 July 1832, dated 1791, bearing the likeness of Washington. This coin must have been a companion piece to Du Ponceau's gift.[94]

The United States assayer in San Francisco, California, Mr. Humbert, coined a $50. gold piece and Franklin Peale exhibited it on 15 April 1851. At the same meeting, Peale also exhibited three cent pieces which were newly coined at the Philadelphia Mint.[95]

On 2 May 1851 William Ewing Du Bois exhibited some metallic currency among which were some specimens of private California minting—five and ten dolllar pieces. These

> so closely resembled the national coin, as to be properly considered counterfeits, with this remarkable feature, however, that they are nearly or quite equal to the genuine issue in value. As the idea of *counterfeiting* seems almost necessarily to include that of *debasement*, or fraud, this unique characteristic renders the pieces highly interesting.[96]

A silver coin of "Haroun Alraschid" from Constantinople was shown and described in detail on 2 May 1851. Three gold rings from the interior of Africa were also shown: the largest was worth $110, the smallest only sixty cents. "They are understood to serve the double purpose of ornament and currency."[97]

The Philadelphia Mint, through Franklin Peale, presented on 19 September 1851 a silver gilt medal in honor of Robert Maskell Patterson. Peale explained the devices and character of the medal and read "the proceedings of the officers of the Mint on the occasion of the retirement of Dr. Patterson" from his position as director of the Mint, with Patterson's reply. [98]

Jacob G. Morris proposed to arrange the coin and medal collection and the curators agreed to let him do so. Franklin Peale notified the members on 21 November 1851 of this arrangement.[99]

21 May 1852

"[S]undry Roman Coins."[100]

Joseph Leidy, in the name of the Southwark Library Company

William H. Dillingham sent on 16 December 1853 some coins to Frederick Fraley asking if the "enclosed Coins" were worth giving to the Society. "My only knowledge of them is from Com. Elliot."[101] Fraley sent them to Charles B. Tregofor the cabinet on 17 December.[102]

Caspar Morris asked to borrow two coins on 17 August 1855 "for the purpose of having copies taken thereof." The members agreed to the loan "subject to the usual guaranty for safe return within a reasonable time."[103]

William E. Du Bois exhibited some Turkish paper currency on 16 November 1855. The first paper money in Turkish history was issued owing to the stress of war, much like American "continental money" of the Revolutionary period.[104]

An aluminum coin was delivered for inspection by William E. Du Bois on 4 January 1856. Some discussion on the use of the metal for coins ensued, for the metal was new and tremendously expensive in the 1850s. By 1856 Du Bois reported that the value of aluminum had "fallen from a gold to a silver valuation, and [was] to be manufactured to some extent in Rouen."[105]

A silver itzebue from Japan which came from San Francisco, where several of these coins appeared following the "opening of trade with that country" was displayed on 4 April 1856 by William E. Du Bois from the Mint Cabinet. A medal struck in honor of Commodore Matthew Galbraith Perry, by the merchants of Boston, to commemorate the opening of Japan was also shown. Franklin Peale praised the superior execution of the medal and attributed high credit to the artists. With these were a 20-shilling piece of James I and an Elizabethan sixpence which had recently been dug up in an earthern pot at Richmond's Island at the mouth of the Saco River in Maine. Thesehad been buried, at best guess, since about 1630 to 1640.

A bronze and a silver medal commemorating Johann Karl Frederic Gauss was presented on 20 June 1856 through the Royal Society of Science at Gottingen. This were struck by order of "His Majesty the King of Hanoveer" in memory of the eminent astronomer and mathematician."[107]   The Royal Geographic Society of London honored Elisha Kent Kane and awarded a medal in "tribute to his zeal and success in prosecuting discoveries inthe Arctic regions." It was delivered to the Society on 18 July 1856 by his father, John K. Kane.[108]

A "Turkish Treasury Note" was displayed on 17 October 1856. It drew ten percentinterest; its circulation was legal; the interest was taxfree; and, the interest coupons were attached at the bottom of the note.[109]

The Royal Norwegian University at Christiana [Oslo] gave a bronze medal on 6 May 1858. It commemorated the fiftieth anniversary of the professor of astronomy, Christopher Hansteen.[110] On 18 June 1858 John E. Le Conte exhibited some Chinese silver "which has the form of a flattened cylinder, bent until the ends meet" with "peculiar marks stamped on it, one of which appears to be in Chinese characters.[111] William E. Du Bois on 21 June 1861 offered for the members' examination two remarkable specimens of current money, one from Austria and the other from Japan.[112]

At the meeting of 7 November 1862 a letter from Joshua I. Cohen was read wherein he presented two photographs of paper currency. One was "from a French Engraving in my possession, the other from a companion Picture for it which I made from my collection."[113]

A medal was received 16 January 1863 from the K. Bayerische Akademie du Wissenschaften. It was issued to honor Frederick Wilhelm von Thiersch in 1860 and was sculpted by J. Ries.[114]

During the American Civil War, tokens were often used. On 18 September 1863, Pliny Earle Chase gave a collection of 303 of them, with a catalogue.[115] On 6 May 1864, Joseph H. Merriam, of Boston, presented eleven tokens; Pliny Chase delivered another 68. [116] W. K. Lanphear, of Cincinnati, Ohio, gave a collection of 315 tokens on 7 October 1864. [117] Pliny Chase offered a revised list of over 2000 tokens on 19 May 1865. He hoped the list would be published; it was referred to a committee.[118]

The Society awarded a Magellanic Premium to Pliny E. Chase on 16 December 1864 for his "discovery of certain new relations between the solar and lunar diurnal variations of magnetic force and of barometric pressure."[119] Chase then made some remarks on the subject.[120] A Committee, consisting of Benjamin Hornor Coates, Alexander Wilcocks, and Franklin Peale, was appointed on 6 January 1865 to prepare a medal for Chase. Progress was reported 20 January 1865 and on 3 February 1865. Peale reported on

16 February 1866 that the medal was ready to be bestowed;   it was awarded by the president of the Society on 2 March 1866.[122]
On 24 July 1866, Mr. Moore wrote John C. Cresson of "a small copper coin, of the weight of forty-two grains, in fine condition, very much like in appearance to the quarter of an eagle of 1798." It was coined in 1803 and the name "Kettle" appeared on it. It was found in a garden in Washington Heights, in New York.[123]

18 December 1868
Thirty-two Russian medals "electrotyped and distributedby the British Museum."[124]
William Blackmore

William E. Du Bois exhibited on 3 December 1869 newly minted silver coins of fifty, twenty-five, and ten cents. These were being coined on the basis of a gold standard, and coins of less than one dollar would "be used only as a subsidiary or fractional currency.[125]

18 February 1870
A medal struck in honor of Stephen Hoogendijk.
The Bavarian Society of Experimental Science at Rotterdam

The engraver of the United States Mint, W. Barber gave to the cabinet on 15 May 1871 a medal of David Rittenhouse. It had been "just completed and struck." Barber presented it for he felt that such a medal belonged to the Society where Rittenhouse had been president "as a grateful return for the privilege of taking the Model from the beautiful Bust in the Society's possession." Moreover,the reverse inscription was taken from the eulogium on Rittenhouse, by Benjamin Rush: "He belonged to the whole Human Race."[127] It was delivered at the meeting of 19 May, the letter read, and the members voted their thanks for it.128
William E. Du Bois read on 1 December 1871 "On a quasi Coin reported found in a boring in Illinois." He presented a photograph of the coin. J. Peter Lesley thought this was another practical joke of the sort which the westerners were apt to play, and cited instances in the oil fields of such jokes. There is a cut of the coin in the *Proceedings*.[129]
On 19 September 1873 a medal arrived from the University of Norway. The legend on the obverse read: "Regni Norwegici Annum millesimium pia celebrat Universitas Regia Fredericiana." On the reverse was: "Tempori Superstes, MDCCCLXXII."[130] Officers of the United States Mint asked the Society for suggestions for "the best device for a commemorative medal of [member Jean Louis Rodolphe] Agassiz." Several members, as a committee, undertook to give the recommendation. The committee reported on 17 April 1874 that, after consideration, it had "suggested a device to the officers of the U[nited] S[tates] Mint."[132]
Samuel Stedman Haldeman exhibited on 3 April 1874 a Sumatran coin which had been found in a bag of coffee in Philadelphia. One side bore the legend "Island of Sumatra. 1804" and the other, in Malay, was inscribed "sa teng wang." He spoke of the difficulties which deciherers encountered from such coins and suggested means of overcoming them.133
A committee reported 10 February 1876 "that it awaited the meeting & action of the Curators for auditing the list of coins in the Cabinet." The curators had been delayed in holding their own proposed meeting.[134]
A letter from Charles Edward Anthon, of New York,[135] was read on 15 February 1876. It concerned a coin struck by Louis XIV in 1670, the date of the settlement of Quebec, thereby making it the first currency of French North America. Anthon wanted to know if the coin would be accepted by the Society and if the history of the coin would be published. The Society accepted, and on 21 July 1876 both the coin and the description were received. The communication was entitled "On a silver Louis of Fifteen Sous, struck under Louis XIV. for circulation." The article was published in the *Proceedings*.[136]
John C. Cresson recommended on 12 May 1876 that the board of officers and the council of the Society notify the United States Mint that it could receive the

"Cabinet of Coins; on condition that the said Cabinet shall be returned to the Hall of the Society" upon demand of the curators. On 17 November 1867, the curators were ordered to see if the coin collection might be accepted by the Mint for "safekeeping and public exhibition."[138] The curators did so and reported on 1 December 1876. The members adopted the report and authorized the curators "to take such further measures as may be necessary" to place the collection in the Mint.[139] Nothing further seems to have been done on this subject and the coins and medals were not placed there.

The Peabody Education Fund ordered a medal of George Peabody from the United States Mint and Robert Charles Winthrop presented on 1 March 1877 a copy for the cabinet. The obverse was inscribed "Education, a debt from the present to future generations. The Trustees of the Peabody Education Fund."[140]

A bronze copy of the Royal Society of London's newly instituted Davy Medal arrived on 18 October 1878. The obverse bore the head of Sir Humphry Davy and on the reverse was the legend: "The Royal Society to [members] Robert Wilhelm Bunsen. Gustav Robert Kirchhoff. In accordance with the will of Humphry Davy, who devoted the testimonial presented to him by the Coal owners of the Tyne and Wear to the encouragement of Chemical research—1877."[141] The members resolved on 15 November 1878

> That the Curators of the Society be directed to make arrangements through the Numismatic and Antiquarian Society of Philadelphia, for the deposit of the collection of Coins and Medals, belonging to the Society in the Pennsylvania Museum of Industrial Art, under agreement that the said collection be properly catalogued and displayed and returned on demand.[142]

The curators reported 6 December 1878 that the collection had been removed to Fairmount Park and secretary Henry Phillips, Jr., receipted its acceptance and sent the Society the thanks of the Numismatic and Antiquarian Society. The Society lent its catalogue of coins and medals to the Numismatic and Antiquarian Society on the same date to help with the preparation of a catalogue and receipt of the collection. The receipted catalogue was received on 20 December from the curator of the Numismatic and Antiquarian Society, Robert Coulton Davis.[144]

Catalogue of Coins Medals &c
belonging to the American Philosophical Society

Medals
Bronze

899	Davy
1	Peabody
2	George I
3, 4, 5, 6	Louis XVI (4)
7, 8	Gustavus III (2)
9	Louis XV
10	Maison Philanthropique de Paris silver
11	David Rittenhouse
12	M. Boulton
12 [13]	[Member Antoine] Lavoisier
14	Segunda Epocha
15 to 45	Russian medals (31)
46	Baron Rokeby
47, 48	Marie Antoinnetta (2)
49	Siewarrow
50	New Haven
51	Norway Millenial
52	Steen Steen Strem Upsal Quadreminiel
53	Napoleon (Aux arts Ia Victoire)
54	Napoleon (La Vaccine)
55	[Member] Lafayette (National Guard)

56	Ferdinand IV
57	Mal[es]cherbe[s]
58	Rousseau (2) 1 — one missing
59 to 64	Monneron (French Revolution) (6)
65	Washington (Sansom)
66	Fred. Thiersch
	John Napier missing
67	Gauss
68	Hooghendyk
69	Washington (Ecccleston)
70	Lord Howe
	Lord Cornwallis (2) missing
71	Oscar of Sweden
72	Leibnitz
73	Preble
Total 78	
74	Washington (Sansom)
75 "	(C. C. A. U. S.)
76	Franklin Institute
77	Gauss
78	Augustin of Mexico [Iturbide]
856	Carolina
79	Nicholas I
80	Berzelius
81	Liebnitz
854	Charles II (Birth medal)
900	Louis XVI 1783 (Peace medal) missing
82	Parrish 1.814 (Peace Medal)
83	Franklin (Bernier)
83	Louis XV
84	One Order

Brass White Metal Lead and Tin

85, 86	Reward of Merit (2)
87	Napoleon & Jose'phine
88	William Penn (Lead)
89	Washington (Heisingtory)
90	Peace medal 1814 (Post nubila phoebus)
91	Countess of Huntingdon (Lead)
92	Jefferson (Lead)
93	Napoleon Antwerp (Lead) (White metal?)
94	Great Britain and Ireland united
95, 96	Erie canal (2)
97	Elector of Cologne
98	Horatio Gates
99	Monastic Seal (Lead)
108 to 113	Casts (Lead) (6)
103 to 107	Clasp medals (Brass) (5)
855, 102	Admiral Vernon (Brass) (2) 1
100	William Pitt (Brass)
101	Monopolizer medal (Tin)

Gilt and Gold

114	Linnaeus (Gold)
115	Battle of Leipzig (Gold) Waterloo—gilt
Essex (Gilt missing)	
116	R. M. Patterson (Gilt)

117, 118	Orders (gold) (2)—Ferdinand VII of Spain
898	Some broken jewelry
119	Entry of the Allies (gilt)

Ottoman Coinage

120 to 123	Mahmoud 1. 2. 3. 4.
124, 125	Suliman 1. 2.
	Khan of the Crimea missing
126	Abdul Mejid
127	Abdul Hamed
128 to 130	Selim 1. 2. 3.
	Orkhan
	Bajozet 1. 2
	Ibrahim 1.
131 to 133	Ahmed 1. 2. 3
	Perim Shah
139	Unknown 1
134	Murad 1. 2. 3. 4.
135 to 138	Mustapha 1. 2. 3. 4
	Moorish of Spain
	Caliph of Arabia
140, 141	Seljukdar

(11 missing of these)
Total 34   33

France

Silver

142	Napoleon Franc
143	Napoleon 1/2 Franc
144	Louis XVI—15 Sols
145	Louis XV Isles du Vent
909	Louis XIV Small piece

Copper and base

147 to 153	Louis XVI Seven pieces
154 to 156	Louis XV Three pieces
157 to 163	Louis XIV Six pieces—one over
164 to 178	Miscellaneous &c. Sixteen 15—one short

Silver 5
Copper & base 32
Total 37

Russia

179	Platinum Six Roubles
180, 181	Platinum Three Roubles (2)
Copper	
182 to 190	Nine pieces

Platinum pieces 3
Copper 9
Total 12

Italy

191	Silver 1	
192 to 200	Copper 9	Silver 1
		Copper 9
		Total 10

Austria

Silver
201   Francis I
202, 203   Charles VI (2)
204   Francis II
205   Maria Theresa
206   Francis & Maria Theresa
207   Besancon
208   Duke of Reichstadt medal

Copper and base
209   Maria Theresa (Base)
210 to 212   M. Theresa Copper (3)
213   Leopold (Base)
901   Joseph of Hungary 1687 (Base)
214 to 222   Unknown 9 Names of 9 given
Copper & base
Silver
Total 23

Prussia
Frederick the Great missing
Base 2
Copper 1
Total 3

South America
One Bank Note
231, 232   Silver 2
226 to 230   Copper 5
Copper 5
Silver 2
One Bank Note
Total 4

North America
233   Rosa Americana (George I)
234, 235   Connecticut (Copper) 2
236   Massachusetts (Copper) (I)
237, 238   Steam coinage medals (Brass) (2)
239, 240   Colonies Francaises 1721, 1722 (3) 2
241   Pitt token Brass
146   Gloriana regni (Silver)
242   New Jersey (Copper)
243, 244   Virginia (Copper) (2)
245   Pattern, cent (Feuchtwanger)
246   Peale medal (copper)
247 to 312   65 Miscellaneous American Coppers
Silver 1
Copper & Base 80
Total 81

Hayti
313   Petion (Base)
314   Christopher (Copper)
Base 1

Copper 1
Total 2

East Indies

315 to 317	Bengal Three silver
318 to 326	Bengal copper Nine
327	Bombay 1/2 Rupee (silver)
328	Pondicherry (Silver) (1)
329 to 331	Persia (Silver) (3)
332 to 337	Unknown (silver) (6)
338 to 353	Unknown (Copper) (16) 4
354	Canton one chopped quarter dollar
	Mocha (copper) (33) missing
355 to 358	Singapore (copper) (4)
359	Cochin China (silver) (6) 1—5 missing
	Cochin China (Base) (2)
360 to 367	Siam (silver) (6)
	Siam (Base) (2)
	Moorish (silver) (1)
368	Madras (silver) (2) 1—

Silver 30
Copper & Base 72 66
Total   102 96

Roman

Denari (Silver and Bullion)

369 to 372	Augustus Caesar 4
373	Augustus & Anthony I
374	Avelius Caesar I
378	Caracalla I
	Constantius I
379–381	Domitian 4 3 one missing
382	Elgabalus I
383	Etruscilla I
384	Faustina Sr. I
385–389	Family 5
	Geta I
390–392	Gordinaus 3
396	Gallienus I
393–395	Hadrian 3
	Herennus I
397	Julian I
398, 399	Julius Caesar 2
400	Maximinus I
401	Marcus Aurelius I
402, 403	Marcus Antoninus 3
403, 404	Philip 2
	Pertinax I
405–406	Postumus 2
908	Postumus Junior I
407	Salonina I
408	S. Valerianus I
409	Sabina I
410–412	Severus 3
375–377	Antoninus Pius 3
413	Titus I

414–417	Trajan 4
418–422	Trajan Decius 5
423, 424	Tebonianus Gallus 2
425–428	Vespasian 4
Total Denarii 68	

Bronze

429–434	Alex. Severus 7 6
	Aelius Caesar I
435	Aurelian I
436–443	Augustus 8
441	Antonia 2 1

Roman. Bronze

866	Kite I
625, 626	Magnus Maximus 2
627–630	Maximinus 4
631	Magnentus
	Marc. Antony & Augustus 1 missing
445, 446	Agrippa 2
904, 905	Antonius 3 one missing
447	Arcadius I
448–457	Byzantine 9 one over
458–484	Constantine 37
485–489	Constans 5
490–499	Constantius II 10
544–553	Claudius 10
554–556	Crispina 3
557	Caligua I
558–561	Claudius Gothicus 4
562	Drusus I
563–566	Diocletian 4
567–575	Domitian 9
	Elagabalus I missing
576–577	Faustina Sr 2
578–584	Faustina Jr. 7
585	Galba I
	Gratianus 2 missing
586	Germanicus 2 1
587–600	Gordianus III 17 14
601–607	Gallienus 8 7 one missing
608–617	Hadrian 10
618	Helena I
619	Honorius I
620	Julian II I
Julia Domna I missing	
621	Lucilla I
622, 623	Licinius Sr. 2
624	Licinius Jr. I
500	Maximus I
501–506	Maxentius 6
507–516	Maximianus 9
516–519	Marcus Aurelius 7 2 missing
906	Marcus Antoninus 2 missing
520–523	Nero 4
	Nerva 3
524–526	Otacilia 4 3

907

527–535	Philip Sr. 9
536, 537	Philip Jr. 2
538–543	Probus 6
632	Septimus Severus I
633	Severrina I
634	Salonina I
641	Trajan Decius I
635–640	Trajan 7 6 one missing
642–645	Theodosius 4
	Titus 2 missing
646–648	Tetricus Sr. 2 one over 3 on other list
649	Tetricus Jr. I
650	Tiberius I

Volusianus I missing

651–652	Vespasian 2
653	Valens I
65455	Victorianus 2
656–660	Valentinianus I 5
661	II 1
662–663	III 2
664–681	Uncertain 18

Total Bronze 277 (281)
Denarii 65
(68)

682	Alexander of Macedon (drachma) silver 1
	Dyrrachium (drachma) silver 1 missing
	Sargossa (drachma) silver 1 missing

Total 3

Miscellaneous

683	Greek Phoenix 1828 (silver) 1
684	Egyptian Besh paralik (Base) 1
685	Egyptian Yarmi (Base) 1
686–687	Egyptian Para (Base) 2
688	Belgian Ducat (Gold) 1
	Turkish Utchik (Base) 1 missing
	Grousch " 1 missing
689 (?)	Roub (Gold) 1

Gold 2
Silver 1
Base 5 (6)
Total (9) 8

England

690	George III Six Pence commemorating 50th year
691	Ibid., (Irish) Ten Pence
Ibid.,	Three Pence missing
865	George II Six Pence Piece with no reverse or copy? Planchet. Very thin
692, 693, 694	Anna Four Pence (Two) Two Pence
695	William III Three Pence Scotch
696	William & Mary Two Shillings and Six Pence
697	Ibid., Three Pence
	James II Four Pieces Gun Money viz Five

       Shillings. missing

698–700	James II Two Shillings & Six Pence, One Shilling. Six Pence
701	Charles II. Ten Shillings Gold.
702, 703	Four Pence (Two)
704	Three Pence
705	Two Pence (Two) One missing

Commonwealth	Two Shillings &
706	Six Pence
707	Two Pence
Charles I	One Penny (Three) missing
708	Three Pence cannot locate
709, 710	One Shilling (Two)
711, 712	Two Shillings and Six Pence (Two)
713	Eleven and twenty Pence Scotch 902
902	See above
863	[ ]d Four Pence Aberyswith Three Pence missing
864	Newark Thirty Pence
714	James I Twenty shillings Gold
715	Five Shillings Gold
862	One Shilling
716	Six Pence
Four Pence missing	
717	Two Pence
718	One Penny
861	Elizabeth Six Pence
719	Two Pence
720	Mary Groat (Two) Philip & Mary one
860	Edward VI One Shilling (Two) missing
721	Six Pence
722–725	Henry VIII Groat (Four) One Penny missing
726	One half Penny
727	Henry VII Penny
859	Henry VI Penny
728	Henry V One half Penny
729, 730	Henry IV Groat and One half Groat
731, 858	Edward IV Groat (Two) one
857	One half Groat
732	Edward III One Penny
733	Edward II One Penny
734–736	Edward I One Penny (Three) Groat missing
737	Anne British Gold Coin
738	James IV (Base) of Scotland
739	John Baliol (Base) of Scotland
Total 72	

Silver Tokens

740	Crown. Chichester
741	Half crown. Chichester
742	Half crown Staverton
743	Half crown Gloucester
744	Two Shillings Bath
745	Two Shillings Attleborough
746	Eighteen Pence Stamford
747	Eighteen Pence Reading
748	Shilling Attleboro

749	Shilling Bristol
750	Shilling Brecknoch
751	Shilling Bilston
752	Shilling Charing Cross
753	Shilling Chichester
754	Shilling Dudley
755	Shilling Frome
756	Shilling Gloucester (Two)
757	Shilling Somerset
758	Shilling Flintshire
759	Shilling Hereford
760	Shilling London
76:1	Shilling Newark
762	Shilling Notts
763	Shilling Northumberland
764	Shilling Warren
765	Shilling Wakeford
766	Shilling York
767	Ten Pence Irish missing
	Sixpence Derby missing
768	Six pence Dorset Total 30
769–853	86 Miscellaneous Copper & Tokens Total
867–879	Plaster Casts IS
883–896	Lead and Copper Casts 20
897	Miscellaneous Rubbish & Copper Pieces about 150
	1.59 worn—of no value

The Numismatic and Antiquarian Society of Philadelphia has deposited in the Pennsylvania Museum and School of Industrial Art the above collection of coins and medals the property of the American Philosophical Society.

R[obert] C[oulton] Davis

Dec[embe]r 19[th] 1878   Curator

        This list is the best extant reference to the coin and medal collection of the Society. Not only is it a copy of the Society's catalogue of coins and medals, which has disappeared, it also states what is missing, and as the missing items were located, they were turned over to the Pennsylvania Museum and School of Industrial Art. And yet, this list refers to the collection's having being placed in the Pennsylvania Museum and relieved the Numismatic and Antiquarian Society of further care of it. The Society, later, made the deposit. Henry Phillips, Jr., wrote a communication, "Some Notes upon the Collection of Coins and Medals, now on Exhibition at the Pennsylvania Museum and School of Industrial Arts, in Memorial Hall, Fairmount Park, Philadelphia" and it was read 7 February 1879 and printed in the *Proceedings*.
        The twenty-first anniversary of the Numismatic and Antiquarian Society of Philadelphia and the twelfth anniversary of the presidency of Eli Kirk Price, were commemorated by a bronze medal, designed by W. H. King. The Society received one of these medals on 4 April 1879. An effigy of Mr. Price was on the obverse and the seal of the Numismatic and Antiquarian Society was on the reverse.[147]
        William and Charles E. Barber donated on 20 June 1879 a medal of Joseph Henry. On 19 December 1879 a gift from the Batavian Society, a bronze medal, was received. On the obverse was the inscription: SOCIETAS. ART. SCIENT. BAT. IN. MEMORIAM. I. SAEC. FEL. CLAUSI. in a wreath, and around the margin was "A. P. VIII. X. MAI. MDCCLXXVIII—MDCCCLXXVIII." On the reverse a palm tree was depicted with mountains in the background with the legend: "Ten nutte van't gemeen Batavia's Genootschap."[149]

Members resolved 3 December 1880 that any notable scientist in any branch of science or the fine or useful arts be nominated by any member "for the bestowal of medals for their discoveries."

> *Resolved,* That such names and recommmendations be placed for consideration in the hands of the President to report to the Society his verdict in favor of one or more of them if proper.

> *Resolved,* That, in case no veto is placed by the Society on such verdict, there shall be a presentation of medals to the persons recommended by the President at a time and manner to be arranged by him.[150]

Medals seem never to have been made, nor presented.
William Morris Davis delivered his gift of ten French bronze medals on 16 October 1885. He gave, also, a listing:

No.   1. The dead Napoleon.
       2. Napoleon le Grand.
       3. Ferdinand Philippe Louis, Duc d'Orleans.
       4. Marie d'Orleans.
       5. Cathedrale de Paris
       6. Liberty enlightened Justice, with Despotism prostrated.
       7. Head emblematic, surounded with heavy wreath of oak and laurel.
       8. A figure of Liberty, looking back...
       9. The three heads of Adam Mickiewicz, Jules Michelet and Edgar Quinet.
       10. Head of Pierre Jean de Beranger.[151]

There is a "bronze medal of Napoleon le Grand a l'Armee francaise" listed on a curator's card.

Frederick Fraley, evidently upset by the deposit of the coin and medal collection by the Numismatic and Antiquarian Society with the Pennsylvania Museum and School of Industrial Arts, sent word on 16 March 1893 that if he were not at the next meeting, he thought "that until some special provision is made" for the safety of the coins and medals "from petty larceny, *it* may be best to allow it to remain with the Numismatic Society. Furniture maker Francis D. Kramer proposed to make a case for the coins and medals for the Society 17 March 1893. The description included "all glass to be double thick american, ease to be made to lock it.[153]

On 23 January 1895 Horatio Robinson Storer, M. D., wrote Henry Phillips, Jr., asking if the Society owned "any medals or tokens...relating to medicine or pharmacy." The reply, "to my best knowledge & belief, no such medals" were in the Society's cabinet was sent on 30 January. [154]

Frederick D. Langenheim, curator for the Numismatic and Antiquarian Society of Philadelphia wrote on 11 April 1895 to Daniel Garrison Brinton that Dalton Dorr, of the Philadelpia Museum and School of Industrial Arts, would like for the Society to deposit the coin collection which was on deposit with them. He would "give your society a receipt accompanied by a detailed descriptive list" should the Society agree to the transfer.[155] This was, it seems, agreed upon and Dorr wrote Brinton on 15 April that Langenheim would give Brinton a list of the coins and medals "which he has selected as being (presumably) the property of the Philosophical Society." Each coin, "except the rubbish," was individually boxed and Dorr would sign the receipt for the coins[157] as soon as the Society approved of the list.

The list was sent on 19 April and the corrspondence was read at the meeting of 19 April. The members authorized the curators to examine the list and "to take a receipt for them from the Pennsylvania Museum, as a deposit in that institution."[158] Brinton then wrote Patterson Du Bois 24 April and asked that a curators meeting be convened as soon as possible to expedite the matter.[159] Du Bois replied on 24 April that he was ill but proposed to call the meeting "early next week." He thought James Cheston Morris might familiarize himself with the documents which the curators should consult. Du Bois did not wish to commit himself to the transfer "without more definite knowledge" of what had been deposited.[160] Brinton promptly replied on 25 April that the transaction concerned merely the Society's coin and medal collection which was "placed in the P[ennsylvani]a Mus[eum], & which is specified on the receipt we accept. All other coins and medals of the Society in the Numismatic and Antiquarian Society[161] remain as the property of the American Philosophical Society.

 The curators reported on 17 May and were requested to continue "their identification and examination" before taking the Museum's receipt. They were given power to act when satisfied.[162] J. Cheston Morris, Richard Meade Bache, and Patterson Du Bois wrote Langenheim on 10 June 1895 that 95 coins and medals were missing from the listing. They asked that the Numismatic and Antiquarian Society "will take such measures as may be deemed by it best to recover the absent specimens." The curators promised all possible cooperation in this endeavour.[163] On 17 June a reply was written by Langenheim stating that he was searching for the missing items and would report to them as soon as possible.[164] Among the items received by the Pennsylvania Museum on 22 October 1895 was one "Large Coin Cabinet."[165] The coins must have been found, for on 25 October 1895 Dalton Dorr wrote that he had another page of the list of coins and medals, which should be affixed to the original list and that he would then sign a receipt for all for the Pennsylvania Museum and School of Industrial Art.[166] Other coins and medals remained missing, however, for on 5 November, 1895 Dorr wrote that he had spent fifteen years getting the deposit of coins to the Museum to the present stage. He promised to "look out for" such coins and medals which, as yet, had not been located by the Numismatic and Antiquarian Society.[167] On 6 December Curator Morris proposed a resolution that "such medals and casts" as the Society had title to, be deposited with the Pennsylvania Museum.[168] By 10 December, Dorr had received the coins and medals and issued an invitation to the officers and members of the Society for a private viewing of them.[169] Dorr wrotet he next day thanking the Society for depositing its collection with the Pennsylvania Museum.[170]

 Meanwhile, Langenheim continued to search for the missing coins and medals and wrote J. Cheston Morris on 20 December 1895 that he would report on this search, [171] "in time for your January meeting." Some undated lists of the 1890s are in the Archives, listing the coins and medals wanting from the listing provided by the Numismatic and Antiquarian Society. As the missing item was found, it was marked as being found on some of these lists.[172] The coins and medals were in the cabinet in the Pennsylvania Museum by 17 March[173] and by 24 March Curator Morris was asked to visit the Museum to check the items against the list.[174] A formal invitation was delivered to the curators 25 March 1898 for "a visit of inspection of our deposits in Memorial Hall."[175] Also, a comprehensive listing of 910 coins and medals, including the cabinet for them, was signed and received 3 April 1896.[176] The curators reported on 10 April that all of the coins and medals, with two exceptions, were now in the Pennsylvania Museum.[177]

 The Pennsylvania Museum had Hans M. Wilder examine these coins and medals; Dorr wrote Morris on 25 August 1898 that the coin "GeoIII Caroline?" was "a copy of the famous Jerrigan's Citizen medal."[178] Wilder wrotehis report to Morris 4 September:

The one marked "Fiorino" is an ordinary Florin [Italy] worth 100 Quattrini (so marked). It was one of the very first denominations struck in 1859, under the provisional Government but otherwise not different from the usual florin.

The "Sanct Vult" (Lucca) is probably a "Barbone" (12 Soldi).

That Indian Rubber from Valparaiso, marked "F. U." is a tramway ticket— PRIMERO FERROCARRIL (URBANO). The number is merely the numbering of the office, just as the numbers on our R[ail] R[oad] tickets.

You showed me another coin struck in commemoration of something (I forget now, what it was) this coin was, similarly to the florin, struck among the first at the change of the Government: otherwise an ordinary coin.

He then wrote of eleven plaster casts, identifying them.[179]

A typed list of 24 items was made on 13 December 1899 and the Society received it: "A Collection of twenty-four bronze medals, plaster casts of medals, gilt medal, iron casts and various coins, numbered and described."[180]   A medal in honor of Edward Jenner which had been issued by the Kings County Medical Society of New York was presented by George Wharton Pepper on 20 November 1896.   The trustees of Princeton University presented a bronze "medal of the University" struck in honor of its sesquicentennial on 19 February 1896.[182]

On 1 October 1897, the executors of the estate of Henry Phillips, Jr., presented two medals and several coins to the Society. At a meeting of the curators on 8 November 1898 J. Cheston Morris delivered this gift of "2 medals & lots of coins." `It was decided that as soon as enough had been received from any source, all such gifts were to be deposited with the other coins and medals in the Pennsylvania Museum and School of Industrial Art. By 13 December twenty-four items had been received and were then deposited.[183]

The Numismatic and Antiquarian Society of Philadelphia presented a medal honoring Eli Kirk Price on 19 January 1900 and thanks were returned for it. Evidently each society had forgotten that this Price medal had been given to the American Philosophical Society in 1879. The medal was ordered framed and hung on the wall.[184] A medal which had been struck in honor of the recent anniversary of Sir George Gabriel Stokes, was received 16 March 1900. The curators were told "to withdraw from deposit all medals struck in honor or to the memory of members of the Society" and to frame and hang them. Henry Pettit wrote J. Cheston Morris on 5 December 1900 that all medals in Philosophical Hall should be kept in the safe, or else be framed and hung.[186]   The curators reported on 7 December 1900 that a medal of Daniel Garrison Brinton issued by the Numismatic and Antiquarian Society of Philadelphia had been received during the year.[187]

On 24 January 1901 additions to the bequest of Henry Phillips, Jr., came to the Society from R. D. Maxwell., executor. Acad Emiae Suae Georgiae Augustae Decord Aet Erno, with Carolus F. Gauss in profile; an Augustin Dupre copper medal with the bust of Benjamin Franklin to the left; some medals which had been sold at the London Exposition of 1851; three Freemasonry medals; a George III copper medal of 1797; a medal in white metal noting the assassination of Abraham Lincoln; and, the Philadelphia Centennial medal of [See also date of 1 October 1897 for notice of the first gift from the estate.]

Preparations for the celebration of the bicentennary of the birth of Benjamin Franklin began early and on 5 February 1904 Isaac Minis Hays reported that" the bill introduced into Congress" for "the striking of a medal" on this occasion was in progress. The medal was struck in 1906 and one was presented, in accordance with the act of Congress, to the Republic of France. Jean Adrien Antoine Jules Jusserand, the French ambassador to the United States, accepted it on 20 April 1906 in Philosophical Hall.[189] On 18 May the members determined that these medals were to be distributed by the committee on the Franklin Bicentennial and medals were sent to various institutions which had sent an address to the Society commemorating Franklin, or had a connection with Franklin: Franklin and Marshall College was named for Franklin; the Library Company of Philadelphia was founded by Franklin; the Masonic Grand Lodge of Massachusetts (Franklin was a mason); Pennsylvania Hospital, which was founded by Franklin; and, William and Mary College which gave Franklin an honorary degree.

The Academie des Sciences, Inscription et Belles Lettres de Toulouse; Anthropologische Gesellschaft zu Berlin; Institute of Engineers and Shipbuilders of Glascow; Johns Hopkins University; K. B. Gesellschaft der Wissenschaften, Prague; State Library of Pennsylvania; Physical Society of London; Reale Academia de Historia, Madrid; Physical Section of the Chemical-Physical Society of the Imperial University of St. Petersburg; Societa Italiana delle Scienze, Rome; Societe Internationale des Electriciens, Paris; Societe Royale de Botanique de Belgique; and the Society of Natural Sciences of Buffalo all received medals, as did the governor of Pennsylvania who was a guest, Abbe Cleveland, George F. Baer, Henry G. Bryant, Viscount James Bryce, Mr. Goss, president of the Scoville manufacturing Company, Waterbury, Connecticut, Charles C. Harrison, Horace Jayne, William W. Keen, J. Rodman Paul, Joseph G. Rosengarten, and Stuart

Wood.[190]   Subsequently, the Society has honored, and continues to so honor, personages from time to time, with this Franklin medal.

28 April 1905
A medal by Dupre "struck in honor of Benjamin Franklin in 1784."

Harrison Morrison

7 February 1908
A silver impression of this same medal.

Richard Alexander Fullerton Penrose, Jr.

3 November 1905
Six masonic medals.

George Rupp

The two-hundredth anniversary of Linnaeus was celebrated by the Royal Academy of Sciences of Stockholm and a medal which was designed by Eric Lindberg, was struck upon this occasion and arrived 20 December 1907.

The committee on general meetings requested 13 March 1908 that the council" consider the advisability of the Society granting a medal in honor of original work." This was referred to a committee.[191] On 8 May Charles Frederick Scott, Eric Doolittle and Amos Peaslee Brown were named the committee. The report was accepted as favorable on 4 May 1909 and the council "voted that the report be favorably recommended to the Society.[192] The medal was not issued.

3 November 1911
A bronze medal "inhonor of the American people and the City of San Francisco" which was struck by the French government "in commemoration of the Earthquake of 1906."

Richard A. F. Penrose, Jr.

Miss Aline Garesche, the last surviving descendant of Peter Stephen Din Ponceau, presented on 2 February 1912 the medal her ancestor won in 1836 as the Volney Prize from the Institut de France, as well as the Cross of the Royal Miliary Order of St. Louis, instituted by Louis XIV in 1693. Leslie William Miller and Samuel Dickson spoke of this gift.[193]

On 24 May 1921 Marie Sklodowska Curie was presented "as a souvenir of this evening" one of the Franklin Bicentennial medals.

7 October 1921
A commemorative medal of the founding of the University of Virginia.

Edwin Anderson Alderman

A medal which "Commemorated Fifty Years of Service to the Commonwealth" which was designedby V. D. Brenner in 1904.

The University of Wisconsin

3 November 1922
The SesquiCentennial medal of the Belgian Academie des Sciences, Belles Lettres et Arts was received.

7 December 1923
A medal struck in commemoration of the Twentieth International Congress of Americanists at Rio de Janiero.

5 April 1926
The Geological Society of London's medal honoring Sir Charles Lyell, designed by L. C. Wyon in 1884.

Joseph Leidy

The council of the Society learned on 19 November 1926 that a gold medal honoring Thomas Balch had been authorized to be awarded "for distinguished service by writing or by active participation in affairs of internationl law or international relations, especially international arbitration."[194]

With the purchase and gift of the immense collection of papers of Charles Willson Peale and his family in 1945 came a medal struck on only one side, made of white metal, depicting three famous Philadelphia physicians in profile: Benjamin Rush, Philip Syng Physick, and Caspar Wistar.[195]

At the annual fall meeting on 17 October 1946, Spridon Dontas of the Athenian Academy presented two bronze medals commemorating the centennial of theArchaeological Society in Athens, Greece, and the Athenian Academy.[196]

In 1952, following the death of Edwin Grant Conklin, two medals were received: one had been presented to Conklin by the National Academy of Sciences in 1943—the John J. Carty medal, and a gold medal which had been presented by the National Institute of Social Sciences.

The Society purchased in 1954 the Benjamin Franklin collection of coins and medals which had been assembled by Abraham Simon Wolfe Rosenbach, the noted rare book dealer.[197]

In 1954 Mrs. George Shull presented a collection including the gold medal which had been awarded her husband, George Harrison Shull, in recognition of his outstanding contribution to agriculture. "That for the origination of hybrid corn" on 29 November 1940 by the De Kalb Agricultural Association; the John C. Scott medal of the city of Philadelphia; and,the National Academy of Sciences Marcellus Hartley medal.[198]

In 1955 medals and twelve plaster casts were purchased:

Adam Smith by designer J. H. Ponscarme for the centennial of the printing of The Wealth Nations

Three contemporary medals honoring the [Joseph Michel and Jacques Etie'nne] Montgolfier brothers' balloon flights

Twelve plaster casts honoring Chretien Guillaume de Lamoignon de Malesherbes, Jean Jacques Rousseau, Comte Honore Gabriel Riquetide Mirabeau, Antoine Laurent Lavoisier, Francois Marie Arouet de Voltaire and Jean-Jacques Rousseau, Marie Antoinette and Louis XVI, Andre Ernest Modeste Gretry, Palladius [Andrea Palladio], les sciences et les arts, Napoleon Bonaparte, Lebrun Cambageres, P. Jolyot de Crebillon, and A. Lagarde de Houlieres.

These last are of English manufacture and were made in Kensington during the reign of George III.

The Poor Richard Club of Philadelphia awarded its fiftieth anniversary medal "for merit" to the Society in 1956.[199] A Benjamin Franklin medal, in white metal, was purchased in 1956.[200]

In 1957 Arthur Bloch presented two United States pennies of 1787. This was the first coin issued by the United States and is called the "Franklin cent," owing to the inscription "Mind Your Own Business" stamped thereon.[201]

With the presentation of the manuscripts of Lewis M. Haupt by his descendant, Miss B. M. Haupt, in 1957, came the Magellanic gold medal which the Society had awarded Haupt for his work on the protection of harbors.[202] Also in 1957 a medal of Lavoisier was purchased. [203]

In 1961 the Societe d'Anthropologie de Paris medal honoring Comte Georges Louis LeClerc de Buffon was received.[204] In that same year, the "Fugio Penny," the "first coin of the United States. Coin authorized by Congress July 6, 1787" facsimile was purchased.[205]

Hans T. Clarke presented in 1964 a two deutsche mark piece of the Bundes republik Deutschland, 1947, depicting Max Planck, and a bronze medal of the Deutsche Akademie der Wissenschaften zur Berlin honoring Max Planck.[206]

The Society began in the 1960s an active policy of collecting papers of eminent scientists. Medals sometimes are included in these collections and they are with the Coin and Medal Collection which is now in the possession of the Society. This small collection is, basically, a recent accumulation, although a few of the medals which were presented earlier are included.

The Rockefeller Institute and James Thomas Flexner in 1964 presented Simon Flexner's papers. Two medals of the 1929 XIII International Physiological Congress, Boston, 1929; an award of the Institut de France, 1937; Institut de France Emile Picard medal "cinquantenaire de son election;" and the Third International Congress for Microbiology medal with Theobald Smith on the obverse were included with the manuscripts.[207]

In 1956 the Society purchased drawings and matrices of medals relating to the American Revolution and the United States by Augustin Dupre. These are described and illustrated in Carl Zigrosser, "Medallic Sketches of Augustin Dupre in American Collections" (*Proceedings,* vol. 101, pp 535ff).

With the collection of Victor George Heiser's papers in 1966 came a small metal box with several aluminum coins for the Culion Leper colony in the Philippine Islands. Dr. Heiser helped with the founding of the colony and he had designed the coins. Also included in this gift was the Order of the White Elephant medal which the king of Siam had awarded him.[208]

With the collection of Wolfgang Kohler's papers in 1967 came the Princeton University Bicentennial bronze medai.[209]   Mrs. Alfred Bendiner presented two medals in 1969 which had been owned by her grandfather, Charles Moore Wheatley: the medals honored the New York Exhibition of the Industry of All Nations 1853–1854 and the Philadelphia Centennial Exhibition of 1876.[210]

From the estate of Isaac Minis Hays came a copy of the 1906 Franklin medal, which the Society had presented to him, the City of Philadelphia medal with William Penn on it (presented in 1908 to Hays), and the Cross of the Royal and Military Order of St. Louis, instituted by Louis XIV in 1693.[211]

The Society determined to dispose of what had been returned by the Pennsylvania Museum of its coin and medal collection in January 1967. Medals of scientists and Franklin coins were retained, however. A dealer was asked to make an offer, but she could not offer much, for "the condition of the coins and medals is a large determinant in their saleable value. A few pieces would command considerably more but they turned out to have only one side, with reverse completely worn off."[212] This was, basically, the same view held by Henry Grundthal, curator of European and ModernCoins, American Numismatic Society. He listed the items, with values; the Society accepted his offer and sold them on 9 April 1973:

England. Box with 3 tin medals. About 1870
6 Islamic silver coins
Virginia half penny
Iowa lodge medal
Russia. 10 Kopecks 1778
Miscellaneous copper coins of little commercial value
Box with late Roman copper coins
5 Siamese tokens
1853 large cent
French minor coins
Japanese Itzebu
Dollar 18590
Massachusetts. Oak tree shilling
2 half cents in poor condition
Trade dollars 1879, 1881, 1882, 1883 proofs
1835 large cent
1793 "   " Holed
1825 Half cent
1794 large cent, 1796 forgery
1787 Connecticut cent
New Jersey cent, Nova Caesarea
United States cent
1878 and 1879 pattern dollars
5 ordinary large cents

Miscellaneous foreign copper and minor silver coins.[213]

John Lewis Haney gave in 1970 the Philadelphia Central High School medal which had been awarded him for service. With Peyton Rous's papers, which were presented in 1970, came the Claude Bernard bronze medal. The Columbia University College of Physicians and Surgeons medal which was inscribed to Hans T. Clarke was included in the gift of Clarke's papers in 1970.[214]

A descendant of Colonel George Morgan, David McCord, gave on 14 May 1979, the gold medal of the Philadelphia Society for the Improvement of Agriculture which had been presented to Colonel Morgan. It had been made by James Trenchard.

At present, there are several medals which must have been presented to theSociety by the organization which ordered them struck. Provenance is lost. However,the Society exchanged publications with many learned societies, was active in the scholarly and scientific worlds, and was well-known as a learned society, so the medals were probably given as a matter of course.

In the present holdings of the Society are:

The Geological Society of London's medal honoring Sir Charles Lyell,designed by L. C. Wyon in 1884

The bicentennial medal of the Academie Nationale de Lyon in 1900

The 1906 Academy of Sciences of St. Louis medal honoring George Engelman, their first president

The medal of the Connecticut Historical Society honoring Thomas Robbins "as a special memorial of the occasion of the 100th anniversary of Robbins's death" in 1906

The dedication medal of the Carnegie Institute of Pittsburgh dated 11 April 1907

The Thomas Jefferson Memorial Association issued in 1908 a Jefferson medal

A bicentennary medal featuring Benjamin Franklin "COMMEMORATING THE 200TH ANNIVERSARY THE SATURDAY EVENING POST FOUNDED BY BENJAMIN FRANKLIN 1728–1928

The New Haven Tercentennary medal designed by Kilenyki

The University of Pennsylvania 1940

Bicentennial medal modelled by R. Tait McKenzie (2 copies)

The medal commemorating the 1941 Philadelphia Coin Club Convention 16–21 August, issued by the American Numismatic Association in honor of its fiftieth anniversary; in 1952 as a part of the American Patriots Series

The American Commemorative Society honoring Franklin's kite-flying experiment in the bicentennial year of the experiment

The 1951 Philadelphia Independence Homecoming Celebration of 1951 medal

The 1952 U. S. Congress medal honoring Franklin on the 250th anniversary of his birth

The 1956 medal commemorating the naming of the Benjamin Franklin bridge connecting Philadelphia and Camden, New Jersey

The 1963 centennial medal of the National Academy of Sciences (two copies)

The 1881 University of Pennsylvania Wharton School of Finance and Economy honoring Joseph Wharton

The centennial medal of the Wyoming Historical & Geological Society with the profile of Jesse Fell and "Centennial of First Use of Wyoming Coal Feb. 11, 1908"

The bicentennial medal of Yale University issued in 1901

The University of Wisconsin's fiftieth anniversary medal 1904 "commemorating Fifty Year of Service to the Commonwealth."

Also in the Coins and Medals Collection, and with no provenance available, are medals of:

John Adams

Chicago Columbian Exposition, 1893

23 Benjamin Franklin medals (8 designed by Augustin Dupre)

9 of the Franklin Bicentennial issued by Congress

A Masonic medal designed by Bernier

One designed by Ralph J. Menconi

One of 1776 with the obverse showing a beaver gnawing on an oak tree

One with the motto: "A Penny Saved is a Penny Earned"

Two of Franklin and Moynton designed by Barre
King George VI medal for service
Hippocrates, designed by E. Du Bose
Horatio Gates
Selina Hastings, countess of Huntingdon
Two Thomas Jefferson medals designed by John Reich (one is a medal given to Indian
     chiefs)
John Paul Jones, designed by Augustin Dupre
Lafayette, issued in 1824
Jean Francois de La Harpe, issued by Galerie Metallique des Grands Hommes Francais
Henry Lee, designed by Joseph Wright
National Academy of Sciences
Louis Pasteur, designed by 0. Roly
William Penn, designed by Lewis Pingo
Petrus Alexiewitz (Peter the Great), designed by Du Vivier
Two Philadelphia Centennial Exposition (one of wood)
Philadelphia College of Medicine (fabric)
Two of William Pitt
Jules Henri Poincaire "Sousciption Internationale," designed by G. Prudhomme
Jean-Jacques Rousseau, designed by F. Dumarest
The Statue of Liberty "A Gift of the French Republic to the United States 1886:"
U. S. Sanitary Commission
George Washington "He is in glory, the world in tears," dated 1799, designed by Nicholas
     Pearce
Two of the sesquicentennial of Washington's initiation as a Freemason, A. L. 5902
One of Berlin iron with a metal loop at the top for hanging
Two of "Commis. Resigned: Presidency Relinq," centennial of inauguration as president of
     the United States, designed by Philip Martin (?) and copyrighted by Augustus Saint
     Gaudens
James Watt, issued by the Royal Cornwall Polytechnic Society Instituted 1833, designed
     by W. Wyon
George Whitfield "Died 30 Sept 1770 at 56 An Israelite Indeed A Good Soldier of Jesus
     Christ"
A medal commemorating the Wyoming Massacre, Pennsylvania[216]
          Even as the Society deposited its Coins and Medals Collection with the
Numismatic and Antquarian Society of Philadelphia, new gifts began arriving, and a new
coin and medal collection began. This collection was augmented with medals of scientists
removed from the original collection after the fragmented remains were returned to the
Society, and today there is a collection of approximately 300 items in the Coin and Medal
Collection catalogued in the Library.
          Of these items the following medals were probably presented before 1878:

J. J. F. Berzelius issued by K. Svenska Vetenskaps Akadicien, Stockholm
Matthew Boulton
Charles, marquis Cornwallis
Humphrey Davy, issued by the Royal Society of London to Robert Wilhelm Bunsen and
     Gustav Robert Kirchhoff
The opening of the Erie Canal
Benjamin Franklin (by Reich?)
Benjamin Franklin and George Washington (presented by Samson?)
Richard Howe, 1st earl
Elisha Kent Kane, issued by the Royal Geographic Society of London(?);
Lafayette presented by John Vaughan
Gottfried Wilhelm Leibniz, presented by the Akademie du Wissenschaften zu Berlin
John Napier, issued by the Royal Society of Edinburgh
Robert Maskell Patterson, issued by the U. S. Mint
George Peabody, presented by the Peabody Education Fund

Edward Preble by John Reich
David Rittenhouse by Barber
George Washington, presented by William Vaughan.
  Subsequent gifts and purchases of known provenance are:

Archaeological Society in Athens and Athenian Academy centennial medals presented by
  theSociety and the Academy
Belgian Academie de Sciences, Lettres et Arts Sesquicentennial medal presented by the
  Academie
Claude Bernard, presented withthe Peyton Rous Collection
Daniel Garrison Brinton, issued by the Numismatic and Antiquarian Society of
  Philadelphia
Columbia University College of Physicians andSurgeons award to Hans T. Clarke
  presented with the Clarke papers
Culion lepercolony coins presented with the Victor George Heiser Papers
De Kalb Agricultural Association medal awarded George Harrison Shull
Volney Prize medal of the Institut de France presented to Peter Stephen Du Ponceau and the
  Cross of the Royaland Military Order of St. Louis, both presented by Du Ponceau's
  descendant Aline Garesche
Benjamin Franklin, purchased 1956 (127 coins and medals purchased as the A. S. W.
  Rosenbach Collection of Frankliniana)
Two Franklin Institute medals awarded to (both in the Rosenbach collection)
Benjamin Franklin, three medals on freemasonry and George III presented by the estate of
  Henry Phillips, Jr.
Institut de France medal to Simon Flexner and Institut de France medal honoring Charles
  E. Picard, both from the Simon Flexner collection
Thomas Jefferson, presented by the Thomas Jefferson Memorial Association
Thomas Jefferson, presented by the University of Virginia
Antoine Laurent Lavoisier, purchased 1957
Abraham Lincoln, presented by Henry Phillips, Jr., estate
American Philosophical Society Magellanic Premium awarded Lewis Muhlenberg Haupt
The Edward Jenner medal which was presented by the Medical Society of the County of
  Kings
Three Montgolfier brothers medals, purchased in 1955, commemorating their balloon
  flights
The National Academy of Sciences John J. Carty medal awarded to Edwin G. Conklin
The National Academy of Sciences Marcellus Hartley medal awarded George H. Shull
The National Institute of Social Sciences award to Edwin G. Conklin
The New York Exhibition of the Industry of All Nations presented by Mrs. Alfred
  Bendiner
City of Philadelphia award to Isaac Minis Hays
City of Philadelphia John C. Scott medal awarded to George H. Shull
City of Philadelphia Central High School award to John Lewis Haney
Philadelphia Society for the Improvement of Agriculture award to George Morgan
Philadelphia Centennial Exhibition medals presented by the estate of Henry Phillips, Jr.
  and Mrs. Alfred Bendiner
Max Planck medal issued by the Akademie der Wissenschaften zu Berlin, and a Max
  Planck two deutsch mark coin, both presented by Hans T. Clarke
Poor Richard Club of Philadelphia fiftieth anniversary medal presented by the Club
Eli Kirk Price, issued by the Numismatic and Antiquarian Society of Philadelphia (2
  copies)
Sesquicentennial medal of Princeton University, presented in 1896
Bicentennial of Princeton University with the Wolfgang Kohler collection (2 copies)
BenjaminRush, Philip Syng Physick and Caspar Wistar on a medal with the Charles
  Willson Peale collection
French Rpublic medal to the people of the United States on the San Francisco earthquake
  and fire of 1906

Adam Smith, purchased in 1955
Theobald Smith with the Simon Flexner collection
Comte Georges L. Leclerc de Buffon from the Societe Anthropologie de Paris
The Statue of Liberty medal
Sir George Gabriel Stokes received in 1900
Two copies of Johann K. F. Gauss medal presented by Henry Phillips's estate
Linnaeus, presented by the K. Svenska Akademie Selskab (?)
The Order of the White Elephant given with the Victor George Heiser collection
Two copies of the XIII International Physiological Congress, Boston, 1929, presented
   with the Simon Flexner collection.[216]

COINS AND MEDALS—References
1. *Trans.*, vol. 2.
2. *Ibid.*, vol. 4.
3. *Ibid.*
4. *Archives.* J Vaughan. List, 15 May 1801; Trans., vol. 6.
5. Com. Rec., vol. 1.
6. Verbal communications.
7. Com. Rec., vol. 1.
8. Donations to Cabinet.
9. *Ibid.;* Com. Rec., vol. 2.
10. *Archives.* T. Jefferson to C. Wistar, 20 June 1806.
11. *Trans.*, vol. 6.
12. Donations to Cabinet, p. 39; Trans., vol. 6.
13. *Ibid.*, p. 20; Trans., vol. 6, p. 20 and new series, vol. 1, p. xliii.
14. *Ibid.;* Trans., vol. 6, pp. 21-22.
IS. *Donations Book; Trans.*, n. s., vol. 1.
16. *Archives.* C. W. Lewis to B. S. Barton, 17 April 1810.
17. Donations Book; Trans., n. s., vol. 1; Donations to Cabinet, p.33.
18. Donations Book.
19. *Proc.*, vol. 5, p. 247.
20. *Ibid.*, p. 255
21. *Ibid.*, p. 264.
22. *Archives.* G. Parish to C. B. Trego, 21 Jan. 1853.
23. *Proc.*, vol. 5, pp. 310, 313.
24. *Ibid.*, p. 314.
25. *Donations Book;* Com. Rec., vol. 2; Trans., n. s., vol. 1.
26. *Archives.* J. Cist to J. Vaughan, 17 Aug. 1818.
27. Donations Book; Donations to Cabinet, p. 33 under date of 21 Aug. 1838; Cur. Don.
Book; *Trans.*, n. s., vo.. 2.
28. *Archives.* C. A. Rodney to P. S. Du Ponceau, 6 Aug. 1818.
29. *Donations Book*; Donations to Cabinet, p. 33; Trans., n. s., vol. 2.
30. *Ibid.*
31. *Donations Book.* Cur. Don. Book; Trans., n. s., vol. 2.
32. Historical and Literary Committee. Letterbooks, vol. 2, p. 47.
33. *Archives.* W. Short to J. Vaughan, 20 Oct. 1824; Don. Book; Cur. Don. Book;
Trans., n. s., vol. 2.
34. Donations to Cabinet, p. 39 under date of 24 Oct. 1826.
35. *Donations Book* Donations to Cabinet, p. 39; Trans., n. s., vol. 3.
36. *Donations Book ;Trans.*, n. s., vol. 3.
37. *Donations Book.*
38. *Archives* . P. Pedersen to J. Vaughan, 6 Feb. 1829; Don Book; Trans., n. s., vol.3.
39. *Donations Book; Trans.*, n. s., vol. 3.
40. *Archives.* H. Middleton to J. Vaughan, 13 April 1831; Trans., n. s., vol. 4.
41. *Donations Book;* 6 May 1831; Cur. Donation Book.
42. *Archives* . N. Collin to J. Vaughan, 28 June 1831; Don. to Cabinet, 16 Sept. 1831.
43. *Ibid.* Dannery to APS, 30 Jan. 1832.
44. *Ibid.* P. S. Du Ponceau to J. Vaughan, 6 July 1832; *Donations Book,* 17 Aug. 1823; Donations to Cabinet, p. 18; *Trans.*, n. s., vol.
4.
45. *Archives* . C. Nagy to J. Vaughan, 20 Aug. 1833; *Donations Book;* Donations to Cabinet; Trans., n. s., vol. 4.
46. *Donations Book;* Donations to Cabinet, p. 41; Trans., n. s., vol. 5.
47. *Ibid.;* Trans., n. s., vol. 5.
48. *Archives* . J. J. Barclay to C. C. Biddle, 1 July 1834.
49. *Ibid.* APS. Report, Sept. 1834; Donations to Cabinet, pp. 16–17.
50. *Ibid.* M. Burrough to APS, 2 Oct. 1834.
51. *Trans.*, n. s., vol. 5.
52. Donations to Cabinet, p. 18.
53. *Donations Book; Trans.*, n. s., vol. 5; Donations to Cabinet, p. 40.
54. *Ibid.;* Trans., n. s., vol. 5; Donations to Cabinet, pp. 5-6, 19–20.
55. *Archives* . APS. Report, 20 March 1835.
56. *Ibid.*, 1 May 1835.
57. *Ibid.;* Donations to Cabinet, p. 20.
58. *Donations Book; Trans.*, n. s., vol. 5; Donations to Cabinet, pp. 9–10.
59. *Archives* . W. B. Hodgson to P. 5. Du Ponceau; 10 April 1835.
60. *Ibid.* W. B. Hodgson. List of coins, 10 April 1835.
61. Com. Recs., vol. 2.

63. *Proc.,* vol. 1, p. 6; Com. Recs., vol. 2.
63. Donations to Cabinet, p. 33.
64. *Archives* . M. Nisbet to F. Bache, 2 Oct. 1838.
65. Franklin Papers. E. Rouvert to F. Bache, 27 June 1840.
66. *Cur. Recs.* J. Lynah to APS, 15 Sept. 1838; *Proc.,* vol. 1, p. 43; Trans., n. s., vol. 6; Donations to Cabinet, p. 32.
67. *Proc.,* vol. 1, p. 70; Com. Recs., vol. 2.
78. *Donations Book*
69. *Proc.,* vol. 1, p. 181.
70. *Ibid.*
71. *Proc.,* vol. 1, p. 187.
72. *Archives* . J. P. Brown to P. 5. Du Ponceau, 10 April 1840.
73. *Proc.,* vol. 1, p. 261; Don. Book; Trans., n. s., vol. 7.
74. Trans., n. s., vol. 6.
75. *Proc.,* vol. 2, p. 24.
76. *Archives* . W. Vaughan to J. Vaughan, 7 April 1841; Misc. MS. Col. W. Vaughan to J. Vaughan, 2 April 1841.
77. *Donations Book.*
78. Donations to Cabinet, p. 10.
79. *Proc.,* vol. 2, p. 149; Don. Book; Trans., n. s., vol. 8.
80. *Ibid.,* p. 201.
81. *Ibid.,* p. 222.
82. *Archives* . J. D. Ellicott to W. H. Dillingham, 4 Nov. 1842.
83. *Proc.,* vol. 4, p. 135; Don. Book, 5 Jan. 1844; Trans., n. s., vol. 9.
84. *Ibid.,* pp. 145–190.
85. *Ibid.,* p. 173.
86. *Ibid.,* pp. 200–201.
87. *Ibid.,* p. 294; *Donations Book.*
88. *Ibid.,* p. 298.
89. *Archives* . Royal Society of Edinburgh to APS, 1 July 1848; *Proc.,* vol. 15, pp. 166–167; *Donations Book.*
90. *Proc.,* vol. 5, p. 143.
91. *Ibid.,* p. 147.
92. *Archives* . K. Svenska Vetenskaps Akademien to APS, 10 Oct. 1850; Proc., vol. 5, p. 233; *Donations Book.*
93. *Proc.,* vol. 5, p. 170.
94. See gift of coins of 6 July 1832.
95. *Proc.,* vol. 5, p. 195.
96. *Ibid.,* pp. 198–200.
97. *Ibid.*
98. *Ibid.,* p. 218.
99. *Ibid.,* p. 230.
100. *Ibid.,* p. 269; Don. Book.
101. *Archives* . W. H. Dillingham to F. Fraley, 16 Dec. 1853.
102. *Ibid.* F. Fraley to C. B. Trego, 17 Dec. 1853.
103. *Proc.,* vol. 6, p. 139.
104. *Ibid.,* pp. 154–155.
105. *Ibid.,* pp. 171–172.
106. *Ibid.,* p. 184.
107. *Ibid.,* pp. 198, 200; *Donations Book.*
108. *Ibid.,* vol. 6, p. 205.
109. *Ibid.,* p. 215
110. *Ibid.,* pp. 308–309; *Donations Book.*
111. *Ibid.,* vol.6, p. 320.
112. *Ibid.,* vol. 8, pp. 263-264.
113. *Archives.* J. J. Cohen to J. P. Lesley, 23 Oct. 1862; Proc., vol. 9, p. 92.
114. *Donations Book.*
115. *Proc.,* vol. 9, pp. 242-258; Com. Recs., vol. 2.
116. *Ibid.,* vol. 9, p. 375.
117. *Ibid.,* p. 425.
118. *Ibid.,* vol. 10, p. 118; Com. Recs., vol. 2.
119. *Proc.,* vol. 9, pp. 487–490.
120. *Ibid.,* pp. 490–495.
121. *Ibid.,* vol. 10, p. 3.
122. *Ibid.,* pp. 6, 8, 204.
123. *Archives.* Mr. Moore to J. C. Cresson, 24 July 1866; *Proc.,* vol. 10, p. 270.
124. *Proc.,* vol. 10, p. 540; *Donations Book.*
125. *Ibid.,* vol. 11, pp 233-34.
126. *Ibid.,* p. 282.
127. *Archives.* W. Barber to APS, IS May 1871.
128. *Proc.,* vol. 12, p. 160.
129. *Ibid.,* pp. 224–228; *Donations Book.*
130. *Ibid.,* vol. 13, p. 260.
131. *Ibid.,* vol. 14, p. 16.
132. *Ibid.,* p. 17.
133. *Ibid.,* p. 16.
134. Officers and Council. Minutes.
135. *Proc.,* vol. 16, p. 197.
136. *Ibid.,* pp. 280–281. For article, see pp. 293–298.
137. Officers and Council. Minutes.
138. *Proc.,* vol. 16, p. 334; Officers and Council. Minutes, 10 Nov. 1876.
139. *Ibid.,* vol. 16, p. 335.
140. *Ibid.,* vol. 17, pp. 313-14.
141. *Ibid.,* vol. 18, pp. 38-39.
142. *Ibid.,* p. 62.
143. *Archives.* Numismatic and Antiquarian Societey of Phildelphia. Resolution, 5 Dec. 1878; and, Numismatic...Society to J. P. Lesley, 6 Dec. 1878; *Proc.,* vol. 18, pp. 86–87.
144. *Proc.,* vol. 18, pp. 87-88.
145. *Archives.* Numismatic...Society. Receipt, 19 Dec. 1878.

146. *Proc.*, vol. 18, pp. 183, 191-206.
147. *Ibid.*, p. 218.
148. *Ibid.*, vol. 18, p 352.
149. *Ibid.*, p. 378.
150. *Ibid.*, vol. 19, p. 196.
151. *Ibid.*, vol. 22, pp. 158-59; "Arch." W. M. Davis to H. Phillips, Jr., 22 Oct. 1885; Curators Cards.
152. *Archives*. F. Fraley to H. Philllips Jr., 16 March 1893.
153. *Ibid.* F. D. Kramer to J. C. Morris, 17i March 1893.
154. *Ibid.*, H. R. Storer to H. Phillips, Jr., 23 Jan. 1895.
155. *Ibid.* Numismatic....Society to D. G. Brinton, 11 April 1895.
156. *Ibid.* D. Dorr to D. G. Brinton, 15 April 1895.
157. *Ibid.* Numismatic...Society to D. G. Brinton 19 April 1895.
158. *Proc.*, vol. 34, p. 166.
159. *Archives*. D. G. Brinton to P. Du Bois, 25 April 1895.
160. *Ibid.* P. Du Bois to D. G. Brinton, 24 April 1895.
161. *Ibid.* D. G. Brinton to P. Du Bois, 25 April 1895.
162. *Proc.*, vol. 34, pp. 338-39.
163. *Archives*. APS. Curators to F. D. Langenheim, 10 June 1895.
164. *Ibid.* Numismatic...Society to APS, 17 June 1895.
165. *Ibid.* Pennsylvania Museum and School of Industrial Art. Receipt 298, 22 Oct. 1895.
166. *Ibid.* Pennsylvania Museum and School of Industrial Art to APS, 23 Oct. 1895.
167. *Ibid.*, 5 Nov. 1895.
168. *Proc.*, vol. 34, p. 487.
169. *Ibid.* Pennsylvania Museum....to APS, 1O Dec. 1895.
170. *Ibid.* Pennsylvania Museum...to J. C. Morris, 11 Dec. 1895.
171. *Ibid.* F. D. Langenheim to J. C. Morris, 20 Dec. 1895. Some undated lists of the 1890s are in the Archives, listing the coins and medals wanting from the listing provided by the Numismatic...Society. See: APS. Curators list (there are five of these); also, Catalogue of coins; n. d.; also, List of lost medals, n. d. As the missing coin or medal was found, it was so marked on some of these lists.
172. *Ibid.* Pennsylvania Museum...Receipt, 11 March 1896.
173. *Ibid.* D. Dorr to J. C. Morris, 17 March 1896.
174. *Ibid.*, 24 March 1896.
175. *Ibid.* W. A. Ingham to APS, 25 March 1898.
176. *Ibid.* Pennsylvania Museum...List, 3 April 1896.
177. *Proc.*, vol. 35, p. 71.
178. *Archives*. Pennsylvania Museum...to J. C. Morris, 25 Aug. 1898.
179. *Ibid.* H. M. Wilder to J. C. Morris, 4 Sept. 1898.
180. *Proc.*, vol. 35, p. 297.
181. Curators Cards; Curators list, 13 Dec. 1899.
182. *Archives*. Curators Minutes, 8 Nov. 1899.
183. Ibid. Pennsylvania Museum...Receipt, 13 Dec. 1899; Curators. List of medals, 13 Dec. 1899; *Donations to Cabinet*, pp. 45–48.
184. *Proc.*, vol. 39, p. 68.
185. *Ibid.*, p. 95.
186. *Archives*. H. Pettit to J. C. Morris, 5 Dec. 1900.
187. *Ibid.* APS. Curators. Report, 7 Dec. 1900.
188. *Ibid.* R. D. Maxwell to APS, 24 Jan. 1901.
189. *Minutes*, 20 April 1906.
190. Officers and Council. Minutes.
191. *Ibid.*
192. *Ibid.*
193. *Proc.*, vol. 51, page v.
194. Officers and Council. Minutes.
195. *Yearbook*, 1945.
196. *Ibid.*, 1946.
197. *Ibid.*, 1954.
198. *Ibid.*
199. Card catalogue for Coins and Medals.
200. *Yearbook*, 1957.
201. *Ibid.*
202. Card catalogue for Coins and Medals.
203. *Ibid.*
204. *Ibid.*
205. *Yearbook*, 1947.
206. *Ibid.*, 1964.
207. *Ibid.*, 1966.
208. *Ibid.*
209. *Ibid.*, 1967.
210. *Ibid.*, 1969.
211. I.M.Hays estate, delivered ca. 1927.
212. *Archives*. C. E. Bullowa to G. D. Hess, 1 Feb. 1967.
213. *Ibid.* H. Grundthal. List, Feb. 1967.
214. Yearbook, 1970.
215. *Ibid.*
216. Card Catalogue for Coins and Medals

Chapter 5
Fossils

In the eighteenth century fossils were considered as a part of the study of mineralogy. The first Encyclopedia published in America defined fossils as, in general, everything dug out of the earth, whether they be natives thereof or extraneous.

Native fossils acording to Dr. [Sir John?] Hill, are substances found either buried in the earth, or lying on its surface of a plane simple structure, and showing no signs of containing vessels or circulating juices...

Extraneous fossils are bodies of the vegetable or animal kingdoms accidently buried in the earth. Of the vegetable kingdom, there are principally three kinds, trees or parts of them, herbaceous plants, and corals; and of the animal kingdom there are four kinds, seashells, the teeth or bony palates and bones of fishes, complete fishes, and the bones of land animals...

These adventitious or extraneous fossils, thus found buried in great abundance in divers parts of the earth, have employed the curiosity of several of our latest naturalists, who have each their several systems to account for the surprising appearances of petrified seafishes, in places far remote from the sea, and on the tops of mountains; shells in the middle of qarries of stone; and of elephants teeth, and bones of divers animals, peculiar to the southern climates, and plants only growing in the east, found fossil in our northern and western parts.

Some will have these shells, &c., to be the real stone, and stone plants, formed after the usual manner of other figured stones...

Another opinion is, that these fossil shells, with all their foreign bodies found within the earth, as bones, trees, plants, &c. were buried therein at the time of the universal deluge...

Others think, that those shells, found at the tops of the highest mountains, could never have been carried thither by the waters, even of the deluge...They imagine, that a year's continuance of the waters of the deluge, intermixed with the salt waters of the sea, upon the surface of the earth, might well give occasion to the production of shells of divers kinds in different climates...

Others think, that the waters of the sea, and, the rivers, with those which fell from heaven, turned the whole surface of the earth upside down; after the same manner as the waters of the Loire, and other rivers, which roll in a sandy bottom... and that in this general subversion, the shells came to be interred here, fishes there, &c.

Dr. [John] Woodward, in his Natural History of the Earth, pursuing and improving the hypothesis, of Dr. Burnet, maintains the whole mass of earth with everything belonging thereto, to have been so broken and dissolved at the time of the deluge, that a new earth was then formed on the bosom of the water, consisting of different strata, or beds of terrestrial matter, ranged over each other usually according to the order of their specific gravities. By this means, plants, animals, and especially fishes and shells, not yet dissolved among the rest, remain mixed and blended among the mineral and fossil matters; which preserved them, or at the least assumed and retained their figures and impressions either indentedly, or in relievo.[1]

This concern for the unexplainable fossils was not new. John Ray, the famous English naturalist, and naturalist Francis Willoughby attempted to create a systematic description of the whole of the organic world. This work in zoology was practically the first original such work since Aristotle. In 1691 Ray published *Wisdom of God Manifested in the Works of Creation* and in 1692 Ray's *Miscellaneous Discourses Concerning the Dissolution and Changes of the World,* wherein he stated that fossils were the remains of once living creatures. Geologist and physician John Woodward followed and agreed with him in his 1695 *Essay Towards a Natural History of the Earth.*

The antlers of the great Irish elk concerned many philosophers at the end of the seventeenth century. A native of western Europe, this extinct species had the most ponderous antlers of any known deer: some antlers spread ten feet wide. Numerous antlers were found in the peat bogs of Ireland. The Royal Society of London, following a discourse on the subject, concluded that the great American animal, the moose, was once common in Ireland. Totally enmeshed in the biblical creation legend, the philosophers concluded:

> That no real species of Living Creatures is so utterly extinct, as to be lost entirely out of the World, since it was first Created, is the opinion of many Naturalists; and 'tis grounded on so good a Principle of Providence taking Care in general of all its Animal Productions, that it deserves our Assent. However great Vicissitudes may be observed to attend the *Works* of Nature, as well as *Humane Affairs;* so that some entire *Species* of Animals, which have been formerly Common, nay even numerous in certain Countries; have, in Process of time, been so perfectly lost, as to become there utterly unknown; tho' at the same time it cannot be denied, but the hind has been carefully preserved in some other part of the World.[2]

In 1739, Charles le Moyne, Baron de Longueil, found the earliest fully documented discovery of fossil vertebrates [e.g., mastodons] in the present United States. The site was near the Ohio River above Louisville, Kentucky [Big Bone Lick]. The next year he returned to France and took the fossils with him, where they were eventually placed in the Jardin des Plantes.[3] Some fossil remains were commented upon by Americans as well. Benjamin Franklin wrote Jared Eliot on 16 July 1747 that the:

> great Apalachian [sic] Mountains, which run from York River back of these Colonies to the Bay of Mexico, show in many places near the highest Parts of them, Strata of Sea Shells, in some Places the Marks of them are in the solid Rocks. `Tis certainly the Wreck of a World we live on! We have Specimens of those Sea shell Rocks broken off near the Tops of those Mountains, brought and deposited in our Library [Company of Philadelphia] as Curiosities. If you have not seen the like, I'll send you a piece.[4]

John Bartram had reported these sea shells to Franklin, and even made a rough map to indicate their location on the high mountains far inland. On his return from Onondago in 1743, Bartram wrote Peter Collinson, of London, that he had seen such fossil shells over much of the country "even on top of the mountains that separates the waters of Susquehanna and Saint Lawrence."[5]

These fossil shells were interesting. David Rittenhouse burned a fossil shell and said that, from the smell of the smoke, it was a shell of an animal, not a mineral creation.[6] John Whitehurst wrote Franklin in 1763 that he was presenting "a few hints, relative to a general theory, or natural history of the earth; principally calculated to prove that fossil shells were originally the offspring of the sea.[7] These "hints" were the outline or summary of the first chapter of his *An Inquiry into the Original State and Formation of the Earth,* which was not printed for another fifteen years [1778].

Franklin, Rittenhouse, Bartram, and other members of the Society discussed fossils and accepted them as being relics of animal life during their "philosophical discussions" and must have spent much time on the conversations. In their rational way they accepted the artifacts as what they were—sea shells.[8] Later, while in France, Franklin wrote the Abbe Jean Louis Gerard Soulavie on 22 September 1782 that the location of "oyster shells mixed in the stone" in Derbyshire seemed proof that Britain had been below sea level at one time and was now elevated"[9]

It was, however, the discovery of the big bones of extinct animals that struck the most responsive chord in scientists. The learned world became particularly excited about the big bones occasionally brought back from the interior of America. Peter Collinson, for example, referred to an article about "the Elephant" [mastodon] in America in a letter to Franklin as early as 5 February 1749/50. Franklin wrote Collinson on 7 December 1762 that he was certain John Bartram had written him "concerning the great bones at the Ohio." Collinson asked Bartram to get more data about the huge bones of six monstrous animals and a "Great Buffalo" which Indian traders George Croghan and Joseph Greenwood located at a "licking place near the Ohio River." Bartram replied that it was a pity the owners of the land "did not send some person that will take pains to measure every bone exactly, before they are broken and carried away which they will soon be, by ignorant, careless people, for gain."

Croghan did ship some specimens, including tusks, to London in 1767 as gifts to Sir William Petty, first marquis of Lansdown and second sarl of Shelburne and to Benjamin Franklin. These great bones and "elephants teeth" pleased the Fellows of the Royal Society of London. Peter Collinson decided that they were from a vegetarian and separate species of elephant, distinct from the mammoth of Siberia as well as the the living creatures of Africa and Asia. The list of this shipment is given in the *Papers of Benjmin Franklin,* vol. 14, pp. 29–39.

Franklin thanked George Croghan in a letter of 15 August 1767 "for the box of elephants tusks and grinders," and marveled that such elephants had not left even a tradition. The American Revolution delayed the answering of these questions, but Thomas Jefferson began: and his *Notes on Virginia* was the reply, and fossils loom large in it. The mastodon or mammoth, Jefferson was sure, was the "largest of all terrestrial beings." He began efforts to collect old bones in 1782 and watched with pleasure the rising interest in remains of ancient animals throughout the country. The American Academy of Arts and Sciences published an account by Robert Annam of bones found on the banks of the Walkill, in New York during the Revolutionary War, and some of them found their way to Pierre Eugene Du Simitière and his museum in Philadelphia. Most of the big finds came from the west; Big Bone Lick continued to yield important collections of bones. However, it was on the Susquehanna that Rittenhouse discovered a tooth. A thigh bone found in New Jersey led the APS to encourage the exploration of that area but with no known result. Lewis Nicola delivered a paper, with drawings, before the APS in 1784 [14] which concerned bones then recently brought to Philadelphia from the Ohio. In this century, George Gaylord Simpson read an extensive and detailed paper on "The Beginnings of Vertebrate Paleontology in North America," with particular emphasis on the role of the APS, for the bicentennial celebration of the Society. He refers to the visit Colonel Nathaniel Ramsay made to Charles Willson Peale's museum and he heard Peale speak of the gigantic bones there. "They attracted the Colonel as he lifted, hefted and handled, speculating in wonder at them." He then stated, bluntly, that Peale should not concentrate on paintings for his museum, for "there were any number like himself... who would get more satisfaction from "such article of curiosity than any paintings, whatsoever."[16]

Like most of the other acquisitions to the Society's cabinet, the fossils were gifts. James McHenry presented on 2 May 1783 "a curious specimen of petrified pine."[17] Lewis Nicola made some observations, on 5 March 1784, regarding the petrified bones brought to Philadelphia by Major Isaac Craig from the region of the Ohio:[18] there were a thigh bone, tusk, and grinder. One year later, William Henry gave "an exceedingly large tusk and one of the grinders of some unknown species of animals," from the same general area of the Ohio.

David Rittenhouse presented on 1 December 1786 an extraordinarily large tooth of an unknown species of animal, but which "appeared to have been of the graminiverous kind" which was found on the banks of the Susquehanna at Tioga.[19] "It is entirely different from the large teeth frequently found on the Ohio.[20] It was given to Charles Willson Peale to have a drawing made which was published later under Peale's name in the *Columbian Magazine.*

On 5 October, 1787 a large thigh bone found near Woodbury Creek in Gloucester County, New Jersey, was described in a paper by Caspar Wistar and Timothy

Matlack. It was part of an unknown species of animal "of enormous size." The article stated that:

> By a comparison of measures, it appears, that the animal to which this bone belonged, must have exceeded in size the largest of those whose bones have been found on the Ohio, of which we have any account, in the proportion of about ten to seven; and must have been nearly double the ordinary size of the elephant.[21]

Wistar and Matlack, with John R. B. Rodgers, were told to search for the missing parts of the skeleton. Nothing seems to have been found. [In 1884 while preparing the Society's minutes for publication, J. Peter Lesley questioned whether this bone was from an hadrosaur].

These gifts attracted others, and on 3 October 1788 Matthias Barton of Lancaster sent "Shells & nuts &c. found at the depth of 7 or 8 feet in the body of a rock, upon the river Susquehanna." Great quantitites of such petrifactions were found in the neighborhood of Sunbury, Pennsylvania, in the high rocky hills. These were followed 20 February 1789 by a collection presented by Captain William Ferguson from Fort Vincennes of "curious petrifactions" and other such fossils from different parts of the West. Additional petrified shells were presented on 6 March 1789 by Reverend Mr. "Becson" [Beeson] from the area near Ringwood Iron Works, in New Jersey.

Timothy Matlack read a description of a large tusk from the West and exhibited two pieces of it on 18 March 1791. John Arndt, of Easton, forwarded a stone to Levi Hollingsworth who presented it to the Society on 16 December 1791. The stone

> was found beyond the Blue Mountains on a high hill running parallel to the Delaware River. This Stone contains a number of Petrified Shells & other Substances was forwarded to me & I wish it to be deposited amongst the Fossils of the Society.[22]

2 March 1792

Two impressions of echinus, or sea nettles, in limestone, sent "in order to obtain your Sentiment of their nature and Quality, whether they are the production of Nature or of art." Many opinions differed on just what they were and that was the reason they were sent to the philosophers. "If you Judge them worthy of your Notice, Please to favour me with the result of your agreement thereon."[23]

David Thomas

16 January 1795

Some petrifactions of wood from Martinique.

Mederic L. E. Moreau de Saint Mery

On 3 July 1796 Thomas Jefferson sent a fascinating account of

> a discovery in animal history of which I hope are long to be enabled to give to the society a fuller account. Some makers of saltpetre, in digging up the floor of one of those caves beyond the blue ridge, with which you know the limestone country abounds, found some of the bones of an animal of the family of the lion, tyger, panther &c but as preeminent over the lion in size as the Mammoth is over the elephant. I have now in my possession the principal bones of a leg, the claws, and other phalanges, and hope soon to receive some others, as I have taken measures for obtaining what are not already lost or may still be found. One of the claw bones in my possession, without it's horny fang, measures 7 inches long, and a larger one was found & has been lost. This phalange in the lion is under 2 inches in length. It's[sic] bulk entitles it to give to our animal the name of the Greatclaw, or Megalonyx. The leg bone does not indicate so vast an excess of size, over that of the lion, but perhaps not more than a double or treble mass. But of this we shall be better able to judge when a fuller collection of the bones shall be made. The whole of them shall be deposited with the Society.24

Jefferson's memoir on the Megalonyx was received on 10 March 1797 and it was resolved to have a committee examine it and have someone make sketches of the bones exhibited with the memoir. At the same time, it was *"Resolved, "* That it is the request of the Society to Mr. [Charles Willson] Peale, he may cause those bones to be put in the best order, for the Society's use."

On 10 February 1797, George Turner presented Several fossils to the Society on. From Cincinnati, Ohio, came some fine fossil coal, which resembled the cannel coal of Europe. Part of one petrified tree—thirty or forty of what appeared to be black walnut trees, were found about 212 miles up the Tennessee River where they had tumbled into the river from the bank on which they grew. With these came specimens of petrified dung. From the rapids of the Ohio River, where "such and various other petrifactions are found in abundance" came a specimen of petrified dung and some petrified ordure "supposed to be human, from the same place."

A paper on the mastodon was received on 22 June 1797 from Judge George Turner and it was turned over to a committee composed of Thomas C. James, Adam Seybert, and Caspar Wistar. The report was made on 17 November and the article was published in the *Transactions.*[25]

Hugh Williamson wrote Jefferson on 24 May 1797 that Mr. Caffery's letter

is in the Hands of Dr. Wistar. You will observe that he promises attention to any Requests I or any other Gentleman may make touching that subject [of big bones]. In fact, I had informed Mr. Jackson his Brother in Law, that it was for the Amer[ican] Philos[ophical] Society that I wished to have as much information as possible on that Subject. A very trusty man who lived at Nashville [Tennessee] a few Miles from the Bones is now in Philad[elphi]a & proposes setting out next Sunday. Mr. William Blount knows him well & will hand him any Letters from any Officer of the Society.26

He wrote again to Jefferson on 28 May 1797 that he was prevented from sending a letter to Caffery:

I intended to advise Mr. Caffery, in sinking for Bones, when he should find one to dig all round carefully so as to be sure of reaching all the Bones of the same Animal, for they must lye nearby in their natural Positions unless Beasts of prey have pulled them away. And as many of the Bones of each Animal may have decayed I wished him to try to collect all that remained of 3 or 4 Animals but the Society as I presume have said all that was proper on that Head.27

The committee reported that Caffery`s letter stated that "many bones of the Mammoth were to be found at Manscoes Lick near the mouth of the Cumberland River." He offered assistance in collecting them and then forwarding them to Philadelphia or New York. The Society ordered on 26 May 1797 that his liberal offer was accepted and he should "take such other measures as may be necessary to procure the Bones ... provided they do not exceed $100.00.[28] By 16 June the committee could report that the Secretary of War would forward the letter to Caffery. He was told that the Society had "long been very desirous of obtaining information respecting the remains of the great Animal which formerly existed in ye western Country." Consequently, the members were desirous of availing themselves of his "liberal offer to collect & transmit by way of the Mississippi such of the large bones as may be found upon searching." The Members thought these bones belonged to the largest land animal yet known, but the bones generally were so scattered "that no compleat idea of theAnimal can be formed." The Society was collecting such bones "not merely for their own gratification but for the information of Philosophers throughout the world & for the credit of our Country." Consequently, "the Society is particularly desirous of obtaining a Compleat Skeleton." Once a complete skeleton was collected "it will be very desireable to have specimens of the largest bones in order to form an idea of the size to which the animal sometime attained."

The Society gave detailed instructions:

If it should not be practicable to obtain all of the bones of the animal it will be very desirable to procure those of the head particularly those which Constitute the upper Jaw, Nostrils & Sockets for the eyes. The Joints of the Back Bone are also very interesting. The Shoulder Blades & Hipbones, the small bones of the limbs & feet & the ribs. The Bones which you cannot refer to any particular part of the Body will also be very important as they may show some peculiarity of structure in the Animal. There have been found two different Species of tusks one nearly round like a horn as you have described, & the other flat like a scythe, compleat specimens of each of these will be very desirable. If the bones after exposure to the air should crack & appear like to crumble away from dryness, perhaps by painting them with oil you will probably prevent it...As some of the bones are liable to split perhaps it will be very proper to bind them round with cords.

The bones of a very large Animal have also been found at Paraguay in S[outh] A[merica]. The Gentleman who lives there ha[s] been so happy as to procure all the bones which were sent to Spain & formed into a Skeleton. As the Animal must have been very interesting on account of Uncommon form as well as size we inclose[sic] a copperplate impression of the Skeleton. 29

The animal was the megalonyx and the copperplate engraving is still in the library.

Secretary John Vaughan also informed Caffery that big bones had been found in upper New York State as well as in a "Salt Petre Cave in Green Bryar County in Virginia." The latter, he thought, might belong to the same type animal as found in Paraguay, "but we do not yet know enough of either to be certain."[30]

At a special meeting of the Society on 4 August 1797 to consider the report of the Committee to Collect Information Respecting the Past and Present State of the Country, the members agreed that the Society viewed as primary objects of research the changes, antiquity and present state of the United States. The members wished, particularly, among other things: "To procure one or more entire skeletons of the Mammoth, so called, and of such other unknown animals as either have been, or hereafter may be discoverd in America."[31]

Then Caspar Wistar received a letter from Nashville, Tennessee, from Francis May, a former student, dated 30 July 1798. He wrote about his:

enquires concerning the Large Bones at Manscoes Lick but must premise that I was unable to obtain every particular relative thereto, as I unfortunately met Capt[ai]n Caffery at the edge of the Wilderness on his way to Richmond. Of course could make but few enquiries. He inform'd me however, that there can be without doubt, several Waggon Load obtain'd by digging and those of varying sizes and that he intended to procure a Skeleton in September next, & if possible, to forward it to Philad[elphi]a by water immediately. I promis'd him my aid in the selection of the Bones, & hope we will be able to accomplish an object so desirable to your respectable Society.[32]

Wistar, William Bache, and Adam Seybert had been appointed a committee to devise the best method of preserving fossil bones.[33] Hugh Williamson had informed the members that such information was needed because someone "in the Western Territory" was about to raise some bones and thought "they were liable to decay as soon as they came into contact with the atmosphere." The report was not made to the Society until 5 December 1799.

On 19 January 1798, Jefferson presented a mastodon bone, "some time ago found in Virginia." The Society then sent their thanks to Jefferson making "acknowledgement of the constant sense they entertain of his valuable Communications & offices of Friendship."[35] Baron Ambroise F. J. Palisot de Beauvois sent on 4 May 1798, also from Virginia, a tooth of a "large non descript animal" which was referred to Caspar Wistar.[36]

Jonathan Williams received a letter from Samuel Hodgdon on 10 October 1798 stating that James Hartford Waggoner "has this day delivered me three

Barrels...which he received of Major Issac Craig for [member] General [James] Wilkinson at Pittsburgh."[37] They weighed 564 pounds and the cartage was $22.56. Williams wrote John Vaughan authorizing payment.[38] James Wilkinson was on the Committee for Antiquities, with Jefferson, Charles W. Peale, etc. and he took the request for specimens seriously because this gift was sent the same year that Committee report was released. The committee reported on 7 December 1798 this gift to the Society as:

The Donation from Gen[eral] Wilkinson consists of Bones & Fragments of the Bones of nondescript animals. There are evident marks of variety as to the age & size of these animals; but whether they be of one or more species the Com[mittee] do not undertake to say. [The committee would only observe:]

1. That the Os calcis (?) & two tarsal Bones must discard the Idea of the Animal to which they belong being of the Buffaloe kind, or indeed of any description having a hoof.

2. The substance & form of the pieces supposed to be horns by the Indians (as appears from General Wilkinson's letter hereto annexed) evidently contradict that supposition; yet it is true that there appears no vestige of a socket in the Jaw, where a Tusk could have been inserted.

3. The uncommon direction of the curve of the Rib, and the appearance of a patella (which fits between the Condyles of an Os femoris and a Tibia,) will doubtless offer matter of curious speculation.

The committee recommended that an able anatomist examine and report on these bones.39

Jefferson's gift of the bones of the unknown animal, the megalonyx, and his paper concerning them was followed on 1 March 1799 by Caspar Wistar's description of the bones.[40] William Shippen reported two weeks later that the descriptions were very accurate:

Agreeably to your request I have attentively examin'd Dr. Wistar's description of the Bones of the unknown animal, and find it very correct & accurate & I am of opinion it should be published with the plates. I also think the Doctors observations are probable and very judicious.[41]

The paper was published in the *Transactions* under the title: "A Description of the Bones Deposited by the President [Thomas Jefferson] in the Museum of the Society."[42] The animal was the megalonyx, the same as had been found in Paraguay. George Gaylord Simpson praises Wistar highly, calling him the father of American paleontology for this work. Julian Parks Boyd wrote an exhaustive study of Jefferson and this fossil. Each of these studies is published by the Society.

Benjamin Smith Barton was granted permission to sketch the mastodon bones on 7 March 1800 "provided it be done in the Society's Hall."

The ultimate accolade must hve been recognized when a letter came from Thomas Peters Smith who was touring Europe, with a statement that, because Benjamin Smith Barton had already been granted permission to sketch the mastodon bones, Georges Leopold Chretien Frederic Dagobert, baron Cuvier, perhaps the most outstanding French scientist of the day, wished to have such sketches made for himself.[43]

On 19 June 1801 the teeth of some extinct animal, with a letter describing it, was received from Thomas Jefferson. Robert R. Livingston, knowing the animal was found in New York State, wrote Jefferson of it, and sent the teeth.

Charles Willson Peale borrowed $500 from the Society to go to upper New York State and disinter a mastodon skeleton there. This story is famous and is well known. The mastodon skeleton was one of the most famous displays in Peale's Philadelphia museum, located in Philosophical Hall. [For a complete account of this incident, see Charles Coleman Sellers's biography of Charles Willson Peale.]

Rembrandt Peale, a son of Charles W. Peale and an artist himself, proposed to travel in Europe to study the great masters of the fine arts. He had been thrilled with the mastodon skeleton his father had dug up and mounted, and Rembrandt Peale had helped with the mounting. He wrote on 5 February [1802?] that engravings of the "Anonymous Skeleton at Madrid" had been acquired by Peale's Museum and "there cannot be the weakest doubt of the Identity of the animal at Madrid, & that to which the bones belonged, presented to the Society by Mr. Jefferson." Rembrandt Peale therefore requested permission to make copies of the bones so he could examine the skeleton at Madrid with the copies in hand.[45] He wrote Robert Patterson 19 February 1802:

> The great object of my intended visit to Europe (besides my Improvement as an
> Artist) is the Establishment of my Father's Correspondence with the Naturalists &
> Museums of Europe, by immediately making Exchanges, with subjects which I
> shall carry with me; as well as the Necessary attention to collect & preserve
> whatever may fall in our way. The Exhibition of the Mammoth Skeleton is intended
> to defray the necessary expences, and it becomes important to render it, with every
> attendant circumstance so interesting as to relieve us from any doubt of its success.
> Of the Skeleton which I take with me, the two largest of the Vertebrae are wanting;
> I have therefore borrowed from my Father one of his large Vertebrae, supplying its
> place with a temporary wooden one.
>
> There are a few Bones belonging to the Philosophical Society, which would render
> my Exhibition in Europe considerably more interesting; if there are no objections to
> my having the loan of them, I shall give my faithful promise safely to return them
> to the Society."[46]

This "loan" did not win the Society's favor, so Rembrandt Peale petitioned the Society on 5 March 1802 "to be permitted to make casts or copies of the Bones of the Megalonyx." Also, he asked on 19 March 1802 to be permitted "to take a cast of the fragment of skull and core of the left horn of some unknown animal of enormous size, lately found in the bed of a creek near the Ohio." Such permission was granted at the meeting of 18 June 1802.

Parts of an "unknown animal of enormous size" [referred to in the paragraph above] was presented by John Brown, of Columbia, Boone County, Kentucky. In his letter to Thomas Jefferson, on 28 April 1802, Brown wrote that he had forwarded the bones to Charles Willson Peale for the American Philosophical Society:

> It consists of Part of the skull bone, the neck joint on the head, the Pith of the left
> Horn, now Twenty-one inches in Circumference, the end off & in a decay'd state. I
> suppose it to hve been part of the head of the Animal whose large Bones are found
> in so many Parts of America & in such numbers formerly at the place called Big
> Bone (Kentucky). It was found by Uriah Hardesty an Honest Citiz[en] who felled
> Hunting in the Bed of a creek (for some months of the Year dry) falling into the
> Ohio River about Six miles below the mouth of Licking river & 12 or 14 miles
> North of Big Bone 2 or 3 miles from the Ohio. (There has not been any other
> Bones discovered near the place.)

Brown supposed Peale might use it to complete his skeleton of the mastodon and give the members the right to "make whatever disposition of it they may think Proper." He concluded by saying he would be "highly Gratified" to know the "Oppinion" of the Society on this gift.[47] There is an entry on a Curators card [ca. 1890]: "Bison, two vertebrae of, from Big Bone Lick, Ky." The minutes list the gift as "Cranium of a Bison?...it remains in the same room with the Mammoth."

Samuel Brown wrote John Vaughan on 10 June 1802 that he believed Charles W. Peale would agree that the skull:

> which I mentioned to him last winter has no relation whatever to his mammoth
> skeleton. It certainly belongs to an animal of the Ox kind and corresponds pretty
> exactly with [Johann George] Gmelin's description of a certain skull found in
> Siberia ... I hope that the bone has arrived at Phila[delphia] before this time and that
> some of our learned Naturalists will favor the world with a correct description of it.
> I enclose you a rough sketch of it [which is wanting today] by Mr. Cadbury who

saw it repeatedly at Cincinnati [Ohio]. He gives it two horns whereas I rather imagine but one remains. This is sufficient to shew that it is no Mammoth.[49]

A specimen of rock salt "embedded with marine shells arrived on 18 [19] November 1802 from Benjamin S. Barton. It came "from the Missouri, where it is in large quantities on the surface of the Earth."

Nicholas Collin reported a letter from Henry Prosperin, the secretary of the R. Societas Scientiarum Upsaliensis, written on 10 December 1802, concerning the exchange of publications with the Society. A rather naive postscript states:

A complete Skeleton of Mahmot (the Mastodon) is very desirable. This would solve the important question, if this animal was carnivorous or herbivorous. The latter appears to me to be the more probable, as it would otherwise have made too great a carnage, except it had been an aquatic animal.[50]

On 7 October 1803 the letter of Martinus Van Marum, the secretary of the Haarlem Society, was received, asking about purchasing some bones of the mammoth. Jefferson sent the Society a letter from W. Lewis of 7 March 1804, describing a bone dug up in Virginia while digging a well. The committee reported 20 April 1804 that "this letter principally refers to minerals which are to be presented to Mr. [Charles W.] Peale."[51] Tristram Patton wrote William Hembel on 16 July 1804 about some sulphate of magnesia he had sent ""o the Chemical Society of Philadelphia." He asked if the sulphate might have a commercial value in Philadelphia, for in and near his property in Virginia there was much sulphate.

This back country abounds with mines and Varieties of mineral waters. A Chemist philosopher here, might be of service to his country. I send you the [drawing of a] size of a claw and bone of a toe (that fits exactly in Socket of s[ai]d Claw) of an unknown animal of the cat kind which were found in my cave and are allowed to be curiosities. The President of the United States wrote a lengthy piece concerning s[ai]d animal, from some of the bones he received from my cave when owned by one Groner.[52]

Patton evidently was asked about the bones for he wrote William Hembel on 17 September 1804 that he was impressed by the delivery of his previous message.

As Mr. John Vaughan has requested please inform him that the bones I described to you, are in my possession, them and some others, found in my cave were intended for the Museum. As Mr. John Lewis proprietor of the sweet Springs sent for the bones, at the request of a number of gentlemen attend at s[ai]d springs who had a desire of seeing them. As the bones were returning back, the person who had the care of them was thrown from his horse, and destroy'd several of them, which appear'd time had made very tender, amongst which the claw received considerable damage.

Some think the claw might belong to some monstrous fowl, am of a contreary [sic] opinion, from three joints of the back bone that I had, which fitted exactly togeather [sic] the hole that held the marrow measured two Inches and half diameter.

Deem it necessary to mention that it was about seven Years since I came to this place, which was then a part of Greenbrier county the bones that were formerly found (it is said) were dispersed some went several hundred miles from here. I believe their were industry made to geather [sic] the bones when Mr. Jefferson received the one you mention that is in the Museum.

My cave is a large opening that goes under ground a great distance and is exceeding dry. There are very large rooms turns to the right and left of the main passage the whole are covered with a solid arch of stone in one of those rooms about seventy or eighty Yards fom the m[o]uth [ ] more [Moore?] first discovered a Salt Petre tells me he was in my cave & made salt petre: about thiry years a goal that time there were merely the whole sceletion [sic] of a Large creature lying on the top of the saltpetre along the bones that I have was found in a room adjoining to the one the sceleton [sic] was in & were about three feet down in the solid clay that appeared never to hae been disturbed by Petremakers which makes me think their may be more of them dug up.

I would send Mr. [John] Vaughan the bones that I have, only am under a promise to send them to James Monroe late governor of that state. He said he would send them to the museum, whether it was to the Society[']s or Mr. [Charles W.] Peal[e']s cannot tell shortly after Mr. Monroe went to France on publick business so that I have been hindered from sending was their [sic] any way I could get clear of my promise, would send them to Phildelphia the first opportunity as I know it was the intention of Mr. Monroe they should go there.

You can likewise inform Mr. Vaughan that should I discover any more bones or hear of any that has ben found I will be particular in getting them and sending them to him through you. [53]

On 7 December 1804 an account of the discovery of mastodon skeletons was read to the Society. James Logan was supposed to have written it in 1762 immediately after the Lancaster treaty with the Indians and Joseph Parker Norris gave a copy of it to Benjamin S. Barton who promptly published it in his *Medical Journal*.

John Bartram wrote to Jemmy, that he is informed by a letter from Col. Boquette [Bouquet], that some Shawnese Indians had brought to Pittsburgh a Tooth weighing 6 pounds and 3/4 & another piece of one, which he calls a Tusk 14 Inches long & the part where it is broke off as thick as a man's arm both in his hands, by which he is confirmed in this opinion they could belong only to Elephants, & requests Jemmy to make enquiry of any of that nation, at this Treaty, how far these Skeletons lye from the Ohio; with sunry other queries, to which he, Jemmy, received the following answers, from two intelligent Shawnese men by an interpreter that the place where they lye is about 3 miles from the Ohio, Salt & moist, about the extent of Lancaster Town, in the midst of a large Savannah, 4 days journey below the lower Shawnese town, on the east side of the river; that there appears to be the remains of 5 Entire Skeletons, with their heads all pointing towards each other, & near together, supposed to have fallen at the same time. When they were asked to describe their several parts, they began with their heads, of which two were larger than the rest. One of these they said, a man could but just grasp in both his arms, with a long nose, & the mouth on the under side. They next mentioned the shoulder blades, which when set on end reached to their shoulders, & they were both tall men. What they called the cup (or socket) of that bone, was equal in size to a large bowl. The thigh bone, when broke asunder would admit of a little boy's creeping into it. They were asked if they had seen long bones they called horns. They answered that they had, & by the distance from themselves to the door, shewed them to be 10 or 12 feet long, & added, that by the bones, they judged the creature when alive; must have been the size of a small house, pointing from a window to a stable in sight. Jemmy then asked if the place where they lay was surrounded with mountains, so as to admit the probability of its ever havine been a lake. They answer'd that hc place was salt & wettish & by having been much tread and licked was something lower than the adjacent land which was however so level to a prodigious extent, that the lick as they called it, could never have been covered with water, & that there were many roads thro' this extent of land, larger & more beaten by Buffaloes & other creatures that had made themselves to come to it, than any thing they saw in this part of the country. In answer to being questioned, if they had seen such bones in any other place, they said they had seen many such, scattered here and there in that large tract of land, some upon the surface, & some partly buried, but all much more decayed by time, than these they had described & not any whole Skeleton. Upon being asked if they had ever heard from any of their old men when these 5 were first observed, or if they or their fathers had ever seen any such large creatues living as these bones were supposed to be part of, they answered they had never heard of them spoke of other than as in the connection they are at present, nor ever heard of any such creature having been seen by the oldest man, or his father. That they had indeed a tradition such mighty creatures had once frequented those savannahs, & that were then men of a proportionable size to them, who used to kill them, & tye them in their hoppesses (?), and throw them on their backs, as an Indian now does a Deer. That they had seen marks in rocks, which tradition said were made by those great & strong men, setting down with their burthens, just such as a man makes by setting down on the snow. That when there were no more of these strong men left alive, God killed these mighty creatures that they might not hurt the present race of Indians, and indeed that God had killed these last 5 they had been questioned about, which the Interpreter said, was to be understood. They supposed them to have been killed by lightning. These they said were their traditions, but as to what they knew, they had told it all.[54]

John D. Clifford wrote from Huntsville, Mississippi Territory on 31 January 1805 and presented many items from several places, among which were:
A common muscle [sic] petrified from Sicily.

A curious bivalve petrifaction, found in a Creek that empties into the Kentucky River. The person from whom I obtained it unfortunately injured the hinge part from an Idle curiosity to see what was within. It is however (I think) unique in its speciae. I have searched several Cabinets for the purpose of finding a shell that resembled it. 55

On 3 May 1805 two teeth from Tioga and Santee were loaned to Benjamin S. Barton for a month so he could draw them. Barton returned them on 21 June 1805.[56] There are eleven sketches of fossil teeth in the Benjamin Smith Barton collection in the library.
Samuel Brown, of Lexington, Kentucky, presented on 1 November 1805 a tooth and pieces of bone found in a "Salt petre cave."[57] He had written John Vaughan 9 April 1805:
A few days ago I had the good fortune to discover (in a Salt Petre Cave which I am working) an enormous Bone which I suspect is of the same species with those described by Mr. Jefferson. I have compared it with the drawing published by the Society, & find that it corresponds with one of them pretty exactly. Another has lately been found but I have not yet seen it. They shall both be sent to the Society via Orleans. I learn nothing more of the Great Bos.58

These bones arrived 20 December 1805 from Samuel Brown and were given to Caspar Wistar for study and a report.[59]
Brown wrote Jefferson:

I take the liberty of transmitting to you by Mr. Fowler the Skull & lower Jaw of an animal whose species, I believe, is unknown to the Hunters and Naturalists of the western Country. It was discovered, some weeks ago, in the Great Salt Petre cave on Rock castle covered with several feet of dry Earth. I have requested the workmen to make diligent search for the remaining Bones of the Skeleton but, as yet no others have been found which could be supposed to belong to this animal.60

Wistar reported on 17 January 1806 that these cave bones "prove to be the Bones of the Head" of the peccary of South America, according to the description by Louis Jean Marie Daubenton in Comte de Georges Louis Leclerc Buffon's works.[61] William E. Hulings presented on 21 March 1806 some impressions of shells which were taken from the mountainous regions of Pennsylvania and New Jersey.[62] William Read wrote to Thomas Jefferson from Charleston, South Carolina, 11 February 1806:

> Observing you attentive to natural Philosophy as well as to other branches of science, I take occasion to present you with a fossil which you may consider a curiosity, & not unworthy of your contemplation. It was found on Rich hope [?] Estate on Cooper River, in forming a canal, 20 feet under the surface of the Earth, resembling decay'd shells, two hundred feet distant from the swamp. I likewise send you a broken one least your Excellency should chuse to direct a chemical analysis on it. From my experiments they prove dentoid. The curious & learned here have concluded them to be the Teeth of some Monster unknown at this date.63

Caspar Wistar reported on 20 June 1806 that he had communicated with Jefferson about "certain bones supposed to be at present in the city of New Orleans." He reported to the members on 19 September that Jefferson would attend to these bones, "found in Ohio."[64] Benjamin S. Barton exhibited on 3 October 1806 a tooth of the mammoth, found in Montgomery Country, Virginia.

Samuel Brown's and Thomas Jefferson's letters about the bones of the mastodon were read on 17 October 1806 and referred to Caspar Wistar, Charles W. Peale and John Vaughan, a committee, which was to correspond with William Goforth, also.[65] L.A. Tarason presented on 21 November 1806 part of the lower jawbone of a mastodon.[66] Jonathan Williams wrote a letter which was read to the members on 16 January 1807 on "Petrifactions on the Falls of the Ohio, near Louisville." It was referred to James Mease, Adam Seybert, and Joseph Cloud.[67]

William Goforth wrote Thomas Jefferson on 23 January 1807:

> I received a letter from Mr. Caspar Wistar junr dated 1 Dec[embe]r 1806 on behalf of the A. P. S. of Philadelphia, requesting information concerning the Head of the Mammoth the Bones of a large animal with Claws an account of other unknown Bones—and also my opinion of the probability of procuring more bones and the method of attempting it—and I was desired to address the answer to you.

> Unaccustomed to correspond[ing] with the learned, my life has been spent in the active duties of my profession, among the labouring class of mankind, and it is with reluctance I proceed to give what little information I am possessed of to your learned body; but relying upon the urbanity of the Society, and actuated by an ardent desire to contribute my mite to the furtherance of Science, I feel much more reluctance to with[h]old it.

> The bones I collected were unfortunately entrusted to the care of a person who descended the Mississippi with [them] some Months since whether he proceeded to Europe with them I am ignorant; as from accident, or from some other cause, I have received no account either of him or them. My answer cannot therefore be expected to contain accurate or exact descriptions of the Bones; but such a general description as I can give from memory follows.

> The part of the Head which was in my possession and which I thought to be the Head of the mammoth appeared small-I only possessed the Maxilla superior, and the Maxilla inferior; with the Teeth. The Maxilla superior was furnished with 4 large Teeth 2 on each side of the Jaws. The 2 nearest the forepart of the jaw were Molares, and had 2 points or cones on each side of the tooth. The other two (likewise Molares) back teeth had three points or Cones on each side of the Tooth making double processes thickly enamelled on the cones or masticating surface.

> The Maxilla inferior was in two parts naturally, teeth the same as in the Maxilla superior and from the appearance of both jaws I concluded they had their full compliments of teeth I judged the Head to which these bones belonged was small

as I had Teeth of the same kind more than five times the size of the largest in either jaw each under jaw with the Teeth weighed 48 lb.

I had a number of Teeth Ribbed Transversly on the Masticating surface and enammelled weighing from 1 1/2 lb. to 12 lb. each.

Of Teeth of the Mammoth kind furnished with double coned or blunt pointed processes on the masticating surface and thickly enamelled and generally 4 processes for insertion in the jaw, as many as a waggon and 4 Horses could draw weighing from 5 or 6 and some 20 lb. each.

One small femoris w[eigh]t 31 lb—4 Ribbs weight and length not recollected they appeared to be so connected with the vertebra as to throw their edge outwards 1 Tusk weighing 100 lb 21 Inches in circumference in the middle which was the Thickest part 1 other Tusk w[eigh]t 150 lb 23 Inches in circumference and measuring 10 Feet 6 In. in length. Its form thus one horn 5 feet long w[eigh]t 21 lb.

The bones of one paw which nearly filled a flour barrel it had 4 Claws and when the bones were regularly placed together measured from the Os Calcis to the end of either middle claw 5 feet 2 Inches.

The bones of this paw were similar to those of a bears foot. When I found these bones I found large quantities of bears bones at the same time and had an opportunity of arranging and comparing the bones together and the similarity was striking in every particular except the size.

The vertebra of the Back and neck when arranged in order with the os sucrum and Coccyges measured nearly 60 feet allowing for the cartileges tho I am not confident the Bones all belonged to one animal and the number of vertebrae I do not recollect.

I had some thin bones of incognita of a monstrous size when compared with my other bones, which I much regret I neither weighed nor measured and a number of large bones so much impaired by time it was fruitless to conjecture to what part of any animal they belonged.

As to the probability of obtaining more bones and the method of attempting it. The best answer I can give will be a relation how and where I procured the forementioned. They were all procured at a place called Big Bone lick about 60 miles below this place and 3 from the Ohio. From my long rsidence in this Country I had long cherished a strong desire to make researches at Big Bone Lick but my circumstances (having a large family and my practice as a physician tho' extensive is not profitable owing to the poverty of the people) would not enable me to bear the necessary expences. About 3 years ago some persons understanding the avidity with which Skeletons of this kind were sought after in Eruope and believing a complete Skeleton of the mammoth might be procured and that it would sell well in Europe were induced to become sharers in the expence of procuring one. I accordingly proceeded to Big Bone Lick with a few hands such as our trifling resources would permit commenced my researches when the Agent of David Ross of Virginia who owns the tract of land forbid me proceeding further since which time I have endeavoured by every means which my contracted situation enabled me to procure liberty to prosecute my search.

Big Bone lick was formerly a Salt Marsh Salt is made there at present. We generally dug thro several layers of small Bones in a stiff blue clay, such as Deer Elk Buffalo and bear Bones in great number many of them much broken, below which was a strata of Gravel and salt water in which we found the large Bones some nearly 11 feet deep in the ground tho' formerly they were found upon the surface. The large bones were not found regularly connected together as those of a carcass which had been consumed by time without disturbance and I was led to form strong suspicions that carcasses of the large animals were preyed upon and the bones scattered here and there. I am so firmly persuaded that large nay almost any quantity of the Teeth Bones and Tusks may be procured that I have long entertained a sanguine hope of bettering my circumstances by procuring skelletons provided I could obtain permission to prosecute my search perhaps it may be in the power of your learned Body to procure me this permission or if the society would wish collections of the Bones of these non descripts for their own use I would undertake to superintend the collection and forward it to Philadelphia or elsewhere for such a compensation as the Society should think proper to allow me for my trouble and quitting my business during the time of the work. I spent about 4 weeks in my former research with 4 and sometimes 5 hands and I expect with proper funds to employ 8 or 10 hands who must be found with victuals and liquor I could completely search the whole Lick. The expense would be about $1.25 for each man. We could take provision from this Town or take a Hunter to kill for us. I have now respected Sir given all the information that Suggests itself and have mentioned the place where the collection is to be made and I hope the Society will endeavour to procure me liberty from David Ross of Virginia to prosecute my search—or that they will close with my proposal as I am confident that the Society will not use the information I have given them to my disadvantage in any manner. 68

Thomas Jefferson enclosed of this letter in his 25 February 1807 letter to Caspar Wistar:

I enclose you a letter from Dr. Goforth on the subject of the bones of the Mammoth. Immediately on receipt of this, as I found it was in my power to accomplish the wishes of theSociety for the completion of this skeleton with more certainty than through the channel proposed in the letter, I set the thing into motion, so that it will be effected without any expence to the Society, or other trouble than to indicate the particular bones wanting. Being acquainted with Mr. Ross, proprietor of the bigbone lick, I wrote to him for permission to search for such particular bones as the society might desire, & I expect to receive it in a few days. Capt. Clarke [sic] (companion of Capt. Lewis) who is now here agrees, as he passes through that country to stop at the lick employ labourers, & superintend the search at my expence, not that of the society, and to send me the specific bones wanted, without further trespassing on the deposit, about which Mr. Ross would be tender, and particularly where he apprehended that the person employed would wish to collect for himself. If therefore you will be so good as to send me a list of the bones wanting (the one you formerly sent me having been forwarded to Dr. Brown) the business shall be effected without encroaching at all on the funds of the society, and it will be particularly gratifying to me to have the opportunity of being of some use to them. But send me the list, if you please, without any delay, as Capt. Clarke [sic] returns in a few days, and we should lose the opportunity. 69

John Vaughan on 6 March 1807 noted that Caspar Wistar had sent Thomas Jefferson "a particular account of such bones."70

Jefferson presented two skeleton heads found at Big Bone Lick and they were described "by the late President Wistar." Caspar Wistar's article, read on 3 February 1809, was referred to as: "On a collection of Bones found at Bigbone Lick, procured at expense of Mr. Jefferson."71 Benjamin S. Barton, Charles W. Peale, and John McDowell were appointed a committee to examine the paper, and on 17 March 1809 the librarian was ordered to advertise for the paper, it "having been accidentally lost." Fortunately, it was located and was published in the *Transactions*.72

15 May 1807
A "Conglomeration of shells from the high hills of Santee."[73]

Cleland Kinloch

17 May 1811
A mammoth tooth from of Santa Fe de Bogota, in South America.[74]

Don Pedro de la Lastre

Benjamin S. Barton exhibited on 21 June 1811 "a large and perfect claw of the Megath[e]rium" which had been located at the foothills of the Cumberland Mountains in a niter cave in Tennessee.

Caspar Wistar delivered from Thomas Jefferson two skulls, mutilated, from Big Bone Lick by Gen. Clark, on IS July 1814.[75] Wistar wrote an article about them: "On the Head Bones of an Animal Found at Big Bone Lick by Gen. Clark," and on 19 January and 16 February 1816 it was referred to a committee of Zaccheus Collins, Josef F. Correa da Serra, and James Mease. It was published in the *Transactions* with two engravings depicting the heads. [76]

Caspar Wistar delivered a paper on 3 March 1815 on "the 0thenoid bone" for publication. The New York Historical Society sent a circular letter 6 March 1817 asking help towards the forming of a collection of "minerals and fossils of the United States. "[77] John Vaughan read on 2 May 1817 "Remarks on the Organic Vegetable remains discovered in Florida," written by Reverend Mr. Henry Steinhauer. The reading was incomplete, but the paper was referred to a committee composed of Zaccheus Collins, William Maclure and Thomas Cooper for evaluation. The

memoir in question is a very full and accurate decription of many varieties of vegetable impressions in shistose and other kinds of Stone; impressions not yet perfectly understood, and therefore not determined and classed. It is of importance therefore to accumulate precise descriptions of such of these origanic remains as have hithero been observed and collected, in hopes that by the accumulated labours of naturalists this branch of knowledge may be rendered less obscure than it now is. The memoir in question deserves to be inserted in the Society's volume as being well calculated to assist in the future classification of these interesting remains.78

From Huntsville, Mississippi Territory, came the gift of J. D.Clifford on 16 May 1817. These fossils were designated "Siliceous Petrefactions of Eschini."[79]

Leonard MacNally, from Dublin, Ireland, sent G. G. Bogart on 28 May 1817 an extract concerning the Irish elk. It was "an extract from a publication very scarce. Very few copies were printed." He offered to help with such data on Irish natural history.[80] Bogart, in turn, sent it to John Vaughan on 20 December 1817 and he promised to communicate information on a moose and on "fossil remains of the states of New York, New Jersey & Virginia."[81] This was Thomas Molyneux's communication to the Archbishop of Ireland, with sketches of antlers, on the Irish elk.[82]

On 18 July 1817, from "Fort Washington, Potomack or Wurburton, Maryland" came a fossil shell of the genus Orca.[83]

7 November 1817
Some petrified wood from Buckingham Township, Bucks County, Pennsylvania.[84]

Solomon W. Conrad

From near Chambersburg, Pennsylvania, George Chambers sent on 21 November 1817 two "specimens of Fossil Reliquiae in limestone," and his letter was referred to a committee composed of Zaccheus Collins, Caspar Wistar and Charles A. Lesueur.[85] William Tilghman wrote John Vaughan on 1 October 1817 that Chambers insisted on packing and defraying all expenses of these fossils. Caspar Wistar had been told of three such specimens, but the "3d, which is in the Street, has been injured, & is not worth sending." There was difficulty in finding a wagon to ship them to Philadelphia for most travel went to Baltimore.[86] On 2 December 1817, however, Chambers wrote John Vaughan that he had "forwarded to you by a Waggoner of the name of Jacob Marks—the boxes containing the Cornera (?) Ammonis desired by you for the American Philosophical

Society...I was assured that they would not be more than 7 or 8 days on the way." [87] Also on 21 November 1817, William Rawle deposited for Mrs. Griffiths of New Brunswick, New Jersey, some ammonites, found sixteen feet deep in a marl pit near Burlington, New Jersey. Thomas Tickell Hewson borrowed some bones to use in his lectures in comparative anatomy on 20 March 1818.[88]

Caspar Wistar died and the fossil bones which he had in his possession on loan from the Society were returned on 15 April 1818:
55 bones belonging to the feet of the mammoth
3 fragments of the ribs of do.
50 bones belonging to the feet legs & spine of Unknown animals
12 fragments supposed to belong to the head of the Mammoth
24 Specimens of teeth of mammoth
13 fragments of teeth & defenses of different animals
3 fragments of the upper jaw of the mammoth containing teeth
5 fragments of the lower jaw of do.
6 fragments of the bony part of horns
2 large horns
2 large defences
2 fragments of smaller do.
4 fragments of the heads of unknown animals
1 head unknown 89
The administrators Dr. Wistar's estate, Mrs. Elizabeth Mifflin Wistar, Richard Wistar and James B. Gibson, delivered these bones and William Edmonds Horner prepared this list.[90]

14 August 1818
Some amber samples found at Cape Sable, Nova Scotia. The donor noted that "a fossil substance being a nidus or a comb of an insect" was in some amber.[91]

Gerhard Troost

3 March 1820
A petrifaction, "apparently the stem of the Arundo Donan;" it was found in the vicinity of Dundorff, Susquehanna County, Pennsylvania.[92]

Redmond Conyngham

18 August 1820
Two specimens of Phytolithes which had been found in connection with coal formations somewhere near Clearfield, Pennsylvania. [93]

Benjamin R. Morgan

21 September 1821
Some belemites from Burlington County, New Jersey.[94]

Zaccheus Collins

The treasurer's records show that on 14 December 1822 Eliza Miller was paid "for Mould & Casts of bones of Megallonex to send to Paris and other societies."[95]

18 July 1823
A "conglomeration of fossil shells."[96]

R. Dietz

John D. Godman was making a study of the mastodon and asked John Vaughan on 18 June 1824 to let him "examine the collection of bones in the Cabinet." He planned to "lay the results of his researches before the Society, when they are sufficiently perfected." The members agreed to let him examine the bones on the same date. James Ellsworth De Kay of New York was "permitted" on 20 August 1824, to "have a series of casts of the bones of the Megalonix which are in the possession of the Society."[97] Charles Lesueur, "under the direction" of the curators was authorized on 21 January 1825 to make drawings of bones in the cabinet which were described in the *Transactions*.

On 18 February 1825 the members "*Resolved*, That casts of M[egalonyx] claws etc., in the possession of this Society be presented to the Lyceum of Natural History of New York."[98] On 21 February the thanks of the Lyceum were received by William Hypolitis Keating. The Lyceum had: "the honor to announce to you that at a meeting of the Lyceum, held this even[in]g, a box was rec[eive]d by Mr. R[embrandt] Peale from the American Philosophical Society, containing casts of the bones & claws of the megalonix. A unanimous vote of thanks was passed to that learned body."

The Lyceum hoped to reciprocate and did. A gift was received on 19 August 1825 from the Lyceum and it was the "cast of Part of the Jaw of a `Megatherium Cuvierei'" which had been discovered in 1824 in North Carolina.[99]

Richard Harlan, on 1 April 1825, read a paper on "an extinct fossil *Tapir;* of a new species of Lepus; or a new genus (osteopera) of the order of Glires." This paper was ordered to be preserved in the Archives. It is still preserved in the Archives and it is endorsed: "not referred [to a committee] as he means to it a Work, now in Press."[100]

Gaspard Deabatte requested permission to take a tooth of the mammoth with him on his projected voyage to Europe. He promised that he would "send back exchanges." The members on 1 April 1825 turned the request over to the curators "with power to take order." On 20 May the curators made their report and stated that "they had presented the tooth to M. Deabatte."[101]

On 13 October 1825 Charles Smith wrote Peter Stephen Du Ponceau from Chambersburg, Pennsylvania and having "lately been over the mouintains," forwarded some fossil shells for the Society. The Shells were found in Mifflin County, near Lewistown, deep in a quarry of Sandstone, on high land. I take them to be antedeluvian— and may furnish much matter of reflection to the inquisitive mind—tho' I believe you have similar specimens.[102]

Dr. Calhoun presented for the cabinet a drawing of a mammoth 2 December 1825. Secretary George Ord received the thanks of the Asiatic Society of Calcutta, written 26 November 1826, to the Society for "the Plaster casts of the bones of the Leg and Great Claw of the Megalonyx" which the Society had presented to the Asiatic Society. Some fossil shells from Virginia and from England were received on 16 February 1827 from John Finch.[103]

During the middle 1820s the Chesapeake and Delaware Canal was being dug. James Mease, on 20 July 1827, presented some fossil shells uncovered by this trench.[104] The Assistant Engineer on the canal construction, Hugh Lee, presented on 19 June 1829 fossils from the "Deep Cut.[105] Another Assistant Engineer, Andrew Alfred Dexter, gave prior to 1831 "a full Collection of Specimens of Fossils" which had been dug from the same "Deep Cut."[106]

Captain Elliot presented some human bones found on the coast of Brazil, near Santos, and Charles Delucena Meigs wrote a memoir on them. Robert Maskell Patterson, Samuel Brown and Nathaniel A. Ware, the committee, reported on 21 December 1827 in favor of publication, although the committee:

abstains from the expression of his [Meigs] unqualified assent to the general proposition of Georges Leopold Chretien Frederic Dagobert] Cuvier that no Human Beings existed, at the period when the Fossil remains of other Animals were involved in one general catastrophe, they cannot help remarking some similarity in the situation in, which the skeletons at Santos are found & those of Guadaloupe as they have been described by [Charles Dietrich Eberhard] Koneg & others. They have been particularly struck with the observations that so great a number of Human Skeletons have been found lying in a regular East & West position both on the Island of Guadaloupe & at Santos in Brazil. The discovery, too, of Axes, Pestels Mortars &c. made of Porphyry & other Rocks so commonly found in the cemeteries of the aborigines of the northern portion of our continent would almost irresistably incline us to the opinion, that all of these monuments must have had a similar origin. It is worthy of remark too, that in the specimens of Rock brought from Santos, we discover small fragments of charcoal which we have often noticed in the recent sandstone formations of which the Capitol at Washington is built; & in almost all mounds or cemeteries of the western states which we have examined. Charcoal shells & burnt clay may be observed not very unlike the concretion from Santos. The Rock at Guadaloupe, it appears, is covered at high water. It may once (and at no very distant period) have been a mound like that of Santos, where the dead were deposited in an east & west position, in a detrius of coraline & siliceous Rocks which may have sunk into the level of low water from the action of Volcanoes, recently extinguished. We have no example of Animal Fossils where such regularity of position exists. The size of the Trees growing on the mound at Santos, by no means, establishes the great antiquity of the concretion. The fertility of a soil enriched by large deposit of animal matter & the influence of a general climate, would soon render such evidences of high antiquity extremely equivocal & unsatisfactory. The percolation of water impregnated with calcarous matter, would in a short period massify or concrete shells, bones & other substances so as to give some appearance of a formation. This process might be effected even during the growth of trees which are found on the mound at Santos. The stalcretion crustations on some of these Bones & shells give strong probability to this conjecture with regard to their origin.[107]

Richard Harlan reported on 1 February 1828 that he was at present examining "a fossil clavicle & part of the sternum of the Megatherium." These fossils had been found in a marl pit on the plantation of William H. Todd of New Jersey.
"The bones of the great clawed animal of Mr. Jefferson, the Megalonyx" were described in a letter from William Cooper to John Vaughan on 31. January 1829. He saw them while they were in the possession of Joseph Dorfeville, of Cincinnati, Ohio. In addition to "one tooth. The Scapula. The humerus. 2 ungueal phlanges. several vertebrae, and a rib. Besides these are several others that I had no opportunity of examining, but which appeared to belong to the same animal." These remains had been located in White Cave, Tennesse, and, up to this date, other than the bones dug from Big Salt Lick and those which were preserved in the Society's cabinet were "the only remains of this animal that have been discovered." The owner wished to sell them, perhaps in France, but Cooper hoped that the Society "which has long possessed the other portions, may be induced to make the acquisition of these also." Richard Harlan spoke on them on 6 May 1831.[108]

6 February 1829
Some fossil bones of a hippopotamus.

Isaac Lea

17 July 1829
Fossils from the "Deep Cut" of the Chesapeake and Delaware Canal.[109]

Andrew Alfred Dexter
Isaac Hays presented a paper "on a new Genus of extinct animal (saurodon)." The committee, composed of Isaac Lea, Zaccheus Collins and R. Eglesfeld Griffith wrote on 15 January 1830 that they had examined "the specimen as well as the description" and, after exhaustive research "believe it to belong to a genus hitherto undescribed." The paper was reported for publication.[110]
A committee, composed of Isaac Lea, Zaccheus Collins, R. Eglesfeld Griffith and William E. Horner, reported on 15 January 1830, on Silvain Godon's paper, "Description of a new Genus & new species of extinct mammiferous quadruped." Thecommittee "carefully examined the description & drawings which seem to have been made with great attention to accuracy." Publication was recommended.[111]
Richard Harlan, on 16 April 1830, read a paper "Note on the New Fossil Genus Tetracaulodon Mastodontoideum" after having read Godon's article. Harlan cited Godon: "The author admits that the specimens he described from Drawings are the remains of a young animmal, and that "in every view," this animal so strongly resembles the mastodon, "but for the singular difference of organization presented by the lower jaw & its tusks." Harlan stated that the lower jaw and molars "certainly resemble those of the Mastodon," much as any "young animal resembles those of the adult individual." The "Tetracaulodon Mastodontoideum," therefore, was a calf of a mastodon, and not a new genus. "In this opinion we are fully supported by our Scientific Correspondents in New

York, who have Carefully examined the original specimen."[112] A curator's card reads: "Cervus americanus Harlan. Metacarpal bones from Big Bone Lick, Kentucky (Jefferson Co1.).[113]

On 16 April 1830 Richard Harlan also commented on the "fragment of a head of a new fossil animal discovered in a Marl pit near Moorestown, New Jersey." Harlan considered this fossil quite interesting, "not only on account of its geological locality, but also as it serves further to establish a new fossil "Genus, the Saurocephalus." Harlan described this in the 1824 Journal of the Academy of Natural Sciences of Philadelphia. He took Isaac Hays to task in a harsh manner and concluded:

We have purposely avoided any criticism on the defective style of the essay here reviewed but the note which on page 475 of the *Transactions,* should certainly have been differently worded, considering the circumstances under which his essay was presented to this Society. In referring to the account of the "Saurocephalus Cancifornis" he states that he has not seen the original specimen and says "We regret that we are compelled to depend upon the account of it by R. Harlan M.D. &c." In presenting to the public his first effort to elucidate an obscure hranch of natural history, he appears to forget that his remark refers to one who has devoted several years to the study of comparative osteology.[114]

On 20 May 1831, Dr. Hays demonstrated "the specific differences between the Mastodon and Dr. Harlan's fossil," in a paper entitled: "Specimens of inferior maxillary bones of Mastodons in the Cabinet of the A[merican] P[hilosophical] S[ociety], with remarks on the genus...of Godman." This paper pointed out the specific differences and a committee composed of John P. Wetherill, Isaac Lea and John Pickering was asked to report on it.

The members ordered, on 16 September 1831, that "a set of the casts of the mammoth bones" and the megalonyx owned by the Society be presented to the Academy of Natural Sciences of Philadelphia.[115] Four days later a letter of thanks was written by the president of the Academy and it was received 7 October. The letter thanked the Society for "a set of casts of the claw and bones of the Magalonyx."[116]

John Vaughan was instructed by Richard Cowling Taylor to let Richard Harlan have access "to the Cabinet of Fossils, which remain at present in the Rooms of the Philosophical Society, as that gentleman has kindly undertaken in conjunction with yourself to promote my wishes with regard to the disposal of the Collection."[117]

18 November 1831

Fourteen plaster casts, had been described in the Journal of Natural Science, of "the Fossil Bones of the Megalonyx laquatus, found in White Cave, Kent County, Virginia.[118]

John Price Wetherill

At the December 2nd, 1831 meeting, Isaac Hays stated that he owned "the best collection of bones of the mastodon known to be in existence, belonging to different museums." Consequently, the members asked him to exhibit them at the next meeting. Meantime, the curators and Isaasc Hays, a committee, were asked "to consider the propriety of making casts." At the 16 December meeting Hays "exhibited and explained the Mastodon bones." Richard Harlan then "described the Mastodon bones in the various museums of the U. S.[119] The Committee reported on 20 January 1832 that John Chitty "an expert moddeler" could make good molds of the originals in the Society's Cabinet, and copies from the casts from the Baltimore, New York, Virginia and the University of Pennsylvania museums. The members agreed to his terms and paid him $135. for the work.[120]

Judge Bry sent some fossil bones which had been found in a hill "50 m[iles] by land and 110 by water from the town of Monroe [Arkansas? Louisiana?]." The hill was 200 yards from the Washita [Ouachita] River and the bones were discovered when, after a lengthy period of rain, half of the hill slid down and "left about 28 of these Bones uncovered, embedded in sea Marl." This gift was received on 20 July 1832[121] and a committee was appointed to examine it. Richard Harlan wrote the report on 21 September 1832:

As far as a cursory examination could enable them to determine, the objects consist of several fossil vertebrae of an extinct species of Saurien, together with a portion of the soil or marl in which they were found; and that subsequent to the appointment of the Committee, a letter from the Donor to the President of the Society containing some account of their locality, has been put into their hands, which has not yet come before the Society, and that the interesting obsevations it contains will be necessarily incorporated into the *description* of the Fossils, which will be presented for publication in the *Transactions*.[122]

        This report, plus another by Harlan on some fossils which Nathaniel A. Ware had forwarded him was read 19 October 1832 and referred to a committee composed of Samuel George Morton, William E. Horner and William Hembel. Ware's fossils were from the junction of the Yellowstone and Missouri Rivers. This committee's report was accepted on 2 November, and publication, with a plate, of Judge Bry's fossils and letter was agreed to.[123]

        Isaac Hays wished to make a drawing of a mastodon tooth to accompany his memoir in a forthcoming volume of the *Transactions* and the members granted him permission to make the sketch on 21 June 1833.

        From La Grange, Alabama, William H. Harrington sent on 13 August 1833 colored drawings of "fossil remains of gigantic vegetables, which are found here in vast abundance." He assured John Kearsley Mitchell that the drawings were "correct representations of some specimens," once artistic license was granted him. He referred to the Reverend Henry Steinhaur's article in the first volume, New Series, of the *Transactions* in his description of "Pytholithus verrucosus." He thought "that there are no less than 4 distinct configurations belonging to the same plant."[124] Six beautiful colored drawings accompany this letter. John K. Mitchell presented the letter, and the illustrations, to the Society 18 October 1833.

        Additional mastodon casts were needed and the 15 March 1833 report of the committee stated that six casts were authorized. John Chitty was paid $114. for making them 10 September 1833 after Isaac Hays wrote John Vaughan: "All the casts being completed and the moulds returned to the Society the whole amount $114, is due and should be paid.[125] The members ordered on 4 October 1833 that sets of these casts were to be sent to the Jardin des Plantes de Paris and to the Geological Society of London. The committee reported progress on this and the curators announced on 1 November 1833 that a set had been sent to the Geological Society of London. These casts were received and on 6 February 1834 a letter was sent, thanking the Society "for the donation of Casts of the Inferior Maxillary Bones of the mastodon & Tetracaulodon.[126] The Curators reported on 4 April 1834 that the gift of casts of the mastodon fossils had been sent to the Jardin des Plantes de Paris.

        On 7 February 1834 the members asked the curators "to examine what arrangements are necessary for the preservation and arranging all of the various donationsthe Cabinet" and to "report at an early meeting."

        John Vaughan told the members on 7 February 1834 that Richard Harlan learned, while in Florence, Italy, that the "Museum of Florence" wished to "exchange the fossil bones of the Val de Arno for the plaster casts" made from the bones in the Society's cabinet. Because several casts were wanting, the curators announced on 18 April 1834 that making such casts cost "not less than $30" and at that price the bones were "now ready for exchange or sale."

        As thanks for he Society's gift, the Musee d'Histoire Naturelle de Paris [of which organization the Jardin des Plantes de Paris is a part] announced that an almost complete skeleton of a Plesiosaurus and Dalicodeines from the cliffs of Lyme Regis, England, were given to Richard Harlan for the Society. News of this gift was received on 3 January 1834.[127] This was "The Great Fossil Saurien, the Maestrich Monitor de Cuvier" or "the Masasauras de [William Daniel] Conybeare."[128] Freight for shipping these gifts was paid to Forstall Bros. & Berthoud 21 January 1834.[129]

16 May 1834
A "Large Collection of Specimens of Anthracite Coal" to better illustrate its formation.[130]

John Pedder

On 27 June 1834 the first shipment arrived of the major gift from the director, the administrators and the professors of the Musee d'Histoire Naturelle de Paris. These 68 plaster casts of fossil bones had been boxed and shipped in two vessels. The first shipment to arrive consisted of bones divided into 28 items. It arrived safely, and a list was sent of the total bones in the shipments:

3. Tete de Paloeotherium crassum (cuv. 055. foss. tome III. pI. LIII et LIV.
4. Sa machoire inferieure   (idem pI. LIII)
5. Tete de Paloeotherium crassum   (non grave'e)
6. Astragale
7. Calcaneum de Paloeotherium Magnum
8. Scaphoide
9. Astragale
10. Scaphoide   de Paloeotherium indeterminatum cuv. oss. foss. pI. XXIX. fig. 4 a 12
11. Calcaneum
12. Astragale de Paloeotherium medium
13. Tibia   idem   idem
14. Pied de derriere gauche de Paloeotherium crassum
15. Portion d'omoplate d'Anoplotherium commune.
16. Pied de devant droit idem   idem
17. Pied de derriere gauche idem   idem
18. Deux molaires sup. de Lophiodon Tapiroide (de Buchsweiler pI. VII, f. 3
19. Portion infe'rieure d'hume'rus de Lophiodon (d'Auvergne)
20. Tate d'Ours a front bombe' (des cavernes d'Iserlohn pre°s Sundwich en vestpha
21. Collection du Crocodile (de Caen,) compose'e de 40 morceaux.
    21A. Portion de colonne Verte1brale
    21B. Ecailles ventrales.
    21C. pierre pour poser les e'cailles
    21D. Bassin (Ischion)
    21E. Portion de bassin
    21F. omoplate droite..21 FF coldien droite
    21G. Portion de machoire infe'rieure
22. Tete de Tortue (du Jura)
23. Tete de Saurien[131]
    These were received in New York from La Havre 16 October 1834 and Richard Harlan was billed for freight charges in France as well as New York. [132] The second part of the gift was received 7 November 1834, when the major portion arrived:
24. Molaires superxeures et canine de Paloeotherium (dept de 1a Goconda
25. Empreinte de tee d'Anoplotherium commune, montrant 1a cervenu.
26. Molaires   Idem   idem
27. Machoire inferieure de Lophisdon, (de Nanterre pres Paris)
28. Portion de Martchoire infe°rieure de idem (de Buchsweiler, animaux voisins de Tapirs, pI. VII, fig. 1
29. Molaire superieure (germe) de Lophiodon (d'origine inconnue) pl. I, f. 3
30. Germe de molaire superieure. idem (d'Alsace)
31. Canine idem   idem   idem
32. Portion de machoire inferieure d'Anthracotherium (de Cadibona)
33. 2' Machoire inferieure idem (d'Alsace)
34. Molaire superxeure
35. Derniere Molaire superieure
36. Germe idem   idem   de Rhinoceros (de Chevilly)
37. Incisive superieure
38. Germe de Tapir (de Chevilly)
39. Molaire inferieure de Tapir (de Chevilly)
40. Molaire de Tapir Gigantesque (Dinotherium) (d'origine inconnue) tome II,

anim. vois. de Panirs
41. Molaire   idem   idem
42. Canine d'Ours (Ursus cultridens) (d'Auvergne)
43. Fragment de canine de Chien
44. Molaire supe'rieure idem   (de Chevilly)
45. Te'e d'Ichtyosaurus communis (de Lyme Regis, comte de Dorset cuv. 055. foss. tome
    V. 2me partie pI. XXIX, fig. 1
46. Tee idem intermedius pI. idem. XXIX fig. 2a 5
47. Portion inferieure d'humerus
48. Cubitus   de Paloeotherium Latum pI. LX fig 1
49. Radius
50. Metacarpien du milieu
51. Metacarpien du milieu de Paloeotherium crassum (tome III, pI. XXII, fig.6)
52. Metatarsien idem idem curtum (pI. XLII, fig. 6)
53. Metacarpien idem idem medium (pI. XX, fig. 3)
54. Astragale de Paloeotherium minus
55. Radius gauche d'anoplotherium commune (pI. LI, fig. l6)
56. Portion d'humerus
57. Portion de Radius d'Anoplotherium gracile (pI. XXXI, fig. I a 5)
58. Portion de Cubitus
59. Astragale
60. Cubitus de carnassier (pI. LXX, fig. 6 et 7)
61. Epaule et partie de l'e'xtremite anterieure de l'Ichtyosaurus communis de Lyme Regis,
    comte Dorset) Cuvier 055. foss. tome V. 2me partie pI. XXX, fig. 5
62. Squelette d'Ichtyosaurus Tenuirostris
63. Cote de Trionyx (tome III, p. LXXVI, fig 2 du Pterodactylus Grandis
65. Humerus de Plesiosaurus
66. Femur idem de Stenay
67. Phalange ongueale d'Iguanodon (de Ia foret de Tilgate)
68. Aiguillon de SiIure. [133]
            John Chitty was paid $21. to repair a fossil skeleton of the Plesiosaurus on
29 July 1834. On 24 May 1837 Chitty was paid $6. for making casts of the Megalonyx
bones.[134] These were made for the Hunterian's Museum by the curators who acted "with
power" granted on 3 March 1837.

1 April 1836
"Specimens of Fossil remains from the neighborhood of Natchez."[135]

William Henry Huntington
17 February 1837
Casts of fossil trilobites of North America. With this gift was a monograph by Jacob
Green, M. D.[136]

Joseph Bruno
            On 3 March 1837 the curators were empowered to make casts of the
Megalonyx for John Collins Warren.[137]

16 November 1838
Some fossils from high in the Andes Mountains in Chile. Two were from "near Coquimbo,
18,000 feet above the Sea," and there were six other fossils "from near Copiapo, 7,000
feet above the Sea, 120 miles from the Coast."[138]

John N. Casanova
            Thomas B. Ashton wrote 11 June 1839 that he was sending the cast of a
fossil jaw, the original of which, is in the Athenaeum of Zanesville, Ohio. The cast was
left with me by W. A. Adams Esq. of that place with a request that it should be placed in
the collection of some scientific institution and I feel that in begging you to present it to the
Philosophical Society of Penn[sylvani]a [sic] I most fully comply with the wishes of my
friend.[139]

A mastodon skeleton uncovered near Bucyrus, Ohio, [later more accurately stated as near Saint Louis and in Missouri] was on display in Philadelphia and the owner wished $440. for it. William E. Horner wrote John Vaughan on 2 December 1839:

The owner of the skeleton of the Mastodon at 398 Market Street is very desirous of bringing his efforts for a sale of it to a conclusion. There is no chance of its being bought either for the Philadelphia Museum or for the University. I feel anxious that it should not leave the city and as a member of the Amer[ican] Philos[ophical] Scoiety will contribute twenty dollars towards its purchase. Dr. R[obert] M. Patterson and member [John Kintzing] Kane have both agreed to contribute somewhat: I know your efficiency in such matters so well, that I sincerely hope so good an opportunity may not be lost of obtaining perhaps the best head of that animal yet discovered. [140]

The treasurer's records show an account of $300 for this purpose 17 to 19 December 1839.[141] By 3 January 1840 "a subscription of members" had purchased the skeleton and donated it to the Society. A committee composed of Drs. William E.Horner and Isaac Hays were asked to "report a description of the same.[142] The report was read on 2 October 1840 and was directed to be published, and it was published in the *Proceedings,* with plates.[143]

The collection referred to, was made by Mr. Albert Koch—a German resident in Saint Louis, for the last five years and has been obtained principally from two localities, Rock Creek, twenty miles south of St. Louis, and Gasconade County, [Missouri] two hundred miles above the mouth of the Missouri river. It consists of two hundred or more Teeth of the Mastodon and of the American Elephant. A dozen or more Lower Jaws of the Mastodon, with very numerous specimens of other parts of the head and skeleton generally, though were is no perfect head.

The most remarkable specimen is a head of an animal, which Mr. Koch calls nondescript, and considers to have been from four to six times the size of an elephant, though Dr. Horner esteems it extremely difficult to establish this. In the present mode of exhibition, the head shows a central oblong amorphous part, which measures six feet in length by two or three in width. It is furnished with enormous tusks, eleven and threetwelfths feet long from their roots, and nine or ten inches in diameter one foot and three inches of their length being inserted into the sockets. These tusks are semicircular, and stand out horizontally, with the concavity backwards. This placed, they are fifteen feet in a straight line, from the tip of the one to the tip of the other...The molar teeth are four in number in each jaw, two on a side; the posterior one is seven inches long by four wide; the anterior, four and a half inches long by four wide. The conformation of the teeth is exactly that of the Mastodon, and the ridges and denticules are sarcely worn at all, a proof that the animal was not old. The upper part of the cranium of this animal is defective....

In the same collection of fossil bones is to be found the skeleton, nearly complete of a Mastodon of very large size: the ribs are wanting, and the upper part of the cranium...

The internal table of the cranium, the brain case, is entire, with a small surface of the contiguous cellular structure of bone in another fragment of the Mastodon. This forms so complete an oval body, that, in Dr. [William E.] Horner's opinion, it is somewhat difficult to conceive that its shape was the result of merely accidental causes; Dr. Horner indeed thinks it rather authorizes the inference, that it had been chiselled or hammered designedly into that shape by the human contemporaries of the animal.

There is also a small head, eighteen or twenty inches long, with tusks ten or eleven inches long in the upper jaw, and four mastodon teeth on each side of each jaw...Whether it ought to be viewed merely as a young Mastodon Giganteum, or another species of the Mastodon, Dr. Horner considers to be at present doubtful... There is an os humeri, probably of a megalonyx, which measures in length one foot eight inches, the ulna of the same animal, and also other bones...

Dr. Horner stated, that his sketch of this rich accumulation of fossil remains, and their examination were very imperfect, and the less instructive to him, for the want of standards of comparison in perfect skeletons, and in plates, neither of which means of elucidation exist in Saint Louis, and he expressed a hope, that their diligent and deserving collector, would furnish the scientific world with exact plates of such as are rare or unknown. [144]

C. G. Forshey, of Louisiana, presented on 3 September 1840: Five species of fossil Coralloides, from Jackson County, Iowa Territory, 1838...Two Cyathphylla and an Orthocera, from the Chert, above the mountain limestone of Copper creek, Iowa, 1838...A cast, in Chalcedonic Quartz, of a Pentamiris, from the Chert of Iowa, 1838.. A Cyathphyllum, and a Corolloides, from Calloway County, Missouri, 1839. [145]

These were received on 2 October 1840.
Leopold de Buch gave on 19 June 1840 three plates of ammonites, having presented his publication on these plates on 15 May.[146] On 19 March 1841 Oscar A. Lawson billed the Society $12. for "Drawing head of Mastodon 3/4 view," the same "Occipital view & portion of spine,": and the "Vertebra & portion of Elephant's head." Also, "Two outlines in profile" were done.[147] He was ordered to be paid 2 April 1841; this was receipted on 7 April 1841.
Richard Harlan notified John Vaughan on 17 May 1841 that the name of the Italian who wished, in 1833, to exchange fossils with the Society was Targioni Toggetti.[148] Isaac Hays read his note to the committee report on the various mastodon bones in the cabinet. This note, on 21 May 1841, as well as the report of the committee, was ordered to be published.[149] On 1 October 1841 Isaac Hays spoke to the members on the "very extensive and highly interesting" collection of fossil and mastodon bones which recently had been brought to Philadelphia by Albert Koch, of Saint Louis, Missouri. There were enough bones to form a nearly complete skeleton as well as "twenty-three lower and eleven upper jaws, of upwards of two hundred teeth." Four of the lower jaws were of the genus Tetracaulodon and one was remarkable for having only one tusk: there was no sign of the other having ever existed.
The fragment of a fourth jaw is particularly interesting, from it apperently belonging to a distinct variety, if not even a new species, of Tetracaulodon. This consists of the chin, and a portion of the left side. In the chin there is a small alveolus on each side. This jaw is strikingly similar to one in the cabinet of the Society, and described by Dr. H[arlan] as belonging to the young of the M[astodon] giganteum...In the latter specimen the alveolus was so small and imperfect, and so different from that in the species of Tetracaulodon then known, that Dr. [Isaac] H[ays] considered it an accidental formation. In the specimen in Mr. [Albert] Koch's collection the alveolus is sufficiently perfect, the lining plate of bone in part remaining, to place beyond all doubt its being a socket for a tusk.[149]

Two upper jaw fragments were of particular interest, having a tusk and part of another "apparently in their original position." This showed the position of the tusks to be the same as in the elephant.

The collection of bones forming the skeleton, called by Mr. Koch the Missourium, though very unnaturally put together, is an object of interest, from the large size and fine state of preservation of some of the bones, particularly the femur and the atlas. The head is far less perfect than the one belonging to the Society. The whole vault of the cranium, except the inner table, is wanting. The two tables of the cranium being widely separated in this genus, the absence of the outer table and the diploe gives to the head a remarkably flat appearance. This, with the smoothness of a great part of the upper surface, resulting from the natural structure of the cells of the diploe, which are very large, led Mr. Koch to believe that the cranium was entire, and that it belonged to an animal different from the Mastodon.[150]

Isaac Hays commented again on 15 October 1841 on the new variety of the Tetracaulodon and showed some fossils and casts of the lower jaws.
He called attention to the circumstance, that the alveoli for the tusks in the first and second of these specimens were alike in form, depth and direction, but that there was a marked third and fourth specimens; the latter being also like each other. In the two former the alveoli are nearly cylindrical, and extend nearly to the inner table of the chin, leaving at their base merely a thin plate of bone: whilst in the two last the alveoli are conical, and so superficial as to leave a space of nearly two inches between their base and the posterior surface of the chin.[151]

Richard Harlan delivered his memoir, "Description of the Bones of a nondescript fossil Animal, of the order of Edentada, allied to the Megatherium, Megalonyx, Clamyphorus, Orycteropus, &c. &c." on 15 October. 1841.[152] The committee's report, read on 5 November, was a detailed description of some of the bones, "friable and light, non petrified, but destitute of animal matter" of the collection made by Koch. This two page printed report concludes: "Dr. Harlan proposes to name this animal, `Orycterotherium Missouriense.'" A note read on 4 February 1842 was ordered to be published with the paper.[153] On 16 March 1842 Richard Harlan left his casts of these bones "near the door of the [Philosophical] Hall" and wrote George Ord to "place them safely on a table until Friday morning.[154] The gift of these twenty-eight casts of the bones of the *Orycterotherium Missouriensis* was made on 18 March 1842.[155]
George M. Justice presented on 16 March 1842 a fossil which came from the island of Antigua.[156] J. P. Wetherill wrote George Ord on 20 April 1842 asking him to let Richard Harlan have the "moulds of the head Bones," as the members had resolved. Ord noted that they "could not be found.[157]
Sir Charles Lyell was lecturing in Philadelphia and on 5 May 1842 Henry Darwin Rogers wrote Ord that Lyell, busy as he was, would "set aside everything else in order to see them, so desirous is he to behold them," if the fossil bones in question could be located.[158]
John Locke wrote Judah Dobson on 12 May 1842 that he was donating "a parcel of casts of fossils, chiefly of our western rocks." The collection of paleontological conchology was "for the benefit of our institutions in Cincinnati," and he wished both to collect and diffuse such information. "These have mostly been made by myself within a few months."[159] The members, on a motion by James Curtis Booth agreed on 20 May 1842, to let Locke "take casts from such specimens of fossils, as in their judgement may not be injured thereby, provided that the moulds" would become the property of the Society.[160]
Isaac Hays proposed 20 May 1842 that the Society have a set of casts of fossil remains sent as a gift to the museum at Darmstadt through Johann Jacob Kaup. This was done and the expenses included $2.25 for the case, $2.50 for paper shavings, and 62-1/2 cents for porterage and shipping, which was paid on 23 July 1842.[161]
John Vaughan's death in 1841 left a decided vacuum—things could not be readily located under the new librarian, George Ord. On 17 June 1842 Richard Harlan announced that no one could locate the molds for the megalonyx bones in the cabinet. He proposed having new ones made "at his own expense, under the superintendence of the Curators." This request was granted on the same day.[162] The twelve bones were turned over to Harlan on 25 June[163] and John P. Wetherill evidently collected them for Harlan 1 July 1842.164 The bones were returned 19 August 1842 and Harlan gave his thanks for the loan. At the same time he asked for the return of his paper "on the fossil remains of the Orycterotherium Missouriense" which had been read before the Society ten months before, but was "no nearer publication at present than it was when first presented to the Society."

Therefore, Richard Harlan planned to take "immediate measures" to make this memoir public.[165]

On 16 September 1842 Isaac Lea exhibited specimens of Lithodomi in rock specimens from Payta, Peru, and Coquimbo, Chile. Lieutenant Rich, of the United States Navy, procured these and Lea spoke of these fossils, like their living counterparts on the beaches of today, which were embedded in rock as high as nearly 200 feet. This same rock, at the same spots, composed of minute grains of quartz which were held together by carbonate of lime, was elevated only a few feet by the earthquake of 1822 and Captain Robert Fitz Roy noted its elevation 1835 as only about eight feet. This rock "tended to illustrate the theory of 'existing causes.'"[166]

On 18 November 1842 Isaac Lea exhibited "a beautiful and nearly perfect specimen of an Ammonite." It came from "Oxford Clay, Chippenham, England," and "the process extending from the aperture was entire.[167]

Charles Alexandre Lesueur's gift of a case of fossils was shipped 20 October 1842 and received 3 February 1843. He had collected them "in the environs of Havre, France." They were received in New York by Edouard Bossange 26 January 1843 and shipped to Philadelphia on the same date.[168]

Isaac Hays on 7 April 1843 discussed three papers which had been read recently before the Geological Society of London concerning the collection of Mr. Koch. The "distinguished naturalist," Robert Edmond Grant, considered the genus Tetracaulodon, well-founded and his conclusions supported Isaac Hays' own conclusions of twelve years before. "As each has obtained his results from the examination of an entirely different series of specimens, they mutually confirm each other." Alexander Naysmith examined the tusks of the "Tetracaulodon Godmanii, T. Kochii, T. tapiroides, and of the Missourium" microscopically. He thought that the Missourium "certainly indicates a distinct species." The third paper was by Koch which "in his opinion fully prove the Tetracaulodon to be a distinct genus." Dr. Harlan entered the discussion with a brief history of the mastodon skeletons in the Philadelphia & Baltimore museums.[169]

The curators were authorized on 21 April 1843, following the motion of Isaac Hays, to make casts "of the Mastodon Chapmani."[170] On 19 May 1843 Isaac Hays moved, and the members agreed, that the "head and other bones of the Mastodon" at the University of Pennsylvania be returned to the cabinet.[171]

Hays reported on 15 December 1843 that S. H. Whipple, of the state of Missouri, had a large collection of fossil bones in Philadelphia of the tetracaulodon. Whipple wished to dispose of them and Hays asked if other members would join him in purchasing this collection.[172] Robert M. Patterson, Robley Dunglison, George Bacon Wood, William E. Horner, Franklin Bache, and the Rev. George Washington Bethune joined Hays, as did John P. Wetherill, John K. Kane, John F. Frazer, Frederick Fraley, Solomon White Roberts, Isaac Lea, William Hembel, and George M. Justice.[173] The collection was presented on 3 January 1844 to the Society.

> These bones were found in the County of Benton, Missouri, about one-half mile from the river Osage, seventy miles south of the Missouri river, at Boonville; in North latitude 38° 10' and in 16° 40' West longitude. The County of Benton, south of the Osage, and bordering thereon, is characterized for its irregular and broken appearance, running up into extensive ridges, rocky cliffs, and flinty knobs. These elevations, though far from being mountainous, nevertheless, afford views of the surrounding country, beautiful, extensive, and in many instances, sublime. Again valleys intervene, through which meander some streams of water, bordered by alluvial bottoms and lofty forests. It was in such a country as this, to all appearance, that the Mastodon delighted to dwell, and there his bones are found most numerous.

> In one of the valleys named, just at the point where a fertile bottom is connected with a more elevated region, is a saline marsh, perhaps of an acre in extent. One half of this marsh is covered by a soil different from that composing the marsh, but partaking of the character of a ridge of land, of oneeight to onefourth of a mile distant, and which runs parallel with the bottom abovenamed. This ridge is

composed in part of a species of limestone, columns of whitch are at intervals left
standing, and in some instances of from ten to twenty feet elevation above the
surrounding portions of the ridge. Between this ridge and the marsh the ground
declines gently, and was formerly covered with oak timber. It is now a cultivated
field. The soil of this field also bears evidence of having been washed, or other
wise conveyed from the ridge. Onehalf of the marsh, as above stated, is covered
with this soil, and to the extent of about ten feet. It was under this deposit, and to
the depth from two to twelve feet imbedded in the marsh, that these bones were
found, lying in the greatest confusion and disorder.[174]

     Mr. Bryan, who had "some fossil bones which he wishes to exhibit" was
recommended on 22 January 1844 to George Ord by Isaac Hays. Hays suggested he
might rent the basement room of Philosophical Hall "lately occupied by the Horticultural
Society.[175] The room was hired and the bones exhibited. On 2 February 1844 Hays spoke
to the members about this exhibit in the basement. These bones were discovered in
Missouri near the place where Koch had uncovered his collection.
     From Boston, John Collins Warren visited Philadelphia and on 10 June
1846 Isaac Hays asked to see the key of the cabinet to show him the mastodon bones.[176]
Dr. Warren reported to Hays of some recently discovred mastodon skeletons in New York
and New Jersey. The one uncovered at Newburgh, New York was stored at Harvard
University. It was complete and assembled—it was a Tetracaulodon. Hays commented on
the "marked differences between this and the skeletons of the mastodon, which he had
examined.[177] John C. Warren asked 22 June 1846 to purchase the casts of the Society's
mastodon bones which Hays had shown him. He wished "copies at my expense of all
these Casts."[178]
     The corresponding secretary of the Academy of Natural Sciences of
Philadelphia, John Cassin, wrote Charles B. Trego on 25 January 1849 inquiring if a fossil
mastodon tooth, brought to Philadelphia in 1843 by Julius Timoleon Ducatel, was in the
Society's cabinet.
     Isaac Lea spoke on 15 June 1849 on some very fascinating reptilian foot
prints which he had recently discovered "in the gorge of Sharp Mountain, near Pottsville,
P[ennsylvani]a." He spoke of the fact of such discoveries and said that "the accumulation
of evidence from various parts of the world soon satisfied the doubts of the most
scrupulous. There is no geological fact better established." Lea had a cast of the foot prints,
with the tail dragging, as well as the pits of raindrops. The sketch of the foot prints was
distinct and "no such animal remains have heretofore been discovered so low" in geological
stratae. These tracks were "8500 feet below the upper part of the coal formation there,
which is 6750 feet thick."[180]
     On 2 November 1849 Isaac Hays proposed, and the members adopted, a
resolution:
    Resolved, That the Curators be authorized to deposit the fossil organic remains,
    belonging to this Society, with the Academy of Natural Sciences: provided that the
    Academy will agree to accept of the deposit and take proper measures for the
    preservation of the specimens; and, farther, shall, by their proper officer, sign a
    receipt for the same, and agree to return them in good condition when required by
    this Society.[181]

     John Cassin wrote on 6 December 1849 that this resolution had been duly
read 27 November and it was decided "That the Curators of this Academy be authorized to
receive said collection of organic remains upon the conditions proposed by the American
Philosophical Society, with power to modify said conditions should it appear necessary.[187]
     Joseph Leidy as the chairman of the curators of the Academy signed a
receipt on 28 November 1849 for "a Collection of Fossil organic Remains, consisting of
Mastodon bones and other specimens."[183]
     On 25 December 1849 the Academy noted:
    A few weeks since our sister institution the American Philosophical Society passed
    a resolution to deposit its collection of organic remains with us. The large number

of mammalian remains in this collection renders it one of the most important deposits which has yet been made to our museum. When received a more particular account will be given.[184]

Franklin Peale and John C. Cresson ordered Charles B. Trego to let John F. Frazer borrow the model of the head of a fossil 12 April 1850.[185] Isaac Hays, Joseph Leidy and William Samuel Waithman Ruschenberger were appointed a committee 2 April 1852 to examine Lea's paper "on the Fossil Footmarks of the Red Sandstone, at Pottsville, Pa."[186]

On 2 April 1852 Joseph Leidy pointed out certain fossils belonging to the Society. One was an almost entire skull of a peccary type animal of a distinct genus. "He also noticed one side of the lower jaw of a fossil tiger, enveloped in oxide of iron, the crowns of the canine and the molar teeth being exposed. The proportions of this jaw indicate an animal of greater size than any specimen heretofore described, of the 'fossil cave tiger.'"

The name of "Felis atrox" was proposed for this animal and Leidy said he planned "to describe these remains more fully hereafter, in a communication for the *Transactions.*"[187] On 7 May 1851 Leidy read his paper "On Extinct Species of the American Lion;" Hays, Ruschenberger and Lea were appointed a committee to examine it. The report of the committee was read 21 May favoring publication.[188]

Some fossils must have been retained by the Society because Isaac Hays suggested 16 April 1852 that a set of casts of the mastodon bones in the cabinet be presented to the Academy of Natural Sciences of Philadelphia. On 3 February 1860 it was moved that "plaster casts of fossils" in the Society's cabinet be deposited in the Academy. Hays delivered a list 6 April 1860 of these plaster casts and recommended that they be deposited in the Academy "upon the same conditions as a deposit formerly made by the Society with the Academy." A complete list of these plaster casts was to be presented at some future meeting.[189]

Some fossil infusoria were exhibited on 18 June 1852 by Martin Hans Boye. They had to be examined under a microscope, of course, and came from "a new locality, half a mile west of Succasunny, Morris County, New Jersey." It was considered a marl but Boye recognized it at once. James B. Fisher examined the area and reported that it appears that it extends over about 5 acres of land, covered with a moderate layer of peat, and the greater portion of it under water. It was first met with in digging a drain, and is said not yet to have been penetrated, at the depth of seven feet.[190]

15 April 1853
Specimens of petrified wood which had been in the Barnum Museum when it had burned. The heat of the fire altered the specimens.[191]

Franklin Stewart
7 October 1853
From the Imperial Society of Naturalists of Moscow, some specimens of "Marrow, from the bones of the Mammoth found on the shore of the river Lena, in eastern Siberia." [192]

Charles Renard
An offer to exchange "e xtinct mammalian fossils" for the Society's Transactions, or other articles or books, was received 20 June 1856 from the Academy of Science of Saint Louis, Missouri.[193]

J. Peter Lesley exhibited 19 October 1860 a fossil plant found near a deposit of quartz crystals and a deposit of silicate of alumnia near the top layer of an anthracite coal bed.[194]

16 May 1862
Some mammoth powder "in use in Germany." [195]

Benjamin Gerhard
Joseph Leidy wrote J. Peter Lesley on 12 May 1863 asking for the "cast of the skull of the Mososaurus" which the Society had agreed to deposit in the Academy of Natural Sciences of Philadelphia.[196]

On 18 December 1863 the curators were told to reply to the request of the Smithsonian Institution for moulds of ethnological specimens.[197] Franklin Peale's resolution of 18 March 1864 that, due to lack of space in Philosophical Hall, the curators be permitted to deposit at the Academy of Natural Sciences of Philadelphia many of the minerals and fossils was acted upon.[198] Joseph Leidy wrote 28 March 1864 that the Academy was "pleased to accept the deposit of the Society" and he acknowledged "the receipt of the Minerals and Fossils, from .... Franklin Peale."[199]

T. C. Juliet wrote in August 1865 that a tertiary shark's tooth had been found at Schuylkill Haven, Pennsylvania, in a piece of coal by a boat captain. Frederick Fraley presented the tooth 16 February 1866 and Horatio C. Wood said that it came from the tertiaries of New Jersey.[200]

James Augustin Greer wrote Josph Henry on 8 May 1866 of his exciting discovery of fossil fishes far above the high water mark in the loess around Vicksburg, Mississippi. This was sent to J. Peter Lesley from the Smithsonian, and Lesley noted: "Replied June 6 JPL."[201]

From Cirencester, England, the Rev. Thomas D. Allen wrote on 15 June 1866 asking for certain information about some "human fossil bones reported to be in the cabinetof the Society."[202] On 18 June 1869, Edward Drinker Cope spoke of some fossils found in New Jersey and he exhibited "the almost perfect cranium of a Mososauroid reptile, the Clidastes prophython." He spoke, also, of other fossils remains. He exhibited a molar tooth on 21 January 1870, along with fragments of a whale skeleton from North Carolina. Meanwhile, great discoveries were being made by the scientists sent out by the government to map and describe the West. Among the scientists were Edward D. Cope and Ferdinand Vandiveer Hayden.

Edward D. Cope showed on 1 April 1870 some black shale from Ferdinand Vandiveer Hayden's collections of 1869 containing fossil fishes. Hayden then spoke of his collections now at the Smithsonian. On 15 April 1870, Hayden showed photographs of fossil fishes of the Green River area and described a new process of photographing these specimens. Also, he showed some geological sketches of the Rocky Mountains.[203]

Edward D. Cope described and exhibited parts of a fossil Bottosaurus found in Burlington County, New Jersey, on 15 April 1870. On 6 May, he discussed and exhibited a Dycynodont cranium from South Africa and compared it with an apparent Dycynodont tusks taken from the Triassic rocks of the Reading Railroad's Phoenixville Trench, thirty miles northwest of Philadelphia. He exhibited on 20 May 1870, as the first found in the United States, "a portion of the dorsal spine of a shark of the genus Asteracanthus of Agassiz, of New Jersey." On 7 October 1870, Edward D. Cope exhibited fossil remains of a new Cretaceous tortoise and described it. With this, he "made some observations on the metatarsal region of Laelaps aquilunguis." He exhibited and spoke of other fossils at the

On 3 February 1871, Edward D. Cope reported that Charles Moore Wheatley had discovered a "bone cave" about twentyfive miles northwest of Philadelphia in the "Calciferous limestone."210 Fossils from this "bone Cavern near Port Kennedy" were displayed 17 March 1871 by Cope. He thought the migration of animals in the New World considering that the higher types belonging to the Eocene and Miocene ages (including the fresh water fishes, Idaho) being all Asiatic, show a land migration over the space now occupied by the North Pacific Ocean when this fauna was destroyed by cold, the sinking of the North Pacific area, and the ice barrier together prevented its restoration. It was, therefore, replaced by a fauna of a lower type from Central America.[206]

Teeth and portions of the jaw of a new Mososauroid, a new genus of a reptile and some slabs of coal slate which contained specimens of a new species of batrachian were exhibited on 3 March 1871 by Edward D. Cope. Cope also exhibited some fossil remains of certain extinct vertebra in North Carolina on 17 November 1871. With this was a communication for publication, with four octavo plates.[207]

Certain fossil remains from Utah were exhibited for the members on 16 February 1872 by E. D. Cope. His paper, "On Bathmodon, an extinct genus of Ungulates" was presented for publication at the same time.[208] At the meeting of 21 February 1873 he exhibited remains of a gigantic Proboscidian (eobasileus) found in

Wyoming. On 4 April 1873 he described and exhibited some specimens of flatclawed carnivore from Wyoming.[209] Drawings and specimens were used by Cope on 16 January 1874 to illustrate his comments on the comparative osteology of the camel and other artiodactyles, extinct and lving.[210]

The secretary, at Cope's request, exhibited on 17 April 1874 parts of a skull of eobasileus galeatus from Bitter Creek, Wyoming. The posterior wall of the cranium was very perfect, retaining one of its horns. "The two middle pair of horns were in separate fragments, as also the two nasal horncores." At the same meeting a fossil walrus cranium from Accomac Harbor, Virginia, was exhibited. It consisted of a "thoroughly fossilized" fragment nine inches long with three well-worn teeth in their sockets on one side and two in the other. To that date this was the southernmost walrus specimen discovered on the Atlantic Coast "and must have been washed ashore from glacial drift." [211]

On 10 September 1875 John L. Le Conte moved that Secretary of the Smithsonian Institution, Joseph Henry, be asked to use whatever necessary funds were at his disposal for obtaining through the skill of Mr. B[enjamin] Waterhouse Hawkins restorations of some of the remarkable fossil forms of the west for exhibition in the grounds of the Centennial Exhibition."[212]

On 2 February 1877, Edward D. Cope described and exhibited a skull,and dental remains of dinosaurs which he found on his most recent western trip. He showed and discussed additional dinosaur fossils on 16 February 1877, "the first ever discovered in Triassic rocks" in the mountains of Utah. He sent J. P. Lesley the manuscript on this latter fossil on 23 February and asked that Lesley announce he would exhibit "some bones of large Saurians from the Missouri River." He did exhibit on 2 March 1877 a thirty-three foot vertebrae column `"of an unusually perfect Elasmosaurus." [213] Edward D. Cope described and showed a cast of the cranial cavity of the Coryphodon elephantopus and commented on the homologies of the organ showing "that the genus to which the animal belongs properly constitutes a fourth subdivision of mammalia lower in type than the Marsupialia." He described and exhibited on 4 May 1877 a cast of the cranial cavity, from near Santa Fe, New Mexico, of a fossil Procamel occidentalis and compared it with the brain of a llama.[214]   His sketch of the plate for this article is in the library.[215]

On 17 August 1877, Cope described and displayed some newly discovered fossils. One was a cast of a garpike which Cope had assigned the provisional name of Clastes cuneatus. It was supposedly of late tertiary date and possibly "a link between the extinct and living genera of that family." Some teeth and other Triassic remains were shown on 2 November 1877 by E. D. Cope. They had been found by Charles M. Wheatley at his Phoenixville, Pennsylvania, copper mines. On 21 December 1877 life size drawings were shown by E. D. Cope of femoral, vertebrae and other bones of "gigantic fossil saurians of the genra Lamarasaurus [camarasaurus], and Amplicoelias [camarasaurus supremus. Amplicoelias altus, and A. latus]." He gave a detailed description of the drawings.[216] An underjaw of a large extinct mammal, roughly mounted, was exibited by him on 1 February 1878.[221] He discussed it and described his discovery of it in Colorado in 1873.[217]

Henry Stafford Osborn from the State University at Oxford, Ohio, offered a donation of some fossils 15 March 1878.[218] From Williamstown, Pennsylvania, W. D. H. Mason wrote describing the "recent discovery of reptilian footprints on a slab of slate rock." This rock came from the Ellen-Goen Colliery. The rock was to be deposited in the Academy of Natural Sciences of Philadelphia.[219] This slab, "bearing the Batrachian footprints" was exhibited on 17 May 1878 by permission of the chief engineer of the Reading Rail Road, Mr. Lorenz. Lorenz proposed the provisional name of Anthracopes Masoni for it until "the discovery of other footprints or remains of the animal, should give occasion for a better determination of genus or species.[220]

J. P. Lesley on 4 October 1878 exhibited plates of Permian fossil plants which had been discovered and described in West Virginia and spoke of the work being done by James Hall, Thomas Sterry Hunt, and others "in harmonizing the geologies of Europe and America." He also exhibited some quasicoprolites from W. D. H. Mason found in the roof slates of the Monmouth coal beds. [226]

On 2 May 1879 Edward D. Cope exhibited a full size sketch of a vertebra of a new species of Camelosaurus and proposed the name C. Leptodirus. He also showed how it differed from the vertebra of Camelosaurua supremus. A limestone slab which contained Trenton trilobites was exhibited on 16 May 1879. It was the property of Isaac Lea which Lea had presented to the museum of the Geological Survey of Pennsylvania.[223]

A slab of roofing slate, "covered with casts of Buthotrephis flexuosa, was exibited by J. Peter Lesley on 5 December 1879.[224] Skulls of extinct mammals were exhibited by Edward D. Cope on 6 February 1880. These were allied to canis, felix, and ursus, among which was the skull of a large cave-bear.[225] They were acquired from the Pacific coast Tertiary deposits.

A life-size drawing of a fossil Eurypterus, found by Ira Franklin Mansfield of Cannelton, Beaver County, Pennsylvania, a member of the House of Representatives at Harrisburg, was received on 1 April 1881. He asked that the drawing be "studied and described" and stated he had found the fossil beneath the Darlington cannel coal bed.[226] On 6 January 1882 Edward D. Cope gave the Society a fossil lower jaw which had been taken from the Colorado basin.[227]

Although interest in fossils remained high, the Society's fossils had been given long ago to the Academy of Natural Sciences of Philadelphia. The plaster casts of fossils remained in the attic of Philsoophical Hall, however. J. Peter Lesley wrote Henry Phillips, Jr. on 10 February 1885 that he could "destroy the casts in the garret, and cart them all away as rubbish." Lesley had tried to give the casts to some western college, but none wanted them.[228]

Jacob Geismar received some brain cases "Specimens belonging to Prof. Cope," on 17 June 1887.[229] On 18 October 1892,. Cope wrote that he would "exhibit specimens of the extinct animals of the West and compare them with living specimens.[230] John G. Morris used a large number of plaster casts" in April 1893 to illustate his talk. J. Sergeant Price wrote on 29 April 1893 (?) that they should be removed for the room was needed for a forthcoming large meeting.[231] On 17 December 1896 J. S. Price wrote J. G. Morris again that the committee on the Hall refused to approve the "placing [of] the plaster casts [of] your headless monster above the door in the Hall." The committee felt that it would be far better placed in the upstairs library.[232]

At the meeting of the curators on 31 August 1898, Benjamin Smith Lyman asked if the moulds of fossil bones and the casts of trilobites could not be deposited either at the Wagner Free Institute of Science or the Academy of Natural Sciences of Philadelphia. It must have been at this time that a listing of casts of fossilsand such was made: the item was described and the donor listed, where known.[234]

The curators moved on 8 November 1899 that "the Plaster Moulds & Casts of Mastodon, Megalonix & other fossils" be deposited, on the usual conditions, at the Academy of Natural Sciences of Philadelphia.[235] From Big Bone Lick, Kentucky, came two vertebrae of a bison and "Vertebra dentation" of "Equus major." These are undated, but were in Philosophical Hall as late as the 1890s. They were, most probably, turned over to the Academy of Natural Sciences and appeared on the listing of deposits given to the Society on 3 June 1901.[236]

On 3 June 1901, Witmer Stone, assistant curator of the Academy of Natural Sciences of Philadelphia, sent a listing of the Society's property in the Academy. The list of the "Vertebrate Fossils" follows:
Ulna & Radius of *Megalonyx descr.* by Jefferson.
Skull of Mastodon Ohioticus.
4 pieces of Tusk of Young Mastodon.
Patella of Mastodon, Big Bone Lick, K[entuck]y.
8 Teeth of   "   "   .
3   "   "   "   and Benton Co[unty] M[iss]o[uri].
18   "   " Elephas Primigenius
Calcaneum of Mastodon   "
Ovibos Bombifrons   "
2 Vertebrae of Bison,   "
3 pieces of Skull and horns,

       Cervus Americanus   "
2 Meta Carpals and 2 Astragali
       Cervus Americanus   "
Axis of Mastodon   Benton Co[unty], M[iss]o[uri].
Several Cervicals, Mastodon   "
Several Dorsal Vertebrae   "
2 pieces of Jaw   "
1 piece " Jaw   "
I Tooth *M. Chapmani*, (type)
2 pieces of Jaw, *M. Americanus*
4 pieces of Jaw, *M. Americanus*, Benton Co[unty] M[iss]o[uri]
50 Teeth
Equus Major, Veretebrae, Big Bone Lick, K[entuck]y
       "——————Tooth,   Natchez
       "——————fragment of jaw, Natchez
Felis Atrox (type) Lower Jaw, Natchez
Ursus Americanus, Skull,   Kentucky cave.

7 November 1924
"[A] 13 lb. section of a petrified limb of a tree, from Montana." Its age was estimated to be "betweeen 250,000 and 1,000,000 years.[237] This is the last fossil item presented to the Society.

Burnet Landreth
          It was evident, that neither the Society nor any of the organizations which had items on deposit, kept good catalogues of the items, or preserved them had they once existed. When the Society, on occasions, asked the Curators to get a listing of the deposits, the answer was often not forthcoming, nor did the Curators have a listing to check the deposit against. The Coin and Medal Collection alone had a catalogue, which survives, yet many items which had been presented to the Society were not in that catalogue. If the fossils ever had a catalogue, it disappeared, and when the Academy of Natural Sciences was asked for a listing, the answers varied enormously. And without a list of their own the Curators did nothing, having no means to check the listings.
          Over the years the members asked the curators to get a listing of the items on deposit—a futile quest, for the artifacts often had been intercollated with the items the institutions themselves possessed. The best explanation, and description, of the Society's holdings in the paleontology department of the Academy of Natural Sciences was delivered on 14 December 1949 by Horace Gardiner Richards, associate curator. He wrote that the bones had been given different catalogue numbers; he then tried to unify them in the list he presented. Some of the larger bones were not available for listing. He questioned three slabs from Pottsville, Pennsylvania, which had catalogue numbers, but he was not certain that they had come from the Society. He further stated that "No attempt has been made in this list to record the various bones of the specimens represented." The information was available in the "catalogue cards in the collection of the Academy."
          Richards listed the bones in 36 lot numbers, and for the sake of convenience, the total number of lots precedes the description of the fossils.
11 *Elephas primigenius* Blumenbach; Big Bone Lick, Kentucky.
8 *Elephas primegenius* Blumenbach; Benton County, Missouri.
4 *Elephas primegenius* Blumenbach.
3 *Elephas primegenius* Blumenbach, Siwalik Hills, India. (collector: Rev. James R. Campbell)
1 *Elephas*; Himalayas, India. (collector: Rev. James R. Campbell)
1 (*Gomphotherium* ?) (Mastodon) chapmani (Leidy). (See *Trans. Amer. Philos. Soc*. Ser. 2 Vol. 4 Plate 22, figs 3 & 4; 1834)
1 *Mammut americanum* (Kerr); Big Bone Lick, Kentucky. (see above Plate 25) (Col lector: Thomas Jefferson)
1 *Mammut americanum* (Kerr); near Pittston, Luzerne Co., Pa.
2 *Mammut americanum* (Kerr). Luzerne County, Pa.

1 *Mammut americanum* (Kerr) (see Trans. Amer. Philos Soc. Ser 2, VoI. 4, p. 334, pI. 28)

1 *Mastodon elephantoides*; Siwalik Hills, India. (collector: Rev. James R. Camp bell)

1 *Mammut americanum* (Kerr); Big Bone Lick, Kentucky. (Collector: Thomas Jef ferson; William Clark) (see Trans A. P. S. Ser. 2, Vol. 4, p. 334, PI. 29)

1 *Mammut americanum* (Kerr); Big Bone Lick, Kentucky (Collector: Thomas Jefferson; William Clark) (same reference as above)

11 *Mammut americanum* (Kerr); Big Bone Lick, Ky. (Collector: Thomas Jefferson)

8 *Mammut americanum* (Kerr); Big Bone Lick, Ky.

1 *Mammut americanum* (Kerr); Big Bone Lick, Kentucky.

114 *Mammut americanum* (Kerr); Benton County, Missouri. (Many bones and molars)

1 *Mammut americanus* (Kerr); Benton County, Missouri. (see Leidy, Contributions to the Extinct Vertebrate Fauna of the Western Territories, PI. 22, figs 5, 6) 1873.

4 *Mammut americanum* (Kerr); Benton County, Missouri

1 *Mammut americanum* (Kerr); Ohio.

1 *Proboscidea;* Siwalik Hills, India

4 *Elephas primegenius* Blumenbach.

1 *Mastodon chapmani* (Hays) (See Trans A. P. S. Ser 2 VoI. 4, PI. 22, fig 3 & 4)

1 *Mastodon collinsii* (Hays) (See above reference Ser. 2 VoI. 4, p. 334 pl. 28)

1 *Megalonyx jeffersonii* (Desmarest) "western Virginia." (see Jefferson, *Trans. A. P. S.* Vol. 4, p. 246–260; Caspar Wistar p. 526–531, pls. 1 & 2)

1 *Megalonyx jeffersonii* (Desmarest) (same reference as above)

1 *Hippopotamus amphibius* L.; VaI d'Arno, Tuscany , Italy.

1 Hippopotamus siwalensis F. & C; Siwalik Hills, India.

1 *Ursus americanus*; from a cave in Kentucky.

1 Bison; Big Bone Lick, Kentucky.

1 *Bison antiquus* Leidy; Big Bone Lick, Kentucky.

1 *Bison Iavifrons* Leidy; Big Bone Kick [sic], Kentucky.

3 *Ovibos;* Natchez, Mississippi

1 *Bison catifrons;* Susquehanna River, Pittston, Luzerne County, Pa.

1 Fish fragments; Paris, France.

1 Fish vertebrae; Paris, France. 244

Of all of these fossils, the only one still in the Society's possession, is the petrified limb of a tree which Burnet Landreth presented on 7 November 1924.

FOSSILS—References
1. *Encyclopedia*, vol. 7, pp. 373-74.
2. Royal Society of London. *Philosophical Transactions*, vol. 57, p. 489.
3. Papers of Benjamin Franklin, vol. 14, pl. 25.
4. *Ibid.*, vol. 3, pp. 149-50.
5. Darlington, W. Memorials of John Bartram & Humphrey Marshall; with notices of their botanical contemporaries, p. 169. The rough map is in the Map Collection in the Library..
6. Hindle, B. David Rittenhouse, p. 285.
7. Franklin Papers, vol. 10, pp. 229-30.
8. Hindle, B. The Rise of the American Philosophical Society 1766–1787.
9. Franklin Papers. B. Franklin to Abbe Soulavie, 22 Sept. 1782.
10. The Franklin Papers is the richest source for materials of this early date which concern both fossils and members of the Society. For letter from Peter Collinson to Franklin and comments by Bartram, see fn., vol. 10, p. 165; for letter from Franklin to Croghan, see vol. 14, pp. 221–122; Franklin to d'Auteroche, see vol. 15, pp. 33-34; the story of Croghan's gift of fossils to his brother-in-law, see fn., vol. 14, p. 28.
11. American Society. Minutes.
12. Shippen, E. Lectures.
13. Franklin Papers, vol. 21, p. 151.
14. Louis Nicola [5 March 1784]. The only reference is in the Minutes.
16. *Proc.*, vol. 86, pp. 130ff.
16. Charles Coleman Sellers. Mr. Peale's Museum, p. 11.
17. *Trans.*, vol. 2.
18. *Ibid.*
19. *Ibid.*, vol. 3.
20. American Museum, Sept. 1789, p. 218.
21. *Ibid.*
22. *Archives*. Levi Hollingsworth to APS, 16 Dec. 1791.
23. *Ibid.* D. Thomas to D. Rittenhouse, 14 Jan. 1792; *Trans.*, vol. 3.

24. *Ibid.* T. Jefferson to D. Rittenhouse, 3 July 1796.
25. Cur. Recs.; Trans., vol. 4, pp. 510ff.
26. MS. Com. H. Williamson to T. Jefferson, 24 May 1797.
27. *Ibid.*
28. Com. Recs., vol. 1.
29. *Archives.* APS to Caffery, June 1797.
30. MS. Com. J. Vaughan to Caffery, June 1797.
31. *Trans.*, vol. 4, pp. 526ff.
32. MS. Com. F. May to C. Wistar, 30 July 1798.
33. Com. Recs., vol. 1.
34. *Ibid.*
35. Trans., vol. 4.
36. Cur. Recs.; Trans., vol. 4.
37. *Archives.* S. Hodgdon to J. Williams, 10 Oct. 1798.
38. *Ibid.* J. Williams to J. Vaughan, 13 Oct. 1798.
39. *Trans.*, vol. 5; Cur. Recs.
40. Cur. Recs., vol. 1.
41. *Archives.* W. Shippen. Report, 15 March 1799.
42. *Trans.*, vol. 4, pp. 526ff.
43. MS. Com. T. P. Smith to R. Patterson, 20 Dec. 1800.
44. Charles Coleman Sellers. Charles Willson Peale, vol. 2, pp. 124–135.
45. MS Com. R. Peale to APS.
46. *Archives.* R. Peale to R. Patterson, 19 Feb. 1802.
47. *Ibid.* S. Brown to J. Vaughan, 10 June 1802.
48. Com. Recs.; Curators Cards.
49. *Archives.* S. Brown to J. Vaughan, 10 June 1802.
50. *Ibid.* Royal Society of Sciences, Upsala, to APS, 10 Dec. 1802.
51. Com. Recs., vol. I.,
52. MS. Com. T. Patton to W. Hembel, 16 July 1804.
53. *Ibid.*, 17 Sept. 1804.
54. *Archives.* Verbal communications.
55. *Ibid.* J. D. Clifford to J. Vaughan, 31 Jan. 1805; Trans., n. s., vol. 1.
56. Com. Recs., vol. 2.
57. *Ibid.;* Trans., vol. 6.
58. *Archives.* S. Brown to J. Vaughan, 9 April 1805; Curators Cards.
59. Com. Recs., vol. 2.
60. *Archives.* S. Brown to T. Jefferson, 4 Nov. 1805.
61. *Ibid.* APS. Report, 17 Jan. 1806.
62. *Trans.*, vol. 6.
63. *Archives.* W. Read to T. Jefferson, 11 Feb. 1806.
64. Com. Recs., vol. 2.
65. *Ibid.*
66. *Trans.*, vol. 6.
67. Com Recs., vol. 2.
68. *Archives.* W. Goforth to T. Jefferson 23 Jan. 1807.
69. *Ibid.* T. Jefferson to C. Wistar, 25 Feb. 1807.
70. Com. Recs., vol. 2.
71. *Trans.*, n. s., vol. 1.
72. *Ibid.*
73. *Ibid.*
74. *Donations Book.*
75. *Ibid.; Trans.*, n. s., vol. 1; Com. Recs. vol. 2.
76. *Trans.*, n. s., vol. 1, pp. 375ff.
77. *Archives.* New-York Historical Society to APS, 6 March 1817.
78. *Ibid.* APS. Report, 15 May 1817.
79. *Donation Book; Trans.*, n. s., vol. 1.
80. *Archives.* L. Mac Nally to G. G. Bogart, 28 May 1817.
81. *Ibid.* G. G. Bogart to J. Vaughan, 20 Dec. 1817.
82. MS. Com. T. Molyneux to Archbishop of Ireland, ca. 1715?
83. *Donation Book.*
84. *Archives.* S. W. Conrad to APS, 7 Nov. 1817; Donation Book.
85. *Trans.*, n. s., vol. 1.
86. *Archives.* W. Tilghman to J. Vaughan, 1 Oct. 1817.
87. *Ibid.* G. Chambers to J. Vaughan, 2 Dec. 1817.
88. Donation Book; Trans., n. s., vol. 1.
89. Com. Recs., vol. 2.
90. *Archives.* APS. Receipt, 15 April 1818.
91. *Ibid.* G. Troost to J. Vaughan, 14 Aug. 1818.
92. Donation Book.
93. *Ibid.;* Curators Donation Book.
94. Donation Book.
95. Treasurers Records.
96. *Archives.* Asiatic Society of Bengal to G. Ord, 26 Nov. 1826.
97. *Ibid.* J. D. Godman to J. Vaughan, 18 June 1824.
98. *Trans.*, n. s., vol. 1, pp. 375ff.
99. *Archives.* Lyceum of Natural History to W. H. Keating, 21, 23 Feb. 1825.
100. *Donation Book; Trans.*, n. s., vol. 3; MS. Com. R. Harlan. Concerning fossils, 1 April 1825.
101. Com. Recs., vol. 2.
102. *Archives.* C. Smith to P. S. Du Ponceau, 13 Oct. 1825.
103. Donation Book.
104. *Ibid.; Trans.*, n. s., vol. 3.
105. *Trans.*, n. s., vol. 3.
106. *Ibid.*
107. *Archives.* APS. Report, 21 Dec. 1827.
108. *Ibid.* W. Cooper to J. Vaughan, 31 Jan. 1829; Curators Cards.

109. *Trans.*, n. s., vol. 3; Donation Book.
110. *Archives*. APS. Report, 15 Jan. 1830.
111. *Ibid.*
112. *Ibid.* R. Harlan. Concerning a new fossil genus, 16 April 1830.
113. Curators Cards.
114. MS. Com. R. Harlan. Concerning a new fossil genus, 16 April 1830.
115. Com. Recs., vol. 2.
116. *Archives*. Academy of Natural Sciences of Philadelphia to APS, 20 Sept. 1831.
117. *Ibid.* R. C. Taylor to J. Vaughan, 29 Oct. 1831.
118. *Donation Book; Trans.*, n. s., vol. 4; Curators Donation Book; Donations to the Cabinet, p. 14; *Journal of the Academy of Natural Sciences of Philadelphia*, vol. 6, p. 269.
119. Com. Recs., vol. 2.
120. *Archives*. APS. Report, 20 Jan. 1832.
121. *Donation Book; Trans.*, n. s., vol. 4.
122. *Archives*. APS. Report, 21 Sept. 1832.
123. *Trans.*, n. s., vol. 4.
124. MS. Com. W. H. Harrington to J. K. Mitchell, 13 Aug. 1833.
125. *Archives*. J. Chitty to APS, 10 Sept. 1833.
126. *Ibid.* Geological Society of London to APS, 6 Feb. 1834.
127. *Donation Book.*
128. *Ibid.;* Curators Cards; *Trans.*, n. s., vol. 4.
129. *Archives*. Forstall Bros...to R. Harlan, 21 Jan. 1834.
130. Donation Book.
131. *Archives*. Museum d'Histoire Naturelle de Paris. Catalogue...of fossil casts, 27 June 1834; *Trans.*, n. s., vol. 5; Donation Book; Cabinet Donation Book.
132. *Archives*. Forstall Bros...to R. Harlan, 16 Oct. 1834.
133. *Ibid.* Museum d'Histoire Naturelle de Paris. Catalogue of fossil casts, 7 Nov. 1834; Donation Book.
134. *Ibid.* John Chitty. Receipt 28 July 1834, 24 May 1837.
135. *Donation Book; Trans.*, n. s., vol. 5.
136. *Ibid.*
137. *Ibid.*
138. Curators Donation Book, p. 37 (J. N. Casanova to J. Vaughan, 15 Nov. 1838); Donation Book; Trans., n. s., vol. 6.
139. *Archives*. T. B. Ashton to R. Dunglison, 11 June 1839.
140. Ibid. W. E. Homer to J. Vaughan, 2 Dec. 1839.
141. Treasurers Records.
142. *Proc.*, vol. 1, p. 166; Trans., vol.7; Com. Recs., vol. 2.
143. Com. Recs., vol. 2.
144. *Proc.*, vol. 1, pp. 279-82.
145. *Archives*. C. G. Forshey to J. Vaughan, 3 Sept. 1840; Proc., vol. 1, pp. 278–279.
146. *Proc.*, vol. 1, pp. 212, 225.
147. *Archives*. APS. Statement...fossils, 19 March 1841.
148. *Ibid.* R. Harlan to J. Vaughan, 17 May 1841.
149. *Proc.*, vol. 2, p. 66.
150. *Ibid.*, pp. 102–103.
151. *Ibid.*, pp. 105–106.
152. *Ibid.*, p. 105.
153. *Ibid.*, pp. 109–110, 147.
154. *Archives*. R. Harlan to G. Ord, 16 March 1842.
155. *Proc.*, vol. 2, p. 157; Donation Book; Trans., n. s., vol. 8.
156. *Ibid.*
157. *Archives*. J. P. Wetherill to G. Ord, 20 April 1842.
158. *Ibid.* H. D. Rogers to G. Ord, 5 May 1842.
159. *Ibid.* J. Locke to J. Dobson, 12 May 1842; Proc., vol. 2, p. 185; Donation Book; *Trans.*, n. s., vol. 8.
160. *Proc.*, vol. 2, p. 191.
161. *Ibid.; Archives*. APS. Bill, 20 May 1842.
162. *Proc.*, vol. 2, p. 197.
163. *Archives*. R. Harlan to G. Ord, 25 June 1842.
164. *Ibid.* J. P. Wetherill to G. Ord, 1 July 1842.
165. *Ibid.* R. Harlan to APS, 19 Aug. 1842; *Proc.*, vol. 2, p. 207.
166. *Proc.*, vol. 2, p. 213.
167. *Ibid.*, p. 235.
168. *Ibid.*, p. 251; *Donation Book; Trans.*, n. s., vol. 9; *Archives*. E. Bossange to G. Ord, 26 Jan. 1843; E. Bossange. Statement, 26 Jan. 1843; also, E. Bossange to G. Ord, 3 Feb. 1843.
169. *Proc.*, vol. 2, pp. 264–266.
170. *Ibid.*, p. 370.
171. *Ibid.*, p. 276.
172. *Ibid.*, vol. 4, p. 30.
173. *Ibid.*, p. 35; *Donation Book; Trans.*, vol. 9.
174. *Proc.*, vol. 4, pp. 35-36.
175. *Archives*. I. Hays to G. Ord, 22 Jan. 1844.
176. *Proc.*, vol. 4, p. 43.
177. *Ibid.*, p. 49; *Donation Book; Trans.*, vol. 9.
178. *Proc.*, vol. 4, pp. 118-21.
179. *Ibid.*, p. 127.
180. *Archives*. F. Peale to G. Ord, 19 June 1845.
181. *Ibid.*, I. Hays to G. Ord, 10 June 1846.
182. *Proc.*, vol. 4, p. 269.
183. *Archives*. J. C. Warren to I. Hays, 22 June 1846.
184. Ibid., J Cassin to C. B. Trego, 25 Jan. 1849.
185. *Proc.*, vol. 5, pp. 91–94.
186. *Ibid.*, p. 110.
187. *Ibid.*, pp. 11–112.

188. *Archives.* Academy of Natural Sciences of Philadelphia. Receipt, 28 Nov. 1849.
189. Academy of Natural Sciences of Philadelphia. *Archives.* Collection 86.
190. *Archives.* F. Peale...to C. B. Trego, 12 April 1850.
191. *Proc.,* vol. 5, p. 261.
192. *Ibid.,* p. 264.
193. *Ibid.,* pp. 261–262, 267, 269.
194. *Ibid.,* vol. 5, pp. 264–265, vol. 7, pp. 175, 326.
195. *Ibid.,* vol. 5, p. 275.
196. *Ibid.,* p. 325; *Donation Books.*
197. *Ibid.,* p. 345.
198. *Ibid.,* vol. 6, p. 198.
199. *Ibid.,* vol. 7, p. 391.
200. *Ibid.,* vol. 9, p. 38.
201. *Archives.* J. Leidy to J. P. Lesley, 12 May 1863.
202. Corn. Recs., vol. 2.
203. *Proc.,* vol. 9, p. 354.
204. *Archives.* J. Leidy. Receipt, 28 March 1864.
205. *Proc.,* vol. 10, p. 204.
206. *Archives.* J. Greer to J. Henry, 8 May 1866.
207. *Proc.,* vol. 10, p. 256.
208. *Ibid.,* vol. 11, pp. 11–117, 278, 316, 368.
209. *Ibid.,* pp. 368, 370, 418, 439–440, 515, 571–572.
210. *Ibid.,* vol. 12, pp. 15–16
211. *Ibid.,* pp. 64, 73–102.
212. *Ibid.,* p. 37.
213. *Ibid.,* p. 194.
214. *Ibid.,* p. 359; vol. 13, pp. 137, 182.
215. *Ibid.,* vol. 14, p. 7.
216. *Ibid.,* pp. 17–18.
217. Curators, *Donation Book.*
218. *Proc.,* vol. 16, pp. 393-94.
219. *Ibid.,* pp. 395, 666; vol. 17, pp. 49–52.
220. *Archives.* E. C. Cope to J. P. Lesley, 5 May 1877.
221. *Proc.,* vol. 17, pp. 9, 231-32, 269, 193–196, 280–281, plates 1–10.
222. *Ibid.,* p. 311.
223. *Ibid.,* p. 709.
224. *Proc.,* vol. 17, pp. 716–719.
225. *Ibid.,* pp. 724–725.
226. *Ibid.,* vol. 18, p. 8.
227. *Ibid.,* p. 238.
228. *Ibid.,* p. 250.
229. *Ibid.,* pp. 364–369.
230. *Ibid.,* p. 414.
231. *Ibid.,* vol. 19, p. 352.
232. *Ibid.,* vol. 20, p. 199.
233. *Archives.* J. P. Lesley to H. Phillips, Jr., 10 Feb. 1885.
234. *Ibid.* J. Geismar. Memorandum, 17 June 1887.
235. *Ibid.* E. D. Cope t~ APS, 18 Oct. 1892.
236. *Ibid.* J. S. Price to J. C. Morris, 1893?
237. *Ibid.* 17 Dec. 1896.
238. Cur. Min., 31 Aug. 1898.
239. *Archives.* APS. Listing of casts...., 189-.
240. *Ibid.,* Cur. Min., 8 Nov. 1899.
241. Curators Cards in the Library.
242. *Archives.* Academy of Natural Sciences of Philadelphia to APS, 3 June 1901; Academy of Natural Sciences of Philadelphia. List, 3 June 1901.
243. Cur. Recs. Horace Richards. List...., 14 December 1949.

Chapter 6

Manufactured Goods

Benjamin Franklin's *Proposals* stated that the Society was interested in the "Improvement of vegetable Juices, as Cyders, Wines, &c....New discoveries in Chemistry, such as Improvements in Distillation, Brewing, Assaying of Ores, &c....all new Arts, Trade Manufactures, &c. that may be proposed or thought of." Until 1800 the bulk of manufactured goods received pertained to agricultural products. During the early nineteenth century, however, many societies were founded throughout the United States to assist manufacturers. Consequently, the gifts to the Society decreased and items brought in for discussion were few and of little importance—except perhaps the making of endless paper and Goodyear's production of rubberized materials.

Two primary concerns of the members in the eighteenth century were the cultivation of grapes and winemaking, and the creation of a native silk industry. To promote these interests, many pamphlets and books were acquired for the library, and some articles were published, but little came of them until towards the end of the nineteenth century when viniculture became a successful industry.

John Morgan presented on 11 March 1768 some plant matter called pappus, or down, which was contained in the pod of the Indian hemp, the Apocynum. Morgan wished to experiment on it. He thought that if it were mixed with cotton it might be spun into threadand subsequently on 1 April he showed the members "some very fine Hemp, soft as Flax." It could be spun into fine single threads and used for making "Sheets and good Sheeting." If three of these fine threads were twisted together, it could be used "to make Stockings of an excellent and durable Quality." Later, on 13 August 1768, the American Society received patterns of "Cloth, Stuffs &c. manufactured in this Province" and agreed that they, upon examination, seemed1 "equal in goodness to any of the kind imported into England.[1]

On 18 March 1768, John Morgan gave the American Society "a Collection of curious preparations for Fishes" which he had received from Lewis Nicola.[2]

The members of the American Society decided on 13 August 1768 that since information had been given them "some time since" that an oil was being extracted from sunflower seeds, and "that several Mills are erected at Bethlehem & Lancaster [Pennsylvania] for that purpose," such information should be made available to the public. Charles Thomson and George Roberts were appointed a committee to study it on 16 September.[3] The account by John Morgan was read and it was recommended that it be published in the "next Newspaper." This sunflower seed oil could "be applyed to most of the purposes for which Olive Oil is used."

Dr. Bodo Otto from Reading, Pennsylvania, sent on 20 September 1768 specimens of sunflower seed oil and cotton seed oil, with a letter about them. Members voted their thanks to him for his "friendly communications" and referred his data to the "Medical Committee to be published under their direction, without loss of time...that people may be induced before the Season is too far advanced to collect some seeds and make some quantities of the Oil."

The articles about both sunflower and cotton seed oil were ordered to be published.[4] The articles on oil from the sunflower seeds, by John Morgan and Bodo Otto, and a note by Thomas Bond on cotton seed oil, appeared in the *American Magazine* for 1769:

The person, who has raised the greatest quantity of the sunflowers with us, informs me, that one hundred plants, set about three feet distance from each other, in the same manner Indian corn is commonly planted, will produce one bushel of seed, without any other trouble, than that of putting the seed into the ground, from which he thinks one gallon of oil may be made. I observed the land, on which he planted the sunflowers, to be of the middling sort, and that he took no pains to hill them, or

even to loosen the ground about them, which from my own observations on some
planted in a neighbor's garden, I take to be of considerable use.[5]

As the sunflower is a plant of great increase, and requires much nourishment, hilling does
not seem so good a method as that of setting the seed or plant in a hole, and when the plant
is about a yard high, to throw in the mould round the stalk, so that the surface of the
ground may be even about it. By an estimate made it appears, that one acre of land wil yield
to the planter between forty and fifty bushels of seed, which will produce as many gallons
of oil. The process for making or extracting the oil, is the same as that of making linseed
oil, which I make no doubt the Society is acquainted with, and therefore shall not trouble
you with it.[6]

This article contains a far longer discussion of the process and uses of the oil, over the
signature of "Charles Thomson, Secretary. Extracted from the minutes of the Society."
Those minutes are assumed to be lost, because they are not in the Society at present.

For about fifty years members were intrigued by the first manufactured
goods presented to the American Philosophical Society held in Philadelphia for Promoting
Useful Knowledge: wine. Then, as now, each taster was a connoisseur and the wine was
drunk and discussed. Francis Alison presented on 21 June 1768 two samples of the
American product. The members sampled it, approved it, and asked him "to obtain the
receipt for making it `that it may be recommended to the Public.'" Robert Strettell Jones, on
the same date, produced a specimen of American wine and the recipe for making it:

> To every Gallon of ye common wild Fall Grapes picked clean of all Stems put a
> Gallon of clear Water, bruising them in the Oaster then strain it into an open
> Vessel, adding two Pounds and one half of brown Sugar, & setting the Liquor in a
> cool Place. Stir it twice or thrice a Day removing any Scum that may arise, untill
> none does arise. Then take a new clean Caske tinctured with Spirit, into which the
> liquor is to be strained, & set in a cool Place. Particular care must be taken not to
> expose Caske while filling to ye open Air.

On 19 July 1768 the Society asked "any Gentleman that would
communicate to them any Method of making Wine of the American grape, without Sugar
or Water or the best way of making it   with that addition." Philip Syng produced another
specimen of wine on 20 September 1768. It was made from the American small black
grape "without water or sugar, in 1767 `which appears to be perfectly sound and delicious
to the Taste.'"

Two samples of wine were presented on 7 October 1768, "the one a year
old ye other two years old, made of the black grape a native of this Province" and the recipe
was given:

> The grapes are gathered in Sept[embe]r before the frost touches them, just when the
> skin begins to have a bluish cast. One heaped bushel of grapes is used to make a
> barrel of wine. The grapes are mashed, then a quantity of water added, which is
> suffered to stand on the grapes two days; then draw it off into the barrel and to each
> gallon put 27 [ ] good Muscavado Sugar. About a quart of good Rum is then
> added, brandy it is thought would be better, when the liquor is sufficiently
> fermented the Cask is bunged up & kept in a cool cellar.

> The wine was fined a few days before drawn by dissolving 2 [pounds?] of Sugar in
> some of the wine & pouring it into the Cask.

> N. B. The Cask should be sweet and seasoned with a little Rum or brandy.[7]

On 11 November 1768 two specimens of wine, one a year old and the other
of the present year, were presented to the Society. Both were made by Morice Pound from
grapes which he had planted. He brought a letter subscribed to by 22 neighbors, "men of
respecable character," who certified that:

> The said Morice had resided some better than four Years in Red lyon hundred in the
> County of Newcastle [Delaware. At that date, what is now Delaware was a part of

the province of Pennsylvania.], during which time though but a poor man, he had cleared 12 Acres of Land and planted 18,000 Vines, that upwards of 8,000 of them are now growing and that about 2050 are in a flourishing state; that in the year 1767 (two years and half from his first planting the Slips) he pressed out above 150 Gallons [of] Wine. Of this wine was one of the Specimens produced.

The American Society was pleased with Pound's achievement and awarded him "Ten Pounds as a reward for introducing so valuable a Culture as that of the Grape" into the province.[8]

From Georgia, on 16 January 1769, came a "Sample of Chinese vetches, six bottles of Soy and six pounds of powdered Sago" from Samuel Bowen. The vetches and soy seeds were distributed but no report seems to have been made on their growth and development.

Type made in Connecticut by Abel Buel was received on 3 May 1769. Benjamin Gale, of Killingsworth, Connecticut, wrote a long letter describing Buel as a man well worth encouraging. Not only had Buel made buttons and jewelry from American crystals, he designed and sent type "already Set, in order to be inserted if the Society think proper in your Chronicle." Gale continued:

when the impression is made on paper the publick will be better able to judge of the performance, if any defects are observable as these are his first performance they must be deemed pardonable, any defects pointed out to him by the Printers his abilities are sufficiently able to Correct...the Discovery of type founding I esteem a most extraordinary attainment which may be rendered a permanent advantage to all N[orth] America.

As your Society was incorporated on a most extensive Plan, and for the most usefull purposes of life, I thought it a Tribute due to them, to give them the first Specimen of his Abilities, and that Americans ought first to be made Acquainted with the Discovery .[9]

The type "Set" was struck and printer Thomas Bradford showed the results to the members. The report was encouraging. The metal was good and "they doubt not he will correct the defects that appear...different sizes, standing out of line, & the impression of some being too faint." Thanks were ordered "for his spirited & useful undertaking" and a specimen of Caslon was ordered to be sent to Buel "for imitation."

"Naso" sent a recipe for "Pompion Ale" from Buckingham County, Virginia, in February 1771. The recipe for the pumpkin concoction was:

Let the Pompions be beaten in a Trough and pressed as Apples. The expressed Juice is to be boiled in a Copper a considerable Time and carefully skimmed that there may be no Remains of the fibrous Part of the Pulp. After that Instruction is answered let the Liquor be hopped cooled fermented &c. as Malt Beer.

The Person who sends this Receipt has made Pompion Ale that has been thought by many to be of Malt, but being no Lover of Malt Beer he confesses he did not like it himself on Account of their Similitude of Taste & Flavour. They differ in nothing but in one circumstance which he believes difficult to prevent. A small Twang of the Pompion remained after the Brewing...N.B. 3 Dozen Bottles were filled two Years ago with Pompion Ale. Tis greatly improved and the Pompion Twang has acquired something of a Mellowness approaching to Musk which is far more agreeable than before.

A very palatable Liquor may be made from Peaches in the above Manner with or without Hops. [10]

Henry William Stiegel, from Manheim, Lancaster County, Pennsylvania, presented some specimens of flint glass which he manufactured, on 21 June 1771. This was fine crystal made it by adding pulverized flint to the liquid glass. The members were very favorably impressed and Stiegel was given a generous testimonial which was used in his advertising and which helped him to gain a grant of   150 pounds sterling from the Pennsylvania Assembly. Stiegel advertised his wares with the admonition, "it is the indispensable duty, as well as interest of every real well wisher of America, to promote and encourage manufactures among ourselves." Another plus was that he would sell his "goods on much lower terms, than such imported from Europe are usually sold." John Bartram and David Rittenhouse bought and used the glass and Bartram "declared that the glass was equal to any that he saw from Great Britain.[11]

On 16 June 1786 Benjamin Franklin received a letter with some silk enclosed, which had been dyed with the American red root [*Lachnanthes Tinctoria*], or Indian paint, also known as the New Jersey tea plant. The letter described the process of making the dye and contained information "on the medical qualities of the root."

Christopher and C. Marshall, who painted much of Philosophical Hall, presented on 16 June 1786 "from their Elaboratory," glauber salts and sal ammoniac. "These salts are equal in quality, if not superior, to any imported, and are sold at a lower rate."[12]

Specimens of white (clear) glass were presented on 6 April 1787 from Mr. Deneufville, of Albany, New York. He offered "the first Proof of a GlassHouse I have been concerned in erecting... near Albany—not as claiming much merit in that art but a pattern of what American Materials will do."[13]

Benjamin Rush wrote a paper on maple sugar and the committee on publications was ordered on 16 September 1791 to see that it was published. By 25 November it had not appeared and the printer refused to publish it until he was given explicit orders to do so. Rush wrote John Vaughan that it would either appear in the Transactions or he would publish it in a pamphlet for the people who were interested in the "sugar lands will render it difficult to detain it much longer from the public eye."[14]

Du Ponceau presented on 20 January 1792 some recently invented French dyes and suggested that the Society should experiment with them.[15] Johann Rodolf Valltravers sent some specimens of hemp, produced by "a new method of carding, Spinning & Weaving raw Hemp, superior to & cheaper than Linnen" by Mr. Dandivan. He recommended that the Society encourage Dandivan to come to America and begin this business. It was discussed at the 15 March 1793 meeting, and Alexander Anderson, interested in animal wool, presented on 3 April 1795, a shawl made from the common Russian goat hair.

Henry Guest wrote about the preservation of meat and flour by charcoal in 1796. He stated that flour purchased in China had charcoal pieces in it and that the flour remained good. He understood that the Negroes in "St. Domingue frequently practice the same." Insofar as charcoal helped preserve meat, he referred to comments by Lorenz Crell and Joseph Priestley. Priestley heard of the technique first from the Russians, and Crell had published on the subject. Guest said that in the West Indies they needed a better way to preserve flour for a longer time than in Europe and he wished the Society would investigate the virtues of charcoal.[16]

Benjamin Schultz wrote of oils prepared from American vegetables, but the committee reported on 7 February 1800 that it could not recommend publication "in its present diffuse and irregular state." However, because the information could prove useful, the Society might publish an abstract.[17]

Joseph Priestley, Jr., presented on 5 October 1801 the composition for enamel which had been "brought [with] some of the Pots with him from England." The ingredients include flint, granite, lead, borax, argillaceous, nitre, calx of tin, potash, red and white lead and white marble.[18]

Benjamin Smith Barton presented on 17 December 1802 a specimen of ware which was formed from clay from Lancaster County,[19] and Benjamin Schultz forwarded on 4 March 1803 a description of, and "on Paper made from refuse Cotton and dyed red." Barton was asked to report on it. Sometime in 1803 a lengthy memoir in French was received on how to make salt water potable.[20]

Thomas Cooper, who had recently immigrated from Manchester, England, told John Vaughan of a process of marking linen with India ink on 20 July 1804. The ink, he said, was not "defaced by bleaching. In a common tea spoonful of aqua fortis mixed with two teaspoonfulls of water, Dissolve 1/8 of silver dollar, or possibly the acid may dissolve 1/16 more. To this solution add as much lamp black & as much gum arabic in powder, as you can take upon an 11 d piece. This will stand the whole process of Bleaching."[21]

A memoir, on the "Method of curing Beef & Pork at Dublin" with salt was received from Bird Wilson on 12 December 1805.[22] In 1805 James Berthoud & Co., of Louisville, Kentucky, had a far more detailed directions for salting and packing beef.[23] On 5 April 1805 Robert R. Livingston's letter, about the manufacture of cloth from seal fur, with specimens sent, was read.

When I was in England Sir Joseph Banks gave me a piece of the furred Seal skin in its native State together with a piece from which the coarse hair was drawn out so as to render the fur uniform & beautiful & a small slip of cloath made from this fur. He could not tell me the process by which the hair was drawn out but I understand it to be heating the skin & then drawing out the hair from the back, the long hair necessarily protruding its roots for that.

This discovery is very important to us who have almost exclusively the Commerce of these skins. They have risen in consequence to eighteen shillings sterling in England, whereas they were worth but two Dollars formerly in China, and perhaps when we know the process we shall find them still more valuable in our manufactories there as an object of foreign commerce.

I send the Society a sample of each of these objects wishing it disperse them as much as possible with a view to promote a discovery of the process.[24]

James Mease was asked to report on this process.[26]

Charles Varle, a French engineer, delivered a paper on "An Easy Method to reduce calcareous matters into lime, saving both fuel and Labour" and it was read 6 February 1807. With this are two sketches of the necessary kiln.[27] A specimen of the "first zinc rolled in America" was received on 16 June 1809 from Joseph Cloud. It was rolled at the temperature between 212° and 3000° F. in an operation directed by Cloud.[28]

Thomas Jefferson forwarded on 4 May 1810 paper made from the *Morus rubra*, the American mulberry, by Silvain Godon. With this was a communication by Godon on the subject.[29] The committee reported on 16 June 1810 that this "communication on the Manufacture of Paper from the Bark of the American Mulberry" was worthy of being published in the *Transactions*.[30]

On 5 October 1810 some French specimens of stereotype and three pages of the letters or matrices, were given by Count Pohlen.[30]

On 17 August 1813 T. M. Forman wrote John Vaughan that "Banne oil," regardless how well purified, nearly always left a sediment in the bottle. He sent some to Vaughan for B. S. Barton to taste and "in order to give it a full chance, it should be prepared in due form with two or three heads of good Lettuce, and some cold *fresh* meat."[31]

John D. Robinson wrote Vaughan on 7 January 1815 describing how vegetable oils were prepared.[32] On 19 March 1819 Joshua and Thomas Gilpin presented a specimen of "endless paper" which they had made. This is still in the holdings of the Society.

From Chatham, Connecticut, Frank Le Baron and others presented on 5 May 1820 a "Glass ink stand Colord by Cobalt." The cobalt mines there were being worked successfully and the manufacture of this glass approached "the metallic state of cobalt." Also, blue thread glass made from Chatham cobalt was delivered.[33]

An extract from the 18 November 1831 *American Farmer* describing Charles A. Bannitz's method of extracting linseed and sunflower oils is in the Library. It was taken from Bannitz's manuscript: "Mode of extracting linseed and sunflower oil;" (1831).[34]

Before 1831 Fairman, Draper, Underwood & Company gave some specimen sheets of "Bank Note Engravings, Busts, Vignettes, &c." At the same general time, Charles Tappan & Company presented some specimens of "their Bank Notes Engraving, &c." which had been submitted to banks.[35]

The efforts to create a silk industry in the United States continued. H. Bry wrote Peter S. Du Ponceau on 6 August 1832 and forwarded:

> a piece of silk, wove by silkworms at my residence. It is a mere object of curiosity, and my second attempt which I intend to repeat, being confident that it can be improved; and that new kind of silk stuff can be made much more even by those valuable insects close attention being paid to them while at work. You can discover by this that it can be made thick or thin ... it never will however be an object of utility.

John Vaughan noted on 17 August 1832 that this was a specimen of silk "Cloth manufactured by Silk Worms on a Plane Surface instead of Cocoons."[36]

From Middleburg, Maryland, William Zollickoffer sent Du Ponceau on 27 December 1833 a specimen of silk which was "the product of worms that were raised entirely upon the Laetuca Sativa, or common garden lettuce." Since there were not enough mulberry trees in the United States to feed the insects, he thought he could help the silk industry by using lettuce, for "every individual who has a little garden" could produce silk. Zollickoffer signed his name and added: "M. D., F. C. P., of the Medico-Botanical Society of London, &c."[37] He wrote again on 26 July 1834 and asked Du Ponceau if the specimen had arrived. He stated that he had "no other desire than the advancement of the arts and sciences, and the benefit of mankind in general, in the prosecution of experimental investigations upon the different subjects that present themselves to my consideration."[38] The members referred the specimen on 15 August 1834 to Du Ponceau and he replied two days later.

Zellikoffer had described the silk as "inferior to none in point of *strength*, beauty and richness of appearance." Du Ponceau refused to comment upon the "beauty and richness of appearance" but mentioned only the strength:

> The silk you have thus produced is greatly deficient in point of strength, the thread can be broken with the smallest effort of the hand which is not the case with silk produced by worms fed on the Mulberry leaves ....

> The society, therefore, could not produce this to the world as a new and useful discovery, the same having been attempted several times in Europe and elsewhere & always found to produce the same results...The lettuce has been tried over and over, it has always produced an inferior silk...So that among silk Culturalists, the use of that species of food is altogether exploded and laid aside.[39]

Du Ponceau reported his reply to the members on 7 November 1834.

George (?) Evans sent John Vaughan on 27 August 1836, " a small skein of silk" which his father had raised:

> from eggs from Italy and sent to this country by Doct[o]r Franklin a short time before the American Revolution. He had previously sent a parcel of Italian mulberry seed which produced the leaves upon which the worms were fed. My Father engaged in the culture of Silk; which he continued three or four years as an experiment; but the revolutionary War coming on the experiment was given up, and never afterwards resumed. I know not the quality of Silk raised; but it must have been considerably as many pounds were manufactured into cloathing for the family during the War and some was sold.

> I was too young at the time to attend to the process of the culture of Silk; but I do recollect an observation frequently made by those who fed the worms that they were five weeks coming to perfection on the Italian mulberry and six on the American.[40]

Marmaduke Burrough presented prior to 1835 "a very large and interesting Collection of fabrics, from the Philippine Islands, Alsan and other parts of Asia. Some were made of hemp and the leaf of the pineapple." Also, some specimens of "the Essential Oils of Croton and Camphor from the East Indies" were included.[41]

Some specimens of hemp and flax from the manufactory of Sands Olcott in Philadelphia was presented on 22 June 1838. Dexter Stone had invented the process as well as the machinery so that both hemp and flax could be spun by "common Cotton Machinery." Stone pointed out that by his process "the rotting or hackling is not required, and all the fibres of Hemp or Flax are converted into yarn, of any required quality or fineness, at a Cost not materially differing from cotton.[42]

On 21 December 1838 a donation of hemp made from the stalk of the pineapple, and a brush "from Japan" which was manufactured from coconut fibers, were received from L. B. Stone.[43]

Franklin Peale delivered some specimens on 19 December 1845 of gum elastic goods manufactured by the New Haven inventor, Charles Goodyear. He spoke of the gum's usual state and how temperature affected it. Goodyear was able to make the gum retain its elasticity regardless of the temperature. The items exhibited included a sheet which took "impressions of a finely engraved copper plate" and a portable map, "which could be put into the pocket like a handkerchief." Bathing mats and "Fancy table covers" were also shown. Peale commented that "the manufacturers were now principally employed in the production of articles of necessity and utility."[44]

On 15 September 1848 Martin H. Boye exhibited some tea specimens which had been artificially colored. He could not detect "any distinct colouring matter, and believes it to have been coloured by the dust of a superior kind of tea. The colour on the outside was a fine green, and exhibits a high lustre, but when this is scraped off, the colour in the inside is much darker."[45]

On 18 April 1851 George M. Justice exhibited a specimen of "flax cotton" made by Mr. Clausen.[46] Justice produced for inspection by the members on 18 June 1858 "sundry substances consisting of paraffine, lubricating oil, burning oil, naptha and benzole." These were made by the Union Coal and Oil Company, Maysville, Kentucky, from cannel coal mined in western Virginia. Capacity was being expanded in order to produce 3,000 gallons daily. The coal yielded from each ton "about an average of 55 gallons of crude oil, from two to three gallons of benzole, and the same quantity of naptha; also nearly 18 pounds of pure parrafine. The burning oil loses nearly onethird in the purifying process."[47]

The endless paper is the only item left in the Society in the category of manufactured goods.

Manufactured Goods—References
1. American Society. *Minutes.*
2. *Ibid.*
3. *Ibid.*
4. *Ibid.*
5. APS. *Memoirs,* vol. 77: The Transactions of the American Philosophical Society &c. Published in the American Magazine during 1769. (1969)
6. *Pennsylvania Gazette,* 6 Oct. 1768.
7. American Society. *Minutes.*
8. *Ibid.*
9. *Archives.* B. Gale to T. Bond, 25 April 1769.
10. MS. Com. Naso to APS; Feb. 1771.
11. Hindle, B. *David Rittenhouse,* pp. 199–200.
12. *Trans.,* n. s., vol. 3,; The American Museum, Sept. 1789.
13. *Archives.* Deneufville to S. Vaughan, 6 April 1787; Trans., n. s., vol. 3.
14. MS. Com. B. Rush to J. Vaughan, 25 Nov. 1791.
15. *Archives.* P. S. Du Ponceau to J. Williams, 20 Jan. 1792.
16. MS Com. Henry Guest. Concerning..., 1796.
17. *Archives.* APS. Report..., 7 Feb. 1800.
18. MS Com. J. Priestley, Jr. Composition..., 5 Oct. 1801.
19. *Trans.,* n. s., vol. 6.
20. MS. Com. Memoir..., 1803.
21. *Ibid.* Verbal communications.
22. MS. Com. B. Wilson to J. Vaughan, 12 Dec. 1805.
23. *Ibid.* J. Berthoud & Co. Directions..., 1805.
24. *Archives.* R. R. Livingston to , 23 Sept. 1804.
25. Com. Rec., vol. 2.
26. *Trans.,* n. s., vol. 6.
27. MS. Com. C. Varle. Concerning..., 6 Feb. 1807.
28. *Trans.,* n. s., vol. 6.
29. *Archives.* S. Godon. Specimen..., 4 May 1810.
30. Donation Book.
31. Misc. MS. Col. T. M. Forman to J. Vaughan, 17 Aug. 1813.
32. MS. Com. J. D. Robinson to J. Vaughan, 7 Jan. 1815.
33. *Donations Book.*
34. Misc. MS. Col. C. A. Bannitz. Mode..., 1831.
35. *Trans.,* n. s., vol. 4.
36. *Archives.* H. Bry to P. S. Du Ponceau, 6 Aug. 1832.
37. *Ibid.* W. Zolleckoffer to P. S. Du Ponceau, 27 Dec. 1833.
38. Ibid. 26 July 1834.
39. *Ibid.* P. S. Du Ponceau to W. Zolleckoffer, 17 Aug. 1834.
40. *Ibid.* G. Evans to J. Vaughan, 27 Aug. 1836.
41. *Trans.,* n. s., vol. 4.
42. *Donation Book;* Proc., vol. 1, p. 63; Trans., n. s., vol. 4.
43. Donation to Cabinet, p. 32.
44. *Proc.,* vol. 4, p. 221.
45. *Ibid.* vol. 5, pp. 3637.
46. *Ibid.* p. 195.
47. *Ibid.* vol. 6, p. 320.

Chapter 7
Mineralogical Specimens

The first encyclopedia published in the United States defines mineralogy as "that science which teaches us the properties of mineral bodies, and by which we learn how to characterize, distinguish, and class them into a proper order." Although, fossils were considered mineral deposits they are listed separately in this volume.

The *Encyclopedia: or a Dictionary of Arts, Sciences, and Miscellaneous Literature* allied chemistry with mineralogy and declared that only lately "since the principles of chemistry were well understood, that mineralogy has been advanced to any degree of perfection." Practically all the pages of this lengthy chapter pertain to chemical analysis of minerals, with a careful discussion of the apparatus essential to their study.[1] The *Encyclopedia* appeared in the 1790s over several years.

John C. Greene, in his an excellent article, "The Development of Mineralogy in Philadelphia 1781–1820," stated that from 1780 to 1820 the development of American science occurred, and that those years "were also the years in which mineralogy became a science." The Society is referred to at times in this article, but the great development of mineral collecting was done by the younger organization, the Academy of Natural Sciences of Philadelphia.[2] Mineralogy was viewed as an adjunct to chemistry, which was taught at the University of Pennsylvania. Prior to 1800 almost nothing about mineralogy is considered important enough to warrant mention by Greene in his study. William Maclure in 1802 "recalled, `a small cabinet of mineralogy' which Dr. [Adam] Seybert brought from Goettingen which cost him 15 dollars was the only one we had to run to in Philadelphia."[3]

Prior to 1800 almost every cabinet of curiosities had a mineral collection: in Paris alone, by the year 1800, there were sixty-one such collections. The desire to, and need for, arranging these collections in a rational manner became more and more apparent, and Greene remarks on the "difficulties inherent in establishing mineralogy as an adjunct of medicine and chemistry." Several attempts were made to classify minerals, and the Society possesses the most famous: Abraham Gottlob Werner, *Letztes Mineral-System;* Martin Heinrich Klaproth, *Analytical Essays Towards Promoting the Chemical Knowledge of Mineral Substances;* Freiherr Jon Jakob von Berzelius, *Attempt to Establish a Pure Scientific System of Mineralogy;* Jean Baptiste Louis de Rome de l'Isle, *Description Methodique d'une Collection Mineraux;* René Just Hauy, *Essai d'une Thorie sur la Structure des Crystaux;* and, Richard Kirwan, *Elements of Mineralogy,* the first extensive treatise on mineralogy in English.

Benjamin Franklin's *Proposal,* founding the Society, stated that it would be interested in knowing about "all new discovered Fossils in different Countries, as Mines, Minerals, Quarries."[4] These professed goals conflicted with the actual interests of many members and those personal interests determined the future of the Society. And yet, some of the members were interested in aspects of mineralogy.

Saltpetre was important during the Revolution; during the ensuing peace, manufacturing became more important. Knowledge of the natural resources of the country was needed, and John Coakley Lettsom, in London, wrote another member: "You ought to institute...a mineralogical Society to try to light the treasures you possess...You possess much but you do not know your wealth." He referred to England's great manufacturing organizations, based on the wealth of minerals in the British Isles. The United States, of course, possessed greater resources, unknown and untapped. Early on, the Society was superseded by other organizations which pursued specific and narrower aims more forcefully than the Society ever would have done. For example, The Chemical Society, founded in 1792, published papers on minerals in the Medical Repository. The Philadelphia Medical Museum published several articles on mineralogy during the 1790s and early 1800s.

Mineral specimens nonetheless had arrived at the Society over the years and some members commented on them and gave other specimens. Nevertheless, however many specimens the Society collected, its mineral collection was neither a large nor an important one, especially when compared with that of the Academy of Natural Sciences of Philadelphia.

18 March 1768
A "Specimen of American Bole." Bole is a friable earthy clay usually red colored by iron oxide. It may be used for dyeing.[5]

John Morgan

25 March 1768
Some asbestos from Chester County, Pennsylvania.[6]

James Alexander

All the curiosities were then placed "in the hands of Owen Biddle until a proper Place is provided to deposit them in."

25 March 1768
A sample of Maryland ochre "which in its native State is a good light blue Paint." However, with some "FireHeat it becomes a good Olive Colour." Even more, "when highly calcined [it] is a good Brown and may prove a very useful Paint."

Owen Biddle

22 April 1768
A sample of yellow ochre from "a large vein of this ore in Cecil County Maryland about 2 Miles from the head of Chesapeake Bay." Some experiments had been made which proved it to be a useful paint and by burning, "it will answer the end of Spanish Brown."

Thomas Gilpin

20 May 1768
Some "curious Specimens of red and yellow Oker," from Chester County, Pennsylvania.

[DONOR UNKNOWN]

1 April 1768
"[V]arious Specimens of Ores." [8]

John Wood

21 June 1768
Specimens of yellow ochre from *Pequea*, Cecil County, Maryland, and from *Pequea*, Pennsylvania.

R. Syng

Benjamin Gale of Killingsworth, Connecticut, sent the American Society on 15 July 1768, through Cadwallader Evans and William Franklin, a box holding six "rough and six polished Crystals the growth of Connecticut." He wrote that Abel Buel, jeweler and lapidary, ground and polished the crystals. He praised Buel, "who from the force of a Natural Genius Invented a Machine for grinding and polish[ing]crystals of Every kind without ever seeing a like machine or having any Instruction from anyone."[9] Also, on 19 August, a collection of "unpolished Crystals of several colours" was received by the American Society.[10]

Isaac Bartram delivered on 19 August 1768 a "Sparr of a Vitriolic Quality" and a "Natural Cylander of Stone," about ten inches in length, which was found on the seashore in Maryland. There were many of this size, and some of greater lengths on the shore.

John Morgan read a paper from Peter Miller of Ephrata on 26 August 1768 to the American Society concerning a "Sample of whitish coloured powder of the Quality of Lead." This sample was found lying between strata of certain rock formations in Lancaster County, Pennsylvania.[11]

3 February 1769
A sample of asbestos.

H. Hollingsworth

On 6 October 1769 members decided to advertise for mineralogical specimens (clays) for the Society. This advertisement was "deferred for some time" on 3 November 1769.

Andrew Oliver sent on 6 December 1771 a small amount of American asbestos, and some was prepared as wicks for lamps, and some as writing paper. This gift was referred to the Committee of Astronomy and Husbandry and American Improvements.

19 December 1771
Some "Earth or Clay."

John Arbo

19 March 1773
Marl from near Wilmington, Delaware and "Alum from the Banks of the Monongahela." These were "thankfully received & deposited in the Cabinet." Another two samples of the same arrived on 19 March 1775.

Thomas Gilpin

18 July 1773
"A specimen of Sinopian Earth [sinopite], Antimony ore, & Alum Bark."

Redmond Howell

A specimen of asphalt which had been found in East Florida.

Mr. Bainbridge

16 February 1781
A paper "on the discovery of a large body of talc, 70 miles from Portsmouth," New Hampshire, along with a specimen. It was listed in the *Transactions* as: "Specimens of Talc from a large body of this fossil."[12]

General Sullivan

October 1782
A specimen of epsom salt, "found `fossil'" in Virginia. James Hutchinson was given it for analysis.

[UNKNOWN]

4 March 1785
Two "very large pieces of chrystal" which had been found in Lancaster County, Pennsylvania.13

William Henry

15 May 1789
A vial of petroleum, "found in Oil Creek which flows into the Alleghany [sic]." Petroleum was found "in considerable quantity" there.

William Turnbull

8 September 1789
Coal, white vitriol, slate, brick, burnt slate, alum nitre, free stone, etc., which had been found in a bank of a stream near Washington, Pennsylvania. Redick wrote that he and a friend, Dr. Baird, were "equally solicitous in making useful discoveries and observations which may [help in acquiring] any rational knowledge, or even rational conjectures, respecting the antient inhabitants of this *World* as well as affording materials for a natural history of it."[14]

David Redick

16 January 1795
Two minerals from the Pyrenees Mountains were presented on by: a piece of copper and a piece of iron ore.[15]

Mederic L. E. Moreau de Saint Mery

5 May 1797
James Woodhouse and Adam Seybert were asked to prepare a listing of the mineralogical specimens.

24 November 1797
Tin and other English ores, crystals, and spars.[16]

Judge George Turner

7 December 1798
"[A] very fine specimen of Talk [talc], from the back part of New Hampshire." The donor wrote a long letter about this mineral, for it was "found in abundance in the back parts of New Hampshire," and the members thought it would "probably prove to be a valuable acquisition to the Arts by supplying the place of Glass where it is required to be secure against heat & fracture," as in lanterns and magazines.

Thomas Passmore

20 June 1800
Three specimens of Iceland crystals [spar] which had been found on a sand bar in the Mississippi River.[17]

Andrew Ellicott

19 November 1802
A specimen of rock salt, "from the Missouri, where it is in large quantities on the surface of the Earth."

Dr. Watkins

19 November 1802
Calcined earth wherein were embedded marine shells.

[UNKNOWN]

Thomas Peters Smith, a young man passionately interested in science and in helping make the United States more powerful and useful, was made a member in 1799. He went to Europe to study and died while returning to the United States. He left his mineral collection to the Society, and John Vaughan and John R. Smith were appointed a committee on 19 November 1802 to inquire about the will. On 6 May 1803 an extract of Thomas Peters Smith's will, "dated at Sea, with Observations by the R[everen]d R. Peters" was presented to the Society by the committee as a partial report. The committee was then authorized to call upon "Thomas Peters Esq. of Baltimore or any other Person who may be in possession of the effects left to the Society...& are Authorized to give such security...to the Administrator." The will was informal, dated "At Sea Lat 41 Long 46 2 Sept. 1802" and was written as a letter to R. Peters:

> To the American Philosophical Society my Collection of Minerals with the propert [sic] Catalogues to be found among my Papers, to be arranged by them, so as to serve as a Scientific Collection but more particularly in a Geological & manufacturing Point of View. They will find among my Papers Descriptions of the various chemical Manufactories, such as Iron Copper Pottery &c. as carried on in the various Manufactories, of Europe I have visited. References are made to such of the Specimens as relate to the Manufactories which they will find properly noticed. Should they find any Information therein contained useful to the Manufactories of my Country I beg them to publish them.[18]

The committee read on 20 May 1803 its "letter of indemnity, directed to Mr. Peters" and the members approved it. By 20 July 1804 the committee which was to arrange Smith's minerals "reported difficulties in fixing on any system.[19] The members ordered the committee to use Richard Kirwan's system [20] based on his second edition, and to report in September. Thomas Peters wrote the committee on 25 July 1803, that he had sent two boxes and one cask which was all he had received:

I should have sent them at the time you wrote, but on looking for a description of the said Minerals I could not find any other than what was in his Journals, which is wrote in so bad a hand that I could not have had an accur[ate] Copy made from it, then I got a person Close to me who was used to the Names of Minerals, therefore I have cut out from the Journal all relating to the said Minerals and also from his own papers, which as you and Others used to the different Names of Minerals you may favor the original list which I have however sent with them, do better than I could do for you. [21]

A copy of Smith's journal was made for the Society and on 27 August 1804 the treasurer paid Edward Ferrer $16.00 for copying "Pages from the Journals of Thomas P. Smith." These lists are in the Library, as are four volumes of Smith's journal of his European tour wherein he notes his observations on the technological improvements in manufacturing and mining.[22]

Nevertheless, difficulties remained in identifying and sorting the minerals and on 19 August 1804 Adam Seybert, Robert Hare, James Woodhouse, Benjamin Smith Barton, and John R. Coxe were named a committee to arrange the Smith gift. On 18 January 1805 it was discharged and Adam Seybert was appointed to arrange the minerals.[23] A committee on minerals named on 4 February 1803 was to examine all future donations. James Woodhouse, John Church, William S. Jacobs, Benjamin S. Barton, John R. Coxe, Thomas T. Hewson, and Robert Hare were the committee. Care had to be taken of the specimens already acquired and Mary Wells was paid $10.00 for "making 600 Mineral pasteboard Cases".[24] This was the first of many such purchases.

With the minerals and journals of Thomas P. Smith came two letters. One was dated 18 April 1801 and was from George Knapp. It concerned samples of English coal which his traveling companion, "Bostonian" Knapp, acquired for him:

Agreeable to the promise I gave you at Paris—I went in search of several specimens of Coal for you & at last with little difficulty I procured some few & have given you a written description of each piece with it. Perhaps the description is not sufficient for your purpose. I found these Colliers to know very little more than they ought about them—they being a class of men not altogether remarkable for their politeness and information. I could get no other than is mentioned. Coals are not housed and separated in London as you expected but are brought in large flat bottomed barges from the Colliers—and distributed from them to whoever would purchase. At first I enquired at several of the Counting houses of the Coal merchants the Masters & Clerks—knew scarcely any thing more than about their being very good & high & recommended themselves & their Coals to me so strongly I could hardly get away from them & found it almost impossible to persuade them that I was no speculator. They however at last told me that if I would go to the Colliers in the pool—off Wapping—where they all lay—I would get the description of the Coal from them...They were the prettiest collection of smutty-faced gentry I ever saw in my life... I hope you have had a happy journey over the Alps—a pied—& wish that you may have acquired all that Mineralogie & other scientific and useful knowledge you seemed so early bent on & indefatigably pursuing. [25]

A letter from James Watt, Jr., to Thomas P. Smith stated that he was sending two boxes of fossils (minerals) on 30 December 1801. He wrote that Smith's "Collection from Dudley" was also forwarded and he had "accompanied it with a few of the excrescences of my own Cabinet." He hoped they would "reach you in safety, although some of your coal specimens are of a very tender kind and were not of a form well adapted for packing."[26] The French government had allocated T. P. Smith some minerals, and the list 27 of 85 items which accompanied them, by Tonnelier, is in the library.[27]

Robert R. Livingston wrote Thomas Jefferson on 26 November 1802 about the use of burnt pyrites as manure, and about clays and spar used at Sevres, near Paris. He forwarded samples, and Jefferson delivered the letter and samples to the Society on 18 March 1803:

> I had heard here that the ashes of Pyrites were used as a manure, but I could meet with no Satisfactory information on the Subject till in a little excursion that I made lately into Flanders I was enabled to See the process & to preserve the Samples I enclose.
>
> I observed two persons at Some distance from the road employed stirring a heap of earth which emitted Smoke but no flame visible at that distance. Leaving my post-chaise & going to them I found that the earth they were burning was a Pyrite Sample No. 1. This was laid upon an earthern floor, in the open air in a bed of about thirty feet long & ten wide and about a foot thick. It was reduced into Small particles like what I enclose & when dry contained Sufficient Sulphure to burn without any addition. When the fire was checked in time it formed the red ashes No. 2 which was more valuable than the bluish No. 3. These ashes were sifted in a fine si[e]ve when they were carried many miles on the back of ashes and used as a manure particularly on grass lands in the proportion of above Six bushels to the acre. The corn was also dried in it after it had been Steeped before Serving & very considerable [fare?] was found from this process. You will observe in this a Striking resemblance to the effects of Gypsum & indeed it almost demonstrates that Gypsum derives its fertilizing quality from the Sulphuric acid. This is probably disengaged by Slow combustion & retained by the earth either in a combined or uncombined State as the earth may or may not be calcarious or as it may or may not contain vegetable matter reducible to ashes with which it would unite. In writing to the agricultural Society of New York upon this Subject I have Suggested to them the Idea of trying diluted Sulphuric & other acids as manures. The effects of which would be more instantaneous probably than any combination of them with earth. Perhaps too this fertilizing quality may not be confined to the mineral acids. If not I have proposed to them a trial of the pyroligneous acid which may by easy process obtained cheaper than any other.
>
> But the Samples enclosed may enable the members of Society to find the earth which I have reason to think by no means uncommon in the United States. I also Send Small Samples of the Clay used in the fabric of China at Sev[r]es to aid the rechereches of Such of their members as may wish to make it an object of inquiry.

Secretary John Vaughan wrote Robert R. Livingston on 23 June 1804 thanking him for the clay and pyrites. Agriculture was making an ever-increasing use of minerals: "at least 10,000 Tons Gypsum are annually consumed in this State alone." Vaughan felt that a new life had been given the Society by the "endeavors we are making to facilitate the knowledge of the new European discoveries." He lamented the lack of public funds for this purpose, but added, "we have nothing to rely upon but the patriotic exertions of individuals, attached to Science & to the promotion of it here." He added that Peter Stephen Du Ponceau "has become very Zealous to forward our views."[28]

At the meeting of 18 February 1803 Benjamin Smith Barton stated that he had tried many experiments in order to see if sulphate of iron was highly nutritious to plants. Joseph Priestley "observed that Mr. Livingston saw the peasants in france [sic] preparing it. They told him they put about six bushels per acre & found it better than Plaster of Paris. Dr. [George] Pearson of London, has also made a similar discovery."[29]

6 May 1803

A specimen of argilla porcella (porcelain clay) which came from the foot of the Catoctin Mountains, near Hagerstown, Maryland.[30]

Benjamin S. Barton

7 October 1803

Some specimens of rock crystal from the La Plata region.

By 2 December John Vaughan reported that a room and a case were in readiness to receive the mineralogical collection. He had hired Jasper Carter, George Flake, and William Broome to make, glaze, and paint the two mineral cases "of 48 lights," thereby spending $150. These were placed in the southeastern room, second floor, which was known as the Minerals Room.[31]

W. Lewis presented on 7 March 1804, through Jefferson, a bone and:

> flint formed in clay. The first visible mark of its formation was a white granulus substance adhering to the clay, and as it [the geological work] progressed, it became more and more compact, until at length it assumed its present form. [Also,] a quartise [quartzite] rock, formed in a similar way, but in soil. The same process attended this stone, & I think that the elegant vegetable lineaments on its inner surfaces prove sufficiently its origin. [Lewis's long letter concerning geological time and formation ended:] Should you deem these I send you, worthy the attention of the Philosophic society, be so good as to give them a conveyance; and after an examination, my desire is, that they be presented to Mr. [Charles Willson] Peale.[32]

After examination, the committee reported on 20 April 1804 that as the letter "principally refers to minerals which are to be presented to Mr. Peale agreeably to the request of Mr. Lewis it appears to them proper that it accompany the minerals.[33]

13 April 1804

Some specimens of cannel coal from England.

[DONOR UNKNOWN]

17 August 1804

Gypsum from Nova Scotia and Havre de Grace.

John Vaughan

Sulphate magnesium from Monroe County, Virginia. It was found in a cave with the bones of the megalonyx.[34]

Tristram Patton

Francis Da Costa, owner of "Mill Grove Farm on Perkiomen Creek [Pennsylvania] half a mile" from the Schuylkill River, presented a specimen of lead ore from the farm on 21 September 1804:

> Its specific weight is 78568, the cubic inch weighs about 5 ounces and the cubic foot about 540.
> From the analysis made of 100 parts, it contains in binary Combinations
> Sulphate of Lead 0.97
> Sulfate of Iron 00.2
> Water 001
> by Separating these different parts, it Contains
> oxide of Lead 0.85
> oxid of iron 00.1
> Sulfuric acid 0.13
> Water 00.1
> The above oxid of Lead being afterward assayed has yielded 75 percent, & one 500 part of Silver; or 3 ounces 1/15 of Silver by hundredweight of Lead. [35]

As far as can be ascertained, this is the first analysis of a mineralogical specimen received by the Society.

Da Costa wrote of the discovery of this lead mine on June 1805:

> The Discovery of mill-grove lead mine on Perkiomen Creek has been made by the wheel of a waggon which struck the top of the vein, on the decline of a hill of about 80 feet high. The Strata round it is a Kind of a red-Soapy-Slate or (Schist), the next to the ore was first a Kind of white-lead, but altered to a quartz intermixed with the

oxyd of iron and carbonated Cala; its first inclinations was about 45° towards Sun rise but Soon altered to 80 do; its power or thickness is now from IS to 20 inches and its direction from 12 to 13 hours, answering nearly to NE by N.

The Shaft being now 13 feet deep the Slaty Rock is become harder and of a yellow rusty Colour, the irony, StalactisedSpar Keeps along with the vein and the ore, being the true *galena* or Sulphurated lead with large fonts, is intermixed with Specks, of quartz and iron, in hard Stalactites.

The analysis made in Paris by Mr. Le Court inspector general of the mints in France, upon a piece which was much like what they call Steel-grain-ore has proved that it Contains 70 p[ercen]t of lead and 500 parts of Silver or nearly 2 ounces and 2' to the hundredweight of lead.[36]

On 1 February 1805 some minerals, "chiefly from Elba," were received from John D. Clifford:
I had the liberty of selecting them together with some others from a large Collection made by a Gentleman employ'd by the French Government to superintend the mine or rather the Iron Mountain of that Island.

There are some Variety of Specimens viz—Large polyhedron Marcassites [sic] of a brown Iron lustre small. Do of the most vivid Colours. Rounded Laminae of different Colours. A beautiful hard Yellow Pyrite with bright facets. Also some other specimens of Pyrites. A small piece of native Sulpher [sic] from Elba. You have also 2 specimens of the general Ore of the Mountain the one of a red brown appearance the other is grey & has a Cavity in it richly Incrusted with ochre.

With the Ores I also added some few other Curiosities—a Species of Steatite Interspaced [?], I believe, with Schorls—this was found on Mount Conisone [?] of the Alpine Mountains. [37]

On the same date some rock crystal, encrusted upon a "ferruginous stone" found in the city of Washington, was received. Adam Seybert, who was ever more interested in mineralogy and taught at the University of Pennsylvania, was ordered on this date to arrange and catalogue the minerals "as he shall think best."[38]

15 February 1805
Three specimens of lead ore from the area around the Perkiomen Creek, in Pennsylvania.
James Mease

Samuel Brown wrote John Vaughan on 9 April 1805 that he was preparing a paper on the nitre caves of Kentucky. He forwarded "a small Bit of our Rock salt petre ore which without any addition of Potash makes excellent nitre. I shall send a large mass of it by water...
P. S. You will greatly oblige me by requesting Dr. [James] Woodhouse or Dr.[Adam] Seybert or both, to analyse the salt sent in the vial & inform me of the result & the relative proportions. I have now many thousand pounds of it prepared & am concerned in a Cave which it is supposed will yield at least a million of pounds. It might be ship[p]ed to Phila[delphia] on reasonable terms. Our workmen affirm that each pound of it will yield a pound of good nitrate of potash when saturated with Potash.

What is the nature & composition of the stone marked No. 1.2. It is found in abundance in some of our Caves. The nodules abound in the Green River Caves. Their formation is certainly very curious.[39]

Samuel Brown presented on 3 May 1805, as he promised, two nodules "abundant in Green River country [Kentucky]." He called "one Salt Petre Rock, which without any addition of Pot ash makes excellent Nitre." The other he sent in a "phial, of which when saturated with Pot ash each pound will yield an equal quantity" of nitrate of potash. The letter was read, and with these gifts were specimens of "fibrous Gypsum and Specimens of Nitrate of Potash and Lime lately discovered in great quantities in Caves in the Neighborhood of Lexington," Kentucky.[40]

The collection of minerals had now grown so large the librarian was authorized on 3 May 1805 to exchange duplicates for specimens needed for the collection.[41]

17 May 1805

Some specimens of Lehigh coal, and specimens of "Black Earth," a new coloring material from a site near Nazareth, Pennsylvania, on the banks of the Lehigh River. With these came a "supposed copper ore" from the Lehigh and some "Saline effervescence" from the chalybeate springs located neare Fort Allen, Pennsylvania.[42]

Anthony Fothergill

Some specimens of gold from Cabarrus County, North Carolina, "purer than the standard of the United States"[43] were received on 21 June 1805, with an assay of part of it by Joseph Richardson at the U. S. Mint. John Vaughan donated these specimens, weighing 7 pennyweights, 7 grains, 21 June 1805 and the assay.

It is with pleasure that I communicate the following statement of the quality of some native gold found in the State of North Carolina & deposited in The Mint of The United States for coinage on the 29 Ult by Richard Trotter a Citizen of that State. No. I consisted of Ingots which had been melted previous to its being brought to the Mint. No. 2 was one entire piece weighing 12 oz: 10, evidently in its natural State and said to have been found in the County of Montgomery twenty miles from that part of he County of Cabarrus where the greater part of the gold has been picked up. Nos. 3 & 4 consisted of Grains of various sizes & are justly represented by No. 5 a Specimen obtained from Richard Trott now in thy possession, from the largest piece contained in this Specimen a small part was cut off & melted with a neutral flux, by this process it lost four p[e]r Cent on the gross weight, the Residue being carefully assayed proved to be 22 Carrats 3 4' g[ra]ms fine as per Statement below. The circumstance of the large piece being inferior in quality to the smaller grains, was unexpected to me, & excited a suspicion in my mind, that the larger lumps are not so pure as the smaller grains. This may be a groundless suspicion, but should opportunities of the like kind occur, I shall endeavour to ascertain the fact.

	Quality of each parcel	Loss sustained in melting
No. 1	22 Carrats 3 grains	
2	22 Carrats 1 grain	4 per Cent
3	22 Carrats 3 grains	10 per cent
4	22 Carrats 2 2' grains	10 per Cent
5	22 Carrats 3 4' grains	4 per Cent.[44]

19 July 1805

Specimens of molybdate lead, discovered in "the Perkiomen vein" in Montgomery County, Pennsylvania.[45]

Zaccheus Collins

19 July 1805
Specimens "of lead ore from the Perkiomen mines" and some cubic pyrites from Lancaster, Pennsylvania.[46]

Anthony Fothergill

Jefferson wrote John Vaughan on 4 May 1806 from Washington that he was about ready to depart for Monticello: "I leave herewith orders to forward them to you by the first vessel, a box containing the minerals from Capt [Meriwether] Lewis."[47] Adam Seybert and John Vaughan were appointed a committee on 15 November 1805 to examine these fruits of the Lewis and Clark Expedition. They reported on 18 November. [48]

On 1 November 1805 Samuel Brown of Kentucky sent "a large mass of argillacious earth" and a piece of pumice to the Society. He wrote on 4 November 1805 from Lexington, Kentucky:

I likewise send you a specimen of Native Nitre found in a Sand Rock cavern. The mass from which it was broken is said to have weighed several hundred pounds. The pieces of Rock contain a strong impregnation of Nitre; the workmen say fifteen percent, sometimes forty. I am now collecting some facts & observations on this subject which in a short time I shall do myself the honor of submitting to your inspection. [49]

6 December 1805
A specimen of feldspar.

Ferdinand Rudolph Hassler

Later that month, on 20 December 1805, a specimen of pure salt was given by Samuel Brown, who wrote "On the Salt Petre Caves on Crooked Creek, &c. in K[entuck]y & the mode of obtaining Nitre from them." This was referred to Adam Seybert, Anthony Fothergill, and James Woodhouse on 7 February 1806, and their report that the paper be published was adopted on 21 March.[50] Jefferson had forwarded Brown's communication when he acknowledged his re-election as president of the Society:

The interest I take in the advancement of the society is indeed without bounds, but my means of contributing to it's purposes very limited. Such as they are, they will on every occasion be devoted to their service.

I avail myself of this occasion of communicating a paper from Doct[o]r Samuel Brown on the Saltpetre caves & rocks of the Western country.[51]

On 7 February 1806 a box of minerals which Robert R. Livingston had procured at Naples, "mainly of volcanic productions," was received. John Vaughan wrote and asked Livingston about these specimens and he replied on 9 March 1806.

I am this moment favoured by your letter of the 26th Feb[ruar]y In which you desire to be informed of the spot on which the volcanic productions that I had the pleasure to present to the philosophical society were found. When I visited mount Vesuvius I observed that the lava assumed forms very different from those which I had entertained ideas of before I examined them myself. That very few of them had the least appearance of the scoria of a furnace as I had been taught to believe; that even that which might be called pumice stone, differed greatly in weight & colour from that which is brought to America; that many of them were ardently crystillized calcarious carbonate, & approached nearly in colour, texture & variety to marble, were capable of the same polish & wrought-like it into tables boxes &c. of great beauty. That appearances are very difficult to reconcile to the common, the certainly erroneous theory of volcanoes. For how were calcarious matter to be found in an encalcined state in these volcanic furnaces, which are supposed to Iiquify & vomit forth the hardest metals, & to mingle them with the most inafreyable (?) earths in a state of fusion? It struck me that an acquaintance with these productions might tend to elucidate the geology of the U. S. & enable us to judge of the agency that Volcanoes might have had in altering its form, or adding to its mineral & fossil productions & what is of more consequence might lead to a discovery of those which are of use; such a[s] tuffa pozzeleno & [sic], which as you know hardens in water & has contributed to render the cement & mortars of the ancients so much more durable than those of the moderns. I therefore ordered an artist at Naples who was usually employed in making these collections, to procure for me a compleat set of Volcanic productions from Mount Vesuvius, which I found to resemble those of the salfa twin (?) & other extinguished Volcanoes in the neighborhood of Baia, except that in the latter the softer parts were eroded, & the harder ones polished by water. The collection I have sent the society were those that he procured; as I had an immediate opportunity of shipping them, I had them packed at his shop, & sent off without examination. But I presume they are a compleat collection of Lava's. The [ ] (as it is called very improperly) sulphur, & oriental salts that I gathered myself in the crater, (having visited it at a very interesting moment when the great laboratory was in full motion, heaving another flame the day before, & when it was preparing for an irruption that broke out a few days after with considerable violence) I intended to have added, but thro' the carelessness of a servant they were left in with specimens of mortar &c. at Rome.

The houses at Naples have for the most part flat roofs which serve not only for pleasure but for many useful purposes. They owe this advantage altogether to pozzelino, which gives the roof the appearance of solid stone. The sort they principally use for this purpose, they call rapello. It is the black sandy irony substance which forms the cone of Vesuvius, thro which you wade ankle deep in climbing to the top of the mountain. Great bodies of it are found wherever Volcanoes have existed. Two parts of this with one of quick lime made a mortar that is difficult to distinguish from stone. In specimens I have had the honor to send to the society may serve to point out the cite of extinguished American Volcanoes, and direct our researchers to this very usefull substance.

Is it not probable, that as Volcanoes were designed the means of elevating Islands & continents from the sea, & perhaps even of transmuting its waters, & aerial fluids into earths, that Pozzelino was intended to stop this progress when this [] was accomplished, & to extinguish the old, as new ones opened? This substance, by hardening in the sea, may close those channels of communication between the ocean and the mountain thro which it receives the principal aliment of its fires. From the Appenines [sic] to the sea, the whole country is volcanic. Rome itself is built upon one, its streets, as with as those of Naples, are paved with lava (for the may be considered as such) the sea has thus been compelled gradually to recede from the foot of this ridge of mountains, as it has receded within the memory of man from Pompeii, which it once washed, & as it recedes the Volcanoes have been extinguished. But what is more remarkable is, that numbers of them, as the sulfurtiera the like avernus & many others in that vicinity, have ceased to burn, tho the recession of the sea has been very smaller. May not this be owing to the agency of the pazzolino, in stopping up the channels of communication with the Ocean?[52]

21 February 1806
Two large specimens of "American Slate."[53]

A. Traquair

20 June 1806
A specimen of "Platina."

Maurice Rogers

38 mineral samples from Ireland.[54]

James Mease

18 July 1806
Fifty-three models "de la Christalographie" after Rome de l'Isle and the publication by Rome de l'Isle.[55]

Ferdinand R. Hassler

Talbot Hamilton wrote on 6 September 1806, presenting various pigments and a specimen of lodestone:
> I send for the acceptance of the American Philosophical Society a piece of Loadstone, brought from Schuyler's Mountain. It possesses considerable magnetic powers and I hope on trial will be found worthy a place in your valuable Cabinet. I have in preparation the Small Model of a Frigate, In order to shew the method [   ] some years agone in swiftering [a m]an-of-War under very distressful [circum]stances, but which method (under [   ]once) she was saved from going to pieces....P.S. The Loadstone was obtained by Mr. Isaac Hulme of Milford Haven Bucks County.[56]

15 May 1807
Gold and silver ore from South America.

James Gould Latimer

From Paris, a case of minerals "which [the donor] collected in Itally, Switzerland and the Tirol."[57] These were delivered by Sylvain Godon, the donor introduced and recommended highly to his colleagues.

William Maclure

James Mease offered on 17 July 1807 to help complete the cabinet by presenting "any specimens from a collection of minerals sent to him by Mr. Donald Stuart." Stuart was collecting for the Royal Dublin Society [Royal Irish Academy]. Adam Seybert, James Mease, and John R. Coxe were to decide which items the Society wished to acquire.[58]

21 August 1807
A box of silver ores and other minerals from Vera Cruz.[59]

Juan Manuel de Ferrer

21 August 1807
Minerals from Niagara and pit coal "from seven Penn[sylvani]a counties... "Westmoreland, Allegheny, Armstrong, Venango, Jefferson, Indiana, Clearfield, and Luzerne."[60]

Robert H. Rose

Anthony Fothergill presented a piece of basaltic rock from the falls of the Passaic River, New Jersey, on 6 November 1807. On the same date a letter from Samuel Brown in New Orleans was read, announcing his forwarding a box of minerals from Mexico; it was received on 4 December 1807:
> I transmitted to the Philosophical Society, by the Ship Hercules Capt. Robinson, a small Box containing Silver Ores & other minerals obtained in the mines near the City of Mexico. They were brought from Vera Cruz by the Hon[ora]ble Daniel Clarke, about two years ago & presented by him to me. You will much oblige me by delivering them, in my name, to the Society.[61]

Benjamin S. Barton, Adam Seybert, and Mahlon Dickerson were appointed a committee on 6 November 1807 to report "On the stone found near Washington" by Silvain Godon.[62] On 20 November 1807 the same men reported that Silvain Godon's "Observations to serve for the Mineralogical Map of the State of Maryland" would be published. [63] It appeared in the *Transactions*. Godon also presented minerals to go with the paper.[64]

James Howell wrote an evaluation of iron ore and forges in Pennsylvania in 1807.[65]

19 February 1808
Minerals from Ava and Ascension Islands.

Captain John Davy

15 April 1808
Some lava from Ascension Island.[66]

Charles Ross

The indefatigable traveler, William Maclure, shipped "a small Box of specimens of Rocks" from Jumilla Province of Murcia, in Spain, on 29 March 1808. The box, he wrote:

Consists of the Specimens of Rocks taken from a chain of small hills two Leagues west of this place situated in the bottom of a valley surrounded by Limestone mountains partly covered by Gypsum and has been once most probably totally - and the Gypsum is recovered by the Limestone. This Chain of hills is about 2 miles diameter isolated in the middle of a gypsum and Limestone Country and would be called by the neptunians of tropore (?) formation consisting of Basalt, Porphiry [sic], Wake (?), Iodestone, & &c. &c. and by the Vulcanists would most probably be considered as Volcanic and different kinds of lava... The Specimens of Phosphate of Lime... with the Specular Iron ore Christilized were taken from one of these hills alternating with the basalt, Wake mandlestone &c. Should I find anything worthy your attention during the rest of my travels in Spain...shall with pleasure forward them to you.[67]

John Vaughan endorsed this letter: "accompanying Specimens which did not come to hand."

1 April 1808
Four pigments from Northampton County, Pennsylvania, on the Lehigh River including "the Coal of which the Black Specimen is a superstructure."[68]

Talbot Hamilton

Two and a half months later, John B. Dabney wrote Thomas Jefferson (20 June) of a volcanic eruption on St. George's Island in the West Indies and sent a basket of the cinders. He and other gentlemen visited St. Georges and toured the area. His lengthy, graphic letter was read at the meeting of 4 November 1808.[69] Thomas T. Hewson and Mahlon Dickerson recommended that even though the letter "contains no philosophic disquisitions, no scientific remarks, on the circumstances connected with the subject, yet as a plain narrative of one of the most awful occurrences in nature," they recommended publication.[70]

On 21 October 1808 members asked Adam Seybert "to report on the minerals of the Society." When he didn't, he was ordered to report "at the next meeting" on 4 November 1808. At the meeting on 18 November 1808, the members accepted Seybert's resignation from his three-year appointment to arrange the minerals.

The committee on William Maclure's paper on geology, "made to the last meeting" recommended on 3 February 1809 that it be published in the *Transactions*.[71]

17 February 1809
A specimen of clay from Amboy, New Jersey and three specimens of copper ore from the mouth of the Perkiomen Creek, Pennsylvania.[72]

William Partridge

The members learned on 23 June 1809 that James Woodhouse, who, with Adam Seybert, had been so active in the mineralogical life of Philadelphia, had died, leaving his collection of minerals to the Society. [73] Specimens continued to be sent; phosphate of lime from Mercia on 23 June 1809; Lyman Spalding's article on the origin of meteoric stones was received on 2 February 1810;[74] on 17 August 1810 several "specimens of minerals found in the neighborhood of Quebec," presented by M. Robert, were referred to Zaccheus Collins for a report.[75]

5 October 1810

A specimen of talc or serpentine from Newburyport.[76]

Samuel Hazard

5 October 1810
Blue iron earth [or azure, or phosphate of iron] from Monmouth County, New Jersey. An article on it by Thomas Cooper was published in the *Transactions*.[78]

F. Pennington

Meanwhile, as the collection of minerals expanded, additional boxes were needed, as was drayage, cases, etc. Records of these can be found in the minutes and in the Treasurers Records.

Silvain Godon, who lectured on mineralogy at the University of Pennsylvania, wrote John Vaughan on 31 January 1811 asking whether the Society intended to:

Grant the Room where the min[era]l collection is exposed, for my next course of lectures, which will take place in March next. You remember that last year several of its members inviting me to make use of it, persuaded that the view of the collection, would be useful for the instruction of those who intend to study this branch of N[atur]al History...

[Godon proposed] to give a compensation for this room, but in case my avocations should not permit me to deliver more Lectures in future, I pray you to mention that I would be glad, to received this concession for the present year, as a compensation for the pecuniary expenses occasioned to me by the Arrangement of the collection, which continued several months. [79]

The Society agreed to this request and asked the College of Physicians, which rented the room, if they would agree. Thomas T. Hewson wrote on 6 February 1811 granting the request, "provided that neither they nor the Agricultural Sociey, who likewise have an interest in the room" are to be expected to cancel regular meetings.[80]

15 February 1811
Some native sulphur specimens from Isle Saba, West Indies.[81]

Silvain Godon

Some specimens of "carbonated Lime magnesized with Talc laminated."[82]

Samuel Hazard

17 May 1811
"[A] large specimen of Rock salt" and various minerals from Santa Fe de Bogota, Colombia.[83]

Don Pedro de la Lastre

20 March 1812
Rock crystal from "Madesgar" [Madagascar].[84]

August Bousquet

In June 1802 there was an eruption of a volcano on Saint Vincent's, West Indies, and George Hallam of New London, Connecticut, was aboard a ship 50 miles away. Sand and dust from the eruption fell on the deck of the ship. Hallam asked Talbot Hamlin to present samples of them on 18 September 1812. Samuel Betton gave another such specimen gathered on the deck of the *Halcyon* which was 80 miles away from the island.[85]

18 September 1802
Minerals from Cornwall, England[86]

Hannah Barnard

2 October 1812
Some lava specimens which General Eaton had collected on the Sicilian volcano, Mount Etna.

Jonathan Williams

20 November 1812
A specimen of lava from Mauritius, Africa, which was brought to the United States by Mr.Desbassaynes.[87]

Thomas Cadwalader

Robert Patterson on 15 July 1814 reported that large pieces of amber had been found in Camden, New Jersey. Some men digging a cellar in a sandy soil containing gravel found the amber and broke it up, but a sample was obtained.[88]

Zaccheus Collins delivered on 15 July 1814 as a gift from Solomon W. Conrad several specimens. One was of zirconite embedded in gneiss found near Trenton, New Jersey. Another was amber from near Crossinks Creek, New Jersey, "occurring in small quantities with Pyrites and Wood Coal." With these were some carbonized wood which was found accompanying the amber.[89]

17 February 1815
Some specimens of carbonate of lead from Wythe County, Virginia, on the Grand Kanawha River.[90] Collins and Robert Patterson were asked to report on them.[91]

R. E. Hobart

3 March 1815
"[A] large specimen of Elastic marble" from New York State. With this was a granular carbonate of lime Jameson and *chaux carbonate sacharoid Hauy*.[92]

Thomas P. Jones

7 April 1815
Solomon W. Conrad's broadside, "Table of the Constituent parts of Earthy Minerals." It was printed on a large sheet in Philadelphia in 1815.[93]

[DONOR UNKNOWN]

Jose F. Correa da Serra had communicated his study on the soil of Kentucky, and on 21 April 1815 the committee reported that it was "highly interesting and ingenious" and recommended the publication of "Observations and Conjectures on the Formation and Nature of the Soil of Kentucky."[94]

Caspar Wistar brought specimens of Wilkes-Barre coal and some specimens of iron ore on 6 October 1815, upon his return "from a Tour in the interior." The coal, which was the same as Lehigh coal, was found in "many hundred places, much used for every Purpose." The iron ore was found under and in contact with the coal.[95] On 15 September 1815 the gift of "Cyanite Iamn. (?) Disthene Hauy" was presented by Joseph Cloud. It came from West Bradford, Chester County, Pennsylvania.[96]

Zaccheus Collins delivered in 1816 some "Blue Iron ore crystallized with Belemnites, mineralized by the same substance" from Gloucester County, New Jersey. Thomas Cooper read an analysis of this mineral on 3 May 1816.[97] The committee which examined the analysis thought it should be published because this ore "is one of the minerals of our country that seems particularly to call for experiment. In Geognostic situation—in external and physical characters it agrees perfectly with the European mineral." The authorities, Martin Heinrich Klaproth, Louis Nicole Vacquelin, and Rene Just Hauy, described the mineral variously. In Cooper's memoir it was:

> Found to be destitute of Phosphoric Acid, and to consist first of Iron in a slight
> stage of oxidation, water and alumine, shewing at least so far as regards American
> specimens that Hauy was right in rejecting the term of [Phosphated Iron].... This
> mineral has also been called Native Prussian Blue, but the prussic acid was sought
> in vain. The origin of the blue colour [Cooper] thinks is from vegetable matters.[98]

Probably around the same date, Collins donated some specimens of molybdated lead which had been found in Montgomery County, Pennsylvania, "in the Perkiomen vein.[99] At the same time, Mrs. Benjamin Smith Barton gave "a variety of minerals" from her late husband's collection (19 April 1816).[100] Gifts continued in 1817.

17 January 1817
Specimens of copper and galena found in Michigan Territory.[101]

Caspar Wistar

7 February 1817
Specimens of rocks from Sarasota and Ballston, New York, which illustrated the geology of that neighborhood.

William Meade

21 February 1817
A "Large Specimen of Muriate of soda from the Island of Hayti found in Solitary at Considerable Depth near the City of S[anto] Domingo."[103]

W. C. Poultney

A circular letter dated on 6 March 1817 was received from the New York Historical Society announcing "their intention to form a collecion of the Minerals and Fossils of the United States." A room was fitted with display cases "with glass doors, one case being devoted to each state." This appeal for specimens noted that it would be most useful "to have the exact localities of the minerals determined, and such further information of the neighbouring country, as the donor can procure."[104]

A committee reported on 15 May 1817 on Henry Steinhauer's paper on phytoliths.[105] Specimens of mineral from Denmark and Sweden were received the same month from J. P. Todd.[106] Later that month. the committee reported on 22 May 1817 that William Maclure's paper on the geology of the United States be published, for after his first paper had appeared, Maclure had "visited a great portion of Europe as a Geologist, and has also visited some parts of the U. S. expressly to reexamine and correct his account of the Geology." The committee recommended publication:

> The Committee feel sensibly the propriety of making the American Philos. Society the medium of communicating to the scientific world, not only the best, but in fact the only good account of the Geolgy of our Country, and they have no doubt but the additional remarks and observations of Mr. Maclure in the present memoir will prove acceptable to every person engaged in this branch of study.[107]

The paper was published, and with it the first geological map of the United States. The members authorized the purchase of models of crystals from John R. Coxe 108 on 20 June 1817; they were purchased a month later for $43.50.[108] On 18 July "Sulphurated of Lime Chrystallized or Gympsum" was also received—from Fort Washington on the Potomac, or Warburton, Maryland.[109]

19 September 1817
Twenty-six specimens of minerals from Sweden and other European countries.

William Maclure

Porphyritic lava from the island of Santorini in the Aegean Sea. [110]

Samuel Hazard

Daniel Drake's letter to Jose F. Correa da Serra on the geology of the Ohio valley was written on 1 October 1817. Drake had made a "vertical chart" of the geology and Correa da Serra asked for a copy, which Drake sent, with a description of the valley. He noted that the slopes were at "a greater angle than is correct." This chart was of the alluvial formation:

> Divided near its middle by the Ohio river, and extends about a mile from either shore, exclusively of the valley of Licking river to the South and that of Mill creek to the northwest. When viewed from any of the surrounding hills this hollow or

expansion appears nearly of a rhomboidal figure [of eight square miles. Drake commented on the terraces of the Ohio and other rivers and added that the naked perpendicular cliffs, which are yet suffering disintegration, and sufficiently indicate that the last retreat of the sea was not a very *remote* period.[111]

The committee directed this memoir to be published on 19 March 1818, delaying their report until the vertical chart could be examined. "This chart aptly illustrative of the acts and observations of the author" formed "a valuable addition to the Geology of our Country."[112]

21 November 1817
Some lava from Mount Vesuvius where a coin had been pressed into the soft lava.
William Rawle

21 February 1818
A collection of crystals and minerals collected from the alpine regions of Chamoux and the neighboring mountains, including a specimen of talc from Saint Gotthard, Switzerland, lava from Vesuvius, and a "piece of sulphureous incrustation, from the lake of Solfatana (?) near Rome."[112]
John C. Montgomery

Two specimens from the Philadelphia area.[113]
Isaac Lea

12 March 1818
John Sergeant sent "two specimens of the marble (as it is called) from which the columns "in the hall of the House of Representatives" were made. One specimen was "polished, and the other in its natural state."[114]
Captain Riley

15 May 1818
Several mineral specimens from the donor's collection "which are wanting in ours,"[115]
William Maclure

17 July 1818
Some minerals from "Tenasee."
Samuel Brown

Bermuda stalactites. [116]
John Vaughan

The Society lent on 7 May 1819 its "Lithographic Stone" to Brown and Otis for "experiments in the art of Lithographic Engraving." The illustration etched on the stone was published in the *Analectic Magazine* of July 1819; the stone is not in the Society today.[117]

21 January 1820
A "Fine specimen of fibrous Graminatite" from London Grove Township, Chester County, Pennsylvania.[118]
Samuel Jackson

On 21 January 1820 very rare cryolite, found only in Greenland, "Alumine fluatic Alkaline," of Hauy, was promised by the Reverend M. Huffel. Zaccheus Collins delivered it on 17 October 1823. Huffel wrote that this mineral came from the western coast of Greenland, "its sole locality."[119] The collection grew with Collin's (21 April 1820) specimen of sandstone;[120] Frank Le Baron's "piece of clay having its surface covered with cobalt,"[121] (5 May 1820) and specimen of plumbaginous carbonaceous slate on 20 October 1820 by Henry L. Abbot. It was found on a branch of the Neshamany Creek, 24 miles from Philadelphia.[122] A piece of "Pudding Stone" [conglomerate] was received on 17 November 1820 from George Blagden.[123]

On 1 December 1820 the committee reported that the Honorable Judge Gibson's "Observations on the Trap Rocks of Conewago Hills, Near Middletown,

Dauphin County," Pennsylvania, and of the "Stony Ridge near Carlisle, Cumberland County, Pennsylvania," was worthy of publication.[124]

Johann Severin Vater sent seven specimens of amber, "some very rare," from Konigsberg on 16 February 1821. One specimen contained a mushroom; another held a moth and a spider; one, a winged ant; one enclosed a round shell; another was between two pieces of wood; one piece was just as it had been dug; and, one was listed as "Amber nut (Lycapodendrum)."[125]

4 May 1821
"A large Specimen of Carbonate of Lime" which had been found around four miles above Harper's Ferry. West Virginia.[126]

Isaiah Lukens

21 September 1821
Gramatite-Hauy and an emerald or beryl mass from New Garden, Chester County, Pennsylvania. "Felspar Foetid" from near Lime Stone in the same county. "Andalusite Felspar A. pyre Hauy" which had been found in granite on the "Coast of China."[127]

Zaccheus Collins

5 October 1821
"Argillaceous Lime Stone" which was used in making the locks in the "N[ew] York Canal in lieu of Roman Cement." This limestone was found near the canal. It was referred to Joseph Cloud and James Mease for examination.[128]

Loami Baldwin

19 October 1821
"Bog Ore" been found under the root of a tree.[129]

Joseph Cloud

19 October 1821
A piece of "Glauberite" from Spain, ten leagues south of Madrid, in Villa Rubin.[130]

William Maclure

William Meade wrote on 14 December 1821 asking permission to deposit his minerals in "any vacant apartment." His collection he said, was the:

Result of many years investigation into the Mineralogical Treasures of this country is now become so extensive that I find it difficult to obtain any situation where it can be placed so as to render it in any degree useful. Many of the boxes in consequence of this difficulty remain at present unopened.

Meade offered to give the Society his duplicates so that the Society would possess "nearly the whole of those that have as yet been discovered" in the United States.[131] His request was referred to George Ord, Robert Patterson, and Zaccheus Collins; it was refused on 21 December 1821.[132]

John James Abert, a United States Army topographical engineer, presented some minerals on 21 December 1821 through Collins.[133]

1 February 1822
Some minerals from Lehigh County Pennsylvania.[134]

William Darby

17 May 1822
Sulphate of magnesia "from the Mercurial Mines at Idri in Triali" (?).[135]

William Maclure

The "Analysis of the Maclurite, or Fluo-Silicate of Magnesia," from New Jersey, which was a new species of mineral, was read by Henry Seybert on 17 May 1822. The mineral consisted of:

Water	01.00	containing oxygen	
Fluoricaid	04.086	02.917	

Silica	32.666	16.430
Peroxide of Iron	02.333	00.715
Magnesia	54.000	20.903
Potash	02.108	00.357
	100.00	
	003.827 Loss	

19 July 1822
Oxide of manganese which had been found in Warwickshire, England. Parkes was a "manufactory chemist" in London.[137]

Adam Seybert, for Samuel Parkes

4 October 1822
"[A] small box containing Specimens of Lava from Mount Vesuvius."

Samuel Vaughan Merrick

17 January 1823
"Sulphuret of Antimony" from Spain.[139]

William Maclure

21 February 1823
A fifteen inch square of "Polished Marble of the Kind used in the Capitol of the U. S. at Washington, for the Columns Breccia."[140]

Charles Bulfinch, architect of the United States Capitol

On 18 July 1823, R. Dietz sent "A Testaceous mass (or Conglomerate of fossil Shells) from Andalusia Island near [Saint] Augustine" together with descriptions extracted from his notes made during the winter months of 1822–1823. Andalusia Island was ten to twelve miles long and one and onehalf miles wide and no more than ten to twelve feet above sea level. Dietz wrote:

A considerable portion of this island is composed of this agglutinated mass, though it is not yet ascertained to what depth. It occurs in horizontal stratified layers, separate at certain horizontal divisions, owing to some foreign matter interjacent between these separations, which prevented their conglutination. The layers are from an inch to a foot & half thick. Their consistency is various, from large shell fragments to pretty small ones, promiscuously deposited; & even aggregations often occur of various sized fragments, together with entire shells in one & the same mass.

Dietz attempted to answer how the uppermost layers became grained; just how deep this conglomerate extended; and the composition of the bottom layers. He knew that the fort at Saint Augustine was built of this conglomerate of square blocks of about 2" 2' feet long, 2 wide & one thick ... It is considered as well calculated for the uses of fortifications, as by its spongy & brittle mixture it will received the [cannon] Balls, without letting them pass through or glance off without being shattered to pieces."[141]

18 July 1823
A specimen of "Novanclar Stone" which came from near Lackawaxen in Wayne County, Pennsylvania.[142]

Jacob S. Davis

23 November 1823
A collection of American minerals "Chiefly from the Eastern States."[143]

Nathaniel A. Ware

20 February 1824
"[A] donation of ores.[144]

Zaccheus Collins

   Adam Seybert read a paper analyzing the "Chrysoberyls of Haddam and Brazil." It was recommended for publication.[145] The members determined on 19 March 1824, following Robert Patterson's resolution, that nothing about the "minerals, fossils &c., in the Cabinet" was to be published "in any work except the Society's Transactions, unless express liberty to this effect be first obtained by the Society."[146]

16 April 1824
A specimen of salt from Santa Fe de Bogota, Colombia.[147]

James Mease, a gift of General Devereaux

30 January 1824
A printed circular letter describing his attempt to make "a collection of the rocks and minerals of Pennsylvania... to arrange [them] in *local* order, according to the geographical divisions of the State." He wrote of the obvious advantages of such a collection and asked for gifts since he "designed to collect specimens of every distinct species of rock and mineral found, in any place in the State."[148]

Peter A. Browne

15 October 1824
"Sulphated Rarytes with ochraceous Iron & Quartz" discovered at a "new locality" near the mouth of French Creek, Pennsylvania.[149]

Zaccheus Collins

15 October 1824
A specimen from Cumberland Township, Rhode Island. The specimen was of "Yenite crystalized in Strait Rhomboidal Prismus."[150] Gerard Troost analyzed the yenite and Robert M. Patterson, Isaiah Lukens, and William Hembel, Jr., reported in favor of its publication on 5 November 1824.[151]

James Mease

16 September 1825
"Sulphuret of Iron in State" which came from Inglesbury, Yorkshire, England.[152]

James Mease, for Mr. Rivinus

Verd antique from Carthage in North Africa.[153]

James Mease, collected by Lt. Glentworth

5 January 1827
A piece of the "Rock of the Pilgrims, at Plymouth, Massachusetts" which the donor had broken off in September 1826. Two weeks later the donor delivered specimens of granite from Hallowell and Portland, Maine. Granite was quarried in each place "in great Blocks by Wedges."[154]

James Mease

20 April 1827
More specimens arrived "from the deep cut" of the canal linking the Chesapeake Bay and the Delaware River.

S. N. Dexter

4 May 1827
Amber from the cut.

Mr. Denke

20 July 1827
Minerals on from the same cut.[155]

Mr. Denke

Members proposed on 15 February 1828 that the curators prepare a catalogue of the cabinet, and John P. Wetherill drafted, and the members adopted, a resolution: "That the Curators be requested to report...a more improved plan of cases for our minerals, and an estimate of their cost."

18 July 1828
Minerals from the "Deep Cut," 52 feet deep, of the Chesapeake and Delaware Canal.[156]

John K. Kane

19 September 1828
Specimens of iron ores from New Jersey Samuel G. Wright had collected for him.[157]

Thomas Cooper

5 December 1828
Three specimens of the "Silicious deposit" from the "great *spring of Geyser*" in Iceland. With these was a specimen of quartz hyatite from the same site.[158]

Peder Pedersen

Additional specimens from the "Deep Cut" continued to arrive. Hugh Lee gave some minerals on 19 June and on 17 July of the same year. They were described as:
A full Collection of Specimens of the different Fossils, Earths and Minerals developed in executing the Deep Cut of the Chesapeake and Delaware Canal, accompanied by a Memoir and a Profile of the Geological Formation of the strata through which the work passed to the depth of 82 Feet. Received through J[ohn] K. Kane, one of the Directors, and Sec[retary] of the Soc[iety].

These were presented by Andrew Alfred Dexter, an assistant engineer.[159]

2 October 1829
A large specimen of *Retin asphalt* from the "Deep Cut.[160]

Andrew Alfred Dexter

Some minerals.

F. Leoming

20 November 1829
A mineral specimen.[161]

William Boyd

Mineralogical additions to the cabinet continued in the 1830s. Caleb Atwater wrote John Vaughan on 13 January 1830 that he was presenting three mineralogical specimens to the Society "in testimony of my gratitude, and high regard for that, most useful and excellent Society." He left them with a Dr. Jones of the United States State Department in Washington. The minerals were reported as:
A quantity of sand, from the bed of the Wisconsin River, obtained by me, in the month of August 1829. Also, carnelions from Praire du Chien, [Wisconsin,] collected on the margin of the Mississippi River, in the summer of 1829, while treating with the Indians, for the mineral region. Also, lead ore, from a mine, at Gratiots Grove, in the mineral country.[162]

Totally overshadowed by the magnificent gifts of Central American Indian artifacts which Joel Roberts Poinsett and William Hickling Keating delivered to the Society, on 2 April 1830, was the entry of, "200 specimens of Minerals from Mexico, embracing many rare and rich specimens of Gold, Silver, Copper, Lead, Iron, Antimony, Mercury, Titanium and Tin Ores: some splendid specimens of the Mexican Fire Opal very interesting Crystallizations of Hyaline Quartz, Amethyst, Carbonate of Lime and Selenite."[163]

7 May 1830
Fragments of the basaltic blocks of the Giant's Causeway in Ireland.[164]

William M. Camac

Peter Arrell Browne delivered on 16 April 1830 a plaster cast of a "Singular impression in primitive marble from Henderson's quarry in Montgomery County," Pennsylvania. A profile of the geological formations between Norristown and Philadelphia, by Browne, had also arrived the same date. Browne had surveyed the area and drawn the "Plate." He wrote:

I send you herewith a cast of a great natural curiosity. A block of marble measuring 30 cubic feet was taken out of Henderson's quarry, upper Merion Township, Montgomery County, at the depth of 60 or 70 feet and sent to Mr. John Savage's marble-saw mill, in Norristown, to be cut into slabs. A piece was taken off about three feet wide and about 6 feet long, and as soon as the surface was exposed to view there was discovered in the solid body of the marble an indentation about 1-1/2 inches long and 5/8 of an inch wide in which were the following two raised

characters **IN** How this impression came there is difficult to divine: the quarry belongs to the primitive rocks: which commencing at this city succeed (as you know) to each other in the following order Gneiss, Micaslate, Hornblende, TalcoseSlate, Primitive Clay slate, a narrow strip of Granite and then the rock in which this singular impression was found.

I shall in a few days have the Specimen in this city and will be happy to exhibit it to your members. [165]

Dr. Feuchwanger offered on 18 June 1830 to sell 500 minerals to the Society at twenty-five cents each. This was referred to a committee which declined the offer on 16 July, stating: "That they do not deem it expedient to make the purchase as they consist of Specimens which we have in our collection."[166] Dr. Feuchwanger then asked Alexander Dallas Bache to withdraw his paper and it was returned on 20 August 1830.[167] On 18 August 1830, Joseph P. Grant sent some minerals from "the Missouri Lead Region" on:[168]

No. 1 was obtained about 16 miles from Galena at a dipping place called the "Big Pitch," or "Big Prospect" in Michigan Territory.

Nos. 2–12 were obtained in Illinois about 6 miles from Galena at a place called "Vinegar Hills."

Nos. 13 & 14 were taken from under the hearth (of bastard limestone) of a Log Furnace at "Colletts Grove" about 18 miles from Galena.

No. 15 was taken up on the Illinois shore of the Mississippi at the lower rapids, about 230 miles above St. Louis.

The Country where the Lead is found is a beautiful prairie, gently undulating, with occasional Groves; soil a rich black loam 12–15 inches thick & below that Clay a little mixed with sand and broken limestone. Where lead exists the clay is generally of an orange yellow and a weed called "the Mesmie(?) Weed" a root several feet long, is usually found. The spots where mineral is found are called "Digging Patches or Leads" (from Lead "to conduct"). [169]

Members agreed to Andres Del Rio's request on 1 October 1830 to be given a small piece of sulphuret of silver for an analysis to be made of it.[170] The analysis, "Silver ores reduced by the method of Becquerel," was referred to a committee on 5 November 1830, and at the same meeting the Society granted Del Rio's request for "any minerals for analysis" which could be spared from the collection.

5 November 1830
A specimen of a calcareous deposit which was taken from the Tartarian Lake only twelve miles from Rome.[171]

Rene La Roche

17 December 1830
Seven minerals.

Lieutenant Allen Deas, U.S. Navy

7 January 1831
Seven copper specimens from the Perkiomen mine.[172]

Mr. Kraff

George W. Featherstonehaugh petitioned for the use of the geological specimens in the cabinet, and on 18 February 1831 the members authorized the curators to provide this service.[173]

3 February 1832
A collection of minerals from the Peruvian Sierra de Pasco mines.[174]

James Mease

17 February 1832
Minerals from Cobija, Chile. were received on, a gift of the U.S. naval officer,. The donor wrote that he knew nothing about the minerals, other than they were from the "mines of Peru & Chili."[175]

Sterne Humphry, U.S. Navy

6 April 1832
Some minerals from Lima, Peru, which had been sent to the donor. On 19 July he presented "some additional specimens contained in the box herewith forwarded" from "Andrew Armstrong, the United States Resident at Lima," who "has resided some time in that Country in a Public capacity.[176]

John Quincy Adams

19 October 1832
A long, handsome lithographic plate of the geological profile of the area rocks between Norristown and Philadelphia, Pennsylvania. The donor was the secretary of the Geological Society of Pennsylvania.[177] A colored version of this plate was given in 1835.

Peter A. Browne

4 January 1833
A piece of salt, 2 x 2-$\frac{1}{2}$ inches which had been cut from a mass of salt rock at the head of the Arkansas River. The river had worn a channel in the salt rock.[178]

Lewis Cass, Secretary of War

Francis Dwight wrote on 21 June 1833 forwarding "these few specimens of ores" from Virginia:
The brown ore was taken from the Orange mines (in Orange County) from a gallery, from 100 to 120 ft. below the earth's surface. Ore resembling this in all particulars, on essay,[sic] over 700 dwts to the 100 lbs of ore. The smaller quartz specimens were picked up in the same county". [179]

Charles Nagy wrote on 20 August 1833 that he had learned of a mineralogical collection "of beautiful specimens, well arranged, I think we could have it at a very convenient price" if so desired by the Society. He added that he would "feel very happy in being an instrument to contribute" to the cabinet.[180] The firm of Forstall Bros. & Berthaud wrote Richard Harlan on 26 December 1833 that "the Calliope has arrived from Leghorn" with the box of minerals he was awaiting.[181] On 15 August 1834, this aforementioned valuable collection of minerals, collected in Germany, Austria and Hungary, arrived as a donation from Nagy.- It contained seventy-two specimens.[182]

27 June 1834
Three specimens of sulphate of strontium from near Bristol, England.[183]

Henry Bright

For more than two months, Andres Del Rio reduced "Sulphurate of Silver by muriate of ammonia and a copper coin." Alexander Dallas Bache delivered this reduction on 17 October 1834.

15 May 1835
A collection of Swiss minerals.[184]

[DONOR UNKNOWN]

2 October 1835
Specimens of zinc from the Picton, Montgomery County, Pennsylvania, copper and lead mine at Perkiomen. The donor prepared it, so it would form "with, brass for weights and measures of the U.S. made under his direction.[185]

John Hitz Ferdinand R. Hassler

6 November 1835
Some specimens from the Acton Mine in the Perkiomen area, of copper, lead, and zinc.[186]

James Rowe

18 December 1835
Specimens of lead ore from Galena.[187]

James Mease

1 April 1836
A specimen of anthracite coal from Illinois.[188]

B. Nelson

Joseph Hopkinson spoke at the meeting of 6 May 1836 about the proposed European trip of Peter A. Browne "with the intention of encreasing his knowledge." He pointed out that Browne had "devoted much of his time and attention to scientific pursuits, especially in the department of Geology." Therefore, he proposed a resolution, tabled for consideration at the next regular meeting:

Resolved, That the President of the Society be requested to address a letter, expressive of the respectful sense entertained by the Society of the zeal and success with which he has prosecuted his studies, and the hope that he may receive in Europe the facilities he may desire for the promotion of the valuable objects of his visit.

19 August 1836
Additional specimens of zinc, copper and lead ores from the Picton Mine at Perkiomen, Pennsylvania.[189]

R. C. Taylor

16 September 1836
Some specimens of pyrites from Burk County, in the "mountain gold range of North Carolina."[190]

James Pedder

17 February 1837
Some mineralogic specimens.[191]

Henry W. Terry

6 October 1837
Two specimens of stone found near Mobile, Alabama with a promise of a "description to be presented hereafter."[192]

W. H. Robertson

17 November 1837
"A Case of interesting Minerals, from Sicily," collected, and given, by the United States consul to Malta.[193]

Winthrop Andrews

5 January 1838
A specimen from Oxford, New Hampshire, of "Augite, in Steatites".[194]

James Mease

5 January 1838
Two specimens from the neighborhood of Charlotte, North Carolina. This new mineral was designated leopardite, as proposed by George William Featherstonehaugh.[195]

Franklin Peale

A letter of 20 January 1838 from John K. Townsend was read on 2 February 1838 with news of a gift of "geological specimens, selected for its use by Mr. Peale."[196]

Robert Hare exhibited fourteen and a half ounces of platinum on 4 May 1838. He had fused this platinum by the use of his hydrooxygen blowpipe. He had "freed another piece of pure platinum from iridium by the process of Berzelius."[197]

21 September 1838
A twenty-one to twenty-three ounce specimen of platinum "being part of a mass of twenty-five ounces, fused by [the donor] in May last, by means of [a] compound blowpipe."[198]

Robert Hare

On 21 September 1838 a gift of thirty-three specimens was received from Thomas G. Clemson. These rocks and ores came from the Halguine district of the island of Cuba, in large part. Rocks came from the Silla de Gebara and minerals ["Sulphuret of Copper, Iron Ore, Chromate of Iron, in large Masses, Oxide of Copper"] came from the "vein and surface " of the Sabana mine. "Euphatide alternating with Silex, Syenite, Mineral combustable" came from the neighborhood of Havanna. From Alabama, there was some bituminous coal from the banks of the Black Warrior River. From Missouri, "PerOxide of Iron from the Iron Mountain, Sulphuret of copper, Sulphuret of Lead, Carbonate of Lead" were received. And from Flemington, New Jersey, came sulphuret of copper.[199] Clemson listed them in his letter:

Philadelphia, August 18th 1838

To John Vaughan Esqr

Sir

I have the honour of presenting through your hands & to the Philosophical Society, Several Suites and Specimens of Mineral Substances which I took from their respective localities with my own hands. I think that they will be found Characteristic and I hope acceptable to the Society. Each Specimen has been labelled with its name connexion and locality.

No. 1 to No. 13, inclusive are rocks and ores from the District of Holguine in the Island of Cuba.

No. 14 to No. 15 inclusive are rocks &c. from the neighbourhood of the Havanna throwing an interesting and remarkable association.

No. 19 to 31 are Mineral substances from the interesting Mineral region of Missouri.

No. 32 is from Fleming in N. Jersey, No. 33 a Specimen of Bituminous Coal from the banks of the Black War[r]ior River Alabama.

Believe in the high consideration with which I have the honour to be your most obedt and humble Servt.

Thos G. Clemson

No. 1 to 13. Rocks & Ores Holguine District Cuba. No. I Characteristic Specimen of Rock from the Silla of Gibara. Those hills are formed of this Rock. The mountain or hill is formed of needles apparently the efforts of Deting [detin] dilapidating Agents. Cuba Dist of Holguine.

No.2. Rock from the base of the Mountains termed Silla de Gibara Gibara Dist. of Holguine Isld of Cuba.

No. 3. Rock showing the connection between the Mass of which the Silla of Gebara are formed and the singular and interesting rock at its base. Holguine.

No. 4. Diallage rock high magnesian found with the metalissorus being in the District of Holguine.

No. 5. Carbonate of Magnesia interesting Magnesian rock: being the chief rock which bears the Metatiferous Veins in the District of Holguine.

No. 6. Carbonate of Magnesia. District of Holguine.

Ho. 7. Serpentine Asbestoid. District of Holguine.

No. 8. Ore from out Crop of Vein, Sabana Vieja Mine District of Holguine.

No. 9. Silex resiniti from out crop of Copper Veins in District of Holguine. There is a striking resemblance between this substance and those varieties of qua[rtz?] found in the environs of Paris in France.

No. 10. Copper Ore (Sulfuret of Copper) & Iron Sabana Vieja Mine District of Holguine.

No. 11.Chromate of Iron (portion) of immense masses which [ ] in the Metaliferous regions.

No. 12.Oxide of copper from Sabana Vieja Mines.

No. 13.Oxide of Copper Surface ore Sabana Viega Mine. Neighbourhood of Havanna an interesting association.

No. 14.Euphotide alternating with Silex Resiniti Combustible &c. Near Havanna Island of Cuba.

No. 15.Euphotide alternating with Silex resiniti and Bituminous Combustible and Pyraxenic.

No. 16.Silex resinite. This rock alternating with the Euphotide and the Bituminous Coal or combustible substance in the Island of Cuba near the City of Havanna.

No. 17.Mineral Combustible found in primuture [primitive?] rocks near Havana Island of Cuba.

No. 18.Combustible (very bituminous) (63% of volatile matter) Chipopota *variety of Coal* found in Vein in Primuture [primitive?] Rocks Near Havana Island of Cuba.

Nos.19–31.From Interesting Region of Missouri.

No. 19.Silica Calcareous rock being that in which the Lead &c. is found in Mineral region of Missouri. Madison Co., Missouri.

No. 20.Ore (perox of Iron.) Pilot Knob Mountain (being the Mass of Ore of which that Mountain is formed and situated 8 Miles from Iron Mountain, Missouri.

No. 21.Per Oxide of Iron from Iron Mountin, Missouri.

No. 22.Brown Hoematite from Metaliferous region, Missouri, Perry County.

No. 23.Sulfuret of Copper &c. Mine La Motte, Madison Co., Missouri.

No. 24.Sulfuret of Copper mixed with Galena & Gangre Mine La Cotte Madison County.

No. 25.Sulfuret of Lead in Rock Mine La Motte, Madison County, Missouri.

No. 26.Cairre Sulfure, Plumb Carbonatic, Courre Carbonatic Mine La Motte, Madison County.

No. 27.Carbonate of Lead Mine La Motte Madison County, Missouri.

No. 28.Ditto.

No. 29.Ditto.

No. 30.Carbonate de Plomb Mine La Motte.

No. 31.Ditto. Flemington, New Jersey.

No. 32.Sulfure de Cuirre. Flemington, New Jersey.

No. 33.Bituminous Coal from Black Warrior River Alabama. [200]

5 October 1838
From the asphalt mines of Seyssel, France, a specimen of asphaltic rock.[201]
								William Strickland

16 November 1818
Minerals from Chile
								John N. Casanova

I have the pleasure for sending to you, for the American Philosophical Society, the accompanying objects of Natural History, which I hope will be accepted by that Scientific Institution.

They are as follows:

Three Specimens of Quicksilver ores from Punitaqui in Chili.

Eight	Do	of Silver Ores from Copiapa Huasca, and Coquimbo Chili
Fourteen	Do	of different varieties of copper ores frog the Provinces of Coquimbo, Aconcagua, and Colchagua, Chili.
One	Do	of Pirytes of Iron from Huacso Chili.
Do	Do	Porcellaneid from Aconcagua, Do
Do	Do	Sulphate of Barytes from Do
Two	Do	Argentiferous Galena from Coquimbo
Two	Do	of Fosiles from the Cordillera, near the Province of Coquimbo, found at 18000 feet above the level of the Sea, and about 130 miles from the Coast.
Six	Do	Do from Do found near Copiasso at about 7000 feet above the level of the Sea, and at 120 Miles from the Coast
One	Do	a Compact of Pebbles found in the Cordillera at about 12,000 feet above the level of the Sea between Mendoza and Chili
One	Do	an Ostrichs egg from the Pampas of Buenas Aires.

One copy of General Observations respecting Cholera."

One Do   of Essai sur le Madar &c. &c.

Being a resident Member of the Asiatic Society Calcutta, and of other Scientifical Institutions of British India, and expecting to return to that Capital soon, I avail myself of this opportunity to offer my services to the American Philosophical Society for any Commission that the said Institution may have to place under my charge.[202]

On 19 April 1839 Henry D. Rogers spoke of a new compound of platinum which he and Martin H. Boye had discovered and were continuing to investigate. Rogers spoke at some length about them and then exhibited specimens of this salt.[203]

Stephen Alexander presented on 3 May 1839 two transparent models of solids, executed in mica. One was a dodecahedron and the other was a pyramid "in which the planes of cleavage upon the solid angles are shown." Alexander D. Bache pointed out:

that these models had all the advantages of those made from glass, with greater convenience in the construction of them. The thin plates of mica are readily marked with a sharp instrument, and easily cut. The parts are put together with diamond cement, it having been found that this is a much better method of connecting the pieces composing the model, than by cutting the sheets partly through and using the mica as a hinge, which renders the sheets liable to split. The forms resulting from the cleavage of crystals, &c., may be represented in these models as in those of glass. [204]

21 June 1839
Specimens of barium, strontium, and calcium. The donor spoke of attempts at extricating these elements and how well he had succeeded.[205]

Robert Hare

Richard C. Taylor sent some "chrome ore (or chromatic of iron)" from Cuba in October 1839. It was "of the finest quality ever discovered in quantity."
It can be obtained in pieces of convenient size; this size being only limited to manageable bulk, for the purpose of ready transportation, in packs or paniers on the backs of mules or Horses. It is conveyed 12 miles in this way down to the landing place of the Gibara River & thence descends in lighters 4 miles to the point or Port of Gibara.

There are fine lodes or veins of Copper ore in the immediate vicinity of the Chrome Bed or Deposit. Several of these copper veins have been opened, the ore being formed of various quartzes.[206]

On 3 January 1840 Robert Hare produced "a remarkably beautiful specimen of potassium, in globular form, assumed by falling into naptha." He spoke at of the process he had used and described misadventures with some of his equipment. On 21 February he exhibited a specimen of silicon which weighed seventeen grains and described his method of amassing it.[207]

20 March 1840
A piece of native Russian platina "from the mines." It weighed one ounce and twenty grains.[208]

Colonel Melnikoff, "of the Russian Service."

Thomas Dunlap wrote John Vaughan on 15 May 1830, "The accompanying specimens of chrystals and pipe iron ore were found at the Iron works of William Reed, Perrysville, Mifflin C[ount]y, Pennsylvania and by him deposited with N[icholas] Biddle, Esquire with whose assent I now beg leave to present them to the American Philosophical Society." [209]

On 2 October 1840 a gift of several minerals was received form C. G. Forshey of Louisiana. He wrote a long letter on 3 September 1840 describing his gifts, which it was printed in the first volume of the *Proceedings*. The specimens were from the "Southern & Western parts of the Union." Among the gifts were specimens of coal, alabaster, and iron ores, "Hematite, Crystallized Nodular Oxide,and Pipe Ore." [210]

From the distillation of coal tar at a high temperature, John C. Cresson exhibited a specimen of napthaline "obtained by a kind of irregular crytallization from the liquid.[211] Andres Del Rio wrote on 13 January 1841 and presented "a small discovery of *magnate of zinc* never seen in Europe." Adding that was grateful for the *Proceedings* of the Society, "I never get any news from Guadalajara [Spain]."[212] He wrote on 4 February 1842 that he read the *Proceedings* and found no comments made on his "mineral chamelion." He was hoping some of the members would have commented on this specimen.

2 April 1841
"A large Specimen of the Red Pipe Stone" from the country of the [Carole, PC Gods require use of word Lakota...] Sioux Indians.[213]

Joseph N. Nicollet

On 1 October 1841 the gift of "a piece of stone taken from the summit of Mont Blanc" was received from Joshua Gilpin. In 1798 this stone had been given to him by Alphonse de Saussure so that he could have part of one of the "highest pinnacles of the

Globe." It was presented in the same box in which de Saussure had placed it originally with a paper noting where it is described in de Saussure's works.[214]

16 July 1841
A specimen of marble from Granada.[215]

Nicholas Patrullo

Robert Hare displayed "various specimens of fused iridium, osmiuret of iridium, and of rhodium" on 20 May 1842. He spoke of the crystallization of these elements and of his work with them.[216]

Isaac Lea brought in some masses of rock from Payta, Peru, and the Bay of Coquimbo, Chile, which Lieutenant Rich, of the United States Navy, presented. Lea said these were particularly interesting because the first tended to illustrate the theory of "existing causes." The rock, a compacted sandstone, was composed of minute grains of quartz cemented by carbonate of lime. A mollusk, Lithodomi, or "Boring Mollusk," was found in it. This specimen was taken from an elevation of 200 feet. These mollusks lived on the sea coast and were "now inhabiting the neighbouring sea coast. The coast had risen to 200 feet, Lea reported, since "the elevation of the coast by the earthquake of 1822, as mentioned by Mrs. Graham, was but a few feet, and that of 1835, as stated by Capt[ain Robert] Fitz Roy, being but about eight feet."[217]

On 21 October 1842 Lea spoke on two specimens of coal from the large anthracite bed in the Pine Grove district in Pennsylvania. One sample had nearly perfect rhombic form with nearly exact cleavages and the other was "scarcely changed from its condition as charcoal." He discussed Sir Charles Lyell's theory that anthracite is converted from bituminous coal "where the beds have been most disturbed," but he disagreed with Lyell—pointing out that the geology of Pennsylvania was different from that of Wales and discussed some of the geological findings of the area.[218]

W. W. Andrews sent on 15 September 1843 a catalogue of the minerals he had forwarded on 17 November 1837.[219] A specimen of earth, "apparently silicious," was exhibited on 15 September 1843 by John Fries Frazer who spoke about it. It had been deposited in a considerable quantity in a chimney of a house in Delaware County, Pennsylvania, by a tornado which passed on 5 August 1843. Frazer thought this deposit raised the question "whether the rain proceeded from a waterspout." He had traced the line of the tornado and discovered it to be a curve. More significantly, when the tornado passed through a wood, small trees escaped but larger trees were "generally prostrated."[220]

Another unusual find was fifteen grain piece of iron removed from a man's eye. He was totally unaware of it, but, from the constant inflammation of the eye, the presence of a foreign substance was inferred. Isaac Hays exhibited this iron and spoke of it on 17 November 1843.

15 March 1844
A specimen of "Dodecahedral oxide of Iron" from Bucks County, Pennsylvania.[221]

John C. Trautwine

18 October 1844
Stalactites from Mammoth Cave, Kentucky.[222]

George M. Justice

John B. Sartori on 29 April 1845 sent a piece of "fixed mercury...in a small box weighing about 16 $\frac{1}{2}$ ounces" asking to examine it so "that they may see the propriety of encouraging this operation which may become an object of a very great importance to our mint in the United States." The specimen was received on 15 August 1845.[223] Robley Dunglison wrote Sartori of his report and Sartori replied on 1 November 1845:

If the analysis made on the sample by your assayer in Philad[elphi]a has been found to contain Zinc & other metals and not a particle of Mercury the operator must have made some mistake. Being once fixed it is a new principle and is like all the rest of metals in general...I can assure your society that there is not a particle of Zinc & or other metals, but pure Mercury ... but if your Society do not wish to purchase it [the process] according to their rules, perhaps the U.S. Mint might think proper to become the purchaser. [225]

This was read on 2 January 1846. Sartori wrote again on 20 September 1846 donating specimens of fixed mercury which he wished to be examined by the U.S. Mint. The specimens were delivered on 5 February 1847; Jacob R. Eckfeldt and Martin H. Boye were asked to examine them. Boye reported verbally on 7 May 1847 that they had examined the three specimens. "The first specimen proved to be an amalgam of tin and mercury; the second, pure tin; and the third an arsiniuret of copper; neither of the latter containing mercury."[226]

A diamond found in north Georgia near Dahlonega was exhibited on 21 November 1845 by Robert Maskell Patterson. Two others had been found in the same area of the gold region of North Carolina some years previously. This diamond weighed 6.8 grains and the specific gravity was 3.54. Mr. Philips, of Philadelphia, had examined it and said it was "very white, and of the first water" bearing a strong resemblance to those of Borneo. It was "a perfect crystal, in the form of a rhomboidal dodecahedron, with the rounded faces characteristic of this gem." It was oval, "somewhat flattened, or having, in the language of the Iapidary, a good spread.[227] Patterson exhibited another diamond on 20 February 1846 "nearly three carats in weight, and considered to be of the first water" from the same area of Georgia.[228]

A specimen of nitric ether was presented by Boye on 5 December 1845. He explained the difference between it and hyponitrous ether and discussed the process of preparing the latter.[229] On 20 February 1846, Boye exhibited a specimen of brown hematite ore containing a small quantity of oxide of cobalt, which came from Huntington County, Pennsylvania, three-quarters of a mile west of Chester Furnace. It contained some manganese. He stated:

The ore was dissolved in chlorohydric acid, the solution neutralized by ammonia, and then the iron precipitated by the boiling, after previous dilution with water. The oxide of cobalt which remained in the solution with the manganese was discovered both by its reaction in the moist way, and by the blue bead it yielded with salt of phosophorus. [230]

On 20 February 1846 when Robert M. Patterson exhibited the second diamond from north Georgia, Franklin Peale said that he owned a specimen of granular quartz which was "supposed to be the gang of the diamond" which was quite flexible. At the next meeting, on 6 March, Peale displayed the quartz. On 20 March Isaac Lea displayed some flexible quartz [Quartz hyalin granulaire Hauy] which came from the area of Spartanburg, South Carolina. It was a foot long "and about the eighth of an inch thick, curving by a gentle force into an arc, the versed side of which measured one full inch." He reported that the specimens "of considerable length of this singularly constructed mineral" could be obtained at this locality. [231]

Boye spoke of, and exhibited, at the meeting of 3 April 1846 several mineralogical specimens from the bituminous coal areas of Pennsylvania. Sulphate of magnesia, both in fibrous crystals and in porous masses, was discussed, as were several specimens of argillaceous carbonate of iron which contained within it sulphate of baryte. From the area of Brighton, on Beaver Creek, came a curious nodular iron ore which consisted "of small oolitic concretions of iron ore...of a light brownish colour" which was imbedded in "a white sparry mass, consisting of a mixture of sulphate of baryte with some sulphate of lime and silica."[232]

Peter A. Browne sent on 16 June 1848 an announcement that the Society for the Development of the Mineral Resources of the United States was being formed. He asked permission to place the Society's name among the correspondents of this new organization. [233]

Robert M. Patterson exhibited for the Society on 18 August 1848 two minerals from the diamond mines of Brazil. He described them thus:

One of these minerals occurs in irregular black lumps of considerable size, and is found in the diamond grounds one or two feet below the surface. It is considered a certain indication of the presence of diamonds, which, indeed, are sometimes found inside of its masses. Its structure is perfectly vitreous, and it appears to be a pure obsidian.

The other, called "Diamond Carbon," or "Black Diamond" is found in the same locality. It cuts all other minerals, including the diamond itself, upon which it acts with as much rapidity as the diamond dust. The specific gravity of the smaller piece is 3.01. These minerals first attracted attention at the diamond mines, about six years ago. The "Diamond Carbon" is sold here at 75 cents per carat of 31/6 grains troy, being about 25 cents per grain, or about six times the value of gold.

Dr. P[atterson] conceives that the "Diamond Carbon" will be found exceedingly useful in the arts, being applicable to all purposes for which diamond dust is now used. [234]

On 20 April 1849 George M. Justice exhibited gold specimens which had been found on the Maryland farm of Samuel Ellicott in Montgomery County, about thirty miles from Baltimore. Three samples had been assayed at the United States Mint and averaged $522 per ton. Quarrying was easy, for the quartz which formed the matrix for the gold was found in a decomposed talcose slate. Although invisible to the naked eye, "much gold appears to be disseminated throughout the gangue.[235]

Two diamonds from Georgia, about $2^1/_2$ carats each, and of very fine water, were exhibited by John F. Frazer on 5 October 1849. The donor believed "others may be obtained from the same locality."[236] A specimen, supposedly of pure zinc which had been obtained by distillation by Charles McEuen, was exhibited on 5 October 1849. It came from the red oxide of zinc from northern New Jersey.[237] John F. Frazer announced on 17 May 1850 that gold had been discovered in the vicinity of Bloomington, Indiana. He exhibited some specimens where the gold was "in association with particles of magnetic oxide of iron; titanite and garnet."[238]

A piece of plumbago from Bucks County, Pennsylvania, Southampton mine, was exhibited by Benjamin W. Richards on 6 December 1850. The specimen, $12^1/_4$ inches long and 3/4 and 5/8 inch thick had been removed from a much longer piece, "remarkable for its purity." He gave brief history of the mine and said that the plumbago was found "better for the purposes of making crucibles, &c. than the imported article, on account of its greater purity, but that, unfortunately, it was expensive owing to the depth of the mine and the difficulty of working it." [239]

On 21 November 1851 H. Boye exhibited some iron pyrites from the "Gap Mine" in Lancaster County, Pennsylvania. They had a "peculiar colour and lustre" and contained copper pyrites and nickel.[240] Charles M. Wetherill's paper "on the occurrence of Gold in Pennsylvania," the "Chemical Examination of two minerals from the neighbourhood of Reading, Pennsylvania," was recommended for publication by John F. Frazer, Robert Bridges, and Charles B. Trego on 16 September 1852.[241]

Some garnets, "beautiful for their fineness of colour and excellence of composition," were exhibited on 5 November 1852 by Charles B. Trego. William A. Hammond, of the United States Army, had procured them "from a volcanic region in New Mexico between the waters of the Rio del Norte and the Gila."[242] On 19 November he exhibited some specimens of copper ore from the same region for the members. He gave these and reported that he "found that smelting establishments had existed in the locality in which the specimens were obtained, but had been abandoned."[243]

Henry A. Boardman exhibited on 7 January 1853 some rock crystal from the Alps "of unusual clearness and beauty. [244]

William E. Du Bois delivered a piece of Australian gold for exhibition on 4 February 1853. He said of them:

The grains are quite different in shape from those of California, being more globular or shotlike; and the proportion of accompanying oxide of iron, and extraneous substances is found to be less by the loss in melting. That loss scarcely exceeds 1-$\frac{1}{2}$ per cent, on the average, while the best shipments of gold from California will average double that loss. [245]

6 May 1853
Silicate of zinc which had been found in the Saucon valley in Lehigh County, Pennsylvania. The product from this bed of ore went to New York "for the manufacture of zinc paint." [246]

Edward Miller

William E. Du Bois exhibited on 21 September 1855 some "new French silver" or the metal aluminium. The French now manufactured it in ingots but, he said, "It is still held at a price little less than that of pure gold." Possible use for this metal for coinage and other things were discussed, "if the price can be brought down, as some anticipate, to 50 cents a pound; or even to 50 cents an ounce." [247]
Du Bois showed on 16 November 1855 some Lake Superior silver ore. One specimen, worth $25, was "pure metallic silver in carbonate of lime," with some copper. The less valuable specimen, worth only $3.75, was of copper and silver "firmly welded together, as it were, are yet free from intermixture."[248] On 4 April 1856 he exhibited specimens of Australian gold in quartz which was "precisely similar in character to the auriferous matrix in California." Such a remarkable similarity was commented upon by Charles B. Trego.
Some specimens of crystallized slag from the Glendon Iron Works at Easton, Pennsylvania, were exhibited on 20 March 1857 by Trego. Although unanalyzed, he thought the crystals were similar to augite. Because the limestone in the area contained magnesia, it seemed that, used as a flux in the furnace, silica and iron would be included "thus furnishing the necessary ingredients for the formation of a substance similar in composition, as well as in crystallization, to augite." [249]
Members adopted on 3 April 1857 John K. Kane's resolution:

Resolved, That Prof. [Charles B.] Trego, Prof. [John F.] Frazer and Thomas L. Kane be authorized and empowered as a committee to proceed to Harrisburg, and there to solicit of the Legislature, if they shall deem it expedient, the deposit with this Society of the geological collection now the property of the State.

John F. Frazer requested to have someone else appointed in his place on 17 April 1857; Frederick Fraley was named. [250]
Du Bois showed a lump of native California gold on 15 May 1857. The dendritic mass was unique in structure "of innumerable specimens heretofore received at the Mint." No quartzose or earthy matter was "in the many interstices of this specimen." [251] On 2 April 1857 Boye showed a series of models constructed by him for illustrating crystal forms and the laws of crystallography and lectured on them. [252]
Joseph Leidy delivered on 20 August 1858 some slate which contained the fossil, Lepidostrobus, thereby "establishing the identity of this coal bed [at Broad Top] at different points of its many outcrops in widely distant parts of the United States." He exhibited also some slate "polished to a perfect mirror surface by the disturbance of the coal bearing structure." [253]
Trego displayed from "the immediate vicinity of the eternal snows of the Himalayas," a mineral deposit gathered from the hot springs of Munnikurrun on 21 January 1859. The specimen came from beneath the water, temperature 196° F., at 7,000 feet elevation above boiling. It looked much like a petrified fungus. He said:
The surface of the lower portion and stem is covered with warty excrescences of a black colour, while the flat surface of the top has a smoothe coating of a brownish-yellow tinge. The interior is composed of delicate shining yellow fibres, closely aggregated, and generally radiating from the central portion or stem. The dark

colouring is oxides of iron and manganese; the fibrous portion is carbonate of lime coloured by oxide of iron; and the smoothe top is carbonate of lime with less carbonate of iron. [254]

3 February 1860
A piece of itacolumite sandstone (flexible sandstone) and showed "very plainly its flexible and elastic properties." [255]

Charles B. Trego

18 May 1860
Some washoe ore, from the Comstock vein. "From its appearance it would not lead any one to suspect that it could be so rich in precious metals." [256]

Mr. Du Bois

A specimen of jasper was presented on 17 October 1862 was taken from a cave in New Hampshire. It was supposed that the aborigines obtained the materials for their flint instruments and arrowheads from this cave, for it was artificially created and was twenty-eight feet long, twelve feet wide and eight or ten feet high. The cave was dug from the granite of "a steep mountain spur, on the banks of the Androscoggin, one and a half miles from Berlin Falls." [257]

Records are scanty for the mineralogical collection after this date, although members still were interested in, and spoke of, mineralogical subjects at various meetings. Specimens were deposited at the Academy of Natural Sciences of Philadelphia, following a resolution by members on 18 March 1864 that "so many of the Specimens of the Collection of Minerals and Fossils belonging to the Society as the curators may select, be deposited in the Cabinet" of the Academy, "provided that they shall be returned on demand, and that the Curators of the Academy shall give a receipt for the same." On 22 March 1864, the Academy agreed, and asked the curators to make the selections. On 28 March 1864 Franklin Peale, for the Society, and Joseph Leidy, for the Academy, signed the receipt for the transaction.[258] No doubt the onset of the Civil War had disturbed the activities of members; the minerals were then deposited at the Academy.

20 July 1866
Titaniferous iron ore from Cumberland, Rhode Island. [259]

Pliny E. Chase

Joseph Leidy on 15 March 1867 gave J. Lawrence Smith a fragment of a meteorite which had been deposited by Joel Roberts Poinsett. "It appears to be an entire meteorite, exhibiting nowhere a cut or broken surface; one end, however, was much crushed, as if the specimen had been used for a hammer." Smith analyzed the fragment and said that most meteorites "of a very highly crystalline structure," such as this, seem to be complete masses, but they are fragments of a larger mass. "It is possible that this iron may be a portion of the large mass recently sent to France from Mexico, by General Bazaine." [260]

Du Bois presented on 19 March 1869 some silver ore from the Black Spider Mine in the White Pine region of Nevada. Du Bois gave an analysis of it and also spoke of other ores and the assay of coins by the Mint. [261] Work for the Centennial Celebration of the Declaration of Independence in Philadelphia was going on, and on 3 December 1875 the members asked that the Society be furnished "at each of its meetings, a report" on the borings near the Centennial structures, "and to furnish the museum of the Society with specimens of the rocks bored through." [262]

17 December 1880
Two specimens of "slag from the site of the earliest iron furnace in Virginia."[263]
R. Alonzo Brock

7 March 1890
A bottle of "Earthquake sand from the Geysers of Summerville, S[outh] C[arolina]." The donor acquired the sand on 31 August 1886.
Henry Phillips, Jr.

Meanwhile, the Society lost some tenants in Philosophical Hall and, while altering the rooms, discussed how to use the extra space. The collections of the Cabinet, many of which were now on deposit in various sister institutions, were considered suitable to fill the areas. But, in early 1893, the remnants of the mineralogical collection in the Hall, as well as other artifacts, were placed in the basement while the second floor received major alterations. While there, carpenters helped clean out the basement and "this has resulted in the destruction of valuable property, among a mass of heterogeneous material some of which must be recognized as worthless." The curators reported that this was done while they "were unaware of what was contemplated, took no part in the proceedings, and therefore are wholly without responsibility for the consequences." [265] The "carpenters had moved with unanticipated zeal & celerity thereby destroying items of the cabinet." [266]

The constantly expanding library needed additional room, and the special committee on the library recommended on 2 April 1897 that a committee of geologists "report... their recommendation" as to the disposition of the "collection of rocks" in the Hall. The curators disagreed,[267] but on 7 May 1897 the report of this special committee was received. The curators were then notified:

That all the specimens which have no labels or designations by which they can be recognised, and which are not of value for other special reasons, be thrown away. Also

That all specimens which can be recognised as to their locality and are of any scientific value (such as the duplicate collection of the First Geological Survey of Pennsylvania) be deposited in the collection of some institution, subject to recall, and a receipt taken therefore. [268]

Edwin J. Simpson, secretary of the Academy of Natural Sciences of Philadelphia, wrote on 14 May 1897 that the Academy did not have "a duplicate set of the rocks of the First survey of the state." [269]

On 17 May 1897 Henry Pettit asked James C. Morris to help the curators dispose "of minerals, &c. now in the central case, north side of North Room." He felt that the curators should act promptly. Because the Society's collections were being reworked and new cases were being built, Pettit felt that the matter of the mineral specimens "should be attended to without delay." Morris asked the members on 4 November 1898 that the curators "be allowed to deposit the collection of rocks and minerals" which were stored in the basement of Philosophical Hall, "in the Wagner Free Institute of Science, or elsewhere, at their discretion." The curators would see that "proper guarantees for their preservation and recovery" would be taken. This was agreed to and on 3 May 1899 the Wagner Free Institute sent a receipt to the Society for 98 specimens deposited therein.[270]

The curators reported on 29 November 1899 that the minerals in the possession of the Society had been removed to the Wagner Free Institute of Science where they "can be better displayed or studied." They added: "In this connection they regret to state that owing to the many movings and vicissitudes which these specimens have undergone, many of their labels & means of identification have been hopelessly lost or destroyed, so that they have become comparatively valueless." The curators, therefore, placed these seemingly valueless items at the discretion of the superintendent of the Philadelphia High School. [271]

Two items preserved in the 1890s, otherwise not identified, had cards describing them: "Specimen of Alum Vermont" and "Niter (specimen of Monmouth)."[272] The Academy of Natural Sciences sent a listing of the Society's property deposited there on

3 June 1901. The entry for mineralogy reads: "442 Trays, as per entries in Academy Catalogue."[273] Even though the Society had disposed of its collection of minerals, Edgar Fahs Smith gave on 6 February 1903 "a specimen of the metal calcium obtained by electrolysis."[274]

In 1949 the curators asked for a report on the mineralogical specimens in the Academy of Natural Sciences of Philadelphia. Horace Gardiner Richards replied on 14 December 1949 when he wrote by hand the only good itemized list of mineral specimens from the Society's cabinet. The preface to this thirteen page list states:

> Since no list of the deposits of the [American] Philosophical Society was found [in the Academy of Natural Sciences of Philadelphia] it was necessary to pick out the individual items scattered throughout the catalog. In all 442 entries were found each representing a tray usually containing a single specimen but occasi[o]nally two or more.

> Instead of giving the entire list of numbers the list is condensed to give under each mineral name beginning with the precious metals the total number of trays and the country or state of origin.

He listed, but not necessarily in this order: *Gold,* native or rock bearing, Virginia, North Carolina, Mexico, Peru, Brazil; *Silver,* native and in various associations and forms, Mexico and Peru; *Platinum,* native, Brazil; Copper, native, New Mexico, Chile, England; *Mercury,* native, Germany,; *Iron,* meteoric and meteorites, North Carolina, Mexico, France; *Sulphur,* native, Montana, Pennsylvania, West Indies, Spain, Italy; *Arsenic,* native, Queen Charlotte Sound, Canada; *Graphite,* Scotland; *Zinc,* native, England, Irididimine (?), Russia; Realgar, Mexico; Stibnite, Spain, France; *Molybdenite,* France; Argentite, Mexico, South America; Galenite, Illinois, Mexico, Hungary; Hanscolite (?), Missouri, France, Hungary; *Sphalarite,* Mexico; Cinnabar, Spain; *Pyrite,* United States, South America, England etc.; *Native gold and sulphur in quartz,* Peru; *Gold in mica schist,* Brazil; *Native gold,* Mexico, Virginia, North Carolina; *Native gold with arsenic,* Mexico; *Auroferous quartz,* Virginia; *Native silver,* Mexico; *Spongy native silver,* Mexico; *Capillary silver,* Peru and Mexico; *Capillary silver with quartz crystal,* Mexico; *Capillary silver on quartz,* Mexico; *Capillary native silver,* Mexico; *Native silver with blende,* Mexico; *Native silver in quartz,* Mexico; *Native silver with sulphuret,* Mexico; *Native silver with blende and pyrite,* Mexico; *Native silver in quartz,* Mexico; *Native silver in Calcite,* Mexico; Copper native silver, Mexico; *Platinum,* Brazil; *Irodosmine,* Russia; *Native copper with copper oxide,* New Mexico; *Native copper,* Chile, England; *Native mercury with sulphuret,* Germany; *Native arsenide (?) with arsenic,* Queen Charlotte Sound, Canada; *Native sulphur,* Sicily, Spain, Nevis Island [West Indies], Montana; *Native sulphur in quartz geode,* Chester County, Pennsylvania; *Graphite graphitic coal,* Scotland; *Stibnite ?,* Spain, France; *Molybdonite,* France; Argentite, Mexico, South America; *Galenite,* Hungary, Mexico, England, Illinois; *Huascolite (?),* Missouri, Hungary, France; *Metallic zinc,* Italy (dep. 1879); *Sphalerite,* England, Mexico; *Pyrite,* England, Chile, Mexico, Peru, Pennsylvania, Rhode Island; *Brecciate and Flint,* England; *Agate,* Germany; *Egyptian Jasper; Silicious sontes (stones?),* Iceland; *Float stone;* France; *Wollastonite in Jarra (?),* Italy; *Pyroxene,* Sicily, Corbie; *Diopside,* Alabama; *Sahlete,* Sweden; *Diallage,* Geneva, Valley of Goats; *Hedenbergite,* Elba, Italy; *Antholite,* Oregon; *Tremolite,* Sweden, Switzerland, Rhode Island, Austria; *Nephrite,* France; *Actinolite (in Talc),* Switzerland, Vermont; *Gadolinite,* Divenden; *Asbestos,* Switzerland, Delaware; *Amiranthus on quartz,* France; *Axenite,* Saxony, Germany; *Beryl,* Iceland, France, Chester County, Pennsylvania, New Hampshire, Brazil; *Chrysolite in sand,* France; *Willemite with blende,* England; *Pyrite,* Alaska; *Chalcopyrite,* Austria, England, France; *Cubanite,* Cuba; *Marcasite,* Mexico; *Arsenopyrite,* Alps, Mexico; *Dufrenoysite,* Switzerland; *Pipargyrite (?),* Mexico, South America; *Tetrahedrite,* Mexico; *Fluorite,* England; *Specular hematite,* Elba; *Micaceous hematite with quartz and calcite,* France; *Argillaceous hematite,* England; *Chrysoberyl,* Brazil; *Cassiterite,* Guatemala; *Rutile in quartz,* Switzerland, France, Mexico; *Pintilated quartz,* La Plata, Brazil; *Pyrolusite,* France, Bohemia, Alps; *Quartz,*

Pennsylvania; *Quartz, Cape May diamond*, New Jersey; *Quartz, black*, France, Austria; *Amethyst*, France, Mexico; *Ferruginous Quartz*, Spain; *Chalcedony*, Germany; *Chalcedony with bitumen*, France; *Chalcedony geode*, Nebraska; *Carnelian*, Lake Pepin; Agate, Mexico, Lake Superior, Oregon; *Jasper Porcelain*, Sicily, France, Ireland; *Jasper, striped*, Massachusetts, Mexico; *Flint*, Brazil; *Flint pseud. after Echinns (?)*, England; *Agated wood*, Antigua, West Indies; *Wood Opal*, Australia; *Opal*, France; *Menilite*, France; *Limonite*, France; *Limonite cast after pyrite*, Lancaster County, Pennsylvania, Rhode Island; *Brucite (?)*, Pennsylvania; *Psilomelane*, England; *Dendritic manganese*, Mexico; *Dendritic manganese in sandstone*, Colorado; *(Leopardite) manganese*, North Carolina; *Auriferous quartz*, Virginia; *Stalactitical quartz*, Austria; *Drusy (?) quartz*, Pennsylvania; *Quartz with chalcedony, ?; Quartz, pseud. after coral*, Europe; *Quartz pseud. after calcite*, Mexico, Hungary; *Quartz, pseud. after gypsum*, France; *Quartz geode; Diallage (?)*, Italy; *Quartz*, Madagascar, Desolation Island, Pennsylvania, Switzerland; *Quartz containing liquid*, Mexico; *Quartz with amiranthus*, Switzerland; *Quartz with Epidote and Asbestos*, France; *Quartz (dodecahedral)* France; *Garnet*, Norway, France, Maine; *Garnet in talc*, Switzerland; *Garnet*, green, France; *Essonite (?)*, Ceylon; *Hyacinth*, Ceylon; *Disurrianite (?)*, Alabama, Maine; *Epidote*, France; *Epidot on quartz*, Alps, France; *Epidote with quartz*, France; *Cassiterite*, Rhode Island; *Piedmontite*, Piedmont, Italy; *Zoisite*, Alps; *Limenite*, Rhode Island; *Axinite*, Pyranees; *Axinite with quartz*, France; *Phlogopite ?*, Vesuvius, Italy; Green muscovite, Maine; *Labradorite*, Labrador; *Feldspar with Amiranthus*, Switzerland; *Feldspar*, France; *Orthoclase*, Simplon, Drachenfel (?); *Lava slag*, Missouri; *Porphory*, Egypt, Sweden; *Obsidian*, Sicily, Mexico; *Marekanite (?)*, Mexico; *Pearlstone in Obsidian*, Mexico; *Pitchstone*, Hebrides, Sicily, France; *Pumice*, Sicily; *Tourmaline (green)* Massachusetts; *Tourmaline (black)* New Hampshire, *Tourmaline*, New York; *Chiastolite*, Germany; *Cyanite*, Tyrol, Switzerland; *Topaz*, Saxony, Germany, Mexico, Brazil, Connecticut, Japan; *Titanite on Adularia (?)*, Sweden; *Staurolite in talc*, Tyrol, Hartz Mountains; Switzerland, Brittany, Maine; *Prehnite*, Scotland; *Apophyllite with Chalcedony*, Sweden; *Matrolite*, Swabia, Germany; *Matrolite in lava*, Italy; *Analcite*, Tyrol; *Harmatome*, Germany, England; *Stiltite*, Iceland, France; *Talc*, Rhode Island; *Celadonite*, Italy; *Kaolinite*, France; *Clay (red)*, Louisiana; *Volcanic mud*, New Granada; *Catlinite*, Sioux Country; *Pinite*, France; *Pinite var. Roseite*, Norway; *Ripidolite*, Maine; *Apatite*, Spain; *Pyromorphite*, France; *Tripite*, France; *Virranite (?)*, New Jersey; *Mastodon Ivory*, Kentucky; *Erythrite*, Saxony, Germany; *Antunite (?)*, France; *Nitre*, Kentucky; *Boracite in Gypsum*, Germany; *Wolframite*, France, Bohemia; *Schulite*, England; *Wulperite*, Carinthia, Austria; *Wulperite vanadiferous (?)*, Chester County, Pennsylvania; *Crocoite*, Cornwall, Pennslvania; *Baroto*, Hungary; *Tourmaline*, Switzerland, France; *Barite*, England, New York; *Celestite*, Sicily, Mexico; *Magnetite*, England, France;

He concluded with: "442 tray a few may have been missed."[275] The only mineralogical specimens in the Society today are a large gold nugget, probably presented by John Vaughn on 21 June 1805, and a stone from the first American capitol building, burned by the British, which was given by Captain Riley in 1818.

Minerlogical Specimens: References

1. Encyclopaedia: or a Dictionary of Arts, Sciences, and Miscellaneous Literature. Philadelphia1798. See article on mineralogy.

2. Greene, J.C.: "The development of Mineralogy in Philadelphia 1780–1820." Proc., vol. 113, pp 283 ff.

3. Ibid.

4. Franklin, B. A Proposal for Promoting Useful Knowledge among the british Plantations in America.

5. American Society. Minutes.

6. Ibid. 18 (25) March 1768.

7. Ibid. By this date the American Philosophical Society and the American Society had united, forming the present American Philosophical Society held at Philadelphia for Promoting Useful Knowledge.

8. *Archives.* J. Wood ...,April 1768.

9. American Society, Minutes, 15 July 1768.

10. *Ibid.*

11. *Ibid.*

12. *Archives.* General Sullivan to APS, 16 Feb. 1781; *Trans.*, vol. 2.

13. *Trans.,*

14. *Ibid.* vol. 3; *Archives.* D. Reddick to B. Franklin, 8 Sept., 1789.

15. *Ibid.* vol. 4.

16. *Ibid.* vol. 5; *Archives.* APS Report, 24 Nov. 1798.

17. *Ibid.* vol. 5.

18. *Archives.* T.P. Smith. Extract ... will, 2 Sept. 1802.

19. Com. Rec.

20. Kirwan, R.: *Elements of Mineralogy.* London: 1784. This work was the first extensive treatise in English on mineralogy. John H. de Magellan, a descendant of the great Magellan, presented this volume on 2 December, 1785.

21. *Archives.* T. Peters to J. Vaughan, 25 July, 1803.

22. *Ibid.* See entries for T. P. Smith.

23. Com. Rec.

24. *Archives.* Mary Wells Receipt, 26 April 1804.

25. *Ibid.* G. Knapp to T. P. Smith, 18 April 1801.

26. Misc. MS. Col. J. Watt, Jr., to T. P. Smith, 30 Dec. 1801.

27. *Ibid.* Tonnelier,-------. Liste, [1801].

28. *Archives.* R. R. Livingston to T. Jefferson, 26 Nov. 1802.

29. Verbal comm.

30. *Trans.,* vol. 6.

31. *Archives.* APS to J. Carter, 8, 9, 19 Nov. 1803; APS to W. Broome, 22 April 1803.

32. *Ibid.* W. Lewis to T. Jefferson, 7 March 1804.

33. *Ibid.* APS. Report, 20 April 1804.

34. MS. Com T. Patton to W. Hembel, 16 July 1804; *Trans.*, vol. 6.

35. *Archives.* J. C. Da Costa to APS, 21 Sept. 1804.

36. MS. Com. 15 June 1805.

37. *Archives.* J. D. Clifford to APS, 31 Jan. 1805; Trans., vol. 6.

38. See: J. C. Greene. Mineralogy..

39. *Archives.* S. Brown to J. Vaughan, 9 April 1805.

40. Minutes, 3 May 1805.

41. Com. Rec.

42. *Trans.,* vol. 6.

43. *Ibid.* Donations Book.

44. MS. Com. J. Richardson to J. Vaughan, 6 June 1805.

45. *Trans.,* vol. 6.

46. *Ibid.*

47. *Archives.* T. Jefferson to J. Vaughan, 4 May 1806.

48. Com. Rec.

49. *Archives.* S. Brown to T. Jefferson, 4 Nov. 1805.

50. *Ibid.* APS. Report, 21 March 1806.

51. *Ibid.* T. Jefferson to T. T. Hewson, 21 Jan. 1806.

52. *Ibid.* R. R. Livingston to J. Vaughan, 9 March 1806.

53. *Trans.,* vol. 6.

54. *Ibid.*

55. *Ibid.*

56. *Archives.* T. Hamilton to J. Vaughan, 6, Sept. 1806.

57. *Ibid.* W. Maclure to APS, 7 May 1807; Trans., vol. 6.

58. *Trans.,* vol. 6; Com. Rec.

59. *Trans.,* vol. 6.

60. *Ibid.; Archives.* R. H. Rose to J. Vaughan, 21 Aug. [1807].

61. *Archives.* S. Brown to B. S. Barton, 20 Sept. 1807.

62. *Trans.,* vol. 6

63. MS. Com. S. Godon. Observations, 6 Nov. 1807; APS. Report, 20 Nov. 1807.

64. *Trans.,* vol. 6.

65. MS. Com. J. Howell. Concerning..., 1807.

66. *Trans.,* vol. 6.

67. *Archives.* W. Maclure to APS, 29 March 1808.

68. *Ibid.* T. Hamilton to J. Vaughan, 29 March 1808.

69. MS. Com. J. B. Dabney to T. Jefferson, 20 June 1808.

70. *Archives.* APS. Report, 18 Nov. 1808.

71. *Ibid.,* 3 Feb. 1809.

72. *Trans.,* vol. 6.

73. *Ibid.*

74. MS. Com. L. Spalding. Origin, 2 Feb. 1810.

75. Com. Rec.; Donations Book.

76. *Donations Book.*

77. *Ibid.; Trans.,* n. s., vol. 1.

78. *Ibid.*

79. *Archives.* S. Godon to J. Vaughan, 31 Jan. 1811.

80. *Ibid.* T. T. Hewson to J. Vaughan, 6 Feb. 1811.

81. *Donations Book.*

82. *Ibid.*

83. *Ibid.*

84. *Ibid.*

85. *Archives.* T. Hamlin to J. Vaughan, 1 Sept. 1812.

86. *Donations Book*; Trans., n. s., vol. 1.

87. *Ibid.*

88. Verbal comm.

89. *Donations Book;* Trans., n. s., vol. 1.

90. *Ibid.*

91. Com. Rec.

92. *Donations Book;* Trans., n. s., vol. 1.

93. *Donations Book*

94. *Archives.* APS. Report, 21 April 1815.

95. Verbal com.

96. *Donations Book*

97. *Trans.,* n. s., vol. 1.

98. *Archives.* APS. Report, 21 June 1816.

99. *Trans.,* n. s., vol. 1.

100. *Ibid.; Donations Book.*

101. *Donations Book.*

102. *Ibid.; Trans.,* n. s., vol. 1.

103. *Donations Book.*

104. *Archives.* New-York Historical Society. Circular, 6 March 1817.

105. *Ibid.* APS. Report, 15 May 1817.

106. D *Donations Book.*on. Book.

107. *Archives.* APS. Report, 22 May 1817.

108. Treasurers Rec.

109. *Donations Book.*

110. Ibid.

111. MS. Com. D. Drake to J. F. Correa da Serra, 1 Oct. 1817; *Archives*. APS. Report, 19 March 1818.

112. *Ibid.*, J. C. Montgomery to J. Vaughan, 2 Feb. 1818; *Trans.*, n. s., vol. 1.

113. *Ibid.* I. Lea to ----, 6 Feb. 1818; *Donations Book.*

114. *Ibid.* J. Sargeant to J. Vaughan, 12 May 1818.

115. *Donations Book.*

116. *Ibid.*

117. *Ibid.*

118. *Ibid.*

119. *Ibid.*

120. *Ibid.*

121. *Ibid.; Trans.*, n. s., vol. 2.

122. *Ibid.*

123. *Ibid.;* Curators Cards.

124. *Archives*. APS. Report, 1 Dec. 1820.

125. *Donations Book.*

126. *Ibid.*

127. *Ibid.*

128. *Ibid.*

129. *Ibid.*

130. *Ibid.*

131. *Archives*. W. Meade to APS, 14 Dec. 1821.

132. Cur. Rec.

133. *Donations Book.*

134. *Ibid.*

135. *Ibid.*

136. MS. Com. H. Seybert. Analysis, 17 May 1822.

137. *Donations Book.*

138. *Archives*. S. Merrick to J. Vaughan, 24 Sept. 1822; Don. Book.

139. *Donations Book.*

140. *Ibid.; Trans.*, n. s., vol. 2.

141. MS. Com. R. Dietz. Notes, 10 July 1823.

142. *Donations Book.*

143. *Ibid.*

144. *Ibid.*

145. *Archives* APS. Report, 15 March 1824.

146. Cur. Rec.

147. *Donations Book.*

148. Misc. MS. Col. P. A. Browne to J. Vaughan, 30 Jan. 1824.

149. *Donations Book.*

150. *Ibid.*

151. *Archives*. APS. Report, 5 Nov. 1824.

152. *Donations Book.*

153. *Ibid.*

154. *Ibid.*

155. *Ibid.*

156. *Ibid.*

157. *Ibid.; Trans.*, n. s., vol. 3.

158. *Ibid.*

159. *Trans.*, n. s., vol. 3.

160. *Donations Book.*

161. *Ibid.*

162. *Archives*. C. Atwater to J. Vaughan, 13 Jan. 1830.

163. *Donations Book.* Trans., n. s., vol. 3.

164. *Trans.*, n. s., vol. 3.

165. MS. Com. P. A. Browne to APS, 16 April 1830; Don. Book.; Trans., n. s., vol. 4.

166. *Archives*. APS. Report, 9 July 1830.

167. *Ibid.* A. D. Bache to S. Conrad, 4 Aug. 1830.

168. *Ibid.* J. P. Grant to J. Vaughan, 18 Aug. 1830.

169. *Donations Book.*

170. Corn. Rec.

171. *Donations Book; Trans.*, n. s., vol. 4.

172. *Ibid.*

173. Corn. Rec.

174. *Donations Book; Trans.*, n. s., vol. 4.

175. Don. to Cabinet; Trans., n. s., vol. 4.

176. *Donations Book; Trans.*, n. s., vol. 4.

177. Misc. MS. Col. P. A. Browne. Profile, 1835.

178. *Donations Book; Trans.*, n. s., vol. 4.

179. *Archives.* F. Dwight to J. Vaughan, 21 June 1833.

180. *Ibid.* C. Nagy to J. Vaughan, 20 Aug. 1833.

181. *Ibid.* Forstall Bros. to R. Harlan, 26 Dec. 1833.

182. *Donations Book; Trans.*, n. s., vol. 5.

183. *Ibid.;* Curators Cards state: "Harm stone."

184. *Ibid.; Trans.*, n. s., vol. 5.

185. *Donations Book; Trans.*, n. s., vol. 5.

186. *Ibid.*

187. *Donations Book.*

188. *Donations Book; Trans.*, n. s., vol. 5.

189. *Ibid.*

190. *Ibid.*

191. *Ibid.; Archives;* W. W. Andrews to J. R. Tyson, 24 Oct. 1837.

192. Don. to Cabinet.

193. *Donations Book.*

194. *Ibid.; Trans.*, n. s., vol. 6; Proc., vol. 1, p. 2.

195. *Ibid.; Proc.*, vol. 1, p. 2; Trans., n. s., vol. 6.

196. *Proc.*, vol. 1, p. 4.

197. *Ibid.*, p. 14.

198. *Ibid.*, p. 42.

199. *Ibid.*, p. 35; *Trans.*, n. s., vol. 6.

200. Don. to Cabinet.

201. *Proc.*, vol. 1, p. 46.

202. *Ibid.*, p. 57; *Donations Book ;Trans.*, n. s., vol 6 (see list on p. Sc).

203. *Proc.*, vol. 1, pp. 94-95.

204. *Ibid.*, p. 97.

205. *Ibid.*, p. 105.

206. Misc. MS. Col. R. C. Taylor. Memo, Oct. 1839; *Proc.*, vol. 1, p. 120; *Trans.*, n. s., vol.6.

207. Proc., vol. 1, p. 166–167, 175–176.

208. *Ibid.; Donations Book ;Trans.*, n. s., vol. 7.

209. *Archives.* T. Dunlap to J. Vaughan, 15 May 1840; *Donations Book ; Proc.*, vol. 1, p. 213; *Trans.*, vol. 7.

210. *Ibid.* C. G. Forshey to J. Vaughan, 3 Sept. 1840; *Proc.*, vol. 1, pp. 278–279; *Trans.*, vol. 7; *Donations Book .*

211. *Proc.*, vol. 1, p. 299.

212. *Archives.* A. del Rio to J. Vaughan, 13 Jan. 1841; 4 Feb. 1842.

213. *Proc.*, vol. 2, p. 40; Trans., vol. 8.

214. *Archives.* J. Gilpin to P. S. Du Ponceau, 19 May 1841; *Proc.*, vol. 2, p. 99; *Donations Book ;Trans.*, vol. 8.

215. *Proc.*, vol. 2, p. 81; *Donations Book ;Trans.*, vol. 8.

216. *Ibid.*, p. 187.

217. *Ibid.*, p. 213.

218. *Ibid.*, pp. 229–230.

219. *Archives.* W. W. Andrews to J. K. Kane, 15 Sept. 1843; *Proc.*, vol. 4, p. 9.

220. *Proc.*, vol. 4, pp. 25–26.

221. *Ibid.*, p. 49; *Donations Book ;Trans.*, vol. 9.

222. *Donations Book ;Trans.*, p. 106.

223. *Archives.* J. B. Sartori to G.Ord, 29 April 1845; Proc., vol. 4, pp. 184, 186.

224. *Proc.,* vol. 4, p. 187; *Donations Book ;Trans.,* vol. 9.

225. *Archives.* J. B. Sartori to R. Dunglison, 1 Nov. 1845.

226. *Proc.,* vol. 4, pp. 226, 301, 307, 335; Misc. MS. Co. J. B. Sartori to G. Ord, 20 Sept. 1846.

227. *Ibid.,* p. 221.

228. *Ibid.,* p. 240.

229. *Ibid.,* p. 215.

230. *Ibid.,* pp. 238-39.

231. *Ibid.,* pp. 240-41, 244.

232. *Ibid.,* p. 247.

233. *Ibid.,* vol. 5, p. 26.

234. *Ibid.,* p. 33.

235. *Ibid.,* pp. 84–85.

236. *Ibid.,* p. 106.

237. *Ibid.,* pp. 106–107.

238. *Ibid.,* p. 150.

239. *Ibid.,* p. 171.

240. *Ibid.,* p. 230.

241. *Archives.* APS. Report, 16 Sept. 1852.

242. *Proc.,* vol. 5, p. 249.

243. *Ibid.,* p. 294.

244. *Ibid.,* p. 305.

245. *Ibid.,* p. 313.

246. *Ibid.,* p. 329.

247. *Ibid.,* vol. 6, pp. 141–142, 148–150.

248. *Ibid.,* p. 155.

249. *Ibid.,* p. 246.

250. *Ibid.,* pp. 248, 251; Com. Rec.

251. *Ibid.,* p. 275.

252. *Ibid.,* p. 303.

253. *Ibid.,* p. 323.

254. *Ibid.,* vol. 7, p. 4.

255. *Ibid.,* p. 175.

256. *Ibid.,* p. 331.

257. *Ibid.,* vol. 9, p. 91.

258. *Archives.* APS. Resolution, 18, 28 March 1864.

259. *Proc.,* vol. 10, p. 259.

260. *Ibid.,* pp. 330-31.

261. *Ibid.,* vol. 11, pp. 92–93.

262. *Ibid.,* vol. 14, p. 661.

263. *Ibid.,* vol. 19, p. 197.

264. *Ibid.,* vol. 28, p. 91.

265. *Ibid.,* vol. 36, pp. 175, 193–194.

266. Cur. Recs.; Curators Reports, 3 Feb. 14 April, 21 April, 5 May 1893.

267. *Proc.,* vol. 36, pp. 175, 193-94; *Archives.* B. S. Lyman to APS, 6 April 1897.

268. *Archives.* I. M. Hays to Curators, 8 May 1897.

269. *Ibid.* E. J. Simpson to P. Frazer, 14 May 1897.

270. *Ibid.* H. Pettit to J. C. Morris, 17 May 1897; Wagner Free Institute of Science to APS, 3 May 1899; *Proc.,* vol. 37, p. 326.

271. Cur. Rec.; *Archives.* APS. Curators report, 29 Nov. 1899.

272. Curators cards.

273. *Archives.* Academy of Natural Sciences of Philadelphia to APS. List, 3 June 1901; A. W. Goodspeed to J. C. Morris, 22 Oct. 1901.

274. *Proc.,* vol. 242, p. 5.

275. Cur. Recs. H. G. Richards. List, 14 Dec. 1949.

Chapter 8
Oddities

Every organization that depends on gifts from the public receives many extraordinary items, especially "sports" or "freaks of nature." The Society, however, got an unusually small number of these, possibly because it was located in a large urban area and was scientifically oriented. Any such item received, and they were few, is listed under zoology. The Society's oddities, rather, are the things which do not fit into the classification of the other collections as arranged in this volume.

During the eighteenth century some gifts were entered in as casual terms as possible. Two samples will suffice: "A collection of natural Curiosities" was given on 4 May 1770 by the widow of William Johnson. The curators were ordered to list the items and return the thanks of the Society to Mrs. Ruth Johnson. The list is no longer in the holdings of the Society. Rednap Howell on 19 March 1773 presented "a number of papers containing sundry specimens of Natural History." That gift has disappeared and no other evidence of it remains. These gifts, and some others, were, most probably, lost when Philadelphia was occupied by the British during the Revolution. Most of the later gifts, following the Revolution, are fairly well described, or listed, in the Society's archives. But, many entries are nonspecific; *lots of bones,* or, *several coins and medals,* for example. These are listed in the specific categories.

David Rittenhouse was responsible for two items concerning electricity. On 17 July 1789 he and Isaac Jones gave "a particular account of the effects of a flash of lightning, June 7, with drawings." Also, Rittenhouse sent through Robert Patterson his "Experiments upon a very small piece of Blacklead Pencil, in the focus of the large lens...in reference to the proposed improvement of Lightning Conductors." Members were shown the specimen of black lead.

16 January 1795
"Four wooden kinds" which were "used by the country people of St. Domingo."[1]

Mederic L. E. Moreau de Saint Mery

Sometime after 1816 the copper plate used to create the Lewis and Clark map in the first publication on this great expedition was received.[2]

18 April 1817
"Plate of Babylonish Brick" taken from a "mosque at the time of Daniel & also the Characters on the Bricks."[3]

Captain Henry Austin

1 May 1818
A "*Stone* from the *First American* capitol, conflagrated by the British" on 24 August 1814.[4]

Captain Riley

The great elm under which William Penn made his famous treaty with the Lenni Lenape Indians was blown down in 1810. The wood was used to manufacture mementos; Roberts Vaux presented on 18 September 1818 a box made from the elm. His letter states that the box was part of the tree "which formerly stood upon the bank of the River Delaware at Kensington, under the branches of which, tradition informs us, William Penn, negociated his celebrated treaty with the Indian Natives, in the year 1682."[5]

3 November 1826
A box which had been made of wood taken up "from the Building of W[illia]m Penn in Letitia Court," in Philadelphia.[6]

John Bacon

2 January 1829
A fragment of a bell of a clock "curiously blistered" by a stroke of lightning.[7]

Isaiah Lukens

15 May 1829
Two locks of "Hair cut from [member] Gen. [George] Washington's head."[8]

John Pierre [Pierce?]

18 June 1830
A "Girdle of a Berber Female" of North Africa. [9]

William T. Hodgson

1830
An "*Etruscan* lamp" ... "picked up in Herculaeum." [10]

Mrs. C. E. S. Peale

17 June 1831
A donation for the cabinet.

James Mease

27 June 1831
Donations.

T. Fletcher and William Short

17 February 1832
"Dresses, War Implements, Paddles of curious Workmanship" from the Fiji and Marquesas Islands. The donor wrote on 3 February that the "two War Clubs are from the Pacific. One from the Mulgrace, and the other from the Fijee Islands....The paddle is from the Sandwich Islands."[11]

Sterne Humphrys

On 18 July 1834 Sylvain Godon presented through Peter S. Du Ponceau, "sundry articles from the South Pacific."[12] He had "lately returned from a voyage to the Pacific." From the Hawaiian Islands was a war club and a piece of "Native Cloth," which had been manufactured from "the Mulberry leaf—Some of the *Figures* are very ornamental; it will. not *stand* water." An ornament worn by women only in the Fiji Islands was for the neck: "the black rings are said to be of *stone* and the *white* rings of Shell." And, from the Society Islands, was a hatchet "not in use at present —hey were formerly used for all purposes, such as cutting trees, building their houses, &c." Godon reported that the twine was "made of the filing part of the *Cocoanut*, and is very strong. Some of these Hatchets are very large."[13]
"Cabinet Donations" were received 19 September 1834 from Mr. Brandis. Du Ponceau presented prior to 1835 some fragments of Egyptian papyrus, containing writing in the Demotic character. They had been found at the ruined city of Thebes by an American officer.[14] Gifts from J. Hitz and [Joseph] Hopkinson were received on 1 April 1836.

20 March 1835
"Chinese combs, &c."[15]

John Vaughan

17 June 1836
An antique "Etruscan" [Greek] kylix found on the estate of Charles Lucien Bonaparte. The ancient capital of Etruria, Vitulonia, once stood on part of that estate. With this came the publication *Musee Etrusque de Lucien Bonaparte, prince de Canino,* complete with plates, of nearly 2,000 articles found in that same locality.[16]

Joseph Bonaparte, Count Survilliers

Before 1838
Three large book cases.[17]

William Short

18 November 1836
A war club acquired on the Fiji Islands and, from the Sandwich Islands, "A common marine Idol, for the head or stem of a canoe."[18]

Thomas Nuttall

On 6 October 1837 a stone cannon ball, the gift of W. H. Robertson, was received. It was: one of Twentythree, said to have been fired at the boat in which Queen Mary and [Henry Stewart, Lord] Darnley made their escape from Loch Leven, and procured from a Fisherman, to whom Sir Walter Scott, some years before, suggested that if the lake was ever lowered, they would be found near a spot marked out by him. The Lake having subsequently been lowered by the proprietor, the Fisherman made the search, and found twenty-one of the Balls with the Keys of the Castle. These are deposited in the museum of the Edinburgh Antiquarian Society. The Twenty-second was found afterwards, and was procured by Mr. R[obertson] for our Cabinet.[19]

This cannon ball was lent to the Historical Society of Pennsylvania and returned on 21 January 1898.

21 September 1838
A mummified ibis in a pottery jar, which had been "taken from one of the catacombs   of Egypt." The ibis looked like "a Sugarloaf." With this were four small models of human mummies two of wood and two of clay.[20]

Lieutenant Percival Drayton, United States Navy

2 November 1838
Four small statues, of Malta stone from "St. Paul's Cave" near Citta Vecchia.[21]

William Winthrop Andrew

Victor L. Godon had been to Egypt with General Lewis Cass and while there he procured the accompanying Ibis, which I have the honor to present to the American Philosophical Society. The excavation from which it was removed is situated 4 or 5 miles to the north of the Great Pyramid: some of the jars were opened on the spot and the contents of several were found to have preserved their form entire, but upon being touched, immediately fell to pieces.[22] This gift was reported 4 January 1839.[22] Franklin Peale and William E. Horner were appointed a committee 4 January 1839 to "open and examine one of the Ibises."[23] The committee was discharged on 1 January 1841.

With the great gift of Benjamin Franklin's papers in 1840 from Charles Pemberton Fox and his sister, Mary Fox, came a painted metal diploma case containing Franklin's diploma from Harvard College.

6 February 1840
A small vase, "reproduced by the galvanic process of Prof. Jacobi...using a fusible metal matrix, which was removed when the form was obtained."[24]

Joseph Saxton

3 April 1840
A "Musical Reed Instrument" of fourteen bamboo reeds which came from Laos. It was described in William Samuel Waitman Ruschenberger's book of travels around the world.[25]

Isaac Lea

16 October 1840
Five notes from Law's Bank of 1820.[26]

Peter S. Du Ponceau

Prior to the publication of volume 7 of the new series of the *Transactions* (1841), W. S. Draper donated a manuscript written on talipot leaves (which were used by the Siamese as paper) in the sacred Pali language.[27]

5 March 1841

A Chinese printing block, given to the donor by W. B. Driver, of Macao.[29] "This block is a fragment, apparently one of several used to print a memorial written by some Chinese official around 1840." It proposed using a group "(probably pirates) against the Barbarians (probably English)."[30]

Robley Dunglison

1 March 1844
A piece of the gun which had burst aboard the *Princeton*. The donor showed the changes wrought iron undergoes under particular circumstances. Fibrous iron became chystalline, but when it was annealed, it became fibrous again. Upon investigation in France, the rails for the Versailles railway were found to become "crystalline, under the jars to which it is subjected." After some more comments, the donor thought the explosion on the *Princeton* "suggested the importance of occasionally annealing pieces of ordnance, as had been found necessary in the case of railway axles, which are annealed periodically."[31]

George W. Smith

4 January 1850
A mass of marine matter which contained a Spanish silver dollar and which was encrusted around a cannon ball. This was recovered from the wreck of the San Pedro, which had been lost on the Spanish main "some forty years ago." [32]

George M. Justice

Robert Maskell Patterson delivered some specimens of dollars from this wreck on 17 October 1845 and read a memoir on the recovery of them by the San Pedro Company, of Baltimore, by use of a diving bell. The silver was very corroded by the sulphur in the powder magazine and none of the coins could be circulated. The cannonballs had lost much weight: those weighing originally eighteen ounces weighed seven and one-tenth ounces. The United States Mint found that by removing the encrustation and black sulphuret and refining the silver, about 94 cents from each dollar was recovered.[33]

16 February 1866
A gift from the United States consul general at Tunis, Amos Perry. It was a fragment of a cover of a Carthaginian sarcophagus. A description of this stone was promised but was not received until 1899 when Thomas Cook Stellwagen, son of the captain who delivered it, wrote an account. It was published in the Proceedings in 1899. Curator Henry Crowther of the Leeds Philosophical and Literary Society wrote 4 October 1899 asking for a photograph of this artifact.

> I am deeply interested in stelae & have been also to Carthage this summer & experienced some of the disappointments expressed by Dr. Stellwagen. Hence with yourselves one feels a pleasure that something, which can reveal to us directly, & not through the Romans, an expression of Carthaginian ideas, has turned up & is preserved.[34]

Captain Henry S. Stellwagen

The Society purchased in 1877 two plaster casts of the coats of arms of the Penn and Calvert families, taken from a post demarking the Mason-Dixon line.
20 August 1880
A piece of the cogwheel of the old Independence Hall clock, the "Stretch"   clock.[35]

B. B. Diney

The superintendent at Columbia College, New York City, wrote on 2 October 1889:
> Recently we came across a perpetual calendar inscribed as follows: "Exhibited at the Centennial Exibition and presented to the American Philosophical Society in Philadelphia by Col. Repetti, Secretary of the Assocazione Cristoforo Colombo, in the name of the author, 1876." It is composed of five sheets of thick card board,

two feet and a half by three feet in size. Each of which is completely covered
with small figures.

I presume that it somehow or other came into the possession of our late President,
Dr. Barnard, at the time when he was compiling his perpetual calendar.[36]

He was asked to return it at the Society's expense, and it was forwarded on 11 October
1889.

On 18 April 1890 Mrs. Jane Rittenhouse Wilson presented a cornelian
watch charm which was reputedly worn by Benjamin Franklin. She wrote that he wore it
while attending "the Convention that adopted the Declaration of Independence." Franklin
gave this charm to "a personal friend, a veteran of the War of 1812, named Daniel Leman,
who gave it to his friend, Mrs. Wilson.[37]

Possibly in 1891, following the death of Joseph Leidy, a plaster death mask
of Leidy was received.

5 February 1892
A locket which held some hair of Andrew Jackson. The thanks of the Society were given to
the donor on 19 February of the same year.[38]

Emily Phillips

Among the coins and medals received by the Pennsylvania Museum on 22
October 1895 from the Society was a "Small earring. Pearl set in gold."[39] No other
reference to this object exists.

Thomas Heath charged Curator James Cheston Morris one dollar on 21 October
1897 "For Repairing Chinese God."[40] Because no entry was ever made for the receipt of a
Chinese god, perhaps this refers to the image of Ganesha, which was reported on 17 May
1811 from William Jones of Calcutta. That donation is the only record of Ganesha in the
Society.

A catalogue of donations to the cabinet was prepared by the curators around
1898. It omits many items, but it does contain one entry which is the only reference to the
gift: "An antique vase, from Carthage, which was presented 16 September 1825 by James
Mease."[41]

1 April 1898
A copy of the Lord's Prayer "said to be the smallest engraving by hand."[42]

Mr. Tappan

A piece of "Ancient glass" was in Philosophical Hall during the 1890s. It
had been taken from the bed of the Somme River.[43] The description in the University
Museum of the University of Pennsylvania reads: "Glass dish. France. Bed of the Somme.
Roman? Bowl fragment. France—peat bog at Marcuil." It was presented by Titian Ramsay
Peale.

On 3 June 1901, Witmer Stone, assistant curator of the Academy of Natural
Sciences of Philadelphia, sent a listing of the Society's property in the Academy. An "Adze
(South Sea Islanders), Step for Stile (South Sea Islanders)," and "Feejee War Club;" as
well as "4 Wooden Images (Egyptian Catacombs)": and "Mummified Ibis (Egyptian
Catacombs)" were the miscellaneous items on the list.[44]

4 November 1904
A "mosaic plaque composed of marbles collected in Rome." It was hung on the wall in
Philosophical Hall by 2 March 1908.[45]

Hon. George F. Edmunds

18 January 1907
Branding iron of William Temple Franklin, "who no doubt was also an occasional visitor" at Wharton's home, Champlost, which was "the favorite residence of Benjamin Franklin when he was in or near Philadelphia."[46]

Joseph Wharton

A letter was read on 2 April 1909 from Dean M. Carey Thomas, of Bryn Mawr College, asking the Society to deposit "a remarkable Greek vase" which the Society owned. The curators were asked to report on this request and they read their report on 7 May stating that it was "inexpedient to comply with the request," and asked Dean Thomas to be so told. The Society notified the Academy of Natural Sciences of Philadelphia on 21 October 1909 that "this Society withdraws from deposit the Cylix presented by Joseph Bonaparte, Ex-King of Spain."[47]

Mrs. Juliana Wood Talcott was thanked on 7 May 1915 for the gifts of "a suit of Persian Armour, and a Japanese embroidered curtain." She sent a translation of the inscription on the armor on 1 November 1915.[48] The curators reported on 3 December 1915 that the important acquisition of the year was this suit of antique armor which included the helmet. "Is is richly ornamented in damascene, and is a good example of Fifteenth Century work."[49] The armor needed attention and Isaac Minis Hays wrote curator Leslie W. Miller that the person who would repair the armor, Shannon, "said it would be necessary to take it away." On 25 February 1920 he wrote Miller that the armor had been returned "in beautiful condition, except for a few holes which I imagine were there before." The Society should take "pains to have it oiled from time to time, and whenever there is any sign of rusting will call on Shannon."[50]

William Guggenheim presented in September 1940 twelve Wedgwood plates commemorating the Bicentennial of the University of Pennsylvania. Each plate depicts some aspect of the grounds or buildings of the University, except one which one shows an incident of a football game. With the gift of the papers of Charles Benedict Davenport in 1944 from the Carnegie Institution in Washington, D. C., came a plaster life mask of Davenport's face.

In February 1949 Harold Braham, acting British consul general in Philadelphia, presented "on the behalf of the Lords Commissioners of the Admiralty, two copper plates of charts which originally formed part of the Atlantic Neptune." These were of Delaware Bay and of Philadelphia County and environs.[51]

Two Benjamin Franklin souvenir spoons were purchased on 26 December 1956.

In 1957 seventeen china plates, made in England by Adams, of John James Audubon's *Birds of America* were purchased. Six are uncolored, and eleven are colored.
A glass bottle with an illustration of Benjamin Franklin's head on it was purchased on 18 December 1958.

A cream Wedgwood pitcher, with a picture of Washington Irving and his house, Sunnyside, on it, was acquired in 1958. This commemorated the 175th birthday of Irving and was a Sleepy Hollow reproduction.

A steel engraved plate of Simon Newcomb was presented by Willman Spawn in 1957–58. When the Drexel Building, situated directly across Fifth Street from Philosophical Hall, was razed in 1957–58, the large bronze plaque which described the history of the building, as well as a fragment of the mosaic floor of the Philadelphia Stock Exchange, located once in that building, where the library had been housed for around twenty years, were presented by the Cleveland Wrecking Company. Later, when the United States Fidelity and Guarantee Building, which had been the temporary home of the library while the present Library Hall was being erected, was demolished in 1959, a mantel and grate were removed and given to the Society by the same company.

29 June 1960
A John Hawksworth memorial ring.

Miss Frances Bradford

Possibly with the acquisition of the Peale-Sellers Collection of papers in 1945 came Franklin Peale's United Bowmen of Philadelphia badge. Franklin Peale was the founder of this organization.

Three coins of admission to Charles Willson Peale's Philadelphia Museum were purchased 8 July 1960, as was the seal of the museum.

1960
A topaz ring, once the property of Mrs. Elizabeth M. Patterson Harris, who was the daughter of Robert M. Patterson.

Dorothy C. Harris

Three decorative items came in 1962 from the estate of William Ezra Lingelbach, former librarian of the Society: two Chinese cloisonne bronze containers (a large bowl and a vase) and a small unadorned fluted footed brass bowl. Two blue cloisonne bronze vases, which had been presented to Mrs. Gertrude Douglas Hess, former associate librarian of the Society, by William E. Lingelbach, were, in turn, presented to the Society in memory of Dr. Lingelbach by Mrs. Hess upon her retirement in 1971.

The council of the Society approved the indefinite loan of the fifth century B.C. kylix to the University Museum, University of Pennsylvania, in 1968.[52] On 5 November 1961 a Staffordshire (?) bowl which depicts Benjamin Franklin and his kite experiment was purchased. With the purchase of the Violetta W. Delafield Collection of Benjamin Smith Barton's manuscripts on 28 June 1970, were several copper plates etched for making prints.

29 June 1970
A cameo which had belonged to James Hall.

Mrs. Lyle L. Jenne

The gift of the Kane family papers in 1970 included a copper plate for Elisha Kent Kane's calling card, presented by relatives Oliver Cope, Thomas Pym Cope, Mrs. Joseph C. Aub and Mrs. Thomas P. Hazard. Mrs. W. Cope gave buttons from Elisha K. Kane's uniform.

A silver tray and cup, presented by the Society to Isaac Minis Hays for his indefatigable labors on the behalf of the Society, were acquired in 1973 with the settlement of the residual estate of Dr. Hays.

Librarian Richard Harrison Shryock delivered in 1976, two pens which had been used by Presidents Richard Nixon, Gerald Ford, and Lyndon Johnson while signing acts pertinent to the Society and the Independence National Historic Park.lob

Julian Parks Boyd presented in 1976 an ivory gavel as a symbol of presidential authority. It is of beechwood and there is a beechwood percussion plate with it.

On 11 August 1982, following its annual meeting, the first ever held east of the Mississippi River, the Lewis and Clark Trail Heritage Foundation presented a plaque, its Award of Meritorious Achievement, to the Society.

The Society purchased the Farmers' and Mechanics' Bank Building in April 1981 for library expansion and a few years later bought a large wooden model of the building, cut away to show how the interior would look after alterations.

There is a paperweight, "composed of a pebble from Samos and a hand from Marathon" with no provenance whatsoever, and a pewter plate which has the coat of arms of William Penn thereon also with no provenance.

Oddities—References
1. *Trans.*, vol. s4.
2. See plate in Library.
3. *Donation Book.*
4. Curator Cards.
5. Donation Book; *Archives.* R. Vaux to APS, 17 Sept. 1818; *Trans.*, n. s., vol. 2.
6. *Ibid.*
7. *Ibid.; Trans.*, n. s., vol. 3.
8. *Donation Book.*
9. *Trans.*, n. s., vol. 4.
10. Curator Cards.
11. *Archives.* S. Humphrys to J. K. Kane, 15 Feb. 1832; *Trans.*, n. s., vol. 4.
12. *Ibid.* P. S. Du Ponceau to J. Vaughan, 17 July 1834.
13. *Donation Book; Trans.*, n. s., vol. 5; Donations to Cabinet.
14. *Trans.*, n. s., vol. 4..
15. *Donation Book.*
16. *Ibid.; Trans.*, n. s., vol. 5; For articles on this kylix, see: William B. Dinsmoor, *Proc.*, vol. 87, no. 1, 1943, pp. 9091, fig. 13; Mary Hamilton Swindler, "Another Vase by the Master of the Penthesilea Cylix," *American Journal of Archaeology*, vol. 13, 1909, pp 142–150, figs. 17.
17. *Trans.*, n. s., vol. 5.
18. *Donation Book; Trans.*, n. s., vol. 5.
19. Misc. MS. Col. W. C. Robertson to J. Vaughan, 6 Oct. 1837; *Donation Book; Trans.*, n. s., vol. 6; Donations to Cabinet, p. 15.
20. *Proc.*, vol. 1, p. 35; *Trans.*, n. s., vol. 6.
21. *Ibid.*, 50.
22. *Ibid.*, 68; *Donation Book; Trans.*, n. s., vol. 6.
23. Com. Recs., vol. 2.
24. *Proc.*, vol. 1, p. 171.
25. *Ibid.*, 190; *Donation Book; Trans.* vol. 7; Ruschenberger, W.S.W. *Voyage Around the World.*
26. *Ibid.*, 284; *Donation Book; Trans.*, vol. 7.
27. *Trans.*, n. s., vol. 6.
28. *Ibid.*, vol. 8; *Proc.*, vol. 2, p. 30; *Donation Book.*
29. *Archives.* APS. Report, 20 Oct. 1843.
30. Catalogue of Instruments, p. 61.
31. *Proc.*, vol. 4, p. 47.
32. *Ibid.*, vol. 5, p. 122.
33. *Ibid.*, vol. 4, pp. 20001.
34. *Archives.* Leeds Philosophical & Literary Society to APS, 4 Oct. 1899.
35. *Proc.*, vol. 19, p. 83; Curators Cards.
36. *Archives.* Columbia University superintendent to APS, 2 Oct. 1889.
37. *Proc.*, vol. 28, p. 100.
38. *Ibid.*, vol. 30, pp. 111, 167.
39. *Archives.* Pennsylvania Museum and Industrial School. Receipt, 22 Oct. 1895.
40. *Ibid.* T. Heath. Bill, 21 Oct. 1897.
41. Cur. Recs.; Curators catalogue [1898].
42. Curators Cards.
43. Ibid.
44. Archives. Academy of Natural Sciences of Philadelphia to APS 3 June 1901, and, List, 3 June 1901.
45. Secretarys Letters. I. M. Hays to C. L. Doolittle, 2 March 1908.
46. *Ibid.* J. Wharton to I. M. Hays, Il Jan. 1907.
47. Cur. Recs. Curators Report, 19 April 1909.
48. Secretary°s Letters. Mrs. Talcott to I. M. Hays, 1 Nov. 1915.
49. Cur. Recs. APS. Curators Report, I Dec. 1915.
50,. Secretary's Letters. I. M. Hays to L. W. Miller, 21 Nov. 1919 and 5 Feb. 1920.
51. *Archives.* H. Braham. Speech, Feb. 1948.
52. Yearbook, 1968, p. 195.

Chapter 9
Zoological Specimens

Few zoological specimens were presented to the Society. Most interest centered on the mastodon and other fossil remains. (See "Fossils"). Medical doctors from Pennsylvania Hospital examined some specimens when some subject of zoological interest was presented. Some items did, however, come into the cabinet.

"A small Box containing a delineation of a few Butterflies of this Island" [Jamaica] was received on 15 November 1770. Samuel Filsted, "an ingenious young gentleman," drew them, and consequently was elected a member. Upon seeing the sketches the members realized "what such a genius is capable of performing should it attempt the Natural History of this Island." These lower and upper views of the butterflies have been lost.

Taylor White forwarded six colored prints which he intended to publish in "a large work intitled _Musaeum Britanicum_." The prints were of the male and female cow deer, the female moose deer, tarandus, elk and "Rain Deer."[1] These prints, also, have disappeared and no trace of the publication has been located. White wrote on 2 February 1772 that he had "already got Painted Drawings of Six Volumes of other Drawings. It has been the amusement of 50 Years. Every drawing is from Nature." He hoped his major opus would "clear the Study of Natural History from which confusion from the writers on that Subject having mistaken one animal for another on calling the same Creature by different Names."[2]

George Gauld packed a "Box of Coral &c." and wrote on 15 February 1773 that he was sending it to the Society. With this coral, he sent a shark's jaw, the skin of a shagreen fish (possibly the skin of a shark or ray), and a porcupine fish.[3] These items, too, have disappeared.

John Archer wrote a long account, on 2 December 1773, of an "uncommon Animal of the amphibious Kind" and presented it, stuffed, to the Society:

As a Collection of the uncommon Production of Nature [seu Dei Naturae] whether of the Animal Vegetable or Fossil Kingdoms may be of Advantage in natural History. I would therefore shew my Willingness to contribute my Mite by presenting the skin of an uncommon Animal of the Amphibious Kind carefully stuffed so as to preserve its natural appearance. I need not therefore trouble you with a Description of its shape. I would only mention that it was of the male Kind & that it was very active & springy as it did when persued leap five or six yards on level Ground. Those who killed it tho't that it made the most of its Tail in Leaping.

A Circumstance that may add to the Curiosity is that it was killed in a Meadow on the Head of a Draught or Branch of Deer-Creek about two Miles & an half from said Creek & between ten & twelve Miles from Susquehanna where there was not a Sufficiency of Water in which it might Swim unless in some few Places where the Falls of the Water in Time of a Flood had washed away the Earth & occasioned little Ponds or deep Places.

I made it my Business to enquire of such persons who lived on the Draughts of Deer Creek & Susquehanna who were acquainted with the Animals w[hi]ch frequented those Waters & of such as dealt in Peltry from other Parts & they informed me that they had neither heard of nor seen such a kind of an Animal.[4]

The Reverend Ferdinand Farmer sent on 15 January 1775 a drawing of a "preternatural birth—a head and face of an Infant" which he received from John A. de Normandie. Another such drawing was received from Dr. Smith on 24 April of the same year, of a "remarkable child." [5]

21 December 1781
"[A]n uncommon human kidney...Although shrunken, it was of not less than three pints capacity." The donor planned to dissect the organ, but wanted the members to examine it before he did.

Thomas Bond

3 February 1784
A collection of calculi taken from horses.[6]

Samuel Filsted

4 March 1785
"[A] huge moose horn," which was "of extraordinary size"[7]

Mrs. Pauli

Robert Davidson sent on 18 April 1788 a lengthy description of a *Lusus naturae.*

I sit down to give you some account of a very extraordinary *Calf, monster, lusus naturae,* or by whatever other name it may be called, which a cow brought forth a few days ago in the neighbourhood of Carlisle [Pennsylvania]. Most of those who have seen this strange creature, both learned and unlearned, have been so much shocked at the first view, that they have not taken time to examine it accurately, and for this and various other reasons no doubt common fame will spread not only some extravagant but even contradictory accounts of the matter. You will by this time wish to know what there is about this odd creature that can so much hurt the feelings of the Spectators? In truth, at first Sight, and to a Spectator who will have only a momentary view, it seems to resemble a human body, laid out at full length upon the floor. Its head is large & much of a square form. The face broad and flat, and having a large mouth, with something that bears a little resemblance to a human chin, strikes a careless observer, as if it were something human. But viewing the head, on every part, it is evidently that of a calf thrown by some means, into a most surprising form. The eyes are not to be seen, until you turn the head on one side, and then you find two of the usual size, and, as far as I can judge, of the usual make, placed nearly where they ought to be and the ears are also very plainly the Calf's, but placed on the back part of the head, pretty near to its short thick neck. It's mouth is of a triangular form; the angle running up towards the forehead is sharp, and on each side of it are plainly to be seen the nostrils, not quite an inch apart; but nose projecting or even apparent it has none. It's tongue is plainly that of a calf. It seems to have no upper jaw: the lower one is furnished with a few teeth. It has four legs, all very short, and bending inwards to the body. They have indeed some rude resemblance of the human at first view; but when you observe on each of the four, the well formed foot of a calf, the resemblance vanishes. The tail is of a proper length, but resembling that of a fox or wolf perhaps more than that of an ordinary calf. Indeed, the whole body is covered with coarse whitish hair, much more like a dog or a wolf than a calf. As it has not been dissected, nothing can be said of internal organization or structure of parts; plain however it is, that from anything apparent in its present state, it cannot be determined, whether nature designed it male or female, perhaps neither...This creature was produced without life, as far as we can learn...In short we know not what to think of this creature; or how it is to be accounted for. Philosophers will no doubt endeavour to form some conjectures, and by comparing this with other monstrous productions that may have appeared in some other parts of the world, may possibly be able to give some satisfactory account of its formation. Perhaps it is best and safest for the greater part of mankind to form no conjecture at all, on this head; but to content themselves with viewing it as one of those unaccountable phenomena, which nature, sometimes produces not perhaps *contrary* to the *laws* of nature, (which we at present but imperfectly understand) but in some way that we are not able to explain, for want of sufficient lights and *data* on which to proceed. At any rate, there appears no sufficient reason to form any conjecture so dishonourable and shocking to human nature, as some superficial observers are apt to form.

This letter was sent to Robert Patterson who delivered it to the Society.[7]

Thomas Pole, a London physician, sent a "Description and Drawing of a remarkable Tumor which had lately occurred in his practice" on 2 October 1789; at the 6 November 1789 meeting "a small fish caught in the Delaware, with a drawing of it" was presented; John Vaughan delivered on 19 December 1789 a gift from his brother, Charles, a "Goose Quill with two Feathers."

On 5 November 1790 Thomas Pole sent a print of "a Boy lately shown in that city [London] as a *Lusus Naturae*; also the representation of an Infant, exhibiting a similar *Lusus,* born in St. Lucia, of black parents." Pole thought the later case "more extraordinary of its variation in Coulour." He considered these people as "admirable Sports of Nature," leading to no practical "Improvement." He concluded:

I am sensible I am not presenting any that is new to the Society yet as a Print may given a juster Idea than A Verbal Description, to some Individuals, who have not had an Oportunity [sic] of seeing such Instances of a partly coloured *Reta mucosum*, it may not be an unacceptable Addition to your collection of curiosities. [8]

Another gift from Thomas Pole, received on 18 May 1792, was a publication, with extra plates. "I beg leave to present to the Society with an exraordinary Case of extra Uterine Gestation just published by my Fr[ien]d Will[ia]m Turnbull." Pole also "sent an extra Set of Plates, that you might have them framed if you should judge them worthy." There were three engravings, all of which are with the publication but only the major plate, drawn by Pole, and engraved by William Skelton, of London, is preserved separately. [9]

From Cincinnati, Judge George Turner sent on 12 January 1794 a collection of shells "from the Territory North West of the Ohio;" they were received 30 May 1794.[10] No listing of the gift is available, for as John Vaughan wrote: "I send you a box of shells received fromn Judge Turner ... The list has miscarried, but shall be applied for." [11]

Mederic L. E. Moreau de Saint Mery presented on 16 January 1795 a ball of hair taken from a mule's stomach and a stone from a cow's. At the same time he delivered a "little" tooth of a whale, three specimens of cochineal from Hispanolia, an insect "called the Dragon" from Martinque, a vegetable fly from Santo Domingo, and an oriental bezoar.[12] James Anderson wrote on wool bearing animals and sent the Society some West Indian sheep wool on 3 April and 17 July 1795.

While touring America and studying the various animals, Palisot de Beauvois gave a description, in French, and a drawing of a new animal discovered in New Jersey. Once translated into English, members judged it worthy of publication. It concerned serpents and Palisot de Beauvois said his "nondescript" reptile was the water rattlesnake, and an engraving of it, with its fangs, was published.[13]

George Turner brought back many items from the North West Territory and presented them to the Society on 10 February 1797. Among these for the most part American Indian artifacts were a "sea-otter skin blanket" from the northwest coast and some natural color porcupine quills. He presented also "An American Swan's foot stuffed." [14]

Palisot de Beauvois presented on 4 May 1798 the tooth of a large nondescript animal. This may have been a fossil and Caspar Wistar reported on it on 22 June.[15] Benjamin Smith Barton gave on 22 June 1798 a report on George Turner's paper on the prairie squirrel,[16] stating that it was difficult to determine that:

The animal described be a new one. Possibly it may be an animal well described by the naturalists of Europe. It is not even certain that it must be a species of squirrel, as we are not presented with a scientific account of it and without such an account, there must be much uncertainty. As the animal is native of our own country, it will not, perhaps, be difficult to obtain a more complete description.

Consequently, he advised delay in publishing the paper "in its present state." [17]

On 1 March 1799 Jonathan Williams delivered a paper on the "Ephoron Leucon" (a sponge) and the committee reported it "worthy of publication."[18] On 6 December 1799 he gave the Society a "large marine excresence." [19]

Benjamin S. Barton exhibited some colored drawings of the rattlesnake on 7 May 1802 and announced his intention to publish a description of these. The colored drawings are now in the APS Library.

The cranium of a bison which had been found near the Ohio River arrived on 18 June 1802 from John Brown, and donation of a box of shells from "Manilla" was received on 3 December 1802. J. B. Armenteros shipped them on 22 December 1801, with a letter to Thomas Jefferson. James Woodhouse, Adam Seybert, Charles W. Peale, and Benjamin S. Barton were appointed a committee to "arrange, number, catalogue and place the shells."[20] It had not completed its task by 1 February when Charles W. Peale was then asked to do the work. [21]

Barton exhibited on 17 December 1802 a drawing of a "New Rat with cheek-pouches from the Indian countries of the Northwest"—killed in 1798. This drawing is in the Library. On 17 December 1802 some specimens of an insect, tinea granella, which was very destructive to "the *grain* of wheat" were received.

From the duodenum of a horse a "calculous concretion" was removed, and Hugh G. Shaw wrote a description of Jonathan B. Smith. The "concretion" was presented to the Society on 21 January 1803 by B. Du Plessis of Philadelphia. [22]

Benjamin S. Barton showed the members on 18 February 1803 a leaping mouse which had been "taken up in the *Torpid State*" near Philadelphia. Barton wrote on the subject and his paper on the "*Dippus* [sic] *Americanus*" was read on 16 December 1803 and referred to Charles W. Peale for comment. This article, and a supplement, were subsequently published. [23]

Barton wrote an article on a new species of North American lizard and it was referred to a committee on 15 April 1803. Edward Stevens (for the committee) recommended publication on 29 August 1803. There is a receipt in the archives from Christopher Rieder, 10 April 1806, for drawing the lizard for Barton. [24]

Thomas Ruston presented on 16 September 1803 a fine specimen of madrepore, a form of coral. On that same date, a buffalo horn was lent to Benjamin S. Barton and the loan was continued on 7 October. Barton returned it on 6 April 1804.[25] Two "Serpent-stones," or bezoars, from Hyderabad, India, were received on 21 December 1803 from Mr. Coates.

Dr. Gillespie wrote a description of a case of "the discharge of two worms from the ear of a child." David Hosack sent it to the Society on 15 June 1804 with a vial which contained the worms. A committee was formed to examine the worms and paper. No further reference is given to these until on 4 December 1807 when the minutes state that the "paper on Insects found in the ear of a Child" was returned "at the author's request. [26] The Society purchased from John Vaughan on 7 December 1804 "a box of curious shells, $9.10.[27] That same month Captain Andrew Newell, of Boston, presented some rare shells and corals from Sumatra. [28]

Anthony Fothergill delivered on 17 May 1805 "Pieces of a Tape-worm." They had been sent to John Vaughan by Mathew Roberts with a letter of 3 May 1805:

> I present you with a production that has excited my curiosity, with a hope that you or some other scientifick character may be able to class it. I think it was one entire animal originally but by actident was mutulated after my first observation of it. I found it in the entrails of a lamb in the beginning of July last.
>
> If you think it worth further enquiry by communicating your or your friends opinions on it I shall be happy in making further communications on the subject. [29]

A skeleton of an Asiatic elephant was received on 20 December 1805 from the Asiatic Society of Calcutta. The members were told that the "attention of the [Asiatic] Society was carried so far as to pay the freight": it was shipped aboard the *Martha*. This gift had interested William Roxburgh for some time, beginning with his letter of thanks for being made a member of the American Philosophical Society on 14 February 1803. He commented on the skeleton of an elephant at that time:

I will immediately write to my friends up the country to endeavour to procure for the Society the Skeleton of an Elephant of a large size, & you may rest assured that every thing in my power shall be done to procure, & send as complete a one as can be got. The enclosed copy of an extract of a letter from Sergoriga, dated 25th February 1802, is the most authentic account of the dimensions, of what may be considered a very large Elephant that you probably meet with.

I have no knowledge of any animal in the Bos or Bison kind larger than the Arnee, the skeleton of the head, & the horns of which, is said to be in the Edinburgh College museum. But I am a very poor Zoologist, & fear that my researches in that way will be of little use. Botany has beeen my constant, and almost chief study ever since I came to India, now verging on thirty years. 30

The enclosed extract read:

It has been generally understood that elephants are not to be met in a wild state on this side of the Ganges. In our neighbourhood however, a herd has been discovered, a male of which attracted no doubt by the females of our camp, has nightly given us much annoyance ever since we came here. Measures at first used to decoy it, for it would carress our females, and allow them to surround it; but a want of skill determined us to destroy it with our artillery, and three successive nights a four pounder was discharged at him with good aim for this purpose. Several grape hit him and one round shot went through his trunk and rightly; notwithstanding which, he stood fronting the gun and allowed it to advance within seven yards of him when a round shot entered his right shoulder and lodged itself in his abdomen. Two more discharges of grape were lodged in the great part in his head, when he at last fell without moving from the spot and at day light (for the 3rd night we had been occupied in this service from 11 till 3 in the morning) we had an opportunity of measuring and [   ] him. His carcase was large beyond any conception. His extreme length from the:

Tip of the top the end of the tail	25feet	1 inch
His girth over the back curve	15	4
From tip of trunk to top of head	9	
From top of head to insertion of tail	10	6
Length of tail	5	6
Girth of tail at the root	1	9
Width of fore foot	1	8
Ditto of hind foot	1	7
Girth of the neck	10	
Ditto arm	5	7
Ditto thigh	5	6
Ditto fore-arm	4	6
Ditto trunk close to the tusks	4	1

Height at the shoulder   10   8

When alive he measured no doubt 12 feet at the back curve.

The tusks lie buried and cannot be touched at present; but they were not large withal
he seemed young and was handsomely proportioned, and clean-skinned beyond
any wild elephant, or indeed tame one I ever saw. People who have heard of
elephants of 12 and 13 feet high will think small of this; but on this subject there is
much deception. Mr. Corse who gave into the Royal Society a memoir on the
generation and growth of the elephant, mentions I recollect that while in Bengal he
made it his business to ascertain the real size of all the large elephants he could hear
of and found one only to measure feet 10.4 high.

Caspar Wistar had written John Vaughan on 26 April 1803 that "any bones
will be acceptable." He would prefer a whole skeleton, but if that were impossible, "the
Head & the feet will be most important, particularly the Head." Wistar did not think $100
too much to pay for such a skeleton. [32]
William Roxburgh wrote John Vaughan on 29 December 1803 that he had
the skeleton "now in hand." He did not know "what the expense of the skeleton may be,
but do not think it can amount to any thing like the sum you mention; however it is time
enough to speak of it when the object is accomplished."[33] On 29 January 1804, Roxburgh
wrote again wishing "the skeleton had been ready...All I have yet received of it is constant
promises. I however, trust it will be forthcoming soon."[34] The skeleton of this Asiatic
elephant was received finally on 20 December 1805. On 17 January 1806 the elephant
skeleton was to be:
placed in the same room with Mr. [Charles W.] Peale's Mammoth, with a
handsome and suitable Inscription to show that it was presented to this Society by
the Asiatic Society...Information to be given of this Arrangement to the Society of
Calcutta. Mr. Peale...perfectly understands that it is not to be advertised, and is to
be at all times accessible to the Members, & he further agrees that no charge shall be
made to those Persons whom the members of the Society may bring to see it.

On 6 November 1807 the Society assured the curators that all expenses of
mounting the elephant would be repaid. [35]
Two horns of the chamois were received on 6 December 1805 from
Ferdinand Rudolph Hassler, "lately from Swizzerland." Also, on 20 December 1805[20]
Thomas Jefferson presented "A Horned Lizard from upper Louisiana."[36] It was referred to
Benjamin S. Barton for description[36] and C. Rieder was paid $10 for a "drawing of the
Spined Lizard." There is a sketch of this lizard, which came from the Lewis and Clark
Expedition, by Charles W. Peale in the library.
Caspar Wistar made a report on 17 January 1806 on two skulls which
Samuel Brown "of Kentucky" had presented.
The first of them appears to be the head of the Common Bear which he believes will
be evident to the Society when they compare it with the more recent head of that
animal now offered for their inspection.

The second specimen he supposes to be the Head of the Perani, or Wild Musk Hog
of South America, & of Mexico. There are two living Animals of that Species now
in the city & their teeth & tusks, which are very remarkable, are exactly like those
of the specimen. [37]

John Vaughan reported a catalogue of the donations by Meriwether Lewis
on 20 December 1805. "The insects and two small animals" were referred to Benjamin S.
Barton for comment.[38] On February 1806 A. Traquair presented a large specimen of
coralline.[39] Charles W. Peale delivered on 8 July 1806 an article on the American antelope,
and with this was a drawing of the beast. Jefferson had given the skin, horns, etc., to

Peale; they came with the Lewis and Clark Expedition donation. Jefferson wrote that he sent "a large box containing skins, skeleton & horns." He added: "I hope you will receive them in good order. The undressed skins arrived here full of worms. I fear you will be puzzled to put them into form."[40]

Benjamin S. Barton and Zaccheus Collins, the assigned committee, announced on 19 September 1806 that Peale's paper was worthy of publication. It was not published, however; on 17 June 1807, Peale withdrew it, "because Captain [Meriwether] Lewis would publish a fuller description in his book."

Benjamin S. Barton borrowed, for one month, on 3 October 1806, the shark teeth "to have drawings taken of them."[41] Thomas Tickell Hewson delivered on 21 November 1806 two preparations of the "eyes of a goose" which exhibited "the membrane of aqueous humor."[42]

Thomas Jefferson fowarded the head of the Arctomys (Maryland marmot) which had been found in Green Brier County, Virginia, and which was sent him by Colonel John Stewart.[43] Caspar Wistar reported on it:

The Head which accompanies this, was presented to the President by Mr. Jno Stewart of Greenbryar county Virginia, who Stated that it was found upon the Surface of the Earth, in his neighbourhood.

It appears to belong to the Arctomyx Monax of Linneus, or Maryland Marmot of [Thomas] Pennant, as will appear by Comparing it with a specimen belonging to Mr. [Charles W.] Peale. The difference in the length of the fore teeth of the upper Jaw, owing to the great length of those in the head sent by Mr. Stewart, has probably been occasioned by a difference in food, for it is reported by Mr. [George] Edwards that the teeth grew to an enormous size, in one which was domesticated by Sir Hans Sloane, so that it was necessary to break them, to enable the Animal to eat. [44]

On 19 February 1808 Captain John Davy gave the Society "some shells from Ava and Ascension Islands." Samuel Harrison wrote Thomas Jefferson on 28 May 1808: "Agreeable to your Request" of a most unusual occurrence which happend in Hebron, Connecticut, in 1770. He received a letter from a friend, S. A. Peters, who wanted a large rock removed and had a miner drill it, charge the rock with gun powder, and detonate it.

The Explosion was very great: The Rock was rent into eight or Ten large Pieces besides many fractional ones. We soon hoisted up the Fragments; at last we came to the two Center and largest Pieces between which the Auger had passed.

Having taken up the Smallest, the largest Piece stood up edgeways. I then went down & viewed the Path of the Auger, which had passed by a Cavity as large as a goose Egg, in which lay a Frog who compleatly filled the Cavity. His thigh was bleeding by Reason of a wound. The orifice was too small to pull him out. The miner soon enlarged the orifice and I took out the Frog, bound up the wound and placed him on some Mud near a puddle of water, which I inclosed with a Board Fence. The Frog was alive and struggling for deliverance when I first discovered him in his Bed; which was as smooth as the inside of a glass Tumbler.

He appeared in perfect & high Spirits, though he had no visible means of living in his Hole four feet & an half down from the Top of the Rock to his bed. (All around him was firm & hard as a flint stone) excepting by what Water, Air & heat that reached him through a small crivice not so large as a Knitting Needle & that Orivice was filled with fine dust from the Top of the Rock down to his Bed in which he lay, in so Close a manner, that with difficulty I dug it out with a steel pointer. I kept the Frog, imprisoned many weeks for the inspection of the Curious.

Jefferson read the letter and forwarded it to the Society.

Peters asked two questions.
1. How the Frog got into the Center of that Rock is a Question not yet answered.
2. How the Frog could live in that dark Recess so far from heat, Air & Water is a
   Question not yet answered.[45]

Charles Willson Peale wrote a report of the paper which was read 4 November 1808. Peale stated that the committee "on full consideration of the progress of said paper, deem it unnecessary to publish" in the *Transactions*.

Robert H. Rose presented corallines from Niagara on 21 August 1807;47 Jonathan Williams delivered a paper on the insect which destroys hives and the committee reported on 18 December 1812 that the paper was excellent, made by a "careful observer," but without the proper scientific knowledge of the insect; it could not be published. However, "It will be made worthy of this honour by the explanations and annotations promised by Dr. [Benjamin S.] Barton, which will give it the rank of a scientific memoir."[48] Barton delivered his notes on 19 February 1813 and the same committee, augmented by Zaccheus Collins, reported that the article by Williams and Barton's notes "both deserve a place in the society's next volume of Transactions."[49]

Benjamin S. Barton died in 1815 and his widow gave the Society on 19 April 1816 the "Skeleton of a Rattlesnake in a glass case." This may be the skeleton Barton drew and deposited in the Library.[50]

The French scientist and traveler, Charles A. Lesueur, exhibited his drawings of fishes native to the rivers and lakes of the United States on 15 November 1816. Members were impressed and voted their thanks to him. A year later, on 17 October 1817, he read "Descriptions of several species of Chondropterigious Fishes, of North America, with their varieties." [51]

On 27 May 1817 Gabriel Crane sent, because he had "seen an advertisment containing a general invitation to make communications to the Society," a description of a worm "having a white body and a brown head" covered with hairs, which was "generated in decaying timber." He thought it resembled "a young and tender root." Unfortunately, he destroyed it while examining it.52 Following Caspar Wistar's death, his widow gave the Society on 15 May 1818 "Three boxes of Insects from China" which had belonged to her husband. [52]

Thomas Say delivered his memoir on the genus Cecindela on 7 November 1818 and the committee reported on 1 November favorably on it.

The Labour bestowed with care in a manner to analyze the various species referable to a single head, is truly valuable and may be said to form the solid material proper to construct the great Fabric of natural History.

Regarding, as the Committee do, the present memoir of this description, they hesitate not to recommend its publication in the Society's Volume. [54]

Nicholas Collin, Zaccheus Collins, and José F. Correa da Serra reported on 3 December 1819 that Say's entomological memoir "appears to be the sequel to a monograph of the same author already published by the society" and recommended publication. [55]

A gift of William Jones, of Calcutta, was received on 17 September 1819. The horns and skeleton head of a wild buffalo of Bengal were accompanied by specimens of coral and "3 Birds these badly found."[56] The labels for these birds remain: "The wild Turkey of New South Wales"; "a pheasant"; and "A green bird of New South Wales." These were "Procured at the five Islands, about 80 miles to the Southward of Sydney." [57]

Nicholas Collin exhibited on 3 December 1819 a worm which was very destructive to apple trees. He had discussed the worm at the 19th of November meeting. On 17 April 1820 Nicholas Marcellus Hentz, a "member of the Academy of natural sciences of Philadelphia" sent from South Carolina through the offices of Lesueur "Some remarks on the Mocking bird" with colored drawings of the Turdus polyglottus of the bird.[58] It was read on 16 June 1820 and given to a committee which reported on 29 November 1822 that it communicated nothing new; after patient and minute examination of the parts "upon the whole, accurate with the exception of there being 10 muscles, 5 on each side of the larynx, instead of six...They must however remark that they do not find any organization in the larynx of the mockingbird any different from that of the order Passeres." Even though the paper was not recommended for publication, the committee praised Hentz's work and said, "They hope he will be induced to continue." [59]

Hentz sent, at the end of 1819, a communication on the South Carolina alligator and on 17 August 1820 a committee reported that the alligator memoir "bears marks of great attention of the author, & of much pains in the dissection, & have no doubt of the accuracy of the description." The committee compared the memoir with all available evidence, including "a small alligator in the possession of one of the committee," but preferred to wait until "a more minute comparison" could be made and until "they procure the heart of a large alligator for dissection. [60]

On 5 October 1821 Charles Smith delivered "two pairs of entangled horns of *Cervus* virginianus," which were interlocked "supposedly in Battle with the heads annexed." They were "nearly perished."[61] They were deposited on 19 October in Charles Willson Peale's Philadelphia Museum so the public might view them.

Insects were presented on 16 April 1824 by Lewis Vanuxem, Allen Armstrong, and General D'Evereux. A committee reported on them on 7 May 1824. [62]

James Mease gave on 15 October 1824 a specimen of the Siren Lacertina in spirits. The specimen came from the Carolinas. Colonel John David Bradburn, United States Marine Corps, asked "an enlightened and liberal priest" in Mexico to write a description of the Aje, from which Mexicans made a beautiful paint. This memoir, dated 29 October 1829, and:

A Case containing a number of the insects called in Spanish Aje, confined in corn husks, and also in cornhusks of a different form, a sample of the preparation from the insect, used here as a paint. When properly prepared it is of a beautiful pink color; and Coll. Bradburn sends it to you, with the insect, in the hope that it may prove useful to his country. The insect must be preserved from the aunt [sic] their natural enemy. [64]

The box and memoir were received on 3 March 1826. On 16 March 1826 Zaccheus Collins wrote John Vaughan that the Aje eggs seemed to be alive and they might be attached to certain trees to see if the insect would live in Philadelphia. "I see in a box not one perfect insect, nor any sample of the pigment."[65] Vaughan translated the treatise and it was read to the members on 17 March 1826.

Charles W. Peale, having moved his museum from Philosophical Hall to Independence Hall, requested the members to let him exhibit the skeleton of the Asiatic elephant which had been presented by the Asiatic Society of Bengal. This request was agreed to on the following conditions:

First—That the bones be joined together, at his cost, in a substantial and proper manner, under the superintendance of the curators of this Society, so as to form an entire skeleton.

Secondly—That, when exhibited, a label be attached to it, stating, that it was presented to the American Philosophical Society, by the Asiatic Society of Bengal; and was by the former deposited in the Philadelphia Museum.

Thirdly—That it may be reclaimed by the Society at any time after *three years* from its first exhibition.

Fourthly—That if the skeleton be not mounted within *one year* from this date, the bones may be reclaimed by the Society, and the agreement made void.

Two of Charles W. Peale's sons, Titian Ramsay Peale and Franklin Peale, received the bones on 6 December 1826. The receipt lists the bones for the "Eliphant—30 Ribs—40 Vertebrae—2 oninata—2 ossa femoris, 2 tibiae—2 Humori—21 Radii 2 ulnae 2 Scapulae 42 bones of hands and Feet 2 teeth 16 fragments—I under jaw—1 Head." [66]

On 2 November 1827 some rattlesnakes on exhibition were described by Richard Harlan. Isaac Lea wrote Robert M. Patterson on 2 November 1827 that he was sending his manuscript with the drawings "of my shells. I have not had time to take the measurements accurately but will fill up the blanks at another time." 67 He probably presented some specimens of unio shells at this time. An article on these shells was printed in the *Transactions*. [68]

A committee examined the paper by J. M. Hentz, "Description of 11 new species of North American insects" and reported on 16 November 1827 that it should be published.[69] A year later, on 17 October 1828, another committee reported on a new paper on insects by Hentz; "Remarks on the use of the Maxilla in Coleopterous insects, with an account of two species of the family telephorida, &c." Publication was recommended and the committee stated that Hentz "evinces as much judgement as he does taste. [70]

On 17 April 1829 a committee reported that Isaac Lea's paper "entitled Observations on the Genus Unio," describing a new genus, was worthy of publication. A continuation of the paper was also recommended for publication by the same committee on 1 May 1829.[71]

Joel Roberts Poinsett gave "a small collection of Mexican Shells" on 2 April 1830.[72] On 20 May 1830 a committee reported that Thomas Nuttall's paper, "Description of a new species of Sarracenia," should be published with an engraving. Nuttall had recently found this "pitcher plant" in Florida and it appeared to the committee "to be new." [73]

Joseph Barabino wrote John Vaughan on 5 August 1830 that he planned to send the Society some insects and shells, but was awaiting a shipment of cork from France in order to line the boxes for the insects. After it arrived, he would ship everything, including the insects, to Philadelphia. [74]

Isaac Lea and Robert E. Griffith were named a committee on 15 October 1830 to exchange "duplicate shells for such as are not in the Cabinet." [75]

On 17 December 1830 Gerard Ralston gave thirteen Cuban insects for the cabinet, and Sterne Humphrys gave on 3 February 1832 some shells "from Mexico (the Coast) & Chili, they are I believe some what rare, but of which you are the best judge."[76] Philip H. Nicklin was permitted to borrow and study "the Shells presented by Lt. Humphryes" on 17 Februay 1832.[77] John James Audubon presented eleven species of marine shells from Florida on 5 October 1832. [78]

Some human bones from Brazil were given by Charles D. Meigs prior to 1835. They are described in the *Transactions*. [79]

The corresponding secretary of the Academy of Natural Sciences of Philadelphia, Samuel G. Morton, wrote Alexander Dallas Bache on 21 July 1836 that the collection made by John K. Townsend was partly at the Academy and the rest was on the way; Townsend was due to arrive in September. He stated:

> It is proposed as most in accordance with his wishes, that the Collections should remain undivided until his return. Of the *Shells*, however, a set has been taken out for the Academy, & if desired by the Philo[ophical] Society, a similar set shall be at once sent to that Institution. [80]

A committee was appointed to confer with Townsend about dividing his collections (he to keep the duplicates and one each for the Academy and for the Society who had subscribed to his journey), and on 20 January 1838 Townsend wrote John Vaughan that Titian Ramsay Peale had selected the geological specimens and shells for the Society and he now sent them. He had delayed, for Peter S. Du Ponceau wished the Indian vocabularies to be altered in arrangement and to be transcribed. Townsend also sent the origianal manuscript of these vocabularies "in order to satisfy the members that no use shall be made of it."[81] Disagreement about the value of these specimens had arisen and the committee reported on 30 April 1838 that Townsend had crossed the continent to the Pacific Ocean, yet, after frequent meetings with him, they noted:

All that they have obtained from him is a small collection of shells, a few ordinary specimens of rocks, and some Indian vocabularies: the whole of trifling value.

Mr. Townsend positively refused to give to the Society any of the Birds and Quadrupeds, &c., of which he has a large and valuable collection; although by his agreement with the Treasurer, Mr. [John] Vaughan, he came under contract to do so. [82]

John Bachman, of Charleston, South Carolina, sent "a small box containing specimens in natural history" on 8 May 1837.[83] There was a "communication" enclosed which the members authorized to be published: "Observations on the changes of color in birds and quadrupeds." [84]

On 20 March 1835 John Vaughan gave some shells to the Society.[85] The firm of Eyre and Massey, employers of Captain Storey, delivered on 5 January 1838 a marine cup called "Neptune's or the Devil's Punch Bowl." It was obtained by Captain Storey "from Singapore embedded in the Sea 12 Fathom water." Storey was on the brig, *Delight,* at the time.[86] This could have been either a giant sponge, a shell fish, the giant Tridacna, or a hollow depression in a coral reef.

On 31 July 1838 William W. Andrews sent the Society "a small case containing the shells of this Island [Malta]. They were received on 19 October 1838.[87] The next month an ostrich egg from "the Pampas of Buenos Ayres" was received from F. N. Casanova (16 November). [88]

C. J. Forshey, of Louisiana, presented on 3 September 1840 shells of the genus Unio from lakes in Louisiana. They were received on 2 October 1840.[89] On 21 May 1841 Isaac Lea showed a living specimen of a Brazilian snail, which had been sent to him by Sterne Humphrys. He commented on "its distinctive character and habits." [90]

Joshua Gilpin wrote Du Ponceau on 19 May 1841 forwarding gifts for the Society. They were received on 1 October 1841; one gift was from his brother, Thomas Gilpin, and himself. It was described as:

About 6 inches of the point of the tusk of a sword fish broken off and left in our Ship Penna. Packet on her voyage home from Calcutta. This tusk was darted into her in the Chinese Seas & occasioned a regular leak on her passage home to Phila[delphia] of about 22 inches in 24 hours & occasioned no small surprize at its regularity but the cause being unknown it was concluded to unload the ship & examine into it when the tusk was discovered the leak stopped & the ship reloaded & sent from Phila[delphia] to Amsterdam....She was unloaded by Mr. George Clynes at his Ship Yard in Kensington & an acount of the transactions published at the time. [91]

On 21 January 1842 two specimens of preserved butterflies from William W. Andrews, United States consul at Malta, were received through the Reverend George W. Bethune of Philadelphia. Letters accompanied these stating that the insects were ninety-six years old. [92]

James McKennan gave on 6 May 1842 specimens of wood removed from a beam from the ruins of Uxmal in the Yucatan. This wood, described by John Lloyd Stephens in his travels in the Yucatan, comes from a tree that bears a delicious brown fruit "about the size and shape of a goose egg." The natives said that the wood would never decay and the tree was called zapodilla.[93] With this gift were specimens of sponge and nineteen specimens of shells, which Isaac Lea selected from McKennan's collection. [94]

Isaac Hays recommended on 19 May 1843, and the members agreed, that the skeleton of the Asiatic elephant which had been presented by the Asiatic Society of Bengal, "now at the museum," be returned to the Society.[95] On 19 December 1845 the curators who were responsible for this were "discharged from the duty." [96]

Specimens of fish from Mammoth Cave, Kentucky, were discussed by George M. Justice at the meeting of 18 October 1844.[97] On 17 September 1847 Samuel S. Haldeman exhibited a spider [Lycossa scutalata]. When the arachnid was impaled by a pin and was dying, "a parasite worm of the genus Filaria, three times the length of the spider," emerged from it. [98]

A "singing mouse" was found in the Northern Liberties of Philadelphia County "some weeks ago." It was in the librarian's room on 17 September 1847 and George W. Smith asked the members to hear it after the meeting. "There does not appear to be any difference of external form between this and the common mouse."

At the 15 October 1847 meeting a committee was formed to investigate this extraordinary creature.[99] A most unusual *lusus naturae* was reported on 2 February 1849 by Benjamin W. Richards. A cow in New Jersey, 35 miles from Philadelphia, produced a monstrous calf "having two heads, four distinct eyes, two mouths, and with but two ears." [100]

Some specimens of Unio were exhibited on 21 June 1850 by Isaac Lea. He removed them from the Little Miami River near Cincinnati, Ohio, and stated that they were "remarkable for their very great size."[101] Lea spoke at the 4 April 1851 meeting of the "great size of certain Naiades" he had found around Cincinnati. One weighed two pounds nine and one-half ounces with the soft part removed. He noted their importance for the geology of the west. [102]

Peter A. Browne wrote on 30 January 1852 that the king of Saxony had sent him "a complete suite of specimens of the fine wools grown in his Kingdom." He offered to show them to the members.[103] The letter was read on 6 February and John Fries Frazer was asked to tell Browne "that the Society will be happy if he will exhibit them at their rooms on Friday next."[104] The committee which examined the wools reported on 2 April 1852 that Browne had given them much aid and information about wool and hair and that he had been studying wool and hair for some years. The collection from Saxony:

> Consists of upwards of six hundred specimens, very neatly put up and labelled, embracing varieties from the principal districts in that country where the growing of wool is pursued as a branch of agricultural economy. These specimens exhibit the quality of wool taken from different parts of the same animal, as well as the varieties from the different breeds of sheep, and the various districts in which they are produced. [105]

Browne wrote that the excellent wool from Saxony was produced by the importation of merino sheep from Spain to improve the flocks. He insisted that sheep which produced wool could not successfully mate with those which produced hair and the excellent Saxon wools with this "uniformity and entirety of fibre" were an "unerring test of *purity of blood*." Browne urged the importation of merino sheep for breeding purposes to improve the wool of the United States.[106] In 1853 Browne published in Philadelphia, *Trichologia Mammalium,* a treatise on the organization, properties, and uses of hair and wool, together with an essay upon the raising and breeding of sheep.

On 2 May 1856 a specimen of Colombian guano was presented by A. S. Piggott of Baltimore, Maryland. He had analyzed the substance, found a high percentage of phosphoric acid, and wrote of varying analyses made of it. [107]

A skull of the helmet hornbill of India, *Buceros scutatus,* was exhibited on 3 October 1862 by Robert P. Harris. A beautiful Chinese intaglio had been carved upon the frontal plate of this male bird. This plate was thick and much like ivory. These carvings were "rendered translucent by some chemical process" and sold to foreigners in Canton. Scientists in the United States refused to believe that any bird produced this ivory-like substance, so this carved skull was acquired for them to examine.[108]

Edward D. Cope exhibited seven Australian and one Maori skulls on 17 June 1870, "probably the first seen here."[109] A cast of a deformed human skull was received on 15 August 1879 from Joseph von Lenhossek of Budapest. It had been described and illustrated in his publication, "Deformities," which was also received on this date. [110]

Joseph Leidy presented sometime prior to 1900 some specimens of shells from the shell heaps at Cape Henlopen, near Lewes, Delaware.[111] The only zoological item still in the Society today is the cast of the deformed skull presented in 1879.

ZOOLOGICAL SPECIMENS—References
1. *Trans.*, vol. 1.
2. MS. Com. T. White to APS, 2 Feb. 1773.
3. *Ibid.* G. Gauld to Dr. Williamson, IS Feb. 1773.
4. MS. Com. J. Archer to R. Harris, 2 Dec. 1773.
5. *Archives.* F. Farmer to ----, 15 Jan. 1775.
6. *Trans.*, vol. 2.
7. MS. Com. R. Davidson to R. Patterson, 18 April 1788.
8. *Archives.* T. Pole to APS, 15 Aug. 1790.
9. *Ibid.*, 3 Feb. 1792.
10. *Ibid.* G. Turner to J. Vaughan, 12 Jan. 1794; Trans., vol. 4.
11. *Ibid.* J. Vaughan to ----` n. d.
12. *Trans.*, vol. 4.
13. *Ibid.*
14. *Ibid.*
15. Cur. Recs.
16. MS. Com. G. Turner to T. Jefferson, 11 June 1798.
17. *Archives.* APS. Report, 22 June 1798; Cur. Recs.
18. *Ibid.*, 1 March 1799.
19. *Trans.*, vol. 5.
20. *Ibid.*
21. Com. Recs.
22. *Ibid.; Archives.* E. Stevens. Report, 29 Aug. 1803 and C. Rieder to B. S. Barton, 10 April 1806.
23. Com. Recs.
24. *Archives.* C. Reider to B.S. Barton
25.
26. *Ibid.; Cur. Recs.
27. Treasurers Records.
28. *Trans.*, vol. 6.
29. *Archives.* M. Roberts to J. Vaughan, 3 May 1805.
30. *Ibid.* W. Roxburgh to J. R. Coxe, 14 Feb. 1803.
31. *Ibid.* R. C. Moore to W. Roxburgh, [1803].
32. *Ibid.* C. Wistar to J. Vaughan, 26 April 1803.
33. *Ibid.* W. Roxburgh to J. Vaughan, 29 Dec. 1803.
34. *Ibid.*, 26 Jan. 1804; Trans., vol. 6. Com. Recs.
35. Com. Recs.
36. *Trans.*, vol. 6.
37. *Archives.* C. Wistar. Report, 17 Jan. 1806.
38. Com. Recs.
39. *Trans.*, vol. 6.
40. *Ibid.*
41. Com. Recs.
42. *Trans.*, vol. 6.
43. *Ibid.*
44. *Archives.* C. Wistar. Account of a skeleton, 5 Feb. 1807.
45. MS. Com. 5. A. Peters to S. Harrison, l0 Jan. 1806.
46. *Archives.* APS. Report, 4 Nov. 1808; Com. Recs.
47. *Archives.* vol. 6.
48. *Archives.* APS. Report, 18 Dec. 1812.
49. *Ibid.*, 19 Feb. 1813.
50. *Donation Book; Trans.*, n. s., vol. 1.
51. MS. Com. C. A. Lesueur. Description, 17 Oct. 1817.
52. *Donation Book; Trans.*, n. s., vol. 2.
53. MS. Com. G. Crane to APS, 27 May 1817.
54. *Archives.* APS. Report, 21 Nov. 1817.
55. *Ibid.*, 3 Dec. 1819.
56. *Donation Book; Trans.*, n. s., vol. 2.
57. *Archives.* Labels, 17 Sept. 1819.
58. MS. Com. N. M. Hentz to J. Vaughan, 17 April 1820.
59. *Archives.* APS. Report, 29 Nov. 1822.
60. *Ibid.*, 3 Dec. 1819.
61. *Donation Book; Trans.*, n. s., vol. 2.
62. Com. Recs.
63. *Donation Book.*
64. MS. Com. Prisciliano Tiran. Concerning aje, 29 Oct. 1825, and, Taylor, Sicard & Co. to APS. 20 Jan. 1826.
65. *Ibid.* Z. Collins to J. Vaughan, 16 March 1826.
66. *Archives.* Peale's Philadelphia Museum. Receipt, 6 Dec. 1826.
67. *Ibid.* I. Lea to R. M. Patterson, 2 Nov. 1827.
68. *Trans.*, n. s., vol. 3.
69. *Archives.* APS. Report, 16 Nov. 1827.
70. *Ibid.*, 17 Oct. 1828.
71. *Ibid.*, 17 April 1829 and 1 May 1829.
72. *Donation Book; Trans.*, n. s., vol. 3.
73. *Archives.* APS. Report, 20 May 1830.
74. *Ibid.* J. Barabino to J . Vaughan, 5 Aug. 1830.
75. Com. Recs.
76. *Donations to Cabinet; Trans.*, n. s., vol. 4.
77. Com. Recs.
78. *Trans.*, n. s., vol. 4.
79. *Ibid.*
80. *Archives.* 5. G. Morton to A. D. Bache, 21 July 1836.
81. *Ibid.* J. K. Townsend to J. Vaughan, 20 Jan. 1838.

82. *Ibid.* APS. Report, 30 April 1838.
83. *Ibid.* J. Bachman to J. Vaughan, 8 May 1837.
84. *Trans.*, n. s., vol. 6, pp. 197ff.
85. *Ibid.*, n. s., vol. 5.
86. *Donation Book; Trans.*, n. s., vol. 6.
87. *Archives.* W. W. Andrews to J. K. Kane, 31 July 1838.
88. *Donation Book; Trans.*, n. s., vol. 6.
89. *Archives.* C. G. Forshey to J. Vaughan, 3 Sept. 1840; Proc., vol. I, p. 278.
90. *Proc.*, vol. 2, p. 67.
91. *Archives.* J. Gilpin to P. 5. Din Ponceau, 19 May 1841; *Proc.*, vol. 2, p. 99; *Donation Book; Trans.* vol. 8.
92. *Proc.*, vol. 2, p. 141; *Donation Book; Trans.*, vol. 8.
93. *Donation Book.*
94. *Ibid.; Proc.*, vol. 2, p. 176; *Trans.*, vol. 8.
95. *Proc.*, vol. 2, p. 276.
96. *Ibid.*, vol. 4, p. 222.
97. *Ibid.*, 106.
98. *Ibid.*, 356.
99. *Ibid.*, 356, 358; Com. Recs.
100. *Ibid.*, vol. 5, p. 69.
101. *Ibid.*, 153.
102. *Ibid.*, 191–193.
103. *Archives.* P. A. Browne to APS, 30 Jan. 1852.
104. *Proc.*, vol. 5, pp. 245, 247.
105. *Ibid.*, 250, 257–258.
106. *Ibid.*, 259–261.
107. *Ibid.*, vol. 6, pp. 189–191.
108. *Ibid.*, vol. 9, pp. 86–87.
109. *Ibid.*, vol. 11, p. 446.
110. *Ibid.*, vol. 18, p. 356.
111. Curators cards.

Chapter 10

The Cabinet Today

At present, not much of the cabinet of curiosities remains in the possession of the Society.

Native American Antiquities

Although the majority of the Native American items are now in the University Museum of the University of Pennsylvania, a few items are now in the Library:

(1) A black slate dodecahedron, perhaps the prized possession of a shaman, was presented by Charles Brown in 1792.

(2) George Turner gave on 10 February 1797 some Miami Indian arrows and the spear which slew Col. Chew.

(3) An Indian earthen bottle or vase from upper Louisiana was donated by H. Peyrouse on 20 September 1805.

(4) Mrs. Frank Speck gave in 1950 a painted gourd and a Montagnais-Naskapi knife and beaded knife case with the papers of her husband, Frank G. Speck.

Antiques

See *Due Reverence*, by Murphy D. Smith, published by the Society in January 1993 (Memoirs 203).

Botany

There is nothing left of this collection today, but the Society retains title to the Lewis and Clark herbarium now in the Academy of Natural Sciences of Philadelphia.

Coins and medals

There is a small, new collection of coins and medals in the Library, catalogued and ready for use. Most of the items pertain to Benjamin Franklin, but there is also a Magellanic Premium medal that the Society awarded Lewis M. Haupt in 1887, which was presented in 1957. These coins and medals are listed at the end of the chapter on coins and medals.

Fossils

A petrified limb of a tree from Montana, presented on 7 November 1924 by Burnet Landreth. The Society retains title, however, to the fossil bones presented by Thomas Jefferson, which are now in the Academy of Natural Sciences of Philadelphia.

Instruments and Inventions

Instruments and models are in the various buildings of the Society on permanent exhibition. There is a printed catalogue for them—*Catalogue of Instruments and Models*, by Robert P. Multhauf (1961)—and a revised edition is planned.

Manufactured Goods

The only item left from the manufactured goods collection is the piece of endless paper which was presented by Joshua and Thomas Gilpin on 19 March 1819.

Maps and Charts

The maps and charts are in the Library, catalogued and available to researchers. The catalogue for them is *Realms of Gold*, by Murphy D. Smith (1991).

Mineralogical Specimens

One mineralogical specimen is in the Society today; a gold nugget, possibly presented by John Vaughan on 21 June 1805.

Objets d'art

The portraits, busts, and other works of art are in the Society, with the exception of a bust of Benjamin Franklin, which was presented to the American Academy of Arts and Sciences. *Catalogue of Portraits and Other Works of Art* (1961) lists the major items. There are, in addition, a large number of photographs of members, as well as many prints and engravings. Both categories are catalogued in the library and available for research. In addition, there is an extraordinary item: the polished porphyry urn presented by Swedish consul member Severin Lorich on 17 December 1819. It came from a manufactory owned by the king of Sweden.

Oddities

Many of the Oddities are still in the Society today. Because they are disparate in description, some have been lumped under arbitrary groupings for inclusion in this chapter.

With the huge collection of the Kane Family Papers in 1978 came a copper plate for calling cards for Elisha Kent Kane, and some of his uniform buttons. These were presented by descendants.

A life mask of member Charles Benedict Davenport was given by the Carnegie Institution of Washington in 1965 with the huge collection of Davenport's papers.

A death mask of Joseph Leidy has no provenance but must have been presented shortly after his death in 1891.

Several engraved copper and steel plates are preserved. Some with natural history subjects on them came with member Benjamin Smith Barton's papers in 1970.

The Society's seal, a copper bookplate for the Thomas William Balch fund purchases, and a copper plate for a letter of thanks by the Society for gifts are in the library. An engraved steel plate of the Benjamin Franklin bicentennial medal was acquired shortly after 1906. Another steel plate for the centennial of the birth of member Charles Robert Darwin came in 1908. An engraved steel plate of member Simon Newcomb was presented by Willman Spawn in 1951–52.

The Drexel Building at Fifth and Chestnut Streets, Philadelphia, (across the street from Philosophical Hall), housed the Society's library for about thirty years. It was razed while the Independence National Historic Park was being formed; in 1957, the Cleveland Wrecking Company gave the bronze plaque which described the history of the building; later in that same year it presented a piece of the mosaic floor of the Philadelphia Stock Exchange rooms (where the library had been housed). There is also the brass plate used on the door of the rooms of the library while it rented rooms there. Later, the same wrecking company presented a mantel and grate from the United States Fidelity and Guarantee Building on Fifth Street, just south of Library Street (where the library now stands) when it was destroyed. The library had been housed in the Fidelity and Guarantee Building during the razing of the Drexel Building and the erection of the present Library Hall.

There are several porcelain or pottery plates. Three plates honoring Benjamin Franklin (one with Poor Richard's maxims); eleven plates of the John James Audubon *Birds of America* series, in color and six uncolored ones; twelve plates commemorating the bicentennial of the University of Pennsylvania, with scenes of the grounds and buildings on eleven and a scene of a football game on one, presented by William Guggenheim; two French eighteenth century hand painted plates of balloon ascensions; and one issued by the Carpenters Company of Philadelphia showing the facade of the old Library Company of Philadelphia building (the present Library building of the Society has the same facade) from a lithograph by Simon Grant.

Some Benjamin Franklin memorabilia were purchased when William Ezra Lingelbach was librarian: a French brass stamp for sealing wax with Franklin in profile; a Staffordshire (?) bowl with a picture of Franklin flying a kite; two French ormulu pendants (drawer pulls?); two Franklin souvenir spoons; and a glass bottle with an illustration of the head of Franklin on it.

Items which once belonged to Benjamin Franklin include a carnelian watch charm, worn by Franklin, presented by Mrs. Jane Rittenhouse in 1890, and, with the massive gift of the Benjamin Franklin papers in 1840, came a metal Harvard University diploma case which held the honorary degree Harvard bestowed on Franklin.

From William Ezra Lingelbach's Estate in 1962 came two Chinese cloisonne items; a large urn and a vase.   A brass fluted footed bowl also was received.Lingelbach had given two small blue Chinese cloisonne vases to Mrs. Gertrude Douglas Hess, associate librarian, which she presented to the Society in honor of Dr. Lingelbach on her retirement in 1971.

Miss Frances Bradford presented a John Hawksworth memorial ring on 29 June 1960 and Dorothy C. Harris give, also in 1960, a topaz ring, once the property of Mrs. Elizabeth M. Patterson Harris, daughter of member Robert Maskell Patterson.

The following items cannot be categorized easily:

Three coins of admission to Charles Willson Peale's Philadelphia Museum were acquired on 8 July 1960.

Mrs. Lyle L. Jenne presented on 29 June 1970 a cameo once owned by member James Hall.

The Carthaginian sarcophagus fragment presented by Amos Perry through Captain Henry S. Stellwagen on 16 February 1866 is in the Society.

Also in the Society today is the plaque of colored marbles picked up in Rome by George F. Edwards and presented on 2 March 1908.

There is a lock of hair of President Andrew Jackson, presented by Emily Phillips on 5 February 1892.

A Wedgwood pitcher with depictions of Washington Irving and his house, Sunnyside, was presented around 1964.

An original nail used in the construction of Philosophical Hall in 1787 was, most probably, retained in 1948 when the Hall was being restored to its original appearance.

In 1830 Titian Ramsay Peale presented an Etruscan lamp (?) which had been picked up in Herculaneum by his wife, Mrs. L. E. S. Peale.

The Society purchased in 1877 two sets of plaster casts of the Calvert and the Penn families coats of arms, taken from the Mason-Dixon line posts.

With the huge Peale-Sellers Collection came, most probably, the badge of the United Bowmen of Philadelphia. Franklin Peale was active in this organization.

William W. Andrews presented on 19 October 1858 four statuettes (two priests, a monk and a peasant woman) cut from Malta stone, taken from Saint Paul's cave, near Citta Vechhia.

From the residual estate of Isaac Minis Hays in 1973 came a large silver cup and tray which had been presented by the Society to Hays.

The Society purchased the Farmers' and Mechanics' Bank building in 1982 and it acquired a wooden model of the building showing the planned alterations in it

www.ingramcontent.com/pod-product-compliance
Lightning Source LLC
Chambersburg PA
CBHW080924100426
42812CB00007B/2359